Fatherhood

Fatherhood

Evolution and
Human Paternal Behavior

Peter B. Gray
Kermyt G. Anderson

Harvard University Press

Cambridge, Massachusetts, and London, England | 2010

Library of Congress Cataloging-in-Publication Data

Gray, Peter B., 1972–
    Fatherhood : evolution and human paternal behavior / Peter B. Gray,
Kermyt G. Anderson.
        p.   cm.
    Includes bibliographical references and index.
    ISBN 978-0-674-04869-0 (alk. paper)
    1. Human evolution. 2. Fossil hominids. 3. Fatherhood. 4. Paternity.
I. Anderson, Kermyt G. II. Title.
        GN281.G7   2010
        306.874'2—dc22   2009044271

For Megan, Sophie, and Stella
—P.G.

For Ann, Keaton, and Mariel
—K.A.

Contents

Preface

> When I was a boy of fourteen, my father was so ignorant I could hardly stand to have the old man around. But when I got to be twenty-one, I was astonished at how much he had learned in seven years.
>
> MARK TWAIN, *OLD TIMES ON THE MISSISSIPPI*

We (Peter Gray and Kermyt Anderson) don't share this view about our own fathers, but Mark Twain's take on fatherhood reveals deep truths. Most importantly, many of us may not think about fatherhood at great length until we become fathers ourselves. The feelings of a growing pregnancy, the arrival of a helpless child, the impact on sleep, the readjustments in a marital relationship—all these things are real to a father in ways they might not be to a son. A younger man might seem ignorant compared to a practiced father.

We have gained fathering experience in two ways. The first is as scholars of fatherhood. We both began studying fathers years before we began writing this book together. Since the late 1990s, we have studied both male behavior and paternal behavior in particular, Peter working in Boston, Kenya, and Jamaica, Kermyt in Albuquerque and South Africa. While numerous practical considerations and theoretical interests drew us into this area of research, neither of us started graduate school with the goal of "I want to write a book on fatherhood!" That came much later, an unexpected consequence of our own interests in fatherhood as a research subject.

A second way in which we have become more knowledgeable about fatherhood is as fathers ourselves. Being fathers of young children colors our outlook on the scientific study of fatherhood and of course immerses us in its day-to-day reality. For Kermyt this fatherhood book and his own fathering behavior are closely tied together. Kermyt's second child was gestating throughout the months when Kermyt was working most feverishly on his contribution to the book. In fact, the book and the baby seemed to be in direct competition at one point to see which would be finished first. For a while, Kermyt was telling friends that he was involved in two major projects, both due in December, neither yet named. The book won the race by only a matter of days. Kermyt's daughter arrived soon thereafter—still in a rush, as she decided to skip the traditional slow labor and instead came out so fast that she was born alongside a highway en route to the hospital.

Peter's two daughters (and Kermyt's son) had arrived in a less dramatic fashion. But their arrival must have had an effect on our perception of the fathers we had already been studying, although in ways difficult to pinpoint. This raises the question, do you have to be a father to write about one? The answer, quite clearly, is no. Does it help? That's more difficult to answer. At some level, our personal experiences with fatherhood surely led us to write a somewhat different book than if neither of us had been dads. You may judge whether the fingerprints of our own fatherhood are visible in the finished product.

Fatherhood

Introduction

Why do we need this book? A tremendous amount of information is available on human parenting. There are books and more books, journal articles, and more journal articles, all covering various facets of human parenting. Yet the vast amount of the scholarship on human parenting focuses on maternal behavior. Browse the nearest library, bookstore, or Web site, and you will find this to be the case. So there is far more ink spilled on motherhood than fatherhood, offering one reason why we might need a book on fatherhood.

This does not mean there is not a valuable, existing body of research on human fatherhood. There certainly is. However, much of the published work on fatherhood, especially that intended for popular audiences, seems to assume that men will read it only if it is interspersed with jokes, sports, and sex. Maybe book publishers feel that more humor than research content is needed to appeal to men's minds. This does not mean that such books are not enjoyable; we find humor and truth in books such as Wilder's (2006) *Daddy Needs a Drink*, but this kind of popular work does not suit our present aims.

A different type of work, both scholarly and popular, takes another approach. These books and articles on human fatherhood discuss excellent empirical research but commonly conclude with advice or advocacy—prescriptions for individual parenting style or for political facets of human fatherhood. Armin Brott's well-received books on fatherhood, such as his (2001) *The Expectant Father*, represent this kind of approach. Unlike such works, this book will not offer advice to individuals or to policy makers; rather, we prefer to synthesize research on human fatherhood in a way that we hope you will enjoy and that will give you pause for reflection.

There *is* a body of scholarly research on human fatherhood under-taken from evolutionary and cross-cultural approaches. This research tells us that in only 5% of species of mammals do males provide parental care. In addition, in all human societies, men spend less time in direct childcare than women. In human hunter-gatherer societies, men tend to spend more time with young children than in most other societies, especially ones in which men make a living herding livestock. A variety of studies have found that men tend to invest more in children if they are the biological parent rather than stepparent. A handful of recently published studies observe that fathers tend to have lower testosterone levels than do single men in the same society. Such findings tend to be scattered across journal articles and edited volumes. Read Barry Hewlett's (1992) edited book entitled *Father-child Relations* or various books edited by fatherhood research guru Michael Lamb, such as his (2004) *Role of the Father in Child Development,* and you will find such data. These books, while excellent, are often highly technical, aimed at an academic audience, and are not easily accessible to a more general readership.

Our goal is to pull together the relevant scholarship on the evolution of human fatherhood into an accessible, readable book. Doing so will articulate the relevance of evolution to human paternal care. We also seek to synthesize this research in a way that will appeal to both academic and popular audiences. We want you to find value in this material, whether you are a father pondering your position, a policy maker trying to decipher why some men pay child support and others do not, or a global citizen questioning why paternal roles around the world seem both similar and different. At the very least, we hope that our synthesis challenges stereotypes of fathers, extends the scope of information on human fatherhood, and makes your fatherly musings more thoughtful.

Data, Data, Data

What kinds of research will be integrated in this book? One source of information is comparative research, or contrasts across species. Because we are primates, we find most helpful references comparing us with nonhuman primates, especially our closest living relatives, the apes. Among the apes, we are most closely related to chimpanzees and bonobos, followed by gorillas, then by orangutans, and then by gibbons and siamangs. We will better describe these species when appropriate in this book; for now, suffice it to say that males in these other species differ from us in their paternal proclivities. By contrasting various facets of our paternal ways with those of our nonhuman relatives, we better understand the similarities and differences.

An occasional source of information tapped in this book will be paleoanthropological. Within this term we include research based on the hominin fossil record, or fossil finds among our relatives since humans split from a shared ancestor with chimpanzees and bonobos around 6 million years ago. The amount of fossil material recovered among our hominin ancestors and cousins during this time frame is small but growing. Combined with information on dates, developmental patterns, and material culture, such as stone-tool kits, this collective body of data provides some inferences regarding the evolutionary history of human paternal care.

We will frequently reference the cross-cultural and historical record on human paternal care and related facets of male behavior. We do so for several reasons. One reason is that we seek an integrative perspective on human fatherhood that does not assume that what happens in the United States or Jamaica or South Africa or China is representative of all humanity. Rather, aspects of human fatherhood show some similar patterns across a wide range of societies, but they also show clear variation too. We wish to fully incorporate this variation into the fabric of the book. And we wish to better understand the bases of that variation, such as why the mode of subsistence in a society can structure the amount and kinds of care that fathers provide their children.

Within this human variation, we give special attention to human hunter-gatherer societies. The reason why is to gain insights into fatherhood ways in socioecological contexts more similar to those in which paternal behaviors arose. Until the invention of agriculture a mere ten thousand years ago, our ancestors were hunter-gatherers who lived in small-scale, face-to-face societies; accordingly, we can profit by studying the ethnographic descriptions of such societies, to gain a better sense of the evolutionary context underlying paternal care. Of course, this does not mean that recently studied human hunter-gatherers are "living fossils." They are fully modern human beings, often interacting with their non-hunter-gatherer neighbors. Modern hunter-gatherers possess tool kits advanced far advanced beyond those of their and our more distant hunter-gatherer ancestors. This might affect the hunting returns of such men and in turn our understanding of male roles, including fatherhood. Still, an evolutionary sense of human fatherhood modeled on the socioecology of hunter-gatherers gives us a far better starting point than, say, a large, highly socially stratified society in which an emperor like Genghis Khan might father hundreds of children across his life span without knowing their names.

Within this cross-cultural and historical record, we will rely on a variety of sources. Some of these are large-scale, nationally representative studies of paternal care in places such as the United States. Some are formalized cross-cultural surveys of human behavior. Some are ethnographic accounts of a specific society, such as the Aka in the Central African Republic.

In addition to ethnographic descriptions, a variety of other types of human behavioral studies will make appearances. We include studies of formal demography, such as patterns of fertility and mortality, in various human and nonhuman populations. These types of studies help address issues such as variation in the number of children men father across and within societies, as well as species differences in male mortality rates, differences that may be linked to family life. We include quantitative and qualitative studies testing predictions regarding human paternal behavior. Guided by the conceptual logic of natural selection, evolutionary theory suggests that biological fathers invest more than stepfathers do; we refer to studies testing this expectation in various human societies. We also draw upon research describing developmental impacts on paternal behavior. Through both in-depth studies in a specific population and cross-cultural surveys, we bring to bear data suggesting ways in which human fatherhood has a life-course perspective to it.

Another source of information occasionally referenced will be human genetics. In this book genetics garners attention because it has provided the traditional means for accounting for inheritance in an evolutionary framework, such as the mechanism of inheritance for traits evolving under natural selection. As anthropologists, we are particularly aware that inheritance does not equal genetics. Culture can also be inherited; so too can epigenetic information, or information that entails biological modifications to genes due to social or other cues. Because of the central role of genetics in biological inheritance, however, we will sometimes reference findings concerning the genetic basis for behavior. Genetic information can also provide interesting information regarding social histories, such as sex-specific migration patterns;

this kind of information is another reason we will occasionally implicate genetics. And if you wish to know who your daddy is, you can turn to genetics for an answer in the form of DNA-based paternity testing.

The physiological evidence of human paternal and related behavior will also be covered. The so-called neuroendocrine system attunes an organism's perceptual, cognitive, emotional, and motor mechanisms to facilitate behavior. Consequently, we can draw upon the handful of recently conducted fMRI studies that provide insights into the neural bases of human paternal care. Moreover, the endocrine system consists of hormones released throughout the body to help organize, regulate, and respond to its world. We will reference new research concerning the hormonal bases of human paternal care.

Many of the data integrated in this book can be situated within an organizing framework proposed by Nobel laureate Nikolaas Tinbergen around 1960. Tinbergen (1963) recognized that there are four complementary approaches to asking and answering any "why" question in biology (such as, why do we engage in paternal behavior?). These approaches address function, phylogeny, mechanisms, and development. Throughout this book, we emphasize functional, or adaptive, explanations of human paternal care. For example, males attempting to channel their limited behavioral effort in order to maximize reproductive success may favor investment in their genetic progeny over stepoffspring. To lesser degrees, we will also touch upon phylogeny (or evolutionary history—such as the comparative primate and paleoanthropological data mentioned above); mechanisms (such as the neuroendocrine mechanisms associated with paternal care); and development (ways in which factors across the life span shape patterns of paternal care).

Organization of the Book

Readers may wonder why we organized the book as we did. How were chapter topics selected? Why did we choose these topics? How did we conceive the order in which these topics are presented? The answers to these questions represent a gestalt of our own reading, research, and personal experience regarding the key aspects of the evolution of human fatherhood. A short narrative of the topical organization could be given as follows.

It seems sensible to begin with an evolutionary account of fatherhood, recognizing the comparative and paleoanthropological evidence

(Chapter 1). This shared evolutionary foundation gives rise to a variety of forms taken by human fatherhood across space and time (Chapter 2). How do men beget children (Chapter 3)? How many children do men father, and why (Chapter 4)? How often are men cuckolded in the process of begetting children (Chapter 5)? How does paternal care impact men's children (Chapter 6)? Male parental investment often occurs in contexts of stepfathering (Chapter 7). How does parenting fit with men's broader social and work lives (Chapter 8)? How is sexuality, from the moment of conception to the postpartum period, linked with fatherhood (Chapter 9)? What psychophysiological impacts does fatherhood have upon men (Chapter 10)? How does fatherhood relate to male health (Chapter 11)? And what does the future hold for fatherhood (Chapter 12)?

We cannot claim to have produced the definitive book on fatherhood in evolutionary perspective. Paternal behavior is a rapidly growing research area, with the result that if we were to write this book in ten years, it would likely vary in many details from the copy you are holding right now. Nonetheless, whether you're a father or mother (and thus have a vital stake in male parental care) or you simply have a father yourself, we hope that this book sheds new light on the mysteries of paternal behavior, and lets you see fathers in a new way.

1

Our Founding Fathers

The geneticist Angus John Bateman conducted seminal breeding experiments in the 1940s with captive fruit flies, experiments that, we will see, have relevance for understanding the evolution of human male behavior (Bateman 1948). When he provided sufficient food resources to his subjects, he observed sex differences in the relationships between fruit fly mating opportunities and reproductive success. He found that the number of offspring a fruit fly male fathered was related linearly to the number of mates to which he was given access. If he had one mate, then he had x offspring; two mates, then $2x$ offspring; three mates, then $3x$ offspring. This relationship did not hold for females, however. Females tended to have approximately the same number of offspring, whether they had mated with one, two, or three males. The additional mating opportunities did not translate into additional offspring for females in the same way they did for males.

Bateman's results probably seem intuitively obvious. The key, though, is that these captive fruit fly patterns appear to generalize quite broadly with respect to sex differences in reproductive constraints in nature. Male reproductive success tends to be ultimately limited by reproductive access to females. For females, resources such as food play a more important role: female reproductive success tends to be ultimately limited not by reproductive access to males but by sufficient resources that can be used for reproduction. A consequence is that males can be expected to compete heavily for limited reproductive opportunities, whereas females are expected to prioritize access to reproductively limiting resources.

This does not mean that Bateman's experiments are the end of the story—far from it. Among animals in the wild, there are cases where it pays females to mate with multiple males. Idaho ground squirrel females bear more offspring if they mate with multiple males; interestingly, in the same litter they may have pups fathered by different males. In other cases, it may benefit females to mate with multiple males to garner favors. If a female can acquire additional food resources by mating with multiple males, her reproductive success may be enhanced. A leading hypothesis advanced to account for chimpanzee females mating with multiple males is that the practice "confuses paternity," thereby allowing a number of males to think they might be an infant's father and in turn be less prone to harming it. Back to fruit flies, though: Bateman suggested that the sexual asymmetries could be traced to differences in gamete size. Females, by definition, possess the larger gamete (the egg), whereas males have the smaller gametes (sperm). Initial sex differences in investment in gametes, Bateman felt, were magnified into sex differences in reproductive investment and hence constraints more broadly.

Decades later, the eminent evolutionary biologist Robert Trivers (1972) argued that the key to understanding sex differences was not in gamete size but in relative parental investment between the sexes. One advantage of Trivers's insights is that they moved the locus of sex differences closer to home—from the very distant focus on gametes to the more readily observable parental care in the wild. In a chapter in the 1972 book *Sexual Selection and the Descent of Man,* he contended that the sex which invests more in parental care will become the reproductively limiting sex. In most species, especially mammals, the sex investing more in parental care is females. As a consequence, males are expected to seek mating opportunities with females. In the language of evolutionary biology, males tend to specialize in "mating effort"—investment in male-male competition, in courtship, and in mate guarding. Females, conversely, tend to specialize in "parenting effort"—investment in the survival and reproductive prospects of their offspring.

A plus of Trivers's framework was that it could account for "sex-role reversals," for species in which the typical sex differences break down. Consider jacana birds. Living in ponds and marshes in parts of Africa and the Americas, these birds possess enormous feet to help them balance upon lilies and the like. Interestingly, male jacanas provide the bulk of parental care. Females drop their eggs off with their males. Males take over, incubating them and fostering their offspring's success. The outcomes of this social arrangement are that males are the reproductively limiting sex. Females compete more among themselves for access to males than males do among themselves for access to females. Females are larger and more colorful than males, thanks to their need to compete among themselves and to advertise to prospective male mates. Jacanas are thus exceptions to typical sex roles that help prove the rule.

Exceptions to Trivers's framework resulted in a reformulation of the basis of sex differences in reproductive strategies. For example, in some species of mouth-brooding frog, males provide more parental care than do females. However, males tend to compete among themselves for access to females more than females compete among themselves for access to males. Such exceptions led to the concept of "potential reproductive rates" as the basis for sex differences in reproductive strategies. The sex with the slower potential reproductive rate is the one over which competition will occur (Clutton-Brock and Vincent 1991).

The sex differences in reproductive strategies that Bateman, Trivers, and others have described resonate with ideas proposed by Charles Darwin. He advanced the concept of sexual selection in the latter part of *The Descent of Man and Selection in Relation to Sex* (1871). As Darwin noted, selection favors traits that enhance survival and reproductive success. Among sexually reproducing species like ourselves, acquiring mates and raising offspring who themselves succeed in obtaining mates present tremendous challenges. These processes have been written into our morphology, physiology, and behavior. We are all descended from a long, unbroken line of males and females who successfully reproduced. As a result, we bear many marks resulting from sexual selection.

Darwin divided what he termed "sexual selection"—selection operating in the sexual and reproductive realm—into two main parts: male-male competition and female choice. He noticed that males commonly battle among themselves in the effort to mate. The antlers, large canines, and extra muscle mass that many male mammals bear compared with that of females serve these competitive ends. Females, conversely, often have the ability to select a mate. A female may look upon the male suitors in her environment and choose the one that best suits her.

The textbook example of female choice is the peacock's train. Peacocks are famous for their elaborate, colorful, and long tails. These are completely lacking in the peahen. Yet Darwin felt that natural selection could not explain the presence of the peacock's tail: it is energetically expensive to grow and maintain, raising the male's nutritional requirements; its mass slows the bird down, making it more difficult to forage and evade predators; and its bright colors are the equivalent of a neon "all you can eat buffet" sign for predators. Darwin argued that the existence of the peacock's train could be traced to female preferences for showy feathers.

Darwin did not delve into the varieties of female mating with multiple males, and he devoted less attention to cases in which male choice operates. Still, he addressed the ultimate bases of animal sex differences in reproductive strategies, bases that would later find great resonance with Bateman's fruit fly experiments and more. These bases allow us to speak of peacocks and human fatherhood in the same sentence.

Patterns of Nonhuman Paternal Care

Approximately 90% of bird species are socially monogamous (a single male and female bonded together, with or without sexual fidelity) and have males who invest in offspring. The peacock is not one of them, but if you have seen pairs of doves or pigeons cooing together, then you get a better picture of the typical avian world. It appears that because birds lay eggs that can be cared for by either males or females, this favors greater male family involvement. A male can sit on eggs, incubating them; can perhaps provide food to a mate while she incubates the eggs; and can later aid in feeding the young and his mate. It should be no surprise, then, that among the vast majority of avian species males and females are about the same size as each other and tend to look fairly similar. If you are in it together over the long haul, there is less need to show off or battle with others in the attempt to seek additional mates.

Mammals, of course, have internal gestation (with the exception of the egg-laying mammals—the duck-billed platypus and the echidnas). Males can hardly sit on fertilized eggs growing in a kangaroo female's pouch or a llama's womb. Males are unleashed. Male investment in offspring can in principle (and in practice often does) end at the moment of ejaculation. Female mammals have the obligate investment through the gestation of their young and must also invest in lactation and care of the young for various lengths of time postpartum. The consequence is that, unlike birds, mammals tend to exhibit sex differences in parental investment and potential reproductive rate. As a result, in only around 3–5% of mammalian species do males and females form long-term bonds with each other (pair-bonds) and do males provide parental care (Clutton-Brock 1991).

The rarity of mammalian paternal care raises other questions: In which species of mammals does paternal care occur? What forms does paternal care take?

A number of social carnivores, such as wolves, dwarf mongooses, and coyotes, have paternally investing males (Clutton-Brock 1991). Males appear to play important roles providing food to pups and mates. In a risky world of hunting, where food is served in the form of valuable, unpredictable, and shareable meals, it helps when there is more than a single adult (the mother) seeking prey on a daily basis. By pooling the risk with an adult male and female, and maybe even other adults and juveniles who do not breed in a social group, selection favors paternal involvement.

Another clustering of paternal mammals occurs among New World monkeys (H. J. Smith 2005). Here, you can find some of the poster fathers of the natural world. Take the titi monkey, of which there are a handful of species inhabiting forests in South America. Not only do male and female titi monkeys sometimes intertwine their tails while perched together on a tree branch, but fathers tend to play important roles carrying their young. A father may lug his little ones through the forest, handing them to their mother for nursing, then putting them back on his shoulders. In experiments with captive titi monkeys, offspring given the choice of heading to their mother or their father will favor their fathers

Among marmosets and tamarins, small-bodied monkeys in South America, we also find numerous species of paternally investing males (Digby, Ferrari, and Saltzman 2007). Here, males play crucial roles in family life. Females commonly give birth to twins. The combined weight of twins may comprise 20% of a mother's body weight at birth. That is akin to a 135-pound woman giving birth to a 27-pound baby. Males help shoulder some of the burden with their young. Commonly, fathers carry the young through the forests they inhabit. As the young are weaned, sometimes the fathers also help provide their young with food, one of the few primate cases in which this occurs. The importance of paternal care in these species has been illustrated through research with captive animals. If cotton-top tamarin fathers are removed from the family scene, mothers often abandon the young. This behavior provides compelling evidence of the importance of paternal care in the form of carrying and provisioning young.

The Descent of Paternal Care: Old World Monkeys and Apes

Paternal care is largely absent among our more closely related primate cousins, Old World monkeys and apes. Take the abundant and pesky rhesus macaque or vervet monkey as examples. Very few males of these species provide any meaningful amount of paternal care. That is the standard protocol for Old World monkeys. Or take baboons living in Botswana. In a wonderful book describing their social lives, males are shown to develop "friendships" with particular females who have offspring (Cheney and Seyfarth 2007). These adult males are typically not the fathers of the young. But by developing a strong relationship, in part by being nice to a mother's baby, a male increases the likelihood of mating with her when she next seeks a mate. Interestingly, in this multimale, multifemale baboon society, males appear to recognize more often than they would by chance alone which offspring they have fathered and come to their offspring's defense when duty calls (Buchan et al. 2003).

What about the apes, to whom we are more closely related than Old World monkeys? Genetic evidence reveals that we last shared a common ancestor with the lesser apes—the twelve or so species of gibbons and siamangs—approximately 20 million years ago (T. Bartlett 2007). The lesser apes live in peninsular and island southeast Asia. These lesser apes tend to form social systems including one adult male, one adult female, and their offspring; adults defend their territories from intruders of their own species who might seek to mate with their partners. Sometimes they do engage in extrapair mating. Yet generally adult males and females of these species tend to be socially and relatively monogamous sexually. Consistent with this, males and females are about the same size; if observing males and females in a shadowy forest, you might have difficulty discerning males from females. Interestingly, however, males are not that involved in paternal care. Of the lesser apes, siamang males appear to provide the greatest amount of parental care. Siamang males may harbor their young on their backs for part of the day. Occasionally, males may provide a morsel of food for their offspring. The remaining species of apes are referred to as the great apes, in part because they are larger than their lesser ape cousins (Campbell et al. 2007; Strier 2007). Of the great apes, we last shared a common ancestor with orangutans approximately 15 million years ago. Orangutans live on two islands—Borneo and Sumatra—in southeast Asia. Important to our story, orangutan males do not provide paternal care. Instead, adult males tend to pursue one of two reproductive strategies. As young adults, when they might be subordinated by fully adult males, males may have a smaller appearance, not so different in size from females. These smaller males may attempt to force copulations upon adult females. They are not preferred mates and thus appear to opt for the only reproductive avenue available, sexual coercion. By being about the same size as females, young males are also agile in their forested environment, allowing them to pursue females wherever they go. Prime adult males, bulked up on testosterone, are larger in size, weighing about twice as much as adult females (Knott and Kahlenberg 2007). Prime adult males have large fleshy cheek pads that facilitate their "long calls" through the rainforest (which make them heard if not seen). They can manhandle young adult males if competing directly but have difficulties pursuing the smaller adult males in trees. Females prefer to mate with these prime orangutan males. Even then, however, these trysts tend to be short lived: males do not stick around to observe their pregnant partners or to welcome their offspring into the world. Orangutan males are the definition of a typical, uninvolved mammalian male.

The other great apes—gorillas, common chimpanzees, and bonobos—live in Africa. We last shared a common ancestor with gorillas around 12 million years ago, and with common chimpanzees and bonobos approximately 6 million years ago. Gorilla males do provide paternal care. Yet the care they provide differs in a number of ways from how we tend to think of human paternal care.

Gorillas tend to form polygynous groups (or harems) based on one or sometimes two adult males, multiple adult females, and their offspring (Robbins 2007; H. J. Smith 2005). Gorilla males exhibit some gentle fatherly ways even if males mark their entry into a new social group in a violent flurry, commonly entailing infanticide. In a polygynous species, the unmated males may wait their opportunity to mate with females, forming bachelor herds. When an unmated gorilla male attempts to break into a group already led by an adult male, the intruder encounters resistance. The mated gorilla, aided by his bulk (and potentially supportive females), attempts to keep the unmated gorilla at bay. Such forms of contest competition between males may account for the huge sexual dimorphism present in gorillas: males weigh about twice as much as females, apparently to utilize this extra bulk during male-male challenges.

If a mated gorilla loses the contest, he loses his keys to reproductive success—the adult females in the group of which he had previously been a part. This may not be good news for the females. It is the nursing young of such females who may now be in jeopardy. A significant fraction of the young present during the arrival of a new male may be killed by the new arrival. Why would he do such a thing? That hardly seems like a good way to entice the mother as a mate. Functional hypotheses for infanticide in gorillas suggest that males may kill young offspring of lactating females in order to terminate females' investment in young to which the new male is not related; after all, he did not father those offspring. Once the young are killed, mothers no longer experience the physiological effects of lactation that can delay a return to ovulation, so they begin cycling sooner. And when they begin cycling, they seek a brawny male that may prevent the attack upon their young from happening again. The new male has already demonstrated his abilities by overcoming resistances of the previous male; the new male may be a good defender in the future. So here a female may mate with the very male who killed her previous offspring.

In established gorilla groups, males play several important paternal roles. Their role of protectors can be appreciated by the dynamics of infanticide described above. Males may also be indulgent with their own offspring. Their little young may play on their backs, finding a quiet calm of encouragement. Gorilla fathers do not help feed their offspring, however; they are not providing resources such as food to their mates or offspring. Gorilla males do not appear to play active roles in the socialization of their young. They are not offering the gorilla equivalent of social guidance (son—be tough—if you don't stand your ground, nobody else will do it for you). The patterns of gorilla paternal care make sense: gorilla males can protect and be indulgent with their young without sacrificing an ability to keep male competitors away. The multiple mothers of their multiple offspring can provide the childcare and guidance their young need. So gorilla adult males may be paternal, but in very limited ways.

Of the living primates, including apes, we are most closely related to common chimpanzees and bonobos. The ancestors of common chimpanzees (hereafter, referred to just as "chimpanzees") and bonobos themselves diverged from each other only about 2 million years ago. So we might imagine a distant ancestor of ours who shared many of the traits present in chimpanzees and bonobos too. Chimpanzees and bonobos have smaller body sizes than we do. Yet when we seek evidence of body sizes among our fossilized ancestors dating back millions of years ago, we find that they were about the same size as modern chimpanzees and bonobos. Such lines of evidence suggest why it is reasonable to refer to contemporary chimpanzee and bonobo traits when attempting to model how our ancestors appeared and behaved near the time, around 6 million years ago, when we last shared a common ancestor with these species.

Do chimpanzee and bonobo males provide paternal care? The quick answer is no. Chimpanzees and bonobos live in multimale, multifemale groups consisting of adults and young (Goodall 1986; Stumpf 2007; Wrangham and Peterson 1996). They form polygynandrous mating systems, meaning that multiple males mate with multiple females. For example, Jane Goodall tells us of a chimpanzee female who mated fifty times in a single day with seven different males. That may be a record even for chimpanzee behavior in the wild, but the contrast with most human sexual behavior is clear. A prime adult female chimpanzee in estrus, or during the fertile time of the ovulatory cycle, displays sexual swellings on her rear that drive males crazy. She tends to mate with multiple males, with some preference, the closer she is to ovulation, for mating with higher-ranked males in the group. Sometimes, as an alternative mating strategy, she may also form a consortship with a single male who attempts to shepherd her away from the group for quiet mating time without the interference of other males. She may accede in the face of brutal sexual coercion.

An outcome of chimpanzee mating behavior is that males may "know" with which females they have mated and, in turn, with which females they may have fathered young. But that is a probabilistic endeavor. A given male cannot say with strong likelihood that he fathered a specific offspring, because a dozen other males may be contenders. It is thus not surprising to find that males do not provide any meaningful amount of paternal behavior, whether provisioning, protection, playing with young, or aiding sons' social development.

The story is somewhat similar in bonobos, but in a gentler way. Bonobo male-female relationships tend to be more balanced compared with those of chimpanzees. Coalitions of adult females, reinforcing their relationships with hoka-hoka (Japanese for the bonobos' brand of female-female sex, which involves rubbing genitals together), can suppress some of the sexual coercion that males might otherwise attempt. The result is that bonobos also mate in a polygynandrous system but without the same degree of sexual coercion observed in chimpanzees. Bonobo males also do not provide a measurable amount of paternal care.

To reconstruct our ancestors' paternal behavior, we begin with mammalian and, closer to home, an Old World–monkey baseline that would suggest very little if any paternal involvement. The lesser apes too exhibit little paternal care, but social monogamy and sexual mono-morphism, and orangutans sexual dimorphism and no paternal care whatsoever. The fossil record of our ancestors from around 6 million years ago reveals larger body sizes than the lesser apes and modest, chimpanzee- and bonobo-like sexual dimorphism. From this we infer that our ancestors around 6 million years ago were living in polygynan-drous mating systems and not providing paternal care. At the start, there is no glimmer of paternal care in our ancestors' eyes.

Early Hominin Social Life

What changed? Here is the moment we draw further upon paleoan-thropological evidence. We call upon fossil finds of our relatives, the hominins (which include us as well as extinct relatives arising after our lineage split from that giving rise to chimpanzees and bonobos). The nature of fossil finds means that there is not a huge amount of material with which to work. It takes a conspiracy of the right time of death in the right place at the right time in history for a hominin to be fossilized and later discovered by us today. As one illustration, in fall 2006 the scientific world held its breath when beholding fossil material from the earliest, best-preserved hominin child ever discovered—who had lived around 3.2 million years ago (Alemseged et al. 2006). Dubbed the "Dikika baby," after the locale in Ethiopia where it was unearthed by Zeresenay Alemseged, a team of experts working on the find shed light on the context of the child's age, gender, burial, and other features of the world in which it lived. Dental eruption patterns suggested that this was a young child around the age of three at the time of death. The best guess, based on the size of the available teeth, was that this was a girl. As well preserved and as complete the skeleton of the child was, it was inferred that she had been buried under layers of sediment perhaps after falling into a stream or other body of water in the midst of a partially forested environment. Did the Dikika child have a father who loved her? Did she have a father who brought meat back to the camp in which she lived and who thus provided some relished fat and protein in her own diet? Did she sleep in a nest next to her mother and father? Behavior does not fossilize directly, and thus we may never be able to answer these specific questions. But we can make some broad inferences about patterns of paternal care during the past 6 million years of hominin evolution, inferences based on paleoanthropological evidence, by looking back in time for clues to the origins of our founding fathers.

Some of the earliest paleoanthropological evidence discovered among hominins refers to a variety of species of "basal" hominins, species whose taxonomic affiliation is not settled, including those hominins, if any, who might be direct ancestors of ours (Klein 2009; B. Wood and Lonergan 2008). These are species arising around 6 million or so years ago, at the dawn of our human lineage's splitting from the lineage that gave rise to chimpanzees and bonobos. Some patterns in the available evidence permit certain inferences regarding these early species' broadly social and more specifically paternal behavior.

The hallmark of a hominin is habitual bipedalism. As the term "bipedalism" implies, that means moving around on two limbs rather than the typical four for a mammal. Evidence from these basal hominins suggests they evolved bipedal ways, but with a twist—apparently, they evolved bipedalism while still spending significant chunks of time living in trees rather than on the ground. For example, fossils from one of these basal hominin species, *Sahelanthropus tchadensis,* exhibit a more vertically oriented foramen magnum—the large hole at the base of the skull through which the spinal cord travels—suggesting an upright, bipedal gait. And yet other species of early hominins display fossil evidence of arboreal ways, evidence such as long, curved fingers and a divergent toe that would help these hominins hold on to tree branches (White et al. 2009). Environmental reconstructions also suggest these early hominins lived in forested environments.

What else can we say about these basal hominins, particularly about their fatherly ways? Unfortunately, not much. We know that in body size they resembled today's chimpanzees and bonobos. We know they were bipedal but spent time in trees. We find that their brains were about the same size as extant chimpanzees' and bonobos'. Few other relevant inferences can be drawn. However, the evolutionary shift upright would later prove quite relevant to human paternal care. If our ancestors had not begun standing upright, freeing hands for other functions, then we would have a tougher time holding our children or procuring things we hand to them.

The basal hominins gave way to the so-called australopithecines. The word "australopithecine" refers to "southern ape." The term was coined by Raymond Dart, an Australian expatriate, who studied fossil material obtained from a limestone quarry in South Africa. The first hint of something interesting in this material was that fossilized evidence of a hominin child—later famously known as the "Taung child"—suggested it had a small brain but was an upright biped. This demonstrated that bipedalism evolved before major shifts in hominin brain sizes. Dart named this species *Australopithecus africanus*. Further australopithecine finds have suggested that at least two groups of australopithecines evolved. First on the scene were the so-called "gracile" (meaning "slender") australopithecines. Counted among these gracile australopithecines are the Dikika child as well as the most famous of all fossil hominin specimens: Lucy, an adult female who lived around 3.2 million years ago. The body sizes of female gracile australopithecines like Lucy resembled those of basal hominins and extant chimpanzees and bonobos. They displayed unequivocal evidence of bipedalism but, like the basal hominins, also continued to provide indicators of spending time in trees. The term "gracile" is in reference to these australopithecines' teeth: they had modestly sized molars and probably modestly sized jaw musculature used for chewing. In those ways they differed markedly from the evolutionary cousins that split from their lineage, the group of "robust" australopithecines. The molars and jaws of robust forms were much bigger than those of their gracile counterparts. These differences suggest differences in diet, with robust australopithecines likely consuming greater amounts of seeds, nuts, and tubers.

Of course this discussion of australopithecines and their diets does not answer the question, did males care for children? One way to address this question is to refer to body-size sexual dimorphism. Just as we have linked sexual monomorphism and various degrees of sexual dimorphism to mating systems in extant nonhuman primates, we can do the same for australopithecines. The general relationship holding across various groups of mammals—from pinnipeds (for example, walruses, sea lions) to bovids (for example, gazelles) to primates—is that monomorphism tends to be linked with social monogamy, and sexual dimorphism with polygyny (Alexander et al. 1979). To be sure, other factors, such as the reproductive benefits of enlarged female body sizes, may play a role too, but a social signal of relative body-size sexual dimorphisms commonly emerges from other such complications (Plavcan 2002). If males must battle among themselves for reproductive opportunities, sexual selection favors sexual dimorphisms such as males being larger than females.

Among australopithecines, female body sizes remain consistent, whereas male body sizes increase, yielding greater body-size sexual dimorphism. The implication is that polygyny may have increased among australopithecines. David Geary and Mark Flinn (2001), pointing out these same patterns, suggest that gorilla behavior might give us a worthy analog for australopithecine behavior. Maybe these relatives of ours lived in groups with a single or small number of breeding males surrounded by multiple adult females with whom these males reproduced. If so, it also seems unlikely to expect that they were providing much in the way of paternal care apart from perhaps protection.

Origin of the Genus *Homo*

Hominin lifeways began to undergo further shifts beginning around 2 million years ago. Enough change in the fossilized bones, archaeological material, and geographic range of these hominins has been documented for researchers to argue for a new genus of hominin—*Homo*, meaning "man" in Latin. Still, researchers debate how to cluster this early *Homo* evidence: how many species were there, and how are these related to each other as well as to later members of the genus *Homo*? We refer to some of these new creatures as "early *Homo*," characterizing their status as the first representatives of the genus in which we living humans are also classified. Like others employing a simplifying picture of human evolution (the "lumpers" rather than the "splitters"), we then recognize a transition from these early members of the genus into *Homo erectus* in Africa, then a transition around 500,000 years ago among African *Homo erectus* into so-called *Homo heidelbergensis*, and most recently a transition within Africa from *heidelbergensis* into modern humans (ourselves: *Homo sapiens*) around 150,000 years ago.

Species of early *Homo* likely derived from gracile australopithecines. Their appearances, as extrapolated from paleoanthropological evidence, suggest continuity with gracile australopithecines but not with robust australopithecines, some of which stuck around until around 1.3 million years ago, overlapping with their *Homo* cousins before hitting an evolutionary dead end. Most important for our purposes, a number of researchers have suggested that early *Homo/Homo erectus* body-size sexual dimorphism appears to have decreased from the highly dimorphic patterns among australopithecines (McHenry 1994; O'Connell,

Hawkes, and Jones 1999). In fact, some researchers argue that levels of dimorphism among *Homo erectus* appear comparable to those found in existing human populations. Harkening to the previously discussed links between sexual dimorphism and mating systems, this suggests that our human tendency toward long-term pair-bonds embedded in mild polygyny may have arisen with early *Homo*.

However, new fossil finds challenge this inference concerning body-size sexual dimorphism as well as other features of early *Homo* and *Homo erectus* lifeways. New fossil material from Georgia, in southwest Asia, has been dated to almost 2 million years before the present. Attributed to some early *Homo* form, it appears to have a more gracile-australopithecine-like degree of body-size sexual dimorphism, because of smaller-than-expected female body size (Lordkipanidze et al. 2007). As the first hominin found outside of Africa, this fossil material has other skeletal features suggestive of a committed biped (rather than one still spending significant time in trees) but also little change in brain size. A female *Homo erectus* fossil pelvis from Ethiopia, dated to about 1.2 million years of age, also suggests a wide-hipped but small-bodied female (Simpson et al. 2008). Suddenly the potential timing of our ancestors' shift to forming pair-bonds around 2 million years ago appears in doubt. Some researchers believe that pair-bonds arose around this time among early *Homo/Homo erectus* ancestors, whereas other researchers believe pair-bonds originated more recently (more on this below).

Other fossil evidence from earlier members of our genus *Homo* helps us better understand these creatures' cognitive and social lives. Some of this evidence concerns inferences about when more helpless and more needy hominin newborns evolved. To be born, rather than snagged in the birth canal, a big-brained hominin baby has to be born with a smaller head than might otherwise be expected. However, the wider maternal pelvis that could enable more prenatal brain growth (and hence the birth of a bigger-brained baby) simply isn't feasible, because of the competing demands of bipedalism on a woman's skeleton. Thus, a larger proportion of brain growth compared with, say, that of a chimpanzee baby must be postponed until after birth. The consequence is that human babies are born more helpless. They may not be able to grip their mothers' hair, like orangutan newborns can, within days after birth. Human babies may be more difficult to carry around. They may command more care, even require more care, than a mother alone can provide (Hrdy 2009).

When in *Homo* evolution did these helpless newborns evolve? Estimates of brain sizes based on fossil remains indicate that early *Homo* had slightly bigger brains than did australopithecines and contemporary apes. However, the enlarged brains both in early *Homo* and *Homo erectus* appear to be mostly accounted for by progressively larger body sizes, with only small increases in brain size relative to body size. The process of slower brain development (and more helpless newborns) appears to have been more important with *Homo heidelbergensis* but did not reach its modern pattern until *Homo sapiens* 150,000 years ago (Thompson and Nelson forthcoming). Accordingly, other caregivers, from grandmothers to aunts, older daughters to fathers, likely took on increased roles, the closer our ancestors came to the present *Homo sapiens*.

Debates Concerning the Origins of Human Pair-Bonds and Paternal Care

Across primates, females are more likely than males to take interest in and care for young. There are various reasons for this sex difference. Female primates in the wild nurse their young for prolonged periods, with mothers typically maintaining proximity to offspring who await their nutritional sustenance. Among Old World monkeys and apes, this means that mothers are almost in constant sight of or contact with their nursing young.

Given the gender differences in reproductive strategies described earlier in this chapter, it is also unsurprising that females take more interest in young. Daughters will be future mothers, so caring for young siblings provides terrific "on-the-job" training that will later enhance the daughters' own caregiving abilities. Older females, especially relatives who may not be currently taking care of their own nurslings, may be helpful, given shared relationships and childcare interests. In contemporary foraging societies, human hunter-gatherer data on childcare patterns, which we discuss in Chapter 2, suggest that older daughters, grandmothers, and aunts tend to provide as much or more direct care of young than fathers do (Kelly 1995). These considerations suggest that if *Homo* newborns required allocare (care by individuals other than the mother), female relatives were as likely as fathers, or more likely than fathers, to provide this care. At least this appears a fair conjecture for direct forms of allocare, such as holding or watching a child.

But how might that fit with the reduction in body-size sexual dimorphism noted above? A general pattern is that long-term bonds between mates (as in social monogamy) are necessary, but not sufficient, to account for paternal care. The baboon males mentioned above represent one of the few exceptions. We suggest that, consistent with the general pattern and new fossil finds indicating more body-size variation in early *Homo* and *Homo erectus* than expected, long-term bonds may have gained importance among our *Homo heidelbergensis* ancestors, but without much direct paternal involvement. However, we readily acknowledge the importance of new fossil finds and other evidence in helping address when human pair-bonds evolved: around 2 million years ago, 0.5 million years ago among so-called *Homo heidelbergensis,* or a mere 150,000 years ago among modern humans.

Long-term bonds may have arisen for various reasons (see Low 2000; Reichard and Boesch 2005). The possibilities have piled up over the decades. The birth of increasingly helpless young required fathers to stick around and help carry their progeny. The male initiated permanent associations with a single female, effectively "mate guarding" the female. The female chose to form long-term associations with a given male to obtain his protective services, protection that could be used to reduce predation, reduce sexual coercion by other males, and reduce the chance of an unrelated male harassing or killing of her offspring. A recent proposal is that the female formed long-term bonds with a male to acquire his services protecting the foods she had obtained and processed (Wrangham et al. 1999).

Among all the proposed hypotheses for the origin of human pair-bonds, the most championed has been that males and females formed relationships thanks to the benefits of male provisioning (for example, J. B. Lancaster and C. S. Lancaster 1983; Lovejoy 1981; Kaplan et al. 2000). This is the "man the hunter" hypothesis of human pair-bonds. Because males provided highly valued game meat to spouses, females chose to form bonds with good providers in order to enhance their own nutrient base and that of their young. Men chose to provision families in order to guarantee reproductive access to a mate and increase offspring survival. With so many hypotheses advanced to account for the origins of human pair-bonds, how can we decide which is best supported?

The first stone tools used by our hominin relatives date to 2.6 million years before the present (Semaw et al. 1997). These are relatively simple cobbles, flakes, and the like. Based on study of "microwear" marks on these stone tools, they appear to have been used to process plants as well as animal flesh. These tools thus provide concrete evidence of hominin meat consumption, whether meat was obtained by hunting or scavenging. Because among chimpanzees and human hunter-gatherer populations it is primarily males who hunt, the supposition has been that "man the hunter" had begun his quest.

The continued elaboration of tool kits since that time suggests increased hunting, plant resource acquisition, and intensive food processing (Plummer 2004). Unfortunately, however, the tools likely used for increasingly efficient hominin food-procurement and food-processing strategies preserve poorly in the archeological record. We find the occasional stone tool, but tools made from plant materials are all but lost in the past. Still, the stone-tool record suggests a remarkable stability in the reliance on Acheulian hand axes, once they appeared approximately 1.5 million years ago in Africa, with the core design little changed for over 1 million years. More-complex hunting implements are not evidenced until the first spear appears around four hundred thousand years ago, and bows and arrows a mere thirty thousand or so years before the present (Marlowe 2005a). A presumption is that this increasingly elaborated hunting technology indicates greater male hunting and an increasingly codified sexual division of labor (a system in which men and women focus on different activities but share with each other the bounty of their success).

Female foraging strategies must have included enhanced technologies, such as the use of digging sticks to access foods, like tubers, that otherwise are unattainable. Advanced food-processing techniques, such as leaching, grinding, and later cooking, would increase the nutritional value of plant foods. The importance of these foods cannot be understated. For one thing, these are foods that could be fairly reliably obtained, with tubers serving literally as plants' "underground storage organs," which people could steal. The existence of a consistent food source enabled females' sharing these foods with males, who in turn were freed to devote more time engaging in high-payoff, high-risk hunting strategies. The availability of a nutrient-dense foodstuff, whether meat or processed plant products, appears to have been necessary to fuel several evolutionary changes in the hominin lineage (Kaplan et al. 2000). We humans have a smaller gut, indicative of a higher-quality diet than would be expected for an ape of our body size (Aiello and

Wheeler 1995). The inference is that our gut sizes may have decreased beginning in earlier forms of *Homo*, thanks to a more nutritionally dense diet, and this in turn may have freed the energetic resources to invest in an enlarged brain. Our adult brains burn about 20% of our metabolic budget, but the smaller brains of chimpanzees burn only around 8% of their budget; our *Homo* ancestors' improved diet made possible our enlarged brain. The more we see this enhanced dietary quality provided by hunting, the more we imagine how women supported men's hunting, how men provided game meat, and how the exchange was fostered by the formation of pair-bonds in a sexual division of labor.

This type of "man the hunter" scenario has long dominated views of male roles in human evolution, including the notion that provisioning has been a long-standing feature of paternal care. Beginning in the 1990s, however, the hypothesis underwent intensive scrutiny. Critics pointed out that hunting big-game animals is an economically risky endeavor (Hawkes 1991). A hunter fails most days, winning the game lottery only on a rare day. Without the support of a mate subsidizing his diet, a male could not engage in these risky activities without starving. And if a father is bent on provisioning members of his nuclear family, he has chosen a poor way to do so, as he usually arrives home a failed hunter.

Human hunter-gatherer data reveal that when men obtain a big-game payoff such as an impala or a deer, then their quarry tend to be widely shared and consumed by all group members rather than simply their nuclear families (Hawkes and Bliege Bird 2002). This pattern of food distribution hardly looks like family provisioning; it looks like group sharing. Consequently, researchers argued for a new interpretation of male hunting, the sexual division of labor, and the nature of human family life. Hawkes and colleagues viewed the acquisition of widely shared game as "showing off" to prospective mates. A successful hunter effectively advertises his value as a mate. Some females provide a reproductive reward to the showoff, becoming his first wife, a polygynous wife, or an extrapair mate. In this interpretation, male hunting has nothing to do with paternal care but everything to do with mating. A corollary is that the evolutionary foundations of human pair-bonds and paternal care reside in alternative scenarios, such as mate guarding: here, males effectively are "parasites" plaguing females and advertising to additional mates through hunting success, rather than acting as worthwhile resource providers.

Other critics pointed out a core problem with the "show-off hypothesis" (Bliege Bird, Smith, and Bird 2001). Even if males use their kills to advertise their hunting abilities to mates, this creates what economists and biologists call a "public goods" problem. That is the problem of group members' receiving the benefits of a certain resource without having to pay the cost to provide it. The reason this is a conundrum is that if individuals can get something for nothing, they will all turn into "free-riders," and thus nobody will ever pay the cost of providing the good in the first place. Consider roads as an example. If you could let your neighbors build and maintain roads while you used them for free, you would be better off than building them yourself. If your neighbors shared the same attitude, they would wait for you to build them, and the roads would never get built. (In societies with strong central governments, taxation can solve this problem; taxes can pay for roads, and free-riders might get stuck in jail.) In the case of hunter-gatherer male hunting, the question is, when all group members may benefit from big game, why should a single female provide the mating rewards to fuel a hunter's continued motivation?

In response to this issue, Bliege Bird and colleagues proposed that hunter-gatherer male big-game hunting represents "costly signaling" of a male's inherent qualities (Bliege Bird, Smith, and Bird 2001). The idea is that a successful hunter advertises to prospective mates that he possesses more-general advantageous qualities (he has "good genes"; he is hard working), which pay for any given female to mate with him. So this advertising strategy overcomes the public goods problem—it pays for a given female to mate with a good hunter—while retaining the advertising essence raised in the "show-off hypothesis." In a number of human hunter-gatherer societies, positive links between male hunting prowess and reproductive success lend support to these views. For example, among Ache male hunters of Paraguay, the better the hunter, the more mates he has (Kaplan and Hill 1985).

We, like other researchers (Gurven and Hill 2009), believe that arguments boiling down male behavior to showing off or costly signaling sell short the real story of human paternal investment. Men in contemporary human hunter-gatherer societies acquire other resources besides big game; smaller game, honey, and other resources are given more to members of a man's nuclear family than to the entire group. So men in hunter-gatherer societies appear to provision after all. Men also provide more resources to biological children than to stepchildren (Marlowe 1999b). If male efforts were mating advertisements alone, males should not care about the paternity status of the young whose mothers they attempt to seduce. But they do, as Frank Marlowe showed with data on paternal behavior among the Hadza, hunter-gatherers in northern Tanzania.

Male contributions to diet appear also to enhance a mate's reproductive output. Human hunter-gatherer females reproduce at faster rates than we would expect for an ape of our body size (Marlowe 2005a). The average time between births, known as the "interbirth interval," is approximately three to four years among recently documented human hunter-gatherers. Compare them to orangutans, who have the longest interbirth interval of any mammal: females without any male assistance take about seven years between births in the wild. Chimpanzees and bonobos have interbirth intervals of around four to five years. If we extrapolated interbirth intervals from female body sizes of these other apes, we would anticipate that human hunter-gatherers would take about seven years between births. The difference in good part appears to be made possible through male food contributions. Across a cross-cultural sample of human hunter-gatherers, the greater the contribution of male resources to the diet, the shorter the interbirth interval. Frank Marlowe (2003) has also suggested, based on Hadza data, that men's provisioning to wives increases in the year or so immediately after she has had a child—what Marlowe calls a "critical period" of paternal provisioning. The other evidence of male provisioning discussed above tells us that some of the resources men obtain are channeled to mates to help them reproduce faster.

A Synthesis of the Evolutionary Origins of Human Pair-Bonds and Paternal Care

So where does this leave us? When and how did human paternal care originate? Based on the evidence reviewed above, we favor the following scenario. In presenting this synthesis, we emphasize the contingent nature of any conclusions—new data and new debates will continue to hone our understanding of these issues.

We infer from the comparative primate data that paternal care was absent at the time our ancestors split from the lineage giving rise to today's chimpanzees and bonobos approximately 6 million years ago. This means our paternal behavior today has been derived recently in evolution.

Consistent with general mammalian patterns of mating systems and paternal care, we suggest that human pair-bonds may have originated in male mate-guarding. We see this process as beginning to move in this direction with early *Homo* or *Homo erectus* around 2 million years ago but demonstrating more-pronounced trends this way with *Homo heidelbergensis* around half a million years ago. As *Homo* adopted fully bipedal ways in more open environments and increased the proportion of the diet obtained from meat sources, group sizes may have increased. During *Homo* evolution, coalitions of lower-ranking males may have agreed upon a compact to mate guard individual females, behavior occurring at reproductive cost to the dominant male, who previously monopolized more mating opportunities, and to the females mated to dominant males. This proposal fits with Christopher Boehm's depiction of our species' "egalitarian" behavior: dominant human males in hunter-gatherer and other face-to-face societies are less despotic than our chimpanzee cousins (Boehm 1999). Females may have acceded to these arrangements if the costs of sexual coercion were not worth resistance. Later, we imagine, the origins of pair-bonds in mate guarding could give rise to facets of paternal care. An outcome is a unique form of mammalian pair-bonding: long-term relationships embedded in a multimale, multifemale social group (rather than, as in the pattern of gibbons, territorial bonds in family groups). We see an important role for males but also for female relatives, such as older sisters and adult females, who provided direct allocare as well (Hrdy 2009).

If pair-bonds were under way, permanent associations may have permitted a greater sexual division of labor and in turn greater male provisioning. Females could subsidize a mate who often failed in seeking resources that she (and he) valued—the rare treats of fat and protein acquired from meat. Males could afford to engage in these riskier economic activities. Females benefited by increasing reproductive output. The compact would need to be mutually beneficial for both sexes not to cheat while apart from each other. Or maybe they would be faithful most of the time, but open to extrapair mating opportunities that could provide complementary benefits. Engaging in economic activities apart from each other for part of the day would make mate guarding tougher.

The formation of long-term bonds would permit other social changes. Assuming that couples slept next to each other at night, fathers would find themselves in proximity to their offspring. This proximity could enhance the development of paternal-offspring attachment. Fathers could spend more time around their children. Through proximity maintenance to mates, fathers too would spend part of daylight hours near children, typically in the presence of the children's mothers too. As children grew older, fathers might play increasingly important roles in socialization, especially for sons. In all of these ways, we see the social presence of fathers in their children's lives as later developments in the evolution of human family life. Our best guess is that these patterns were more prominent with *Homo heidelbergensis* around half a million years ago but didn't really achieve modern patterns until literally the emergence of modern humans 150,000 years ago.

Paternal investment may have shaped other important reproductive outcomes during hominin evolution. The food contributions by men to partners may have enabled them to reproduce more rapidly, thereby enabling mates to achieve higher lifetime reproductive success thanks to shortened interbirth intervals. The presence of males as deterrents to predators and perhaps males of enemy groups may have contributed to the reductions in human hunter-gatherer juvenile mortality we find compared with that of wild chimpanzees and Old World monkeys. Hunting weapons and fire may be particularly good deterrents to would-be predators, so effective in fact that the most feared animals among contemporary foragers tend to be venomous snakes (rather than, say, leopards or jaguars).

All this being said, contemporary forager data reveal that adults die, couples separate, and family relationships are in flux (Blurton Jones et al. 2000; B. S. Hewlett 1991a). Traditional conceptions of human paternal investment privilege intact families and so-called genetic fathers (those men who have biologically fathered coresidential children). Mixed families of step- and genetic children probably have a deep ancestry. So likely do extrapair matings, especially among younger couples, further fostering blended hunter-gatherer families (see Winking, Kaplan, et al. 2007). Yet hunter-gatherer data also point to the evolutionary novelty of at least one common feature of contemporary paternal investment—passing along inherited wealth like livestock, farmland, or money to children. Hunter-gatherer subsistence patterns lack, until more-recent complex foragers like the Nootka of Vancouver or Ainu of

Japan, the stores of wealth that allow fathers to accumulate goods to give to their offspring.

Our view of the evolution of human paternal care also hinges on assumptions concerning hominin life spans and mortality patterns (Boone 2002). Critics of the "hunting hypothesis" have largely sought to displace a primary role for fathers with that of grandmothers. The argument is that grandmothers make particularly effective caregivers—measured both as providers of direct care (for example, babysitting) and as providers of indirect care (for example, providing food resources such as tubers)—benefiting their grandchildren (Hawkes et al. 1998). However, the strength of that proposal depends on how likely we imagine postreproductive grandmothers to have fulfilled these roles among our ancestors. Based on contemporary hunter-gatherer evidence, ethnographers proclaim that after a forager woman survived to reach adolescence, chances are that she would live twenty years beyond her reproductive capacity (Gurven and Kaplan 2007); often, it is assumed this long life span and postreproductive capacity can be projected back to early *Homo* nearly 2 million years ago. However, bioarcheological evidence for old individuals is largely lacking, leading other researchers to assume that extended life spans and hence any significant role for postreproductive grandmothers does not appear until our species appears in Africa around 150,000 years ago (Caspari and Lee 2004; Kennedy 2003).

We find more persuasive the view that extended postreproductive hominin life spans emerged recently—with ourselves, *Homo sapiens*. We view the rapidly expanded cultural arsenal—from more-efficient hunting tools to improved knowledge of predators' behavior to better food-processing techniques—of *Homo sapiens* as contributing to reductions in environmental insults and in turn juvenile and adult mortality, thereby enabling more older postreproductive individuals to survive in contemporary hunter-gatherer groups than, say, among hunter-gatherers of 150,000 years ago. This means that we tend to favor a perspective that sees pair-bonds, a sexual division of labor, and paternal care as playing more important dimensions throughout *Homo* evolution but especially in the past 150,000 years of our species' existence, rather than an extreme view that foregrounds grandmothers at males' expense. Reductions in mortality also allow more fathers to survive to watch their children grow and thus to play more important roles in socialization.

We are enthusiastic that current debates concerning the origins of human pair-bonds and paternal care may benefit from the addition of new data in comparative genomics (Bradley 2008). Several physiological systems have been linked to mammalian social behavior, including underlying genetic mechanisms such as the vasopressin receptor (more on that in Chapter 10). Moreover, humans display physiological evidence of reduced "sperm competition" (more on that too in later chapters), which raises the potential of identifying and attempting to time with a molecular-clock approach when this reduction occurred (and thereby permit inference of a shift toward sociosexually monogamous pair-bonds among our hominin ancestors [see Carnahan and Jensen-Seaman 2008]). Already, comparisons of the human and chimpanzee genome, with genomes of gorillas and orangutans not far away, have demonstrated patterns and timing of human evolutionary events, such as the loss of our body hair; we anticipate that similar sorts of analyses may help address the evolutionary story of human paternal care too.

However the precise evolutionary details of human paternal care unfolded, it is clear that patterns of human fatherhood stand out in comparative perspectives. Paternal investment is a distinguishing characteristic of our species. We number among the small fraction of mammalian species in which males play important roles in raising offspring. These shifts toward paternal investment appear to have occurred recently within hominin evolution. The limited available evidence highlights potentially important transitions among our ancestors around half a million years ago *(Homo heidelbergensis)* as well as the time of our species' origin in Africa around 150,000 years ago. All this being said, however, it is equally obvious that human paternal care exhibits variation both cross-culturally and within cultures. In the next chapter, we shift our focus from the founding fathers to the range of variation in human fatherhood.

2

A World of Diversity: Cross-Cultural Variation in Paternal Care

The Aka live as hunter-gatherers in the Congo Basin rainforest in central Africa. As Barry Hewlett's account of their paternal care has revealed, these men are remarkably involved fathers (B. S. Hewlett 1991b). When the amount of time fathers spend with their young children is quantified, Aka men hold them 22% of the time they reside in camps and are within an arm's reach throughout the bulk of the day inside or outside of the camp. Aka fathers also sleep in close proximity to their infants. As a consequence, a father's world incorporates his young progeny throughout the vast majority of waking and sleeping hours. The amount of time Aka men spend in contact with or near their young children surpasses that in any other known society. However, Aka fathers do not engage in any rough and tumble play with their children. They also do not engage in negative reinforcement or discipline; an infant who hits another infant may be moved to another place, but his or her father (or mother) will not hit the child or say no (B. S. Hewlett 1991b).

A variety of factors help account for the patterns of Aka paternal care. One of the most important is the nature of Aka subsistence activities. As we shall see, fathers in hunter-gatherer societies such as the Aka tend to devote more time and effort to holding and caring for their infants and toddlers than do men in other types of societies. Furthermore, Aka men and women cooperate in using nets to hunt forest antelope and other animals; these activities mean that spouses are often in close contact, and a nursing infant can be readily handed to a father. Because the subsistence nature of Aka society requires cooperation more than competition, fathers can also afford to be indulgent with their young children (the children do not need to be trained to rise up a highly competitive social hierarchy), and by spending so much time with their children, fathers may feel less compelled to play vigorously with them.

We have two goals in the present chapter. The first is to survey cross-cultural variation in paternal care. To do this, we rely heavily on quantitative cross-cultural comparisons, in part to canvass the breadth of variation, though this approach does come at some expense of discussions of specific cases. The second goal of this chapter is to help account for some of this cross-cultural variation. While it is notable itself that human fathers around the globe care for their children (as the previous chapter highlighted), a variety of factors underlie cross-cultural variation in paternal care. So with these twin aims in mind, let us survey the variable landscape of paternal care.

Measuring Fathers

Before we can document and explain cross-cultural variation in paternal care, we must first attend to some conceptual housekeeping. We need to define what we mean by "paternal care." We need to clarify the forms of paternal care that we wish to compare and explain cross-culturally. We also need to describe the kinds of data that are useful for this chapter's purposes. So before we jump into addressing cross-cultural variation in paternal care, we first address these important measurement issues.

We adopt a loose view of paternal care as the time and resources given by a man to his children. This loose view acknowledges the variable ways in which researchers from various disciplines approach and define "paternal care," "paternal involvement," "paternal investment," or the like. Throughout this chapter (and later ones), we will include data accrued from these various approaches, so our purposes are best met employing a broad definition of paternal care. Psychologists, as well as some sociologists, typically focus on male involvement with children, involvement in which men interact directly with them. Involvement can be active, including such actions as holding, feeding, and changing diapers, or it can be passive, including such behavior as just being nearby (B. S. Hewlett 1991b). Measures of father involvement may include things like how much time a father spends holding a baby or talking with a child and how frequently the parent and child eat a meal together. Evolutionary biologists, conversely, often focus on parental investment in offspring. Parental investment includes allocations of resources (such as time, food, or money) that increase the fitness of existing offspring. In practical terms, "fitness" means anything that will improve children's chances of survival, make them healthier, and increase the probability of their making a living and finding a mate when grown up. Investment is obviously a much broader category than involvement. One can invest in a child without being physically near (by procuring food, building a home, or working for an income). Evolutionary biologists generally conceive of parental investment as having an opportunity cost; that is, there is something else the parent could have done with that investment, and allocating it to a child means it cannot be used for something else.

Nonevolutionary social scientists, in particular economists and some sociologists, also focus on investment in children, generally in reference to explicit financial expenditures, such as child support payments by nonresident parents, or college tuition. These scientists acknowledge the opportunity costs involved in these payments, as well as the beneficial effects these expenditures tend to have on offspring. They differ from evolutionary biologists in that they are not generally thinking about long-term fitness benefits for the offspring involved.

Finally, psychologists often make use of measures of emotional closeness or parental warmth, as well as scales measuring people's beliefs or attitudes about parenting. Examples of these include statements like "I am very close to my child," "My child confides his or her problems to me," and "Fathers should be heavily involved in the care of children," all answered on a scale measuring the extent to which the respondent agrees or disagrees with the statement. These measures are distinct from both involvement and investment, and they can be criticized on the grounds that they are vague and cannot be empirically validated. Yet they also clearly tap into some aspect of parenting, in particular dimensions that may not be captured by quantitative estimates of involvement or investment.

What features of paternal care should we measure and compare? One scheme biologists advanced for the study of mammalian paternal care is a distinction between direct and indirect paternal care (Kleiman and Malcolm 1981). "Direct care" refers to holding, carrying, and closely interacting with a child in ways benefiting his or her survival. "Indirect care" refers to more-removed forms of aid, such as provisioning, providing inheritances, and offering protection against predators or other dangers. This contrast between direct and indirect care provides a useful start to distinguishing facets of paternal care, a distinction we use to structure major portions of this chapter's contents. We devote whole sections to cross-cultural variation in direct paternal care and to cross-cultural variation in indirect paternal care. However, the contrast between direct and indirect care also harbors some gray areas. Social and moral training can be tricky to place in such a dichotomy. This aspect of paternal care is of greatest importance in humans but of questionable relevance in nonhuman mammals, which is one reason it may not have been a necessary component of the direct/indirect care framework. We devote another section to cross-cultural variation in social and moral training, to give due justice to this side of human paternal care. Finally, we also cover several dimensions of paternal care—from involvement in the birth process to corporal punishment—where it seemed most sensible to do so along this unfolding look at variation in paternal direct care, indirect care, and social and moral training.

Various types of data enable documenting and explaining cross-cultural patterns of human paternal care, although we emphasize quantitative cross-cultural comparisons throughout the present chapter. We commonly draw upon the Standard Cross-Cultural Sample (SCCS). The SCCS consists of 186 cultures differing in linguistic group, region of the world, and subsistence, in order to capture a wide, representative array of human cultural diversity. In this sample, one can grasp a crude but comparable view of paternal care among polygynous societies of pastoralists (who herd livestock such as cattle) in eastern Africa, rural horticulturalists (who practice shifting cultivation of crops) in Brazil, recent hunter-gatherers in Australia, or highland farmers in Nepal. Although few variables are available at the level of detail we might desire (for example, paternal proximity is categorized on a 1–5 scale for a given group, though variation within that society is ignored), the SCCS has the advantage of encompassing a great range of cross-cultural variation in geography, subsistence type, and population size.

In other instances, we compare features of paternal care across countries. With qualitative or quantitative data amassed by countries or other political units (for example, states or regions), some patterns in paternal care can be discussed. In these types of comparisons, we might encounter qualitative variation in national differences in fathers providing moral guidance to their sons and daughters. These data tend to be not only less detailed but also motivated by bureaucratic considerations (that is, the needs of governments for such data), but these data still enable comparisons of paternal care at a different scale. Some of these comparisons appear more legitimately "cultural" (for example, a comparison between a southeast Asian and western European country) than others, depending on the specifics.

As a final note on measuring paternal behavior, we devote little space this chapter to discussing uninvolved fathers or even "parasitic" fathers (fathers who drain resources from a child and perhaps the child's mother). The kinds of studies reviewed in this chapter do not enable ready comparisons of the fraction of fathers in different societies who shun paternal investment altogether. Elsewhere in the book, we touch upon issues of less-involved fathers, including fathers' variable contributions to child support, and patterns of father-offspring sexual abuse. To be sure, the full spectrum of cross-cultural variation in paternal care includes these darker sides of paternal care in addition to the more tangible and positive contributions highlighted here.

The Birth of a Father

The birth of a child is the birth of a father and of a father's possible direct care contributions. Are men involved in these earliest of paternal moments cross-culturally? A generation ago, in countries like Sweden or the United States, men were rarely immediately present at their children's births. In a dramatic shift, the vast majority of fathers in these same countries are now present at the bedside when their children are born (J. Draper 1997). Clearly part of that sudden change can be traced to greater couple mobility and to the reduced availability of female kin to serve similar roles. Yet this change also invites the question, how do patterns of male involvement at birth vary in broader cultural context?

Surveying the SCCS for evidence of paternal involvement at birth, Lozoff (1983) found relevant data for 120 of the 186 societies in the sample. In 27% of these societies men were present at birth. However, even when present, fathers rarely did anything but observe. Those patterns are notable because human mothers typically give birth with the assistance of others, but more often that assistance is provided by trained specialists (for example, midwives) or female relatives (Trevathan 1987). Most male involvement at birth appears oriented less toward immediate care of the newborn and more toward socially recognizing a man's paternity or providing indirect or emotional support to the mother. As a provocative illustration, one researcher of the Huichol (of Mexico) wrote that men assist in childbirth as follows: "When a woman had her first child the husband squatted in the rafters of the house, or in the branches of a tree, directly above her, with ropes attached to his scrotum. As she went into labor pain, the wife pulled vigorously on the ropes, so that her husband shared in the painful, but ultimately joyous, experience of childbirth" (Berrin 1978, 162). However, this remarkable Huichol "tradition," circulated as fact on the Internet, is apparently a fabrication designed to sell local art.

In a smaller sample of sixty societies similarly representing diversity in subsistence, geographic, and sociopolitical diversity, Huber and Breedlove (2007) investigated both direct and indirect assistance to mothers during birth. Of different relatives, grandmothers and aunts provided the most immediate assistance to the mother at birth (for example, by massaging her), followed by fathers. However, fathers provided the most indirect assistance (food and shelter, for example) to mothers during birth, even more than grandmothers did. Several factors helped account for cross-cultural variation in men's investments: in societies with higher paternity certainty (that is, societies in which the men are most likely to be the actual fathers of their supposed children), fathers provided more direct but not indirect care to mothers; and in societies more oriented toward male ancestry and inheritance (patrilineal bias), fathers provided more direct and indirect care to mothers at birth. These patterns can be understood as reflecting male interest in channeling their resources to biological relatives, particularly within a male lineage. None of those male investments included donating their testicles for use as pulley devices.

Cross-Cultural Variation in Direct Paternal Care

With the birth day past, how does men's direct involvement in childcare play out cross-culturally? For us to address this question, it may be best to begin with hunter-gatherer direct paternal care. Because recent and contemporary hunter-gatherer societies better resemble the socioecological context in which human paternal care evolved than other types of societies do, we may profit by investigating patterns of direct paternal care among hunter-gatherers, then comparing patterns of hunter-gatherer paternal care with patterns across a wider array of societies.

In recent decades, a number of researchers have closely eyed fathers and their children while tabulating quantitative data on the amount of time fathers spend with their young children. Among the hunter-gatherer Hadza of northern Tanzania, for example, Frank Marlowe (1999a) discovered that fathers in camps spend around 5% of their time holding their children aged nine months or younger. These Hadza data are fairly consistent with hunter-gatherer paternal holding data across other societies in Africa, such as the Bofi, and in Australia, where researchers have done similar research (Fouts 2008; Marlowe 1999a). The main hunter-gatherer exception to these direct care numbers is the Aka, who hold their children for 22% of the time these fathers are in camp (B. S. Hewlett 1991b). The Aka pattern of husbands and wives cooperatively net hunting appears to help account for their unusual direct care patterns compared with those of these other foraging societies.

In an analysis employing the SCCS, Marlowe (2000) documented both cross-cultural variation in direct paternal care and several factors underlying it, including data from hunter-gatherers as well as from other kinds of small-scale societies. As revealed in these analyses, fathers in hunter-gatherer societies provide more direct infant care than do fathers in horticultural, agricultural, or pastoralist societies; the contrasts are most extreme with pastoralists. Fathers in hunter-gatherer societies also provide more direct care of children than do fathers in these other societies. In this same data set, at least two variables additionally cross-cut subsistence bases of societies in association with direct paternal care. The more polygynous the society (that is, the greater the proportion of men who have multiple wives), the less direct paternal care is provided. Moreover, the greater male aggressiveness is within a society, the less direct paternal care is provided.

What should we make of these cross-cultural patterns of direct paternal care? The finding that hunter-gatherer men invest more in direct care than do men in other societal types is important to evolutionary arguments concerning human paternal care. Because of the greater relevance of hunter-gatherer lifeways to evolutionary scenarios, these hunter-gatherer data suggest some merit to projecting direct paternal care into an evolutionary past. The hunter-gatherer data additionally question why direct paternal care would diminish in other economic systems, such as pastoralism. As for the other findings, the greater the polygyny within a society, the more men may be spending their effort seeking additional mates rather than investing in their current ones and offspring, which would help account for the negative link between polygyny and direct paternal care. If men are called into male-male competition to achieve status within a group or to aid in between-group coalitions, this may inhibit their ability to provide direct paternal care. Using a more limited sample of eighty societies from the SCCS, Mary Katz and Melvin Konner (1981) effectively reached similar conclusions concerning factors accounting for variation in direct paternal care. They suggest that "where the male's role includes polygyny and/ or military activities, he does not contribute to childcare, regardless of women's contribution to subsistence. When these are absent, he contributes if the mother is busy with subsistence activities especially if the family is not extended. When the father is absent and the mother's workload is high, grandparents and siblings help with childcare" (175). The bottom line is that subsistence factors, male involvement in warfare, and the mating system all help account for variation in direct paternal care.

The results of these cross-cultural analyses highlight variation in direct paternal care primarily across small-scale societies. Through complementary kinds of analyses conducted among samples in larger countries, we can compare patterns of direct paternal care across more urban and technologically varied societies. Summarizing a variety of such studies among two-parent families in countries such as Japan, India, Malaysia, and Brazil, Jaipaul Roopnarine (n.d.) demonstrates variation in the amount of daily time men spend with their young children. Men in India are near their children an estimated three to five hours a day, the highest time of any group in the sample. At the other extreme, Japanese fathers average about twenty minutes a day with their children. In between are samples from urban Malaysia, where fathers spend an average of about an hour and a half daily caring for their one-year-olds, and Jamaica, where fathers report about an hour of daily care of one-year-olds.

While a host of factors underlie this international variation in direct care across Japan, Malaysia, India, and elsewhere (and we will talk more about these factors throughout the book), one pattern is robust across all samples in which direct care has been assessed. There is not a single society reported in which men's time devoted to direct care of young children surpasses the time women devote to direct care. In Roopnarine's (n.d.) compilation, fathers devote anywhere from 20% (in a Malaysia sample) to 78% (in a U.S. sample) of the time that mothers spend giving direct care to young children. In smaller-scale societies, mothers similarly devote more time than fathers do to direct care (Kramer 2005). Indeed, grandmothers and older siblings sometimes spend more time in giving such care than fathers do. In a rural Mayan community in Mexico, mothers provide 46% of direct care, fathers 2%, and older daughters 32% (Kramer 2005). Moreover, in some societies, such as the Hadza, the Bofi of the Central African Republic, and the Khasi of northeast India, the more time fathers devote to direct care, the less time maternal grandmothers do, and vice versa. These data suggest that a mother benefits from others' help but that a variety of caregivers, including but not restricted to fathers, can assist (Hrdy 2009). This research also reminds us of an obvious fact: fathers are not mirror images of mothers. Instead, fathers face parenting with the evolved baggage of a male mammal, including weighing the optimal use of their time to mating versus parenting effort, and orienting with a male-specific physiology to parental tasks.

In view of a male-specific parental orientation, we might imagine a variety of factors that impact fathers' direct care of children. Take the following account of paternal care among the Yanomami, an Amazonian group that mixes horticulture with hunting and gathering: "In the morning Yanomami fathers play with their children, male and female, for 15 to 30 minutes while their wives tend to domestic tasks. They place their children in the hammock, raise them up, speak to them in the typical high-toned baby talk, kiss, and fondle them. Their repertory of affectionate behavioral patterns is qualitatively identical to that of mothers. Fathers also feed their children prechewed food. They use social body grooming behavior less frequently than mothers (delousing, cleaning off, removal of pimples, etc.) and engage in more play and athletic activities with the children. The children respond most positively to these play bouts with the father" (Eibl-Eibsfeldt 1989, 224–225). From this account alone, we are prompted to ask about possible differential interactions of fathers with boys versus girls, and the specific kinds of activities in which fathers engage, such as physical play. Certainly, we can posit other variables that might be important to patterns of direct paternal care.

Age of a father's child, for a variety of reasons, could be one relevant factor. If the child's mother serves as primary caregiver of an infant she nurses frequently, then the father's role may increase once a child has been weaned. Yet older children also become increasingly independent and less vulnerable,and thus require less direct care from parents, with older siblings and others able to help too. When we bring data to these possibilities, among Kipsigis agropastoralists in Kenya, men have little involvement in infant care, meaning that interactions can only increase as the child ages. Accordingly, children's participation with their fathers for many activities, such as playing, eating, and doing chores, increases from birth to age four (Harkness and Super 1992). Among Bofi foragers in the Central African Republic, we also find fathers playing greater roles as their children age: while their one-year-olds spend about 4% of their waking hours in physical contact with fathers, four-year-olds spend about 15% of their waking hours in physical contact with fathers (Fouts 2008). Interestingly, however, men in the United States may actually decrease their involvement over the same age span: given more-limited family care networks and shorter nursing durations, U.S. men spend more time with their highly dependent young but less time as children grow older and become less needy of direct care (Harkness and Super 1992). Covering a much wider age range, Mark Flinn (1992) observed that fathers in Trinidad "interact slightly more with adolescent and adult offspring than with infants and preadolescents" (66). Finally, among the Hadza, Marlowe (1999) reveals how several measures of direct paternal care change across children aged zero to five: paternal proximity, play, and nurturing all drop as children age, but communication is not clearly age related.

Another factor that could impact a father's direct care is the gender of his child. Inherent differences between boys and girls may elicit different parental responses. Fathers may have sex-specific reasons for biasing variation of care into either boys or girls (for example, by training a son to hunt or farm). Accordingly, in many societies, fathers provide more care of sons than of daughters. Hadza fathers, for example, spend more time with sons than with daughters (though there is no sex bias on the part of mothers) (Marlowe 2005). Similar patterns are observed in the United States. Kathleen Harris, Frank Furstenberg, and Jeremy Marmer (1998), using a national sample of American families with children ages eleven through sixteen, examined an index of parental involvement, which was composed of measures of behavioral involvement (such as activities done together) and emotional involvement (such as closeness and affection). Fathers scored significantly higher on the parental involvement index for sons than for daughters, whereas mothers showed no differences in involvement depending on their child's gender. Traditionally, in Korea fathers focused more on sons, but in part because of currently small family sizes, Korean fathers are now equally involved with sons and daughters (Shwalb et al. 2004).

Yet another factor that may impact direct paternal care is the type of caregiving activity. Do fathers engage in different types of caregiving behavior when compared with mothers? To take a specific example, do fathers play differently with their children—engaging particularly in rough, physical play—than mothers do? Researchers contemplating this question, and answering with observations culled from various societies around the world, often, but not universally, find that fathers engage in more physical play than mothers do (as is the case among the Yanomami described above). Among the Tsimane of Bolivia, for example, fathers devote a greater proportion of their direct caregiving to children aged zero to five to playing (and comforting) than do mothers (Winking, Gurven, et al. 2009). Integrating much of the U.S. research on parental play, Daniel Paquette (2004) observes that fathers spend a higher proportion of their time with children, and particularly sons, in physical, active play. However, among the Aka, fathers do not engage in rough forms of physical play like tossing infants in the air (B. S. Hewlett 1991). This form of play is also less prominent in urban samples of fathers living in India, Taiwan, Malaysia, and Thailand (Roopnarine n.d.).

Paternal Presence after Dark

To shine light on direct paternal care across a full day, we also need to consider the roles of fathers after dark. What happens after nightfall, particularly in places lacking electric lighting? Researchers have traditionally said less about direct paternal care at night, in part because paternal activities are less readily observable. However, sleep-wake cycles suggest that regardless of the waking hours fathers spend with their children, if fathers should sleep nearby, they might be exposed to child stimuli (smell, sounds, touch) in visceral ways across many hours a day.

Ball, Hooker, and Kelly (2000) summarize results from several cross-cultural surveys of father-child sleeping patterns. In a survey of eighty small-scale societies within the SCCS, fathers in 31% of these societies co-slept (shared same bed or other sleeping surface) with mother and child; in 29% fathers slept apart but in the same room; and in another

31% of societies fathers slept apart but in a different room or dwelling. In this same sample, infants always co-slept with mothers. Interestingly, similar patterns of mother-offspring sleeping proximity hold among Old World monkeys and apes, underscoring how unusual Western sleeping practices of placing infants alone in their own room to sleep are (Small 1998). That said, the cross-cultural patterns clearly reveal wide variation in fathers' sleeping proximity to infants. Yet where fathers sleep in proximity to infants, mothers are also present, suggesting that this form of paternal care is a triadic (mother, father, baby) phenomenon.

In another cross-cultural analysis of father-child sleeping arrangements, sleeping proximity was related to the strength of paternal relationships (Ball, Hooker, and Kelly 2000). In twenty-six of forty-nine societies in which fathers slept in close proximity (for example, next to the children or in same room) to their infants, these fathers had close relationships with them, whereas fathers in only five of twenty societies had close relationships to their infants if fathers did not sleep in close proximity to infants. As a fascinating illustration of links between sleeping arrangements and paternal involvement, Lev-Wiesel (2000) compared fathers' perceptions on an Israeli kibbutz in which some children slept in a communal sleeping area and others at home. The fathers whose children slept at home reported higher paternal involvement and satisfaction than the fathers whose children slept communally did.

Changes across Time in Direct Paternal Care

In the cross-cultural patterns we've explored so far, we see differences in paternal care in slices of time. Clearly, however, men's direct care can change within a given cultural context over time. The rapidly changing paternal involvement at birth in countries such as Sweden and the United States is just one example. In countries like the United States, some data sets enable documenting shifts across time in other dimensions of paternal care. Using time diaries in which men recorded their activities, Suzanne Bianchi (2000) found that American men in 1965 spent 0.4 hours per day doing things when the primary activity was childcare. In 1998, that had increased to one hour per day—an increase of 250%. That amount of time pales compared with the time mothers spent on childcare, which was 1.5 hours per day in 1965 and 1.7 hours per day in 1998. Still, it is a large relative increase: the ratio of men's childcare time to women's childcare time increased from 0.24 in 1965 to 0.55 in 1998. American men spend half as much time on childcare as women—but they are far more involved than they were three decades before.

Bianchi (2000) also examined changes in time spent with children in any activity—that is, not just during direct childcare but at any time when children were present. Mothers' overall time with children was 5.3 hours in 1965 and 5.5 hours in 1998. Fathers still lag behind mothers but have increased overall time involvement from 2.8 hours in 1965 to 3.8 hours in 1998. The ratio of fathers' to mothers' overall time with children has increased from 0.51 to 0.65. Thus, American men now spend about two-thirds as much time with children as women do. However, Bianchi notes that her data measure overall time with children, not time per child. Because family sizes were smaller in 1998 than they were in 1965, this implies that time involvement per child has increased even more—especially for fathers.

This pattern of increasing paternal involvement with children is not unique to the United States. Anne Gauthier, Timothy Smeedeng, and Frank Furstenberg Jr. (2004) examined time diaries from Canada over four periods, ranging from 1971 to 1998. They found that men's time spent on personal care given to children (including health care) increased from 14.8 minutes per day in 1971 to 44.9 minutes in 1998. Play time also increased, roughly doubling from 15.4 minutes to 32.3 minutes. In this same study, the authors examined time diaries from sixteen industrialized societies, including the United States, Canada, Australia, and thirteen European nations. They found that fathers' time spent in childcare increased from 0.5 hours per day in the 1960s to 1.17 hours per day in the 1990s. Women's childcare increased as well over the same time period, from 2.06 to 2.79 hours per day. In both the United States and Canada, fathers may have been increasing their direct care in recent decades because of changes in economic and wider family life: lower fertility and greater job mobility mean other female relatives are less available to help care for the little ones, leaving men to pick up more of the childcare slack.

Cross-Cultural Variation in Indirect Paternal Care

Fathers can do more than spend time with their children in activities like playing, holding them, or sleeping next to them. Fathers may also provide indirect sources of investment that benefit their young, whether at some cost to the father or not. The bulk of attention in this area falls upon paternal resource provisioning. What kinds of resources—food, livestock, money—do fathers provide their children, and how do these kinds of investments vary cross-culturally?

Answering this question can be tricky. While we have been able to present quantitative data on men's time spent in direct care or proximity to children, can we quantify fathers' resource investments in their children in ways fostering cross-cultural comparisons? Marlowe (2000) attempted to do just this with the SCCS by using the relative contribution men make to subsistence (for example, 50% of caloric intake is from foods men obtain) as a measure of male provisioning. This type of measure has difficulties, however: these data don't disentangle whether the foods men get are given directly to children (or to mothers, who convert them into food for children—either way, this constitutes indirect paternal care) or to other individuals (for example, to other women). Still, some of the patterns stemming from this analysis seem reasonable and consistent with other types of data from specific societies (see Low 2000).

Across the SCCS, men's contribution to subsistence differs across subsistence mode (Marlowe 2000). Men in pastoralist societies contribute the most to subsistence, followed by men in agriculturalist and hunter-gatherer societies. Men in horticulturalist societies contribute the least to subsistence. Because men in pastoralist societies hold the main societal stores of wealth—livestock—they oversee crucial sources of indirect investment: livestock can be used as food sources (for example, milk, blood, meat) or as bride wealth to help male relatives marry (more on that below). Men in agriculturalist societies focus their efforts on land acquisition, land clearing, crop harvesting, and in other ways that may serve as indirect forms of paternal investment. Hunter-gatherer men target food resources, particularly game and honey, that in part serve as indirect care. Finally, the low levels of indirect subsistence contribution among horticulturalists stem from women's widespread role of engaging in many of the essential crop-based activities.

Apart from subsistence mode, the marital system is also linked to indirect paternal care in this cross-cultural sample. In the rare cases of polyandrous marriage systems, in which a woman is married to multiple men, men's subsistence contribution is at its highest. These few cases include resource-strapped societies like in highland Nepal, where brothers marry a single wife, a practice allowing them to keep a family parcel intact and also to invest heavily in agricultural production (Low 2000). Men's contributions to subsistence are next highest among societies with monogamous marriages (a man married to one wife), followed by societies with slight polygyny (marriages in which a man has more than one wife) and lastly those with more widespread polygyny.

Male indirect care can also include protection, whether against predators, other individuals within one's social group, or members of enemy out-groups. Unfortunately, few data are available to quantify male protective services as sources of indirect paternal care. Marlowe (2000) observes a positive association between the degree of polygyny and male aggressiveness in the SCCS. Combined with the earlier finding that in this same sample greater polygyny is associated with less male subsistence contribution, these data suggest that fathers who provide fewer subsistence resources but who do provide valuable protective services through their aggressive behavior may be able to marry polygynously. The fact that among the bellicose Yanomami of the Amazon Basin the men who have killed ("unokai") have more wives and more children than nonkillers suggests support, at least in some cases, for male aggressive services to be harnessed in threat deterrence or group attacks (Chagnon 1988). Cross-culturally, these protective facets of indirect paternal care may have been most important in the Amazon Basin and New Guinea Highlands, areas where, until recently, remarkably high rates of between-group violence and death prevailed. In most areas of the world today, indirect paternal care less commonly entails protective services; police forces and other external agents are more likely to serve those functions.

The Wealth of Fatherhood

Apart from subsistence contributions and protection, the other major forms of variable human indirect care are material resource transfers to children. A father may provide resources to his children, such as money, livestock, or land, while he is alive or after his death. However, the possession of substantial material resources does not occur among mobile hunter-gatherers. Consequently, this facet of human indirect paternal care is recently derived in our evolutionary history, though unfolding in interesting ways cross-culturally.

Resources provided by fathers can help their children marry. A couple may require resources to help them get started—land on which to grow crops, livestock to milk for food, money to help make a down payment on a home. A son may need to turn over resources to a bride's parents in order for them to allow her to marry him. The expenses of a wedding ceremony itself may also benefit from a father's helping underwrite its costs. So how do fathers help, cross-culturally, with these marital endowments? The most common requirement cross-culturally (in 38% of societies in the SCCS) is that a male seeking a hand in marriage provides bride wealth—resources offered to a bride's parents in exchange for their consent. A young suitor often obtains help from his male relatives, especially his father, to leverage the costs of bride wealth. A pastoralist Kenyan Ariaal father may provide his son with camels, sheep, or goats, to help his son to acquire a wife. So this is a concrete way in which indirect paternal care can aid a son's marital prospects in life.

In unusual pockets of the world—parts of Eurasia—another form of wealth transfer at marriage has arisen. This is the dowry, a marital down payment offered by the parents of a daughter. The dowry is typically used to help the new couple establish themselves with resources such as land or household items. It is not given to the bride's parents (unlike bride wealth). Dowry can be found among most western European populations (though times are rapidly changing, with less of these formal wealth transfers at marriage still taking place) and occurs alongside bride wealth in a number of south Asian societies. Attempts at reconstructing the cultural evolutionary roots of dowry suggest it arose within a societal ancestor common to most of western Europe, perhaps among the religious elite (Fortunato 2008).

What about other paternal resource transfers? Cross-cultural variation in inheritance patterns indicates that patrilineal inheritance (inheritance via the father's line) is more common than matrilineal (via the mother's line) inheritance or bilateral (through both parents' lines) (Murdock 1949). These patterns have their own underlying logic. Patrilineal inheritance often occurs alongside patrilocality (a couple's living near the father's family) and polygyny. Among the pastoralist Gabbra of East Africa, for example, a polygynously married man can thus live near his co-wives, his livestock, and male kin with whom he has alliances useful in mobilizing to defend livestock from neighbors who might want to steal it. Matrilineal inheritance, conversely, often occurs when the services men provide (for example, their involvement in distant warfare or the nature of the community's subsistence) take them far afield from their wives. Men in these circumstances are less immediately available and have lower paternity certainty.

Interestingly, shifts in the economic factors underlying these different inheritance patterns can also alter the patterns of inheritance. A wonderful example occurs when matrilineal African societies adopt livestock as new sources of subsistence. In a comparative study of sixty-eight southern African societies, when livestock are adopted, then inheritance shifts from matrilineal to mixed or patrilineal inheritance (Holden and Mace 2003). Among the urban South African Xhosa, with whom one of us (Kermyt Anderson) worked, paying bride price (or lobola) is still aspired to by many youth, even though marriage is declining, and nonmarital birth rates have increased tremendously. Anderson found strong support for bride price among the urban high school teachers and students with whom he worked; they felt that paying lobola was a sign that the man respects the woman.

At least two other features of patrilineal inheritance warrant attention. One is that, even while inheriting resources through the father's lineage, a man has multiple ways to pass these resources on to offspring (L. Barrett, Dunbar, and Lycett 2002). A father might practice primogeniture (giving all the wealth to the first born) or ultimogeniture (giving all wealth to the last born), or give his wealth to all sons to share evenly, keeping intact family lands, as in the polyandry example, or splitting up resources into smaller shares, for example, smaller plots of land. Daughters may also receive an inheritance through the paternal line, with an allocation equaling that of sons or being a fraction thereof (as, for example, in Islamic law). Each of these options has its relevant merits, depending on which participant's view one takes. A firstborn son's marital and reproductive prospects would benefit in primogeniture, but later-born sons would suffer reproductive consequences. Interestingly, in a number of historic western European samples, later-born sons were more likely to become celibate religious figures (L. Barrett, Dunbar, and Lycett 2002). Currently, one of the best predictors of male homosexual orientation is having lots of older brothers (Blanchard 2008). If later-born male siblings face stiffer competition (in the womb, during childhood, for resources as adults), they may be less likely to acquire mates and may have fewer offspring.

One other feature of patrilineal inheritance is that it also appears to be closely related to marital system. Monogamous marriage is often associated with bilateral inheritance or weak patrilineal inheritance. Polygynous marriage and patrilineal inheritance commonly go hand in hand. Indeed, Guy Cowlishaw and Ruth Mace (1996) showed that, cross-culturally, when marital systems change, so too do inheritance patterns. As an illustration, a shift toward monogamous marriage within a society is associated with low or no patrilineal inheritance bias in fifteen out of twenty cases. Conversely, a shift toward highly polygynous marriage within a society is associated with strong patrilineal inheritance bias in fourteen out of sixteen cases. The idea is that in societies where polygyny is common, a father may garner resources to acquire multiple wives, in addition to helping sons with resources they use to marry. Of course, this system can also give rise to new forms of father-son conflict ("Son, I'd rather take a fourth wife than help you marry a first wife"), leading to later ages of marriage for sons.

A good illustration of the ongoing importance of indirect paternal care in the form of resource transfers is the family will. The creation of a will provides vivid testimony to how one prioritizes the allocation of limited material resources. From several North American studies of wills, multiple patterns emerge in their designations of inheritance (Judge and Hrdy 1992; M. S. Smith, Kish, and Crawford 1987). Parents will more of their assets to children and grandchildren than to their own parents, and to lineal relatives (that is, descendants) rather than to collateral relatives like siblings or nieces and nephews. These patterns are consistent with maximizing the reproductive success of one's descendants. Fathers are also more likely to will resources to their wives to use and then allocate to children, while mothers are more likely to will resources to their children than to their husbands. These patterns reflect the facts that mothers typically outlive fathers and that older fathers, unlike postmenopausal mothers, might remarry and reproduce again in the event of a spouse's death, diverting resources from the first wife's children.

Cross-Cultural Variation in Social and Moral Training

If fathers can perform variable direct and indirect forms of parental care, they can also serve as important social and moral agents. Apart from the kinds of paternal care described so far in this chapter, another common theme in the cross-cultural patterning of paternal care is the role fathers play by providing social and moral guidance to their children. Take the Martu Aborigines in the western desert of Australia (Scelza forthcoming). Despite the massive social and economic changes experienced in Martu society, fathers still play important roles during adolescent initiations. Along with other group members, fathers help plan and conduct the circumcision rituals which enable a male to take a step closer to manhood. Accordingly, the presence of an adolescent male's father is associated with an earlier initiation: 15.4 years of age on average versus 16.7 years without a father present. Earlier male initiates also begin reproducing earlier, the kind of benefit an evolutionary perspective embraces.

Cross-cultural attitudes toward fatherhood commonly entail some element of paternal social and moral agency. Just as in the Martu case, fathers are often expected to help guide their children to social success. Fathers may offer social and moral training, sometimes reinforced by giving discipline, sometimes by setting an example. This guidance may begin early but often escalates in significance, especially with sons around the time of adolescence. In many east Asian societies, for example, fathers are expected to command respect and a sense of family piety, in part through cultivation of strict, emotionally distant relationships with children (Shwalb et al. 2004). In the past, these paternal roles fostered success of the lineage in agricultural, trade, or bureaucratic sectors; today, these patterns of paternal socialization increasingly focus on training children to succeed in a competitive labor market.

What about paternal socialization in a wider cross section? Employing the SCCS, Bobbi Low (1989) investigated children's training across a variety of primarily small-scale societies. Results revealed a number of differences between the training of boys and that of girls, and in relation to the social stratification and degree of polygyny of a given society. For example, two of the values most inculcated in girls are sexual restraint and industriousness, whereas for males the values most commonly inculcated are self-reliance and fortitude. Among boys living in socially unstratified groups such as small-scale hunter-gatherers or horticulturalists, the higher the degree of polygyny (which should also be linked with higher male-male competition for mates), the more males are taught to be obedient and industrious, to exhibit fortitude, and to be aggressive. Among boys living in socially stratified societies (for example, agriculturalist societies with elites and commoners), boys are expected to adhere to a different set of values—to be self-reliant and industrious but not aggressive—as the degree of polygyny increases. The point of these analyses is that they illustrate how the values children are expected to adhere to make sense in specific socioecological contexts. How do parents get their children to adhere to these values? Also relying on the SCCS, David Levinson (1989) finds that exhortation (for example, lecturing, setting an example) is most commonly used for boys and girls, followed by physical punishment. Among ninety societies, about 75% practice some form of physical punishment of children, but only about 35% of these ninety societies commonly employ physical punishment. Unfortunately for us and our discussion of fatherhood, these analyses do not reveal the relative role of fathers inculcating values in their children or the methods they employ in doing so (that is, whether fathers use physical punishment or not).

A cross-cultural analysis of adolescence provides more clear insight into fathers' social and moral roles. In their survey of adolescence, a survey relying on the SCCS, Alice Schlegel and Herbert Barry III (1991) reveal some of the important social and moral functions fathers serve, particularly for their sons. In 66% of societies comprising the sample, male adolescents spend most of their time with adult males, including fathers; 84% of adolescent girls, conversely, spend most of their time with adult females, including mothers. These data reveal the sex-differentiated patterns of association, patterns that foster adolescent sons' learning from fathers. Indeed, as revealed in another item from this sample, "for boys, the father is the single most important agent in 79 percent of 173 cases, while the mother is most important for girls in 85 percent of 171 cases" (Schlegel and Barry 1991, 39). Fathers serve more emotionally distant, domineering roles in the lives of their adolescent children at the same time that fathers devote significant time to economic and social activities with their sons. The nature of father-adolescent interactions largely suggests that fathers model or teach appropriate adult behavior rather than employing outright coercion to make their point.

The patterns of father-adolescent interactions vary to some degree according to subsistence mode (Schlegel and Barry 1991). Fathers engage in relatively more contact with adolescent sons in hunter-gatherer and horticultural societies than in agricultural societies. Fathers also have more domineering relations with both their sons and their daughters in horticultural and agricultural societies than in hunter-gatherer societies. Finally, fathers have more intimate relations with their sons in hunter-gatherer societies than in horticultural and agricultural societies. Some of these patterns across subsistence mode relate to the lack of heritable property among foragers. More commonly among hunter-gatherers, a son must demonstrate his hunting prowess to satisfy a prospective bride; that task, unlike transfers of livestock or land, fosters gentler father-son interactions and more reduced conflicts than in other types of societies.

Fathers' roles as social and moral agents are clearly changing in many societies. The authority on which a father rested his opinions can be undermined in the face of rapid social and technological change. Rather than a father modeling locally appropriate economic activities, a son may show his father how to plug into the latest computer technology. The expansion of state or religious education has also displaced some of fathers' role in providing social guidance. Involvement in education removes sons spatially from their fathers' presence, limiting any meaningful degree to which a child can watch his father at work. When all of these elements are put together, we can see why the expansion of formal education and paid employment challenges many elements of paternal socialization. In Barry Hewlett's (2000) formulation, these kinds of international trends in countries like the United States and Japan suggest an ongoing reduction in the importance of fathers' transmitting knowledge to their children, and particularly sons, compared with societies of hunter-gatherers, horticulturalists, and agriculturalists. Increasingly important indirect paternal care, in such circumstances, relies more on what fathers are carrying in their wallets, providing in their wills, and devoting to their children's education to foster success in a competitive, international labor market.

The Development of Dad

Where and when in development does a father originate? What factors shape the kind of father a male will become? In light of the cross-cultural variation in paternal care observed, researchers have sought to locate early social influences arising during the first few years of life that might shape a given male's likelihood of later being an involved or a removed father. An earlier form of this developmental model focused on a distinction between, at poles of a spectrum, "father absent" and "father present" societies (P. Draper and Harpending 1982). The idea was that in a society or even a family within a society in which an involved father helps care for his son early in life (for example, by interacting with him, sleeping near him), the son will develop into a doting father. Conversely, if a son has a distant relationship with his father (for example, having little interaction with him, not sleeping near him), then the son would internalize this absence and later replicate the pattern of being a more distant father. This framework built on earlier views that when men needed to form strong male-male coalitions to foster success in intergroup aggression, this might act against involved fathering.

Several other development frameworks sought to shift the emphasis from a father's absence or presence shaping subsequent paternal proclivities to an emphasis on "risk" more broadly construed (Belsky, Steinberg, and Draper 1991; Chisholm et al. 2005). The idea was that factors including, but not limited to, father absence or presence early in a son's life would serve as important cues indicative of relative risk in the local socioecology (that is, the nature of the family/community/economic group in which the child is embedded). The greater the risk suggested by relevant cues, the more oriented a male would later be to male-male competition and mate seeking and the less oriented he would be to involved family life. Effectively, a son would perceive in a risky environment the need to "live fast and die young" in the attempt to successfully reproduce in the local environment. These kinds of models are consistent with many of the available data, including intergenerational consistency in forms of paternal care discussed throughout this chapter.

These models are important for several reasons. They suggest that the kinds of variation in paternal care observed throughout this chapter have roots in early social experiences. Each of us, if transplanted at birth into a different cultural milieu, such as that of the Hadza or Yanomami or that of urban Korea, would internalize our early social experience in ways shaping our later social behavior, including paternal care. Adoption studies tell us that indeed this sort of practice occurs (Richerson and Boyd 2005). The behavioral development of east Asian babies adopted into U.S. households early in life strongly reflects the social environment of their adoptive parents. The same was true of American colonial and early U.S. children captured and raised by Native Americans; moreover, the effects of internalizing the local Native-American behavioral codes were strongest among the youngest captives, who were raised for the longest period of time by their new parents.

Another reason these developmental models are important is that they suggest "sensitive periods" in development during which we might be particularly responsive to experiences and stimuli that impact later patterns of paternal care. The Belsky, Steinberg, and Draper (1991) model suggests that experiences during the first five to seven years of life are particularly important in shaping later reproductive and parenting behaviors. Both prenatally and in the first few years postnatally, we lay some of the emotional foundations of our personality and behavior (Cozolino 2006); exposure to social or solitary sleeping contexts, to physical play or the lack of it, to responsive caregiving or to unresponsive may have longer-term impacts on our behaviors, including the ways we later parent.

As illustrations, recent research has investigated the effects of early social experiences on children's hormone levels (more on hormones in Chapter 10). These studies do not disentangle effects on sons versus daughters, nor do they tell us whether these effects persist until adulthood; still, they represent new findings that lend tangible support to the physiological effects of early social experiences. In a survey of seven daycare studies, children had elevated afternoon levels of cortisol (which is viewed as a stress hormone) at daycare compared with levels on days not spent in daycare (Vermeer and Van IJzendoorn 2006). How to interpret these findings is unclear, however. Perhaps elevations in daycare cortisol are associated with children's raised physiological arousal because they are around more children, and the ways they are adjusting will be adaptive in later social worlds filled with other peers in school and with unrelated individuals at work. Or maybe these children are really overextending their stress responses, given their young ages and this evolutionarily novel context of lots of similarly aged, unrelated peers and of unrelated caregivers. To take one other example, children initially raised in socially deprived eastern European orphanages but subsequently adopted into warm, loving households elsewhere still exhibited alterations in oxytocin and vasopressin levels about three years on average following adoption (Fries et al. 2005).

All this being said about the importance of early social experiences impacting subsequent behavior, we also bear in mind the bigger developmental picture. Any complex human behavioral trait (like components of paternal care) represents how heritable predispositions partly based in relevant genetic variation interact with environmental factors such as social context throughout one's life. So even if early social experiences matter in shaping a male's later patterns of parental care, we can reasonably expect that other effects throughout life also shape his paternal care. Later childhood social experiences, adolescent initiation and socialization processes, current cues in the social environment (for example, the nature of a man's relationship to a mate) can all affect that same male's paternal care. Indeed, a massive amount of the research in this book emphasizes the effects of factors of recent or immediate salience on predicting paternal care (for example, the factor of whether the man believes he is the biological father of a given child). We also consider the experience of fatherhood as an adult developmental phenomenon in itself. In many cases, becoming a father transforms a man, including other features of his life, like his physiology, sexuality, and health. Because a man does not undergo pregnancy, birth, or extended lactation, the experiences shaping his parental behavior are particularly contingent on developmentally salient social cues. In turn, the variation in these cues helps account for the cross-cultural variation in paternal care we have highlighted throughout this chapter.

In summary, this chapter has surveyed cross-cultural variation in paternal care. We have considered variation in paternal direct care, indirect care, and social and moral training. From involvement at birth to bequests at death, men clearly play variable roles cross-culturally in enhancing their children's survival and reproductive success. We have seen that economic factors, intergroup aggression, and features of the mating system can help account for variation in men's parental care. Experiences throughout development provide important influences on a male's later paternal proclivities. Still, for adults, the most pressing constraint on fatherhood is finding a mate. In the next chapter, we focus on the long-term partnerships in which men become fathers.

3

Men and Marriage

In order to become a father, a man must eventually secure the assistance of a woman (and vice versa, for a woman to become a mother). While the advent of sophisticated assisted reproductive technologies such as in vitro fertilization (IVF) have made it possible for conception to occur without sexual intercourse, it is unlikely that this technology will ever become the predominant form of procreation for the human species. For starters, such technologies tend to be prohibitively expensive. More important, most people enjoy sex. Despite advances in recreational technology that were unimaginable to our forebears—video games, MP3 players, wired coffeeshops, and whatnot—sex remains an extremely popular form of entertainment. Forecasting the future is always a dangerous proposition, but we feel we aren't risking much by predicting that sexual intercourse is here to stay.

Sex is not the same as procreation, of course. Any given act of sexual intercourse has a fairly low probability of producing a baby. The acceptability of short-term sexual relationships varies across cultures; some societies allow sex only after marriage, which typically follows a long engagement and, often, a substantial transfer of resources (such as bride price or dowry) from one family to another. Other societies are more permissible, allowing sex after only a brief courtship. Among the 186 cultures in the Standard Cross-Cultural Sample (SCCS), 35% either marry girls at or before puberty or insist on female virginity at marriage, while 40% allow premarital sex (authors' calculations from the SCCS). The other 25% technically prohibit premarital sex, but it is weakly censured and occurs frequently. Nonmarital sex is also available, particularly to men, in virtually every society, in the form of commercial sex workers, who require neither prolonged courtship nor extended commitment.

And yet even when sex is permissible within short-term relationships, reproduction within those relationships is rare. As we'll discuss below, most babies are conceived in the context of long-term partnerships. People do get pregnant from one-night stands, but it's a very small fraction of pregnancies; in general, people are not having babies with complete strangers. Rather, people form long-term economic, romantic, and sexual relationships. In most cultures such relationship are called marriages. We do not have the space to provide a comprehensive review of the factors influencing union formation and dissolution; entire books could be (and have been) written on that topic. But in this chapter we will overview some of the main features associated with marriage (broadly defined), with an emphasis on how they relate to fatherhood.

Definitions of Marriage

So what is marriage? It's tricky to define; as with art, you know what it is when you see it, but no two definitions agree. Marriage occurs in virtually all human societies. It typically involves the long-term union of (at least) one woman and (at least) one man, though same-sex marriage is legal in a growing number of societies, and most societies allow men to have multiple wives. Beyond that, the details vary tremendously. In many societies, marriage involves a ceremony, often officiated by a religious leader. In state societies, couples have the option of a nonreligious civil ceremony. Both religious and civil ceremonies legitimize the union, providing legal rights and protections as well as social legitimacy. But in many cultures, no ceremony is required: the couple simply moves in together, and they are considered married.

In contrast, weddings are grand and elaborate affairs in many societies. One of us (Anderson) once attended a wedding in Calcutta, India, that lasted five days. Each day revolved around a different ceremony, with the groom formally introduced to the bride's family one day, the groom formally meeting the bride on another day, and so forth. Large feasts were held on each of the five days, with an opulent display of gifts. In the United States, wedding ceremonies are not nearly so prolonged, with most lasting a mere hour or less. But they are nonetheless extravagant, with the average cost for a wedding in 2008 estimated at $28,732, not including the honeymoon or the rings (Wedding Report Inc. 2008).

In contrast, in many small-scale societies the wedding ceremony is much less formal or elaborate. Among Ache hunter-gatherers of Paraguay, marriage occurs when a man and a woman begin sleeping together at the same fire at night (K. Hill and Hurtado 1996). Among !Kung hunter-gatherers of the Kalahari Desert, first marriage, which typically occurs when the girl is prepubescent and the boy a young teenager, is marked by modest ceremonies that include friends accompanying the couple to their new hut and rubbing them down with oil the next morning (Shostak 1981). These first marriages, however, are typically short lived, and like the Ache, the !Kung often remarry several times, with no particularly grand ceremony marking each new nuptial.

Trial marriages are common in many cultures, allowing a couple to test whether they are a good match before they are considered married. Among the Taramiut Inuit, when a couple decides to marry, the man moves in with his fiancée's family. If a baby is produced within a year or so, the couple is considered married, and they move to the husband's camp. If no baby is forthcoming, the man eventually moves out (Garburn 1969).

In most developed countries, cohabiting unions, in which couples live together but are not legally married, are increasingly common. Sociologists have characterized these relationships as "trial marriages," informal, marriagelike unions that are typically a transitional stage: most couples either marry or go their separate ways, with relatively few remaining in permanent nonmarital cohabitational relationships. In the United States, for example, the majority of American couples live together before they marry (Bumpass and Lu 2000). Among men ages twenty-six to thirty, 8% are currently living in a nonmarital cohabitational relationship (Bernhardt and Goldscheider 2001), while rates for women in roughly the same age group, twenty-five to twenty-nine, are higher, at 21% (Bumpass and Lu 2000). In Europe, cohabitation rates vary by region. In northern Europe (Scandinavia plus Iceland), 81% of unions (this includes both cohabitation and marriage) begin as cohabitational relationships (Kalmijn 2007). In western Europe 58% of unions begin as cohabitations, while in southern Europe only 18% do (Kalmijn 2007).

There is some debate whether cohabitation is becoming an alternative to marriage, with cohabitation becoming a stable relationship in which some people will remain all of their lives. In general, this does not seem to be the case, though it may be true for a minority of cohabitors. In Europe, high cohabitation rates are associated with delayed marriage, but most people do end up marrying—they just do it later, after cohabiting for several years (Kalmijn 2007). In Sweden, many couples put off marrying until after the birth of a first child, but they usually marry before the second one is born (Bernhardt 2004). In the United States and Canada, half of cohabiting relationships end within about two years; of these, roughly equal numbers break up or transition to married life (Bumpass, Sweet, and Cherlin 1991; Z. Wu and Balakrishnan 1995). Only about 10% of cohabiting couples remain together, unmarried, after a decade.

Many reasons are given for the increase in cohabitational relationships and nonmarital childbearing. It may be that the current generation of young adults, many of whom came from divorced households, do not value the institution of marriage or trust in its permanency or validity. Additionally, the increasing cost of marriage may discourage many young couples from entering a formal marital union or at least cause them to postpone marriage (Smock, Manning, and Porter 2005). Cohabitational unions differ from formal marriages in many important respects—they are more fragile, and they lack the cultural and legal standing of formal marriages—and sociologists and policy makers are careful to distinguish between these two types of unions. From a cross-cultural perspective, however, cohabitation relationships are essentially identical to the informal marital unions present in many cultures. As our emphasis in this chapter is on long-term unions, regardless of the legal standing of these relationships, we will often include data on both formal marriages and cohabitational unions when discussing "marriage," though we will take care to distinguish between them when appropriate.

Marriage Rates

Marriage rates vary tremendously across societies and are influenced by many factors. Age at first marriage is an important influence on a society's marriage rate: in cultures in which people tend to marry earlier, more people get married. Among !Kung hunter-gatherers of southern Africa, the median age at first marriage is 19 (Howell 2000). Among Ache hunter-gatherers of Paraguay, the mean age at first marriage in the precontact forest period (before the Ache were settled on reservations) was 15.2 for women and 20.2 for men (K. Hill and Hurtado

1996). In many developing countries the average age at marriage is quite young. In the 1960s, for example, the average age at marriage for women in both Libya and India was 16.8, while it was about 22 in both Ceylon and the Philippines.

In many European countries, marriage is becoming less and less common, and a significant fraction of the population never marries. In the 1960s, for example, 16% of Swedish women and 28% of Spanish women ages twenty-five to thirty-four had never married (Strassmann and Clarke 1998). In the United States, age at first marriage has steadily increased in recent years, as more and more couples choose to delay marriage and live together instead. In 1967, 7% of American women ages twenty-five to thirty-four and 14% of American men in the same age bracket were single (Strassmann and Clarke 1998), while in 2001, 38% of women and 50% of men ages twenty-five to thirty-four were single (Kreider 2005). Despite delays in marriage, most Americans eventually do marry. While 84% of men and 72% of women ages twenty to twenty-four in the United States have never been married, by ages forty to forty-nine only 14% of men and 10% of women have never married (and the proportion falls to less than 7% by the fifties) (Kreider 2005).

Why Marry?

Why do we marry, or more broadly, why do we form long-term, relatively exclusive relationships with a sexual partner? Humans are not unique in forming long-term attachments to a partner. We find reproductive partnerships in which males and females form attachments long enough to raise offspring and provide biparental care among 13% of teleost fish, 20% of amphibians, 2% of reptiles, over 90% of birds, and fewer than 5% of mammals (Clutton-Brock 1991). Interestingly, some of these avian species, such as swans and geese, include same-sex couples who may even raise offspring together (for example, two females raising offspring sired by a departed male) (Roughgarden 2004). These nonhuman reproductive arrangements clearly lack the cultural dimensions and meanings of human marriage, yet there are undeniable parallels present as well.

Our closest relatives, the great apes, do not form long-term pair-bonds. They also exhibit a high degree of sexual dimorphism; males are larger than females. Yet in terms of obtaining food, male and female great apes are quite similar: they both do basically the same things to acquire the food they need. (The main exception to this is hunting among chimpanzees, which is essentially a male domain.)

Humans, as noted in Chapter 1, are only mildly sexual dimorphic. Men are generally larger and heavier than women, but on nowhere near a gorilla-like scale. Behaviorally, however, we exhibit a much greater level of sexual dimorphism than our primate cousins (Low 2000). The traditional gender breakdown of foragers is often described as "men hunt, women gather," and while that is not an ironclad rule, it is generally true. Regardless of ecology or subsistence pattern, every society observes a division of labor by gender, though the details of which gender performs which activities often varies. Some behaviors, such as lumbering, mining, and butchering animals, are predominantly male activities across cultures, while fetching water and firewood is usually women's work. Things like milking animals, tending crops, and making pottery and baskets can be both men's work or women's work, but in most cultures they are typically done by either one or the other (Low 2000).

Economists argue that households comprised of opposite-sex adults make sense if there is a division of labor by gender (Becker 1991). If you live in a culture in which gender norms dictate that men and women do different things, then the most efficient way to fulfill all of the economic activities that are required to run a household is to have both men and women in the same household. From an economic stand-point, marriage is about cooperation. It allows individuals to share in the economic labor of their partners. Gender specialization allows individuals to focus on increasing their skills at specific tasks, thereby resulting in greater overall household productivity than if each person tried to be equally good at all tasks.

Marriage is also about sex, at least to a certain extent. In cultures that prohibit sex outside of marriage, marriage allows people to legitimately have sex. Even in cultures where nonmarital sexual encounters are allowed, marriage (or its equivalent) grants each person some degree of sexual exclusivity regarding their partner. The frequency and quality of sexual intercourse declines with marital duration (Liu 2003), though across cultures married couples report having sex more frequently than unmarried persons do (Laumann et al. 1994; Wellings et al. 2006). Sexual exclusivity is in the eye of the beholder, and there is frequently a double standard, in that men are more likely to have multiple spouses (and thus multiple lifetime sexual partners) than women are. But sex is a recognized element of marriage, and in most cultures it is acceptable or desirable for a married woman to become pregnant.

Marriage is thus also about children. Marriage provides legitimacy to children; children born out of wedlock may have fewer legal rights and may even be unable to inherit property or social standing from their father. The production of offspring is often a very explicit goal of marriage. Leslie Buckle, Gordon Gallup Jr., and Zachary Rodd (1996) characterize marriage as an implicit reproductive contract, representing a trade-off between the sometimes conflicting reproductive fitness goals of men and women. Failure to have children—which is almost always blamed on the woman—is cross-culturally a valid reason for divorcing or for adding a second wife to the marriage (Betzig 1989).

Fertility also frequently occurs in long-term, marriagelike cohabiting relationships. This phenomenon is not new; in eighteenth-century Europe, for example, 19% of first births in Germany and 37% in England were to unmarried women (J. W. Wood 1994). In contemporary Sweden, 23% of men living with biological children and the children's mothers are in unmarried relationships (Bernhardt and Goldscheider 2001). In the United States, 12% of reported pregnancies are to women in nonmarital cohabiting relationships (Laumann et al. 1994). In the Caribbean, a large fraction of children are born to nonmarital unions, accounting for over 85% of children of men under thirty and 45% of children of men over fifty (Roopnarine 2005). As we noted above, we treat these unions as marriagelike, because they typically involve relatively long-term relationships—but at the same time, nonmarital unions tend to be less stable over the long term. For example, in Western countries children whose parents are living together but unmarried will spend roughly three times as many childhood years living with single mothers as children whose parents were married at the child's birth (Heuveline, Timberlake, and Furstenberg 2003), something we will discuss in more detail in Chapter 6.

Marital Choice

Cross-culturally, the rules for whom you can marry—and how many spouses you can have at one time—vary tremendously. One rule that is found in all cultures concerns whom you cannot marry. Specifically, there is a universal incest taboo, although incest is defined differently across cultures. All societies prohibit marriage and sexual relationships between biological parents and children and between biological siblings.

There is tremendous variation in the acceptability of cousins as spouses. In the United States, first-cousin marriage is often looked upon as somewhat inappropriate, and it is illegal in twenty-seven states (S. Stritof and B. Stritof 2008). In contrast, no European country prohibits marriage between first cousins, and cousin marriage is both allowed and preferred throughout the Arab world. About 36% of marriages in Saudi Arabia are between first cousins, and another 22% involve more distant relatives (Khlat 1997). Across the Arabian Peninsula, the percentage of marriages that are consanguineous—that is, involving a blood relative—ranges from 35–60%, while in north Africa 30–40% of marriages involve relatives. While these are all Islamic countries, cousin marriage apparently predates the spread of Islam in those countries; cousin marriage rates are similarly high among Lebanese Christians. Overall, 48% of cultures in the SCCS allow first-cousin marriages, and first cousins are preferred marriage partners in 32% of societies (authors' calculations).

In contemporary nation-states the only requirements people must meet in order to get married, apart from the incest laws, are to be above the age of legal consent and not to be currently married to anyone else. The permission of other family members is not required, nor can these family members lodge legally binding objections to the union. Even criminals, who lose many of the privileges of citizenship, retain the right to marry.

Romantic love may or may not play a role in marriage. The belief that falling in love should precede getting married is reflected in an old children's jump rope rhyme. The rhyme implies that love precedes marriage, and this is true in many societies. The main criteria that most Westerners expect in a good marriage is romantic love. Being in love is considered essential for a happy marriage, and falling out of love is one of the main justifications for divorce. Financial stability is considered important but not sufficient, and the perception that a woman married a man for money and not for love is generally perceived as the basis for an unhappy relationship.

Yet in much of the world, love is not a required precursor to or component of marriage. The decision to marry is not made by the couple involved, at least not by themselves; their families have a lot to say about it and may engineer the process entirely. In many societies, marriages are arranged by older kin, who seek a match that has good social attributes, such as wealth, education, social class or caste, and so forth. In no other species do relatives wield such influential roles in the mate choice of sons and daughters. Arranged marriages occur in 48% of the cultures in the SCCS and are the predominant means by which marriages occur in 30% of cultures (authors' calculations). They are most common in India, China, Japan, and eastern and southern Europe. In arranged marriages, couples may not be in love with each other; they may never have met before the marriage was arranged. They often do not meet before the wedding itself. In this case, the jump rope rhyme would more properly be "First comes marriage, then (possibly) comes love": love is expected to follow marriage rather than precede it.

How Many Spouses?

The majority of the world's citizens live in large, industrialized nation-states in which monogamy—marrying only one spouse at a time—is enforced by both custom and law. The question of how many spouses you can have is a ludicrous one for citizens of those societies. (Although in a sense you can have as many as you want, provided you only have one a time. Elizabeth Taylor has been married eight times—and she hardly holds the record.)

The Ethnographic Atlas (Murdock 1967), a compendium of data on over 1,200 societies that was begun by George Murdock in the 1960s and is periodically updated, lists 186 cultures, or 15% of the world's cultures, that allow only monogamous marriages (J. P. Gray 1998). These numbers suggest that an adherence to strict monogamy is a minority opinion, cross-culturally speaking. In most societies, not only is marrying more than one spouse an option, but it is the cultural ideal. The most common pattern is polygyny, in which men are allowed multiple wives. This marriage system occurs in 85% of societies (J. P. Gray 1998). However, just because men can marry more than one wife, it doesn't mean they all do. That would be possible only if the sex ratio were extremely imbalanced. Even most polygynous marriages begin as monogamous ones, with a second wife added to the union later.

Polygyny is associated with wealth; men who have more resources are more likely to have multiple wives. Indeed, it has been suggested that this pattern is the reason men across cultures tend to pursue wealth or culturally defined high status: not as an end in itself but as a means to acquire more wives and, subsequently, more offspring. Among the Kipsigis of Kenya, for example, wealthier men have greater total lifetime reproductive success (Borgerhoff Mulder 1987). On the Micronesian atoll of Ifaluk, wealthier men and those with greater social status, such as chiefs, have more children (Turke and Betzig 1985). The same was true of nineteenth-century Mormons (Heath and Hadley 1998) and Swedes (Low 1994) as well. Even among hunter-gatherers, who have very little material wealth, better hunters have greater reproductive success, as seen, for example, among the Ache (Kaplan and Hill 1985). Many men cannot afford multiple wives, even if they live in societies that allow it.

The other type of marriage system is polyandry, in which women have multiple husbands. This system is extremely rare, being found in only four cultures, or 0.3% of societies (J. P. Gray 1998). Polyandry is associated with cultures living in the high-altitude Himalayas, such as ethnic Tibetans and the Ladakhi of India. The general explanation for the occurrence is polyandry is the need for a diversified household economy, due to harsh ecological conditions (Durham 1991). In Tibet, for example, a household containing several men can engage in a greater variety of economic activities, such as agriculture, herding, and salt trading, than a household with just one man. To reduce conflicts of interest among husbands, Tibetans generally practice fraternal polyandry, in which husbands are all brothers (Beall and Goldstein 1981; Haddix 2001).

Mate Selection Criteria

Whom we marry, then, is subject to a host of culturally defined constraints. Whether you or your parents choose your spouse, whether you can have one spouse at a time or several, whether your family is obliged to make a substantial payment to your spouse's family—these vary across cultures, and most of us are subject to the rules of the society we live in. Yet within those constraints there is still often a great deal of latitude. Most of us have the choice of more than one person for a mate, yet we can generally narrow the field to a single individual. What characteristics do people look for in a life partner, and what traits influence which person they pick (or is picked for them)?

People tend to partner with individuals who are like them in many respects. Most couples come from similar socioeconomic, religious, ethnic, and cultural backgrounds, a phenomenon referred to as homogamy (for example, Mare 1991). To some extent this is because we are most likely to meet people who move in the same circles we do. And people from backgrounds similar to our own are likely to be more acceptable to our families. But even within the same social circles, there are often dozens if not hundreds or thousands of potential mates. What draws us to certain individuals and not others?

In many respects, men and women both look for the same thing in a mate. David Buss and others (2001) report the results of a study that asked American men and women to rank eighteen different traits in order of their importance in a marriage partner. The questionnaire was administered to different populations (often targeting college students) six times between 1939 and 1996. Across the decades, both men and women ranked personality characteristics such as "dependable character," "emotional stability, maturity," "pleasing disposition," and "mutual attraction/love" as their most important characteristics in choosing a mate. In fact, those four traits were the top-four mate preference traits for men in every decade sampled and were among the top-five ranked mate preference traits for women for every decade, with the exception that "mutual attraction/love" was ranked number 6 in importance by women in 1956.

Although men and women both rank the same traits highly in a potential partner, they also tend to look for different things in a spouse. Men place greater emphasis than women on physical characteristics, such as attractiveness, symmetry, and a good waist-to-hip ratio (that is, the woman's hips are significantly wider than her waist). These traits all signal youth, health, and reproductive capacity. It makes sense, evolutionarily speaking, to value partners who are capable of producing offspring, and physical characteristics are one of the key proxies men use to evaluate this in prospective mates.

Psychologist David Buss (1989) examined mate preferences from a sample of over ten thousand respondents living in thirty-seven countries. He found that men valued good looks in a potential partner more than women did in thirty-four out of thirty-seven countries. (In the remaining three countries, there was no difference between men and women; in no country did women value good looks more than men did.) Consistent with men valuing potential fertility in their partners,

Buss (1989) found that in all thirty-seven countries, men preferred partners who were younger than they are. On average, husbands were three years older than wives for the twenty-seven countries in Buss's sample that had demographic data on age at marriage. In the sixty-year American mating preferences study by Buss and others (2001), men rated "good looks" more highly as an important characteristic in a mate than women did.

Women, in contrast, tend to prefer men who can provide resources for them and their offspring. Female fertility is to a certain extent influenced by access to resources; women with more resources (or with wealthier husbands) have more children, at least under traditional circumstances. For example, historical data reveal a strong association between female fertility and farm wealth in historical Ireland (Strassmann and Clarke 1998) and Sweden (Low and Clarke 1992). (The relationship between wealth and fertility has reversed quite recently in many industrialized societies, something we will discuss in more detail in Chapter 4.)

In the study of sixty years of mating preferences (Buss et al. 2001), women ranked "good financial prospect" as more important in a mate than men did for every decade studied. In a cross-cultural sample of mating preferences (Buss 1989), women were more likely than men to value partners who were a "good financial prospect" and showed "good earning capacity" in thirty-six out of thirty-seven countries. This finding is consistent with the preferred age difference that Buss found: women prefer slightly older men as husbands, because in most socioecological contexts it takes men longer to acquire the physical and social skills and capital to be good and consistent providers. These preferences are found even in samples of cohabiting couples in the United States, who tend to have more liberal and egalitarian views towards traditional gender roles. Pamela Smock, Wendy Manning, and Meredith Porter (2005) reviewed research that examined whether cohabiting couples marry. In every study that included men, male income was a significant predictor of marriage; no study found an effect of women's income but not men's. In an accompanying qualitative study of 115 cohabiting couples, Smock, Manning, and Porter (2005) found that both men and women stressed the importance of men's economic situation, rather than women's, as a prerequisite for marriage. The couples in this sample were generally unwilling to marry until the man had a stable and reliable source of sufficient income, regardless of the woman's financial status. Similar results have been found for Sweden, where male income is a significant predictor of marriage; each additional US$1,000 of income increases the likelihood that a man is married by 4–5% (Bernhardt and Goldscheider 2001).

Studies on gender-specific mate preferences have generally been carried out in developed countries or literate and educated subsamples within developing countries. Relatively little work has been done on mate preferences in subsistence-level societies. A notable exception is the study by Elizabeth Pillsworth (2008), who compared data on mate preferences in two populations: the Shuar, an Amazonian mixed horticultural/foraging population, and undergraduates from the University of California at Los Angeles (UCLA). She found that the UCLA sample replicated the results found by Buss and others: men valued physical attractiveness more than women did, while women valued resource-related traits more than men did. But among the Shuar, Pillsworth found no gender difference in the importance of either trait. Both Shuar men and women place little emphasis on physical attractiveness in a mate, while both men and women place great emphasis on the ability to provide resources. However, when Pillsworth asked the Shuar to rate specific individuals on their desirability as long-term partners and on their personal characteristics, she found that women, but not men, valued provider qualities in a partner, while both men and women valued personality and physical attractiveness.

Pillsworth's work with the Shuar suggests that more research should be done on mating preferences among subsistence populations, in order to confirm or reject the patterns we see in more developed societies, as well as in developing but nonsubsistence level. Perhaps physical attractiveness is not more important to men than women living in premodern conditions. Even among the Shuar, however, we see that women value men who are economic providers. The importance of provisioning in foraging populations is underscored by a study by Frank Marlowe (2001), who examined the relationship between male provisioning and female fertility among 161 subsistence-level societies. He found that societies in which more of the diet was contributed by men have shorter interbirth intervals, lower juvenile mortality, and higher female fertility than societies in which men contribute a lower proportion of the diet. By providing resources to women, men increase their fertility and the survival of their offspring, resulting in increased fitness for both men and women. From an evolutionary perspective, it makes sense for women to value men who are good providers.

Marriage Markets

Another factor that influences whom we choose as partners is simple supply and demand. Economists have applied the principles of market economies to mating dynamics to describe what they call "marriage markets" (Becker 1991). Let's imagine a population of 100 women, each of whom can be unambiguously ranked in terms of attractiveness (not just physical attractiveness but other attributes as well) as a mate, from lowest to highest. Imagine a group of one hundred men, all similarly ranked. Each of the one hundred men would prefer to marry the most attractive woman in the group, but there's only one of her. Similarly, each of the one hundred women would prefer to match up with the most attractive male in the group, but there's only one of him. Because the most attractive man prefers the most attractive woman, and vice versa, they end up pairing up with each other. The second-most attractive woman and the second-most attractive man might prefer the most attractive opposite-sex individual, but because the top-ranked individuals have already chosen each other, the second-ranked ones pair up. This process is called "positive assortative mating," and the end result is that the most attractive men pair up with the most attractive women, the folks in the middle match up with their respective counterparts, and the folks at the bottom pair up with each other.

Applying the concept of markets to marriage dynamics lets us understand why some traits reduce the probability of marriage or remarriage. We have already mentioned that women value economic resources in a mate more than men do; not surprisingly, then, men with fewer resources (measured by such proxies as low income and low education) are ranked lower in the marriage market and are less likely to marry (see, for example, Low 1994 for nineteenth-century Sweden; K. G. Anderson 2000 for the contemporary United States). Men value youth in a mate and typically marry women a couple of years younger than themselves; as women age, their probability of marrying decreases. In nineteenth-century Sweden, wealthier men married younger women (Low 1994). Education can raise one's standing in the marriage market.

In India, for example, men are the primary breadwinners, so parents' investments in the educations of sons increase the sons' standing in the marriage market by increasing their earning ability (Shenk 2005).

Previous fertility can lower one's ranking in the marriage market, especially for women. Using a nationally representative sample of American women, one of us showed that women whose first birth was nonmarital were less likely to subsequently marry, and spent about ten fewer years between ages fifteen and forty-five married than women whose first birth occurred during a marriage (K. G. Anderson and Low 2003). Buckle, Gallup, and Rodd (1996), using a sample of respondents from Albany, New York, found that divorced women with children are less likely to remarry than either divorced women without children, divorced men with children, or divorced men without children. Divorced mothers rank lower on the marriage market partly because women with children tend to be older than women without children and also because many men are unwilling to invest in other men's children.

Some women with children do remarry, and the men in those unions become stepfathers to the woman's children. We will discuss stepfathers in more detail in Chapter 7. For now, we'll note that if women with children are ranked lower in the marriage market than women without children, then it follows that they are more likely to marry men who are themselves ranked lower in the marriage market. One of us applied this logic to a study using a nationally representative sample of American men and found that men who become stepfathers (that is, who marry women with children) tend to have less education and lower income and were more likely to have been previously married than men who marry women without children—all traits associated with lower standing in the marriage market (K. G. Anderson 2000).

Many other factors influence marriage markets. The increase in nonmarital births and divorces in the United States and Europe in recent decades means that more single women have children, so the presence of previous children will be less detrimental to them in terms of their ability to remarry. If single women with no children are relatively rare, men will be more willing to marry women who already have children. Men who marry women with children may have fewer children over time than men who marry only women with no children, but men who marry with women with children have much greater fertility than men who never marry at all (K. G. Anderson 2000).

Imbalanced sex ratios may change marriage-market dynamics as well, in favor of the scarcer gender. Marriage markets that favor women result in more women marrying higher-quality (in terms of education and income) men (Lichter, Anderson, and Hayward 1995). The so-called marriage squeeze, in which one sex has difficulty finding a mate, often affects men adversely when population growth rates are falling. If men prefer to marry women two to three years younger than themselves, and fewer children are born each year, then there will be more men born in year x than there are women in year $x + 2$. Two decades later, when those men begin looking around for a spouse, they will find tight competition for the available women in their preferred age range. This situation is particularly acute in countries like China and, to a lesser extent, India, which as a result of sex-specific abortion have a glut of men. The resulting sex ratio is skewed in favor of women, an effect exacerbated by the falling birth rates in those countries. Chinese women can be very choosy about finding a mate, because they have many available suitors to choose from, while many Chinese men, in the absence of polyandry, will be unable to obtain a spouse. Some people have suggested that the glut of men in many countries may be a public health concern (Hudson and Den Boer 2002). What will all those extra men do?

While many populations have a surplus of men, this situation is not universal. Many American cities have a shortage of single men; in these cities, men are less likely to marry women following the birth of a child than in cities where men are more common (Harknett 2008). This situation is particularly acute for African American women, who often face a shortage of eligible men within their communities. At the University of the West Indies, viewed as the premier university in the Caribbean, approximately 80% of students are women. At lesser extremes in the United States and Canada, about 60% of college students are females, meaning that the market may favor male preferences versus females'. College-educated women will face challenges finding a mate with the same level of education as they have, leaving many of them with fewer options and difficult choices, such as accepting mates with less education or remaining single.

Costs of Marriage

As we discussed in Chapter 2, marriage often involves a substantial exchange of resources. In cultures where resources are transferred from one family to another (through practices such as bride price or dowry), it can be difficult to get married unless you can meet those cultural obligations. As a result, poorer individuals may be unable to marry. For example, among the Kipsigis, subsistence agropastoralists in Kenya who raise crops and livestock, earlier-born sons are more likely to marry sooner than later-born sons, because there is less money available to pay the bride price required for the marriage of later-born sons. However, having older sisters increases the odds of a Kipsigi man marrying, as he can use the bride price that his sister receives to pay for his own marriage (Borgerhoff Mulder 1998). Cross-culturally, bride price is associated with polygyny; when men vary in wealth and can marry multiple wives, market forces increase the price of attractive wives, forcing poorer men out of the marriage market and allowing wealthier men to acquire surplus women (Low 2000).

Dowry, in which goods or resources are transferred from the bride's family to the groom's (or sometimes to the bride herself, to be taken with her to her new household), makes daughters more expensive than sons, because women require large sums of money to marry off. This means that it can be very expensive for women to find a husband. Dowry is associated with ecologies in which women contribute less to the household economy, such as agricultural societies that rely on the plow (which is generally considered men's work) (Gaulin and Boster 1990). In these circumstances, women are perceived as more of a burden. Dowry functions as a form of female competition for mates, allowing daughters to marry up the social scale and obtain high-quality husbands so long as their fathers can afford sufficient dowry (Gaulin and Boster 1990).

Even among hunter-gatherers, who rarely have the resources in hand to facilitate explicit exchanges of goods such as bride price or dowry, there may be expectations of an exchange of women from one group to another. When women's labor is valued, a group cannot afford to lose a woman (through her marrying a man from another group) unless they receive one in return (through an exchange of females). Among the Mbuti of central Africa, for example, as one scholar has noted, "when a boy chooses a wife he becomes obliged to find a 'sister'—actually any girl relative—to offer in exchange to his bride's family for one of their bachelor sons. This can be quite a chore, as it may be difficult to find a 'sister' who is willing to marry the youth his in-laws have in mind as a groom, and whom the groom himself will also like" (Turnbull 1961, 121).

Fertility within Marriage

We noted at the beginning of this chapter that most fertility occurs within the context of long-term relationships. This makes sense:
because children are dependent for eighteen or more years, women
should be reluctant to have a child with a man who is a stranger whose
ability and willingness to invest in offspring has not been proven or
vetted. However, demonstrating that few pregnancies occur in the
context of casual flings or one-night stands is difficult, as we know of
no database that tracks these encounters. Several lines of evidence do
suggest that, however permissible casual sex may be in some societies, most people do not reproduce in the context of short-term relationships.

In the United States, for example, most Americans have several
short- to medium-term sexual partnerships before settling into a longer-
term union, typically either marriage or a cohabiting union. Among
Americans born 1963 to 1974, 56% of men and 45% of women whose
first union was a marriage had at least one sexual partner before marriage, with 21% of men and 8% of women reporting five or more partners (Laumann et al. 1994). The percentages are even higher for the
number of sexual partners among people whose first union was cohabitational: 80% of men and 68% of women had at least one previous
sexual partner, and 36% of men and 20% of women had five or more
(Laumann et al. 1994).

In terms of conceptions, Edward Laumann and others (1994), using
a national sample of Americans, report that 12% of reported pregnancies were to women in nonmarital cohabiting relationships, 68% were
to married women, and 20% were to women who were neither married
nor cohabiting. Not all pregnancies result in live births, and women
who do not have male support are the most likely to terminate pregnancies (K. G. Anderson, Kaplan, and Lancaster 2007; E. M. Hill and
Low 1992). In the national sample analyzed by Laumann and others
(1994), only 47% of nonmarital, non-cohabiting conceptions produced a live birth, versus 62% of pregnancies of cohabiting women and
77% of married women. If we weight the number of pregnancies by
their outcomes, we see a further shift in favor of marriage as the context for live births: 75% of live births in this sample were to married
women versus 9% to cohabiting women and 15% to unmarried non-
cohabiting women. We cannot conclude, however, that 15% of children

are born to short-term relationships such as one night stands. That figure probably includes many women who got pregnant from steady boyfriends with whom they do not live; the actual rate of live births resulting from casual sexual encounters is presumably lower, though we cannot pinpoint it with more accuracy.

Similar results come from Gladys Martinez and others (2006), who report men's marital status at the time of their first child's birth for a nationally representative sample of American men. They find that 66% of first births were to married couples, 18% to cohabiting couples, and 16% to unmarried individuals who were living apart. Martinez and others (2006) also report that for births within the past five years, 70% of marital births and 61% of cohabiting births were wanted at the time of conception, versus only 36% of nonmarital, non-cohabiting births. Thus, the births that occur to unmarried couples who do not live together are typically not planned or wanted. Despite the fact that most Americans have multiple sex partners, they generally reserve baby making for long-term relationships.

Social Fatherhood through Marriage

Marriage is also the main process through which people acquire social parenthood, that is, the responsibility of parenting a child who is not one's actual offspring. As noted above, whenever an individual forms a union with someone who has children from a previous relationship, that individual becomes a stepparent. Because of high rates of nonmarital fertility, divorce, and remarriage not only in the United States and Europe but also in many other countries, especially in urban settings, a significant fraction of men will end up being stepfathers to children who are not genetically related to them but to whom they have a social relationship, defined through their relationship to the children's mother. We will discuss the nature of this relationship, as well as the prevalence and consequences of becoming a stepfather, in Chapter 7.

Another prominent form of social parenthood is adoption. In the United States and Europe, adoption is usually thought of in terms of a married couple (or in some cases an unmarried individual) legally adopting a completely unrelated child. In the United States, less than 3% of children under eighteen live with adoptive parents (Kreider 2003). While there is a perception that many adoptive parents adopt foreign-born children, only 14% of adopted children under eighteen in America are not born in the United States, while 18% are of a different ethnic group than that of their adoptive parents (Kreider 2003). Adoption in the United States is associated with marriage; 78% of adopted children live with two married parents, while only 5% live with a single parent who has never been married (Kreider 2003). Adoption is also associated with socioeconomic status; adoptive parents in the United States have greater income and higher education and are more likely to own a home than parents of either biological children or stepchildren (Kreider 2003).

In most societies, the adoption of a completely unrelated child is rare. In high-fertility societies it is much more common for a couple to take on parental responsibility for a child who is related to them in some manner but who is not their biological child. This relationship may be called adoption but is really fostering, and it occurs for several reasons, including recipient families' having "not enough" children, or perceived advantages in the recipient household, such as better schools nearby or a greater ability to invest in children (such as having more resources) (K. G. Anderson 2005; Silk 1980). The practice is widespread in Oceania, where up to 31% of children may be adopted (Silk 1980). Adopted children in Oceania are overwhelmingly likely to be related to the adopting household, most at the level of first cousin or closer (Silk 1980). In the Micronesian atoll of Ifaluk, for example, high-status couples are more likely to have their children adopted by lower-status relatives, allowing the high-status families to have more children and greater reproductive success over the long term (Betzig and Turke 1992).

Fostering is a common practice throughout sub-Saharan African countries (Lloyd and Blanc 1996), and occurs for many different reasons. Fostering may occur when a child is orphaned, that is, when one or both parents die, although a significant fraction of fostered children are not orphans (K. G. Anderson and Beutel n.d.). The HIV/AIDS epidemic has resulted in an increasing number of orphans, particularly in Africa. For example, in 2003 14% of black South Africans had experienced the death of a father before age sixteen and 4% of black South Africans had experienced the death of a mother before age sixteen (Operario et al. 2008). As the HIV/AIDS epidemic continues, rates of single and double orphanhood among black South Africans are expected to increase (Nyambedha et al. 2003). Many of these children are fostered to distant kin, such as aunts, uncles, grandparents, or cousins, or to older siblings. The extent to which members of foster households are regarded as social parents varies across cultures, and marriage is not necessarily a required precursor to foster parenthood. We will discuss in more detail the consequences of father absence on children's outcomes in Chapter 6.

Union Dissolution and Divorce

Humans are not the only animals that form long-term unions for the purposes of raising offspring. Some animals, such as swans, form pair-bonds for life, and will not repartner even if a mate should die. Humans are not typically like that; while there are societies in which spouses nearly always remain together until death do them part, divorce occurs in most human cultures. Among the 85 cultures in the SCCS with data on the frequency of divorce, divorce occurs rarely or never in 29% of societies, while in 46% it is common or universal (authors' calculations). Divorce can be conceived as a tug-of-war between male and female interests; marriage represents a compromise between these competing interests, but when the costs of remaining together exceed the benefits, the union ends. Divorce is common among hunter-gatherers as well as more technologically advanced cultures. Data collected among Aka, Hadza, and !Kung hunter-gatherers suggest that 25–40% of marriages end in divorce (Blurton Jones et al. 2000; B. S. Hewlett 1991b). The Ache have fairly informal marriages; they are easily dissolved and new ones easily formed. During the precontact forest period (before the Ache were settled on reservations in the 1970s and lived solely as hunter-gatherers), Ache women had had on average ten spouses by the time they reached thirty, while Ache men had had about seven by that age (K. Hill and Hurtado 1996).

Divorce is influenced by societal factors as well as individual ones, that is, by macro social forces as well as micro ones. The "era of unrestricted divorce" began in the United States in 1970, with parallels in many other countries, following the liberalization of divorce laws that made it possible for virtually anybody who wanted a divorce to obtain one (Cherlin 2008). Nevertheless, the increase in divorce rates in industrialized counties cannot simply be blamed on no-fault divorce laws, as divorce rates had increased dramatically, in the United States at least, before such laws were introduced. Many factors contributed to the increase in divorce, including increasing rates of women's employment and increased women's income, as well as the relative erosion of men's wages (Cherlin 2008). Whatever the cause, as divorce rates increased, divorce itself became more acceptable, to the point where currently about half of American marriages end in divorce.

A great deal of research has examined the correlates of divorce and union dissolution. Factors such as age, money, and personality play a role in divorce. For example, divorce is associated with early age at marriage, as well as with low socioeconomic status (including low income and low educational level) (L. K. White 1990). Personality conflicts, including disagreements over money, increase the likelihood of divorce (L. K. White 1990), while, cross-culturally, "displeasingness" is cited as the fourth most common reason for divorce (Betzig 1989).

Because most fertility occurs within the context of long-term relationships such as marriage, it is perhaps not surprising that children— or lack of children—play a role in divorce. In a survey of 160 cultures in the Standard Cross-Cultural Sample that had data on conjugal dissolution, Laura Betzig (1989) found that infertility is the second most common reason given for divorce. In societies that allow polygyny, the problem of an infertile wife is often solved by adding a second, presumably fecund, wife to the union (Betzig 1989). But in cultures that enforce monogamy, infertility often results in divorce. Betzig (1989) examined a cross-cultural sample of thirty modern societies and found that divorce rates are highest for couples with no children in twenty-five societies (83%), while Helen Fisher (1989), using thirty-one years of data from forty-five countries, found that the modal number of children at divorce was zero, occurring in 62% of societies.

It is possible, of course, that lack of children may not cause divorce. Rather, the causal arrow could point in the other direction—couples who sense they are going to get divorced may be less likely to have children. But even if that is true, it only serves to underscore the relationship between marriage and fertility. If you have a partner you do not like or who has other undesirable qualities, such as being a potentially poor investor or parent, it makes sense to separate from that person and start over with someone else before having children. And in fact this is what many couples do. The potential reproductive benefits of divorce (that is, being able to have children with someone else), however, decline as the potential for future reproductive opportunities decline, and this is reflected in gender-specific patterns of divorce instigation. In England and Wales, for example, women are overwhelmingly likely to initiate divorce at younger ages, but this declines steadily with age. Men initiate very few divorces at young ages but are increasingly likely to initiate divorce as they grow older (Buckle, Gallup, and Rodd 1996). A man in his forties can potentially increase his reproductive output by remarrying a younger woman, while a woman in her forties who remarries a younger man will not have any more children than a woman who stayed married to her initial spouse.

The costs and benefits of leaving a partner to establish a new relationship are influenced by the sex ratio. If opposite-sex partners are scarce, and you have a partner already, you are probably better off remaining with that partner than leaving and trying to find a new one. Similarly, if potential partners are abundant, and same-sex competitors scarce, you might have an easier time leaving your current relationship and "trading up." Katherine Trent and Scott South (1989), in a cross-cultural analysis using data from sixty-six countries, found that high sex ratios (more men than women) predicted lower divorce rates. Nicholas Blurton Jones and others (2000) examined divorce rates for four hunter-gatherer societies: the Ache, the Hiwi, the !Kung, and the Hadza. The measure for divorce is necessarily crude, and the researchers ranked these societies in terms of relative frequency of divorce, from the lowest (the Hiwi) to the highest (the Ache). They report that the two societies with more females than males (the Ache and the Hadza) have the highest divorce rates, while the two societies with more males than females (the Hiwi and the !Kung) have the lowest. Because of the small sample size and crude measures used, this result must be treated with caution, but it suggests that among small-scale populations, men are more likely to leave marriages when there are plenty of other females available and less likely to leave them when females are scarce. A. Magdalena Hurtado and Kim Hill (1992) built a mathematical model, based on Ache and Hiwi data, suggesting that men's having a positive impact on child survival will stabilize pair-bonds only when mating opportunities are scarce, implying that the sex ratio impacts divorce rates more strongly than men's impact on children. (We will discuss the relationship between paternal investment and children's outcomes in more detail in Chapter 6.)

Also consistent with the idea that fertility influences union dissolution is the relationship between infidelity and divorce. We will discuss paternity confidence in greater detail in Chapter 5, but basically men tend to be sensitive to the potential for infidelity because they will pay great evolutionary costs if they unknowingly raise other men's children. To avoid this, men place restrictions on women's ability to have extramarital affairs, and punish infidelity (actual or perceived) through violence and divorce (Daly and Wilson 1988). Betzig (1989) found that, cross-culturally, infidelity was the most common reason given for divorce.

Because adultery impacts male and female fitness separately (female infidelity decreases the probability that a man is the father of his wife's children while male infidelity does not alter whether a woman is the mother of her own children), we expect to see a gender bias in the reaction to adultery. And in fact we do: female adultery is much more likely to result in divorce than male adultery. In England and Wales, for example, men are much more likely than women to name adultery as grounds for divorce, and in fact adultery is the most common grounds for divorce named by men (Buckle, Gallup, and Rodd 1996). Among the eighty-eight societies in which adultery is given as a valid reason for divorce, divorce followed adultery by either partner in twenty-five of these societies (28%), by only the wife's infidelity in fifty-four societies (61%), and by only the husband's infidelity in just two (2%) (Betzig 1989). Men are much more likely to end a relationship if women are unfaithful than women are to end it if men are unfaithful.

Men use violence and aggression to control women's behavior and in particular to prevent or punish infidelity. Men may react violently to perceived infidelity, in addition to or instead of divorce. It is significant that perceived female infidelity is the leading cause of spousal homicide (Daly and Wilson 1988). Yet men's use of violence may backfire, precipitating divorce as women seek to end the relationship. In England and Wales, cruelty was the most common grounds for divorce among women, who were far more likely than men to mention this as a reason for ending the marriage (Buckle, Gallup, and Rodd 1996). Cruelty and male attempts to control women may explain why women are more likely than men to file for divorce at every age up through sixty (Buckle, Gallup, and Rodd 1996); even though the reproductive advantages of divorce are lower for women (in terms of the probability of remarriage and subsequent fertility), the reproductive costs of remaining married may often be greater for women.

Cross-culturally, cruelty or mistreatment is the third most common reason for divorce (Betzig 1989). In her cross-cultural data, Betzig noted that cruelty as grounds for divorce is ascribed exclusively to men in forty-five out of fifty-one cultures and to both spouses in five cultures, and in no culture is cruelty ascribed exclusively to women. She also notes that ethnographic material supports the suggestion that male cruelty often results from female infidelity, or at least male perception of it. Women who are unable to leave their partners may resort to more drastic measures; spousal homicide committed by the wife most often results from previous physical or psychological abuse, of either the woman or her children, or fear of future abuse (Daly and Wilson 1988).

If lack of children leads to divorce, it should follow that having children decreases the odds of divorce. And this is true to an extent. Divorce is virtually nonexistent in the year following the birth of a first child in the United States, though we do not see a dampening effect of birth on divorce following subsequent births (L. K. White 1990). Cross-cultural studies suggest that when fathers are highly involved with children, marriages may be less likely to end in divorce (Seccombe and Lee 1987). As we will discuss in Chapter 6, this may result from paternal care being a form of mating effort, with women preferring to remain with men who are high investors in children (and, conversely, being more likely to leave men who are poor investors) (K. G. Anderson, Kaplan, and Lancaster 1999). One American study found that divorce is less likely following the birth of a boy than a girl, an effect which may result from men being more involved with sons than daughters (Morgan, Lye, and Condran 1988).

The relationship between fertility and union dissolution is somewhat different for cohabitors than for married couples, at least in the United States. For many couples, cohabitation is a premarital state; a large fraction of cohabiting couples subsequently formalize their relationship through marriage. Although most births occur within marriage, a significant fraction occur to cohabiting couples; as Pamela Smock (2000) notes, a large proportion of what surveys identify as births to "single mothers" actually occur within unmarried two-parent households, while Larry Bumpass and Lawrence Lu (2000) argue that the recent increase in nonmarital births in the United States is due to increased cohabitation rates and not to increases in births to women without partners. While most cohabitors either break up or marry, a small fraction are lifelong cohabitants, remaining unmarried but not separating. One Canadian study found that fertility increased the probability that a cohabiting couple would remain cohabiting, rather than separating or marrying (Z. Wu and Balakrishnan 1995). One nationally representative American study found that a pregnancy among cohabiting couples increased the likelihood of marriage but had no effect on separation (Brown 2000), while Lawrence Wu, Larry Bumpass, and Kelly Musick (2001) found that American cohabiting unions were twice as likely as marital unions to dissolve following a first birth. In Sweden, cohabiting couples who are pregnant are more than twice as likely to marry as nonpregnant couples, although this is not universal, as the average age at first birth is less than the age at first marriage (Duvander 1999).

Tibetan Polyandrous marriages provide an interesting case study for conflict of interest among spouses, because of the unusual situation of several social fathers helping to raise children within a single household. Polyandry does not increase female fertility, and it decreases male fertility, especially for younger co-husbands, who typically father fewer children than their older brothers do (Beall and Goldstein 1981). Although cultural rules may stipulate that all men in the family share fatherhood responsibilities equally, in practical terms there is an unequal distribution of fertility within the family, with the oldest co-husband likely to have fathered the first several children in the marriage. As a result, polyandrous Tibetan marriages are more successful if the co-husbands are full siblings rather than half siblings or unrelated males; co-husbands who are full siblings at least are raising nieces and nephews, if not their own children, while more distantly-related co-husbands are expected to invest in more distantly related offspring, leading for further tensions and conflicts within the marriage (Durham 1991). When economic circumstances permit, men readily leave polyandrous unions to set up their own monogamous marriages (Haddix 2001). Polyandry represents a compromise, in which men make the best of a bad situation. Sharing a wife is less desirable than having one all to yourself, but better than having none at all.

Starting Over: Remarriage Following Divorce

The end of one relationship may open the door to another, and many cultures allow individuals to remarry following divorce. Among Americans ages fifty to fifty-nine, 63% of men have been married exactly once, 23% exactly twice, and 8% three or more times. The corresponding values for women are similar: 65% have married once, 22% twice, and 6% three times or more (Kreider 2005).

Serial monogamy allows men and women to practice what is in effect lifetime polygamy, even if they live in a culture where monogamy is the only available marital arrangement. This kind of polygamy can have tremendous impacts on fertility, particularly for males, for if they remarry younger women, they can greatly extend their reproductive life span (Low 2000). In a sample of preindustrial Sami, nomadic reindeer herders from northern Finland, Pekka Käär and others (1998) found that men were more likely to remarry than women. Furthermore, remarriage increased male fertility but had no effect on female fertility. Remarriage extended the reproductive life span of Sami men by about five years, giving them an additional 1.4 children, compared with men who married only once.

In summary, marriage is an important element of fatherhood because most reproduction occurs within the context of long-term unions. Marriages may be made for love or arranged by families for economic purposes, and marriages can involve only two adults or far more. Many factors influence whom you marry, including incest taboos, cultural expectations, wealth and income, sex ratio, presence of children from previous unions, and age. Many factors also influence whether a marriage will end, including lack of children, perceived infidelity, and violence and cruelty. At some level, whether two people have that magic spark or whether they lose it is a phenomenon that defies empirical analysis, but we hope we have provided some insight into the major social and cultural factors that influence both marriage and divorce. In the next chapter we'll examine more closely the factors that influence whether people have children and, if so, how many they have.

4

Fathers and Fertility

What factors influence whether or not men have children and how many they have? Every biological father is the progenitor of at least one child, but why do some men stop at one or two, while others have a dozen? After all, men produce far more sperm than they could ever turn into babies. An adult male produces about 85 million sperm per day, somewhere in the neighborhood of one quadrillion—a thousand billion—over the course of his life. Obviously, no man has fathered anywhere near that number of children. The highest recorded fertility is accredited to King Moulay Ismail the Bloodthirsty of Morocco, an eighteenth-century despot who is reported to have had at least 888 children (Einon 1998). Virtually all men achieve fertility levels falling far short of this record, and even King Ismail's output has been disputed on technical grounds (Einon 1998). In this chapter we will explore the factors that contribute to fertility and survey the variation in fertility that has been observed across cultures and through time.

Historically, demographers and biologists studying fertility have focused on women (J. W. Wood 1994). To a certain extent this makes sense: women are the ones having babies, and the processes of female fertility are what you might call highly visible, in that everybody around her, including the woman herself, knows she is having a baby. Men are a step removed from fertility; they help create the baby but do not carry it, and some men may not even know about all of the children they have fathered. Thus, measures of male fertility may undercount offspring production. Because every child in a society has both a father and a mother, biologically speaking, if you track female fertility you must be keeping track of male fertility as well. But as we will discuss below, male fertility can differ from female fertility in important ways. We will start with a broad overview of the factors influencing human fertility, with the acknowledgment that the patterns presented here are generally drawn from studies of women, not men.

Factors Influencing Fertility

The words fertility and fecundity are sometimes used interchangeably, but they have very different meanings within different branches of science. For the purposes of this chapter, we adopt the usage of demographers (Weeks 2008; J. W. Wood 1994): "fertility" is the production of a live birth or the number of children born, while "fecundity" is the biological capacity to reproduce, or reproductive potential (J.W. Wood 1994:3). (Note that this usage is the opposite of the way many medical and biological researchers use these terms.) Fertility is easier to measure than fecundity—all women, and most men, are aware of the birth of a child, and most adults can accurately report how many children they have had. Fecundity is a bit trickier to measure, because it is not easily observable. You cannot casually glance at a women and tell if she's ovulating, nor can you readily assess whether a man has a healthy sperm count without getting personal. Self-reported data are not reliable, so measuring fecundity requires methods of investigation that are more burdensome (such as daily urine or saliva samples) or even invasive (such as blood draws or tissue samples). Fecundity is also not an all-or-nothing issue but can fall along a range between full fecundity and sterility (Weeks 2008).

Fecundity is obviously an important precursor to fertility; a person with no viable gametes will not have children. Heritable factors, such as a genetic predisposition to sterility or subfecundity, may influence fecundity. Other factors—such as libido—may be influenced by genetic factors as well. Heritability may also influence fertility. Current research on twins in the United States and Denmark suggests that a portion of variation in fertility and in age at first reproduction is due to genetic factors (Rodgers, Rowe, and Buster 1999; Rodgers, Kohler, et al. 2001).

However, social and cultural factors influencing fertility are much more prominent than genetic ones. Social factors translate the potential for children into actual offspring. Demographers have organized the factors affecting fertility into a list of proximate determinants of fertility (for example, Bongaarts 1978; K. Davis and Blake 1956; J. W. Wood 1994). This framework is important to studies of cross-cultural fertility patterns, because social factors, such as the acceptability of nonmarital sex or the age at first marriage, are to a large extent responsible for variation in fertility patterns across societies. These proximate determinants were conceptualized to explain differences in fertility at the population level, but they can be used to explain individual differences within populations as well.

Perhaps the most influential version of the proximate determinants of fertility was devised by John Bongaarts (1978), who divided them into three groups. The first group includes factors affecting exposure to intercourse. What this boils down to, not surprisingly, is that the fewer years of your life you spend in a sexual relationship, the fewer children you will have. Factors such as delayed age at first sex and greater time spent between sexual relationships result in fewer offspring, relative to individuals who had an earlier age at first sex or who spent virtually all of their reproductive years in sexual relationships. For example, in a study of lifetime fertility patterns of American women, one of us found that the older a woman was when she had her first child, the fewer children she had; for every seven years a woman delayed beginning reproduction, she had one less child (K. G. Anderson and Low 2003).

The second group of proximate determinants of fertility are factors that deliberately control fertility within sexual unions. These factors include contraception and induced abortion. While the effectiveness of contraception varies, there is a close cross-cultural relationship between contraception use and completed fertility (Pritchett 1994). Included in this category is surgical sterilization, which is fairly common among couples who have achieved their desired family size. For example, in 1995 26% of U.S. women ages fifteen to forty-four had undergone tubal ligation, while 12% of men in the same age range had had vasectomies (Chandra 1998). Induced abortion is also widely used to control fertility. In Russia and Belarus, for example, more than 60% of pregnancies are terminated through elective abortions, making abortion the leading form of birth control in those nations (Henshaw, Singh, and Haas 1999). Globally, about 26% of pregnancies end in elective abortions; the United States is right at the global average (25.9%), while Europe is much higher (48%) and Africa much lower (15%) (Henshaw, Singh, and Haas 1999). Abortion ratios display a U-shaped distribution with respect to maternal age, being highest in the teenage years (when many women are not yet ready to start a family and may not have secured reliable male commitment to raising their children) and lowest in the twenties and thirties before climbing again in the forties (when many women have achieved their desired family size and are also electing to terminate pregnancies that may have complications such as Down syndrome) (E. M. Hill and Low 1992).

Bongaarts's third group of proximate determinants are natural-fertility factors, processes that limit fertility in the absence of deliberate control factors such as contraception and abortion. Simply having sex is not enough to ensure conception; women who are sexually active will not become pregnant if they are not ovulating, and ovulation may be suppressed for many reasons. For example, breast-feeding can induce postpartum infecundity lasting several years if breast-feeding is frequent and regular (J. W. Wood 1994). Temporary celibacy within sexual relationships (attributed to biological factors such as erectile dysfunction or to social factors such as temporary separation and postpartum abstinence) also decreases the odds of conception. Coital frequency may also influence conception: couples who have sex more often are more likely to conceive (Wilcox, Weinberg, and Baird 1995). Coital frequency tends to decline with relationship duration, so that couples who have been together a long time have sex less frequently than couples who have just begun their relationship (J. W. Wood 1994).

Woman are sterile before menarche and after menopause, and the ages of those two transitions vary both within and across populations. It generally takes a year or two for women's cycles to stabilize following menarche, resulting in a period of adolescent subfecundity during which conception is unlikely (J. W. Wood 1994). Other factors, such as weight loss or high levels of physical activity, may also suppress ovulation (Ellison 2003). Other factors work to increase the probability of ovulation. For example, women who have more frequent contact with men, independent of coital frequency, have shorter, more stable cycles and are more likely to ovulate (Veith et al. 1983).

Even if conception occurs, there is the risk of spontaneous uterine mortality, or miscarriage. Rates of fetal loss are difficult to measure, especially during the first week following conception, when the fetus is not yet producing human chorionic gonadotropin (hCG), the chemical signature that is used by most pregnancy tests to detect conception. Nevertheless, it is estimated that as many as 60%—and some mathematical models put it as high as 80%—of conceptions terminate naturally, often before women are even aware they are pregnant (Holman and Wood 2001).

Bongaarts's framework calls attention to the various steps involved in producing a baby. Two cultures may have similar fertility levels but reach them through very different pathways. For example, Ireland in 1960 had a total fertility rate of 4.0 (Potts 1997). This level is similar to that among some hunter-gatherers, such as the Batak of the Philippines (3.9), the Inuit of Greenland (3.7), or the Northern !Kung of southern Africa (4.3) (B. S. Hewlett 1991a). Yet the proximate pathways by which these similar fertility levels are reached vary tremendously. Virtually all fertility in Ireland occurs within the context of marriage (Strassmann and Clarke 1998). The Irish delay marriage, thus delaying the start of reproduction. For example, in 1961 37% of Irish women ages twenty-five to thirty-four were not married; by ages thirty-five to forty-four, 23% were still unmarried (Strassmann and Clarke 1998). Once they marry and being reproducing, the Irish then space births fairly closely together. Most hunter-gatherers, in contrast, marry and begin reproduction at fairly early ages, soon after menarche, but they space births out fairly far apart (J. W. Wood 1994). For example, among the Northern !Kung, 56% of women are married by age nineteen, and 90% by age twenty-four (Howell 2000). Although they marry and start reproducing far earlier than the Irish, the !Kung achieve only slightly higher fertility because they space children farther apart, with the modal interbirth interval being four years (Howell 2000). Similarly, when two populations have strikingly different patterns of fertility, the proximate-determinants approach lets us pinpoint why; for example, the cultures may have different rules influencing entry into sex, age at weaning, or the acceptability of induced abortion.

Fertility Patterns

What were fertility patterns like in the ecological conditions under which humans evolved? Let's begin with a hypothetical question: what would human fertility patterns look like in the absence of birth control? Let's say you had a society in which women reach menarche at age fifteen and menopause at forty-four, which would give them thirty reproductive years. If all women in the society first get pregnant at age fifteen, each pregnancy lasts nine months, and they all conceive again three months following each birth, women in this society would give birth to thirty babies over their life span. Most readers will recognize that conceiving again three months after every pregnancy is an unrealistic assumption; while some women do get pregnant a few months after their most recent birth, it's unlikely that would occur consistently to every woman in a society over the entire reproductive span. If we assume women in this hypothetical population got pregnant fifteen months after each birth, thus spacing children two years apart, women would each have fifteen children over their lives. That is not biologically unfeasible, for individuals at least—many people have a great-grandmother or great-aunt who had fifteen babies, or know someone who does.

But while individual women may be able to produce that many offspring, no human society has ever maintained an average of fifteen live births. We cannot directly observe the fertility patterns that hunter-gatherers experienced, for example, twenty thousand years ago, before the advent of agriculture, but we can collect data on existing natural-fertility populations, that is, populations that do not use birth control and do not take deliberate steps to stop reproduction once they reach a desired family size (J. W. Wood 1994). One survey of seventy natural-fertility populations found mean completed fertility of 6.1 births per woman (J. W. Wood 1994).

Fertility in all of these subsistence societies falls well short of the theoretical biological maximum, although a few societies have come closer to it. In the early 1960s, Shipibo horticulturalists in Amazonian Peru gave birth to 9.94 children per woman (Hern 1977). The Hutterites, a communal Anabaptist group who migrated to the United States from Europe in the nineteenth century, experienced even higher fertility. In the 1940s the Hutterites had an average completed fertility of 10.9 births per woman (Eaton and Mayer 1953). Because of their high nuptiality (virtually every Hutterite woman was married by age twenty), short interbirth intervals, and long reproductive life spans (continuing reproduction into their forties), Hutterites exhibited near-maximum fertility for every age group except fifteen to nineteen. This historical high-water mark did not last long, however; by the 1970s Hutterite fertility had dropped to roughly half of its peak level (Nonaka et al. 1994). The reasons for this decline are not clear. Hutterite women began to delay marriage by about four or five years, but fertility within marriage also decreased, especially at older ages, suggesting Hutterites may have begun adopting birth control to protect women's health (Nonaka et al. 1994).

At the other end of the fertility spectrum, many nation-states now exhibit astoundingly low levels of fertility. Replacement-level fertility is typically defined as 2.1 children, enough so that each woman will have, on average, two children who reach adulthood, sufficient to replace both herself and the father. The widespread use of contraception, as well as delayed marriage and surgical sterilization once desired fertility is reached, has resulted in the average fertility of many nations falling well below the replacement level. Of the 194 nations with fertility data published in the *World Fertility Chart* (United Nations 2008), 67 (34.5%) have total fertility rates of 2.0 or less. Global fertility averages out to 2.6 children per woman, but there is tremendous regional variation. Of the 40 European nations, only one—Albania—has fertility above 2.0, giving Europe an average total fertility of only 1.4. Asia and Latin America are both higher, at 2.5, while Africa currently averages 5.0 births per women. Only two of Africa's 54 countries (3.7%) are at or below replacement level, versus 4 of the 21 countries in Latin America (19.0%) and 16 of the 50 countries in Asia (32%). Currently, the record for the lowest fertility in the world is held by Macao, at 0.8 births per woman, with Hong Kong running a close second place, at 1.0 births. Third place, at 1.2 births, is a ten-way tie, held by nine eastern European and former Soviet Union countries (such as Belarus, the Ukraine, Poland, etc.), along with South Korea. The United States, in contrast, has the highest fertility in the developed world at 2.01 children per woman, just brushing up against replacement level. (Canada, in contrast, has a fertility rate of only 1.5.)

Globally, fertility has dropped quite sharply over a fairly short time period. In 1970, average fertility was 4.5 births per woman, nearly two children higher than it is now (United Nations 2008). If we examine the 189 countries for which we have data for both 1970 and 2000 (drawn from United Nations 2008), we find that nearly every country has lowered its fertility over that time span. Oman had the highest fertility in the world in 1970, at 9.3 births per woman; in 2000, Oman's fertility was 3.6, only 38% of what it had been three decades earlier. In 1970, 33 of the 189 countries in the sample (17%) had a completed fertility of 7.0 children or above. In 2000, only 2 countries (1%) did: the Democratic Republic of the Congo (7.3) and Niger (7.1). Five countries went against the prevailing trend and increased their fertility across this time period, and only 2 (the Democratic Republic of the Congo and Chad) increased fertility more than 3% from their 1970 rates. A total of 48 countries (24% of the world's nations) decreased their fertility by more than half over this time period. The global trend has been toward reduced fertility, and nearly every country has been swept up in that trend.

The record holder in terms of fertility reduction is the People's Republic of China. Within thirty years, China's fertility dropped from 5.7 births per woman to only 1.4, a reduction of 76%. Much attention has been focused on China's one-child policy, begun in 1979, in which the government offered substantial financial incentives for women to restrict their fertility to only one birth. However, by the time the one-child policy was implemented, Chinese fertility had already dropped by more than half, from about 6.1 in 1965 to about 2.7 in 1979 (Weeks 2008). In 1971—when fertility levels had already begun a substantial decline—the government began the *wan xi shao* family-planning education program, stressing later *(wan)* births, longer *(xi)* birth intervals, and fewer *(shao)* children (Weeks 2008). This policy summed up, in a nutshell, the proximate-determinants approach to fertility, by stressing that later age at first reproduction and longer birth spacing will result in fewer children. As a result of these family-planning programs, Chinese women and men exhibit high rates of contraception usage, with about 87% of married women using contraception (Hesketh, Lu, and Xing 2005). Nearly half (46%) of married women use the intrauterine device (IUD) as their form of birth control, with female sterilization utilized by 37%. Male sterilization (vasectomy) is a distant third, used by only 8% of married Chinese couples in 2001, while use of the condom (6%) and oral contraceptive pill (3%), so widespread in the United States and Europe, is almost negligible in China (Hesketh, Lu, and Xing 2005).

China's one-child policy has attracted a great deal of attention and criticism, in large part because of the perception of heavy-handed governmental interference in people's reproductive choices. Most women are offered no choice of contraception, and 80% simply use the method that their family-planning worker recommends (Hesketh, Lu, and Xing 2005). There is a widespread impression that many women in China undergo coerced abortions to keep them from exceeding the one-child limit, and while that undoubtedly happens, the abortion ratio in China is estimated at 27.4 abortions per 100 pregnancies, a rate barely higher than that of the United States (Henshaw, Singh, and Haas 1999). Another area of controversy arising from the one-child policy is the sex ratio, which is heavily biased toward males. Currently in China there are 115 boys born for every 100 girls (Hesketh, Lu, and Xing 2005).

In urban areas, the bias is even more extreme for second children, with 130 boys born for every 100 girls (Hesketh, Lu, and Xing 2005). These numbers reflect a strong preference for sons in Chinese society, and there is concern that the one-child policy encouraged female infanticide, though the evidence in support of this is equivocal (Hesketh, Lu, and Xing 2005). Certainly, sex-specific abortions as well as underreporting of female births have contributed to this sex-ratio bias (Weeks 2008).

Male and Female Fertility Differences

How do men fit into this picture? While every baby has a father as well as a mother, there are important male/female differences in fertility patterns. While average male fertility and average female fertility must be the same within a population, there is more potential variance in male fertility than female fertility: a fraction of men may have much greater fertility than any woman could achieve. Men produce far more gametes than women; in the roughly 280 days it takes a woman to ovulate, conceive, gestate, and give birth, a man may produce perhaps 25 billion sperm. A man who had sexual access to a different reproductive-aged woman who was not pregnant, not on the pill, etc., each day of that time period would have a shot at producing up to 280 offspring in the time it takes a woman to produce one child. His actual fertility would fall far below this, because women are not fecund most days of their cycles, not every ovum exposed to semen results in a conception, and many conceptions do not result in a live birth. Using published data on each of these factors (Einon 1998; R. G. Gould 2000), we calculate that a man having sex with a different woman over each of 280 days could realistically expect to father between four and ten children. This calculation still far outweighs the number of children most women could produce over the same time period.

Thus, a male's fertility is in effect limited by the number of females he can impregnate. For a woman, conversely, access to more sexual partners will not increase her fertility (unless her primary partner is infertile). No matter how many partners she has, a woman cannot manage more than one birth every nine months or so. The highest recorded female fertility is credited to a Russian woman, the first wife of one Fyodor Vassilyev, who between 1725 and 1765 had sixty-nine live births, spaced out over "only" twenty-seven pregnancies (Clay 1989).

(Amazingly, sixty-seven of these children survived infancy.) King Moulay Ismail the Bloodthirsty had nearly thirteen times as many children as Vassilyev's wife did; he achieved this high fertility through his harem of around five hundred women, by whom he averaged 14.3 children per year (R. G. Gould 2000). Thus, multiple partners increase male fertility, while having little effect on female fertility. Among polygynous Mormons in the nineteenth century, each additional wife increased male fertility by over six children, at least up through four wives; beyond that, fertility leveled off and began to fall, possibly due to increased male age as well as reduced resources available for these later wives (Heath and Hadley 1998). In polyandrous cultures, in contrast, women with multiple husbands do not have more children than women with only one husband (Beall and Goldstein 1981).

In monogamous countries, male fertility is necessarily constrained by the limits of female fertility. Although men produce sperm throughout their lives (with reduced levels at higher ages), an older sperm-producing male will not have additional children if his wife or partner is past menopause. This limitation has an obvious loophole: men may have children throughout their lives if they repartner with younger women, following either the death of or divorce from their first wives. Consider two historical examples: the eighteenth-century German composer Johann Sebastian Bach had twenty-six children, while the American patriot Paul Revere, born roughly a generation later, had sixteen children. These men both lived in monogamous societies, where they were restricted to one wife at a time. They both achieved their high levels of fertility by remarrying much younger women following the death of their first wives, thereby extending their own reproductive life spans. Perhaps the starkest example of this is Fyodor Vassilyev, introduced above, whose first wife bore him sixty-nine children. He subsequently remarried, and his second wife gave birth to an additional eighteen children, spaced across eight pregnancies, giving him a lifetime total of eighty-seven children (Clay 1988)—hardly a record, but impressive nonetheless. (Consider that he achieved roughly 10% of King Moulay Ismail's fertility, but with only two women, as opposed to Ismail's five hundred.) Serial monogamy can thus increase men's fertility even if cultural rules forbid polygyny.

An additional way in which male fertility differs from female fertility is that women's reproductive physiology is much more sensitive to energetic conditions than men's. Pregnancy and lactation are both extremely energetically expensive; conceiving, bearing, and then breast-feeding a child represents a huge energetic commitment from a woman, typically lasting several years (Ellison 2001). Thus, when food is scarce or a woman's energetic requirements are high (for example, from high levels of physical exercise), ovulation may be disrupted (Ellison 2003). Sperm production, in contrast, is much more robust to energetic demands or availability; men have to be close to starvation before their testes shut down (Bribiescas 2006). Men and women are both likely to suffer decreased fecundability in response to an illness or disease, but the effect is much smaller for men than for women.

Fecundity drops with age for both men and women, but in different ways. Women experience permanent sterility with menopause, the timing of which varies across populations but typically occurs by age fifty (J. W. Wood 1994). In contrast, fecundity declines gradually in men, and there is no sharp cutoff. A seventy-year-old man still has about 50% of the reproductive capacity of a twenty-eight-year-old man (J. W. Wood 1994), and men are thus technically capable of producing babies at very old ages. If we compare age-specific fertility for Yanomamo men and women (using data from Melancon 1982), we see that young Yanomamo men have lower fertility than women do (men ages twenty to twenty-four have only 52% as many babies as same-aged women do). Male fertility levels lag behind that of women at younger ages because it takes men additional years to acquire the resources and social standing they need to obtain a mate. Once they are having babies, however, men keep at it for longer than women. Yanomamo male fertility at ages forty to forty-four is about 2.6 times that of women. Polygyny among the Yanomamo allows men to marry younger women and keep producing children at older ages. Yanomamo men have 2.92 children between the ages of forty-five and seventy-five, over fifty-four times what Yanomamo women have over that same age range.

The Demographic Transition

Fertility patterns in modern industrialized countries differ tremendously from what humans experienced for most of our evolutionary history. Traditionally, people experienced high fertility (a lot of babies were born) as well as high mortality (a lot of those babies died). Contemporary hunter-gatherers have about 5.5 children, but 20.3% of them die by age one, and 43.4% die by age 15 (B. S. Hewlett 1991a).

For example, the life expectancy at birth of Ache females during the time the Ache lived in the forest was 37.1, and 11.6% died during their first year of life. Between 3% and 7% of Ache girls died each year up through age seven, so that by age eight, 34.7% of girls ever born had died (K. Hill and Hurtado 1996). Horticulturalists and agriculturalists have slightly higher fertility—estimates are 5.4 to 6.1 children for horticulturalists and 6.6 for agriculturalists—and rates of infant and child mortality that are similar to those observed among hunter-gatherers (Bentley, Jasienska, and Goldberg 1993; B. S. Hewlett 1991a). This pattern of high fertility and high mortality probably characterized most of human evolutionary history: people had a lot of children but most of them died, leading to no or fairly slow population growth.

During the nineteenth century, following the Industrial Revolution, demographic patterns began to exhibit a shift, never before seen in human history, called the "demographic transition" (J. R. Weeks 2008). Populations began to move from a regime of high fertility and high mortality to one of low fertility and low mortality. Mortality rates began to drop first, so that people were still having a lot of children, but a lot more of them survived. A population explosion was the result. Eventually birth rates declined as well, coming in line with mortality rates, so that, as mentioned above, a large number of countries now are having fewer children than are required to replace the parents.

The demographic transition was first observed in postindustrial Europe, but it has occurred all over the world. As we noted above, nearly every country in the world has reduced its fertility over the past three decades, with fully a quarter of the world's countries reducing fertility by half. These sudden drops in fertility were made possible by the availability of reliable contraception, as well as surgical sterility and, in many countries, legalized abortion (Potts 1997). But modern technology only explains how fertility levels dropped, not why they dropped. People will not use birth control unless they desire to limit their fertility, and there is a close negative association cross-culturally between desired fertility and contraceptive use (Pritchett 1994). Any theory of low fertility levels must explain not just how fertility dropped but why.

Many theories have been proposed to explain the demographic transition, though none has met with universal acceptance. Demographers generally are not able to predict demographic transitions in advance; they can only point them out after they occur. We know that demographic transitions are associated with education; more educated, wealthier, and more socially successful segments of the population reduce their fertility levels first, with less educated, poorer, and less socially successful strata eventually following suit (Borgerhoff Mulder 1998; Low 2000; Potts 1997). This pattern is true cross-culturally as well, with more-educated countries having lower fertility than less-educated ones. Using a sample of 127 countries that had data on total fertility rate and female literacy rate (UNICEF 2007), we find a strong negative correlation between fertility and literacy, with female literacy accounting for 60% of the variation in total fertility rate (author's calculations; correlation $r = -0.775$, $p < 0.0001$). Whether education actually causes reduced fertility or is simply an easily identified proxy for the true cause is unclear.

In order to understand why fertility levels have dropped in so many societies, we need to understand why they were once so high. Why did preindustrial families tend to have so many children? It wasn't simply due to lack of birth control; many lines of evidence suggest people in pretransition societies desire large families. And in many cultures, the idea of actively working to suppress one's fecundity is nonsensical; you might as well try to change the color of the sky. Cultural norms reinforce pronatalist beliefs, with many societies valuing fertility; individuals are often not considered fully adult until they become parents.

Clearly, with high infant-mortality rates, one would need a large family simply to ensure that at least one or two children would reach adulthood. But this raises the question, why have children in the first place? That is, what good are they? The costs of fertility are obvious, and include the risk of death during childbirth, the high costs of raising children, etc. What are the benefits of fertility, beyond the simple enjoyment many people get from being parents? For one thing, children may be valued for their labor. In preindustrial societies, children can perform economic activities (such as gathering food, tending animals, or caring for children) that contribute to the household economy and simultaneously free up adults to perform other activities. One prominent explanation for high levels of preferred fertility is the wealth flows theory, associated with demographer John Caldwell (1976), which posits that children may be a form of retirement insurance in places where government social security does not exist. When you are too old to work, your children can take care of you. And indeed, in many cultures, particularly (though by no means exclusively) in Asia, people expressly articulate a desire for children (often a son) who can take care of them when they are elderly (Skinner 1997).

Evolutionary theory proposes a somewhat different perspective on why people have children. From an evolutionary point of view, children are ends in and of themselves—at least, if they survive to produce more children. You could say that children are a stepping stone to producing grandchildren (and great-grandchildren, etc.). Anthropologist Hillard Kaplan (1994, 1996) raised the question of whether it would make sense, in evolutionary terms, for older adults to "free-ride" off their children's labor (and drain their children's resources), as posited by the wealth flows theory. Consider two alternative strategies: one in which a parent keeps funneling resources into children and, eventually, grandchildren, and another in which the parent funnels resources into children until the parent reaches old age, when the flow of resources reverses and the children invest in the parent. Which strategy would be favored by natural selection? Assuming that children who put resources into their parents have fewer resources to invest in their own offspring, the one-way resource flow—from parent to offspring—seems the one that would be favored by evolution, because it will produce more offspring (and grandoffspring, etc.) over the long term.

Kaplan decided to examine whether wealth in traditional societies really does flow from children to parents when parents are older, as is commonly supposed. He did this using data from three indigenous South American societies, the Ache, the Piro, and the Machiguenga, who make their living from hunting, gathering, and (among the Piro and Machiguenga) simple horticulture. In these subsistence-level societies, wealth is measured in food and is not stored. Income can be measured as calories produced or acquired, while expenditures are measured as calories consumed. While thinking of wealth in terms of food may seem awkward or counterintuitive to some readers of this book, who are used to dealing in currency, real estate, and material goods, we must keep in mind that until the agricultural revolution all human beings lived as hunters and gatherers, unable to accumulate resources apart from the fat, muscle, and other tissues of their own bodies. Studying these recent subsistence-level communities should tell us something about the transfer of resources in the types of ecologies humans lived in when our demographic patterns and preferences evolved.

Kaplan found that, not surprisingly, young children were an economic drain on their parents. In terms of food production, children ate more than they produced and had to receive food from their parents (and others) in order to survive. It is not until ages eighteen to twenty that Ache, Piro, and Machiguenga adults begin to produce more food than they consume. After this age, they produce a net surplus, and continue to do so *through the rest of their lives.* No period of "retirement" exists in these communities, no age at which elderly adults stop producing food and live off of the labor of their adult children. Among the Machiguenga, for example, sixty-year-old adults produce 4,600 calories per day but consume only about 2,500 calories, leaving a net surplus of 2,100 calories—45.6% of their daily production—that could be shared with their children and grandchildren (Kaplan 1994).

Thus, the available empirical evidence suggests that in populations deriving a significant portion of their food from foraging, wealth flows in one direction: downward, from parent to offspring. People do not have children to support them in their old age, because there is no age at which parents require such support; parents work until they die. Children do not become self-sufficient until around ages eighteen to twenty—by which time they are often parents themselves. (The median age at first birth among the Ache, for example, is nineteen for women and twenty-four for men [K. Hill and Hurtado 1996].) By the time foragers produce enough food to feed themselves, they find they are not producing enough to feed themselves *and* their children—and thus they are still dependent on their own parents' assistance. Children are not economic assets in a parent's old age; rather, they remain an economic drain on parents throughout their lives. Because people in these societies do not have children to support them in their old age, the wealth flows hypothesis cannot explain the high levels of fertility observed in pre–demographic transition societies.

So what does account for high fertility in traditional societies? The same processes favored by natural selection in other sexually reproducing species also come into play in humans (for example, Turke 1989, 1991). Organisms face a fundamental trade-off between offspring quality and quantity—you can have many low-quality offspring or fewer high-quality offspring. Humans, along with other primates, choose to invest highly in offspring; we have chosen quality over quantity. In traditional societies, parental investment produces improved offspring—they are more likely to survive, are healthier, are better able to acquire food, etc. However, this relationship holds up only to a point, beyond which there is a diminishing return from parental investment. In other words, beyond a certain level of investment, the next unit of investment results in less improvement (in terms of offspring quality) than the previous unit did. Eventually the situation will reach the point where the parent will receive greater fitness returns from investing in a new offspring than from investing resources in an existing offspring (Kaplan 1994, 1996). Hence, the parent has another child—resulting in the observed levels of high fertility. Human populations could, in principle, maximize quantity and minimize quality, producing as many as fifteen children per woman. Hunter-gatherers and horticulturalists strike a balance between the two, favoring increased quality at the expense of quantity, and thus produce about six offspring—enough to increase the likelihood of a few surviving to adulthood but not so many that parents couldn't afford to raise them all.

Reduced Fertility in Modern Economies

So why do people in industrialized societies tend to have so few offspring? If children had been economic assets in preindustrial societies, we could explain the demographic transition in terms of the decreased value of children's labor, particularly in market economies where children have to attend school for many years to acquire economically valuable skills. But, as Kaplan (1994, 1996) has shown, children do not support their elderly parents in subsistence economies, so that explanation is not sufficient. Kaplan argues that the transition to market wage-labor economies may hold the key to the explanation of lowered fertility. He points out what economists have known for a long time: in wage-labor economies, there is an increasingly positive relationship between education and income. Someone with a tenth-grade education earns more, on average, than someone with a ninth-grade education, and someone with an eleventh-grade education earns more than someone with a tenth-grade education. But the difference in income between eleven and ten years of schooling is greater than the difference between ten and nine years of schooling (Lam 1999). The wage benefits of education increase dramatically at higher levels of schooling; although the difference in years of schooling between a high school graduate and a ninth grader is the same as that between somebody with three years of college and a high school graduate, the income difference is much greater for that latter pair than the former. For example, in South Africa a black male with an eleventh-grade education earns twice as much as a black male with an eighth-grade education, while a black male with a college education earns 4.9 times as much as an eighth grader (K. G. Anderson, Case, and Lam 2001). If you are a parent investing in a child's education, you get greater returns on your investment—more bang for your buck, so to speak—the more education the child completes.

Kaplan suggests that the different proximate cues that parents use to determine levels of investment in offspring—and we're not really quite sure what those are—lead to different levels of parental investment in traditional versus wage-labor societies. In traditional societies, parents recognize when they begin to receive diminishing returns from their investments, and they transfer their resources to new offspring. In market economies, however, the point of diminishing returns may never be reached. Education is incredibly expensive, and the cost of a college education in the United States was 6.6 times higher in 2007 than it was in 1970 (U.S. Census Bureau 2007). Higher education has become a financial black hole that sucks up increasing amounts of money; in the United States, for example, the average annual cost of college attendance (including tuition, room and board, books and supplies, etc.) was $11,300 in 2003 (U.S. Census Bureau 2007b). And yet increasing levels of schooling produce increasingly larger returns to offspring income, so that rather than cutting off investment and transferring it to a new child, the parent keeps pouring resources into the existing child. The increased cost of raising children means that the number of children must be reduced (Borgerhoff Mulder 1998)—hence, we observe greatly reduced fertility levels. The global increase in education, especially for girls, is surely one of the factors that has driven the drop in fertility observed for most countries.

What is particularly interesting is that the reduced fertility observed in modern environments does not appear to be optimal, from the perspective of producing grandchildren. Kaplan and others (1995), using a sample of men in Albuquerque, New Mexico, who reported their fathers' fertility as well as their own, found that men who had the most children (a dozen, in their sample) had the most grandchildren. Nonetheless, the most common level of fertility observed in the sample was only two children. If the goal is to maximize grandchildren, men should be having twelve children—but they aren't. Other studies have also shown that reduced fertility does not maximize long-term reproductive success in industrialized countries (for example, Low, Simon, and Anderson 2003; Vining 1986). There is an apparent disconnect between the cognitive mechanisms parents use to allocate resources (mechanisms that originated in our evolutionary past) and the actual levels of fertility that would maximize fitness in contemporary market economies.

The relationship between resources and fertility has thus been turned on its head. While in traditional societies men acquired resources to obtain greater sexual access to females and more fertility, in modern cultures, ironically, high socioeconomic status is associated with the lowest fertility (and the oldest age at first birth). There is still some indication that, at the proximate level, income and status still result in greater reproductive opportunities for men—or at least what would have been greater reproductive opportunities, in the absence of birth control. Daniel Pérusse (1993), using a sample of men in Quebec, Canada, found that men with higher social status had both more sexual partners and greater frequency of sex than men with lower social status. Although their actual fertility was not greater, men with higher status had more potential conceptions. This research suggests that some elements of the traditional proximate pathways still hold true, even if other proximate mechanisms are in place to prevent conception.

In summary, while every man has the biological capacity to produce countless numbers of offspring over his life span, no man has achieved such boundless fertility. Social and cultural factors typically restrict most men to one or a few spouses or long-term sexual partners throughout their lives, though some men may have access to more women and thus achieve higher levels of fertility. Even without modern birth control, fertility in traditional populations was far lower than what was theoretically possible. The advent of wage-labor economies and the corresponding increase in the cost of raising and educating children have driven our fertility preferences to all-time low levels. From our current vantage it is difficult to forecast whether desired family size will continue to decrease or perhaps level out. Changes in fertility patterns will have important implications for overpopulation and the extent to which our species might overextend our resources.

5

Who's the Dad?

It's an oft-told tale: a woman is pregnant—but the man who thinks he is the father isn't. No one knows when fences were invented, but we imagine that no sooner was the first one erected than two neighbors were leaning over it and discussing this issue, which continues to be a central focus of gossip, soap operas, and daytime talk shows, as well as great literature. In 2007, for example, media frenzy was sparked when, following the death of former model (and potentially rich heiress) Anna Nicole Smith, no fewer than seven names were put forward as possible fathers of her newborn baby girl. Salacious interest only increased when paternity tests revealed that the man on the child's birth certificate was not the father. Even when large inheritances are not at stake, the question of who is (and who is not) the father of a given child evokes a profound response from people in every society.

Why Paternity Confidence Matters

Why should a man care whether he is the father of a particular child? If you've read this far in the book, you know that human males exhibit extremely high levels of parental care, relative to most other mammalian species. Male parental care evolved because of the reproductive payoffs: among our ancestors, males who invested in children left behind more offspring than males who didn't. But the strategy of investing in offspring as a way of getting one's genes into future generations backfires if the putative genetic offspring the man is investing in actually aren't his children at all. (We'll address the question of investment in stepchildren, whom the man realizes up front aren't his, in Chapter 7.) In effect, a man who ends up unknowingly raising another man's offspring pays all of the cost while receiving none of the evolutionary benefits, while the actual genetic father freeloads, enjoying the benefits without paying the costs. The English word "cuckold," used to describe a man whose wife is unfaithful to him, derives from the cuckoo, a bird that has raised evolutionary freeloading to an art form. The cuckoo is known as a brood parasite because it lays its eggs in other birds' nests, leaving those other birds to care for and raise the hatchling cuckoos, at no cost to the cuckoo parents. It is perfect metaphor for what happens to some men when they unknowingly raise a child fathered by another man.

In a world of perfect information, a man would know for certain that he is the father of every child attributed to him and that he is not the father of every child he thinks is not his. Unfortunately the real world is far messier, allowing room for mistakes. While actual paternity (that is, the state of being the genetic father of a child) and paternity confidence (a man's own evaluation, not necessarily consciously articulated, of whether he is the genetic father of a child) may agree, they need not entirely overlap. Some men may be sure they are the father of children when they actually are not, while other men may be convinced they are not the father when they actually are. This potential ambiguity raises the stakes—not only must men be vigilant against cuckoldry, but they must ensure they do not make incorrect decisions about nonpaternity, for mistakes could prove costly from an evolutionary perspective.

Defining and Measuring Nonpaternity

If paternity is the situation of a man being the biological father of a given child, then nonpaternity is the opposite: the man definitely is not the child's biological father. For an individual, this is an all-or-nothing phenomenon: a man either is or is not the father of a particular child. At a population level, however, nonpaternity is usually expressed as a rate or percentage, reflecting the proportion of men in the population whose putative children are not theirs. We can thus state, for example, that nonpaternity in Switzerland has been reported at 0.83% (Sasse, Chakraborty, and Ott 1994), whereas a sample of French families has revealed a nonpaternity rate of 2.8% (Le Roux et al. 1992).

Nonpaternity is measured through paternity tests, though it would be more accurate to call them "nonpaternity tests." These tests do not prove that a man is the father of a given child; rather, they prove that he is *not* the father. If the test is highly accurate (more on that below) and the man has not been shown to not be the father, then we presume he actually is the father. Confused? Perhaps a simplified example would help. You are probably familiar with the ABO blood-typing system. Your blood type is determined by three alleles, and each person has two copies of these alleles. You may have two copies of the same one or two different ones. The O allele is recessive to both A and B, so if your genotype is AA or AO, your blood type is A. Similarly if your genotype (your genetic makeup) is BO or BB, your blood type is B. Your blood type will be O only if you have two copies of the O allele, while if you have one A and one B allele, your blood type is AB, because neither of these alleles is dominant over the other.

In the early twentieth century, it was recognized that the ABO blood-typing system could be used to demonstrate nonpaternity. Suppose you have a mother who has blood type O (genotype OO) and a man who is AB (genotype AB). The baby's blood type is O. Can the man in question be the father? No. The mother contributes an O allele and the father contributes either an A or a B, so if he were the father, the baby's genotype would have to be either AO or BO. Let's look at a second example: the mother is type O, the putative father is AB, and the baby's genotype is AO. Is the man the father? Well, he could be. But the test doesn't prove he is. There are millions of other men with compatible genotypes (AB or AA) who could also be the father. Proving nonpaternity is easy; proving paternity is hard.

The ABO system is not very efficient for demonstrating nonpaternity; because there are a limited number of blood types, some of which are very common, paternity tests based on ABO blood type can detect only about 18% of men who are actually not the fathers (Sussman 1954). (The other 82% of men who were not fathers could not be identified as such, because their blood type was similar or identical to that of the real father.) There are actually dozens of separate blood-type systems in addition the well-known ABO system; using many of these at once increases the chances you will correctly identify that a man cannot be the father (that is, multiple-system paternity tests will have a higher probability of exclusion). Tests using multiple blood groups were available by the 1950s but were not widely used, because the laboratory work was expensive (Marsters 1957). Later, in the 1970s, the HLA system (which uses antigens that are part of an individual's immune system and which provide each of us with a fairly unique HLA "signature") was used to detect nonpaternity; this method had a greatly improved probability of exclusion, eventually allowing researchers to correctly exclude 95% or so of non-fathers. By the mid-1980s, paternity tests began to use DNA to identify nonpaternity, increasing the ability to exclude men as fathers 99.99% of the time (for example, Helminen et al. 1988; Jeffreys, Turner, and Debenham 1991). In other words, for 10,000 paternity tests involving men who are not the fathers of children, 9,999 of them will be correctly excluded as the father; only 1 man in 100,000 who is not the father will fail to be excluded. With such high levels of specificity, DNA paternity tests have taken on the dimension of omnipotence: any man who cannot be excluded as the father is considered to be the father, because the odds of failing to exclude a true non-father are so slim.

Modern nonpaternity tests are therefore highly reliable and can detect nonpaternity with a high degree of accuracy. They are also increasingly popular. A 1973 survey of American laboratories offering paternity testing found that only a few thousand tests were performed per year, making up a small fraction of the laboratories' total casework (Polesky and Krause 1977). By the early 1980s, when paternity tests were still based on the HLA system, between 25,000 to 30,000 paternity tests were performed in the United States each year (Smouse and Chakraborty 1986). The introduction of DNA tests led to a rapid increase, with about 120,000 tests performed in the United States in 1990 (Pena and Chakraborty 1994), and 280,000 a decade later (Bishai et al. 2006). In 2007 an over-the-counter paternity test was introduced for sale at drugstores, which will undoubtedly accelerate the growth of this rapidly expanding industry even further.

Nonpaternity Rates

How common is nonpaternity? In other words, how many men are raising children they think are theirs but who actually aren't? This question is surprisingly difficult to answer. As noted above, actual paternity and a man's perception of paternity may overlap, but they need not do so. While many men's assessment of paternity accurately reflects actual paternity, some men have accepted children who are not theirs, while other men have denied paternity for children they actually fathered.

Many sources (including medical textbooks) cite nonpaternity rates in human societies as being 10% or greater, prompting Sally MacIntyre and Anne Sooman (1991) to note that "rates of nonpaternity have taken on the character of urban folk tales—pieces of conventional wisdom which are widely believed but have little basis in fact" (869). Upon inspection, there turns out to be little empirical basis for these claims. A well-cited review from 1995 found a worldwide median nonpaternity rate of 9% but used a sample of only ten studies (Baker and Bellis 1995). What exactly do we mean by asking what nonpaternity rates are? Are we speaking of nonpaternity rates in a general population? For a specific population? For the entire human species? Do we envision a random sample of households, in which father/child pairs are administered paternity tests? These methodological dimensions are rarely addressed but have important implications for the results we would expect to see. For example, we might expect higher levels of nonpaternity in a population that allows nonmarital sex than in a population that makes nonmarital sex a capital offense.

While random population samples of nonpaternity have not been collected, there is a common form of data collection which can potentially provide great insight into nonpaternity rates. Family genetic studies routinely collect genetic samples from mothers, fathers, and children, often for the purposes of identifying genes associated with specific diseases or other traits. Once they have obtained their data, the first thing researchers do is to identify (and discard) cases of nonpaternity, which would otherwise confound their analyses. In the methods section of their papers, geneticists typically state that they have discarded cases of nonpaternity—but they often do not provide any more detail than that. Some studies, however, are more specific, identifying either the number of cases of nonpaternity exposed or the rate of nonpaternity in their sample. One of us collected a sample of twenty-two studies published between 1950 and 2003 that stated nonpaternity rates (K. G. Anderson 2006). The median nonpaternity rate in these studies was 1.7%, meaning that 1.7% of these men could be excluded as the biological fathers of their putative children. Broadening the sample to include fourteen additional studies that were unpublished and in some cases based on hearsay or that were otherwise methodologically vague increased median nonpaternity to 3.3%—still far below the widely quoted 10% figure.

Does this figure represent the "true" nonpaternity rate? Probably not. The men who participate in family genetic studies and other studies that collect DNA are likely to be biased with respect to their level of paternity confidence—that is, their perceived paternity. These studies rely on volunteers, and men who are convinced they are not the father of a child (or who have significant doubts) are probably less likely to participate in those kinds of studies. In fact, they're probably less likely to still be in a relationship with the child's mother and to be socially recognized as the father. So Kermyt Anderson (2006) argued that those samples were biased toward men with high paternity confidence, who are likely to think that they are the father of their actual children. In contrast, he collected published data on thirty-one studies derived from commercial paternity testing laboratories. The men involved in those DNA tests are likely to have at least some doubts regarding the likelihood of their being the fathers of their putative offspring. Anderson therefore argued that this sample was biased toward men with low paternity confidence. The median nonpaternity rate for this sample was 29.8%—far higher than the 10% typically cited.

So the question remains, how common is nonpaternity? How many men are unwittingly raising children who aren't their own? We find that around 2–3% of men with high paternity confidence can be excluded as fathers, while about 30% of men with low paternity confidence could be excluded. The "true" rate must lie someplace between those two extremes. To answer this, we would need to know the percentage of men in a population who have high and low paternity confidence. If we know, for example, that 90% of men in a population had high paternity confidence and 10% had low, simple algebra can be used to calculate an average nonpaternity rate of 6.5%. In order for the true rate to be 10%, 23.5% of men—nearly a quarter of the population—would have to have low paternity confidence. How likely is that?

Surprisingly, very little is known about men's own assessment of paternity. It is apparently much more straightforward to collect DNA or blood samples from men and test their actual paternity than to ask them point-blank if they think their children are actually theirs. Only two published studies have done this, to the best of our knowledge, and one (Fox and Bruce 2001) unfortunately provides no information about the distribution of their measure of paternity confidence. The other study was a face-to-face survey of about 1,350 men living in Albuquerque, New Mexico, a survey in which men were asked to list all of the pregnancies and live births that had been attributed to them (K. G. Anderson, Kaplan, and Lancaster 2006). Later in the interview, each man was asked to indicate whether he was certain that he was the father of each pregnancy, certain that he was not, or uncertain that he was or was not. Lumping together the men who expressed any doubts that the offspring might be theirs (including each man who was uncertain he was the father and each who was certain he was not the father), we found that 1.46% of men in the sample had at least some doubts that they might not be the fathers. This sample probably underestimates low paternity confidence, because men would have been likely to omit naming pregnancies for which they could have been the father but felt certain they weren't. Still, using this figure for low paternity confidence in Albuquerque, and the earlier figures for actual nonpaternity among men with low and high paternity confidence, we can estimate that the actual nonpaternity rate in Albuquerque is about 3.7%. This estimate is still far lower than the 10% figure commonly referenced.

This is not to say that there are no populations in which nonpaternity could be 10% or higher. Cultures in which men are frequently absent or in which there are high rates of short-term sexual unions and/or simultaneous sexual partners are likely to have higher rates of nonpaternity. We would expect greater nonpaternity in urban than rural locations, in settings characterized by migratory labor patterns, and in situations in which large numbers of men are either incarcerated or in the military. We might thus expect nonpaternity to vary across racial/ethnic as well as socioeconomic groups. In a rare empirical example of variation in nonpaternity among different populations, Lee Schacht and Henry Gershowitz (1963) calculated nonpaternity rates among newborns at a single hospital in Detroit, Michigan. They calculated that actual nonpaternity rates (taking into account that their blood group–based tests would not detect many cases of true nonpaternity) were 1.49% for whites in their sample and 10.1% for blacks.

Little other research has examined the correlates of nonpaternity rates. In his survey of worldwide nonpaternity rates, Kermyt Anderson (2006) found no variation across global regions, although his sample was strongly skewed toward developed countries. David Bishai and others (2006), using a sample of nearly ten thousand American paternity tests, found that very few characteristics of the child, mother, or father predicted the outcome. Race/ethnicity, father's age, child's gender, and child's age were not associated with the results of the paternity test. The only statistically reliable predictor was mother's age, suggesting that older women are more accurate when identifying the fathers of their children than younger women.

Cuckoldry, Conception, and Traditional Ideas of Paternity

Until recently, cultures across the world lacked detailed knowledge of the biochemistry of conception, but most were aware than sex caused pregnancy, that menstruating women were not pregnant, and that a long interval after menstruation often indicated pregnancy (we will discuss beliefs about conception in more detail in Chapter 9). In many cultures, menstruating women are obliged to follow strict etiquette that limits their contact with men and non-menstruating women; this etiquette includes being barred from participation in religious rituals, abiding by restrictions on certain kinds of labor, and residing in separate menstrual huts (Strassmann 1992). The Old Testament, for example, states that menstruating women are unclean and must keep themselves apart from others (Leviticus 15:19–22). Among the Dogon of Mali, a subsistence agricultural society, women are obliged to visit menstrual huts and limit contact with their family during menses (Strassmann 1992, 1997). As a result, menstruation among the Dogon is not a private event but a publicly acknowledged activity, so that everyone in the village is aware of a woman's stage in her cycle. Beverly Strassmann (1992) has suggested that menstrual taboos among the Dogon function to increase paternity confidence: because only non-pregnant women visit the huts and cease visitations once they become pregnant, the timing of pregnancy is known to the entire community, and thus the father can be assigned with a high degree of confidence.

Nonpaternity is a result of female sexual behaviors, specifically, a woman's having multiple sexual partners during the same period of time or in a very closely spaced sequence. This situation is sometimes characterized as "infidelity" or, in the nonhuman (especially avian) literature, extrapair copulation (or EPC). However, while the terms "infidelity" and "EPC" imply straying outside a commitment between just two sexual partners, pregnancy and thus nonpaternity can occur in broader contexts: for example, after a one-night stand or intercourse with a commercial sex worker, neither of which imply any medium- or long-term commitment from either partner to each other. As we discussed in Chapter 3, the vast majority of human pregnancies occur in the context of medium- to long-term relationships, which typically imply sexual fidelity (at least from the female partner). Men in most cultures place great emphasis on female sexual fidelity and chastity; David Buss (1989), in a sample of mating preferences in thirty-seven countries, found that men in twenty-three (62%) of the countries in his sample prefer partners with no previous sexual experience. Women with more promiscuous sexual histories are unlikely to obtain a commitment for paternal care from a male. It is highly unlikely, for example, that a commercial sex worker who found herself pregnant would attempt to obtain child support from one of her customers, knowing that he would be extremely dubious about being the father. (Although with modern DNA testing it is possible to identify fathers with virtual certainty, which raises the possibility of a prostitute's obtaining child support from a man who paid for her sexual services, we know of no case of this having been done yet; however, it is likely to have occurred someplace, particularly in areas where prostitution is legal.)

Accurate data on sexual infidelity—or, to put it less judgmentally, simultaneous multiple sexual partners—are notoriously difficult to get. In nonhuman animals you can use observational data to assess the frequency of extrapair copulations (although even this is not accurate, as DNA analysis in the 1980s revealed far higher rates of nonpaternity in many bird species than would have been suspected based on observed EPCs [for example, Petrie and Kempenaers 1998]). Researchers interested in humans have to rely on self-reports, which are likely to underreport sexual partners outside of established unions. In nationally representative samples of married American women, rates of self-reported extramarital sex range from 11.6% to 15.0% (Laumann et al. 1994; Wiederman 1997). We would expect even higher rates of multiple partners among nonmarried women.

Female sexual infidelity is required for nonpaternity to occur, but not every episode of female sexual infidelity will result in nonpaternity. The fact that reported rates of marital infidelity are much higher than reported rates of nonpaternity support this. In order for a woman to conceive a child by a man other than her primary partner, she needs to have sex with him around the time of ovulation. In order to present a convincing case that her main partner is the father, she needs to maintain a sexual relationship with him as well. Many episodes of marital infidelity probably occur during periods when spouses are separated or not physically intimate (perhaps already well on their way to divorce), so if a pregnancy were to occur, the husband would have little doubt that he is not the father. Both ova and sperm are fairly short lived, with 50% of sperm lasting one day or less and 50% of ova surviving only twelve hours (Royston 1982). Thus, an insemination that occurs long before or after ovulation is very unlikely to result in conception (Wilcox, Weinberg, and Baird 1995). Traditional human populations lacked precise knowledge about the timing of ovulation, but they tended to recognize that the pool of candidates for the father of a woman's child was restricted to men who had had sex with her after her last menstrual period prior to her pregnancy (see Chapter 9 for more details).

Thus, for one man to father a child and another man to think he is the father, a woman must have sex with two men within a matter of days or a week or so at the most. Data on the frequency of overlapping sexual partners probably reflect a bias toward underreporting, but rates of concurrent sexual partnerships in nationally representative samples have been reported at 12% in the United States, with higher rates for never-married women (19%) and lowest rates for currently married women (4%) (Adimora et al. 2002). One nationally representative British study found that 9% of women ages sixteen to forty-four had had concurrent sexual partnerships in the previous year (A. M. Johnson et al. 2001).

Indirect evidence on the prevalence of closely spaced double matings comes from the study of heteroparity, or dizygotic (that is, fraternal) twins with different fathers. Heteroparity occurs when a woman experiences superfecundity, which is the release of multiple eggs at ovulation, and these eggs are fertilized by different men; that is, she has sex with more than one man while her ova are fertile (Ambach et al. 2000). Heteroparity involves nonpaternity for at least one man: the putative father of both twins, who is actually the father of only one. (It is possible that he is the father of neither and that two other men impregnated the woman in question, though this must be extremely rare.) Robert Wenk and others (1992) estimated that heteroparity occurs in about 2.4% of dizygotic twins. Note that this rate falls within the range of nonpaternity (1.7–3.3%) reported above for men with high paternity confidence. W. H. James (1993) speculates that "erotic circumstances might sometimes cause multiple ovulations" (258) and suggests that rates of superfecundity may be higher when women have multiple sexual partners.

The evidence thus suggests, at least tentatively, that sexual infidelity and nonpaternity, while related, are also distinct. Nonpaternity cannot occur without an extrapair copulation, but not every EPC results in nonpaternity.

When females mate polyandrously—that is, with multiple male

partners—sperm competition may result, in which sperm from multiple males compete to fertilize an ovum (Parker 1970). Like lottery tickets, more sperm increase one's probability of winning. Because sperm production is to a certain extent a function of testis size (for example, Simmons et al. 2004), species that mate polyandrously tend to have larger testes, controlling for body size (R. L. Smith 1984). Gorillas, for example, have a harem mating system, in which a dominant male excludes other males and retains sole sexual access to a group of females. Gorillas have very small testes for their body size, because their sperm rarely have to compete with other sperm for access to ova. Chimpanzees, in contrast, have a polygynandrous mating system, in which every male in the group mates with every female (multiple times, over the course of days). Sperm competition is very important among chimps, and they have very large testes for their body size. Where do humans fit into this continuum? How important is sperm competition among humans? Humans have slightly larger testes than would be expected for a primate our size, suggesting we were mildly polyandrous in our recent evolutionary past (R. L. Smith 1984). Testis size is unlikely to change rapidly and would not keep pace with the significant changes in human mating systems that have occurred worldwide since the adoption of agriculture about ten thousand years ago.

Thus, nonpaternity results from sexual infidelity, often in circumstances that lead to sperm competition. What cues do men use to evaluate paternity, that is, to determine their level of paternity confidence? We turn to that topic in the next section.

Cues Used to Evaluate Paternity

Women do not face the prospect of being unsure if a child belongs to them. The mechanics of internal fertilization ensure that mothers will always be certain of maternity; there has surely never been a woman in labor who wondered as the baby passed through her birth canal, "Is this really my child?" Men, in contrast, can never be fully positive of paternity; unless the man and woman lived alone on a desert island, there is always a possibility, however remote, that some other man was responsible for the pregnancy. How do men evaluate whether they are the father of a particular child? Surprisingly—or perhaps not, given how sensitive these questions are—little research has directly examined what cues men use to assess paternity. Two likely possibilities are the behavior of the woman herself around the time of conception and the resemblance between the man and the child (J. N. Davis and Daly 1997).

Men in most cultures do not know exactly when women are ovulating, and the exact timing of conception is not well understood in many traditional cultures (see Chapter 9 for details). In contrast to many mammals (including many nonhuman primates), whose females are sexually active only during a narrow window of time that coincides with conception, a human female can and does have sex throughout her cycle, making it difficult for a man to monitor her activity (and to keep all other males at a distance) when she is most likely to conceive. Nonetheless, when a woman becomes pregnant and a man is informed he is the father, he probably uses cues of her behavior around the time she would have conceived as a guide to whether he is likely to be the father. If he was away for months before and after the start of the pregnancy, he is likely to conclude he cannot be the father. If he was present but knows she had other sexual partners, he may alter his assessment of paternity accordingly. If he is absolutely certain that he was her only sexual partner, he should accept that he is the father. Of course, some men are more suspicious than others, while others are very trusting. Some men will suspect infidelity if their mates were apart for only the briefest period, while others have complete confidence in their partners even if the couple was separated for long durations. It is likely that many men make up their minds about the likelihood of being the father of a particular child in part on their perceptions of the sexual fidelity of their mates and on the degree of trust and commitment within the relationship.

Rather than waiting for the baby to be born, presumably most men make up their mind about paternity when a woman says she's pregnant. One of us was involved in a study that looked for variables associated with low paternity confidence by men (K. G. Anderson, Kaplan, and Lancaster 2006). Using the sample of Albuquerque men described above, we found that a man was more likely to have low paternity confidence—that is, to think that the child was not his—if the pregnancy was unplanned or if the couple was unmarried. Men are more suspicious of pregnancies resulting from relationships in which the couple has less commitment to each other or was not planning on having children immediately. These factors are consistent with the proposal that men use cues of partner sexual fidelity to assess paternity confidence.

While men probably make up their minds about paternity before their children are born, after birth they have an opportunity to reevaluate this relationship based on resemblance. Mirrors did not exist in most traditional societies, but people could see their reflections in pools of water and could also view family traits present in their relatives. Phenotypic matching has been proposed as a mechanism of kin recognition in nonhuman primates, and captive chimpanzees can match unfamiliar mother/son pairs based on physical resemblance (Parr and De Waal 1999). The polyandrous Nyinba of Nepal use physical resemblance to determine which of a woman's co-husbands is the actual father, while in Sierra Leone, Mende men used resemblance to deduce adultery (Levine 1977, cited in Durham 1991; Strassmann 1992).

Moreover, other people could observe and comment on resemblances (or lack thereof) between men and their putative children. Several studies conducted in hospitals in the United States, Canada, and Mexico have found that the mother's relatives are more likely than the father's relatives to say that the new baby looks like the father—presumably hoping to reinforce his paternity confidence and downplay any doubts he may have (Daly and Wilson 1982; Regalski and Gaulin 1993; McLain et al. 2000). Some evidence suggests that men pay more attention to resemblance than women do and are better at detecting it (Volk and Quinsey 2002). One study even found that a priori beliefs about paternity influenced men's perceptions of resemblance (Bressan and Dal Martello 2002), which reverses the usual notion that men assume paternity based on resemblance. Whether children actually resemble fathers more than mothers is open to debate. A well-publicized 1995 study found that one-year-old babies resembled fathers more than mothers (Christenfeld and Hill 1995), but several subsequent attempts to replicate this study have failed (Brédart and French 1999; Bressan and Grassi 2004; McLain et al. 2000; Oda, Matsumoto-Oda, and Kurashima 2002). Furthermore, it is not even clear whether babies should preferentially resemble fathers or not. Yes, it can reinforce paternity confidence—but if another man is the father, then strong paternal resemblance actually signals nonpaternity, which may be detrimental to the child (Brédart and French 1999; McLain et al. 2000; Pagel 1997). Because male investment is important to offspring, children and their mothers share a common interest in sustaining investment from a male, regardless of whether he is the biological father. While perceived resemblance is likely to play a role in influencing men's assessment of paternity, no study has yet examined this question directly.

Does Nonpaternity Influence Paternal Care?

In 350 BCE, Aristotle wrote in his *Nicomachean Ethics,* "These are the reasons, too, why mothers are fonder of their children than fathers; bringing them into the world costs them more pains, and they know better that the children are their own" (Aristotle 1908, 9.7). A corollary of this might be "fathers are fonder of some children than others, because they are more certain they are their own." It is widely recognized that men are less likely to take care of children whom they do not acknowledge as their own (for example, Alexander 1974; Trivers 1972). Among birds, many studies have examined whether males decrease paternal care in response to reduced probability of paternity. While the predicted effect is often found, it is often lacking as well, leading to a fair amount of head scratching among ornithologists, as well as criticisms that many studies have not manipulated paternity confidence in an ecologically appropriate manner for the species being studied (Schwagmeyer and Mock 1993; Sheldon 2002). Testing this fairly simply hypothesis in birds has proved more difficult than expected.

Among humans, a woman's husband is generally acknowledged as the father of her children. So firm was this idea that many countries severely limited the ability of a man to challenge paternity and establish his putative children as bastards. British law in the matter was based on the Seven Seas Rule, which "held that if a married woman became pregnant while her husband was anywhere within the British empire, her progeny was considered legally his. Thus if a woman became pregnant while her husband was away on a two-year sea voyage, *no one could contest the legitimacy of her child* even if the couple had not seen one another, much less had conjugal relations, during those two years" (Rudavsky 1999, 127; emphasis added).

However, as noted above, extramarital infidelity is a common justification for divorce, and in recent decades legal tradition has held that men are not responsible for putative children that are not in fact theirs (Wilson 1987). This responsibility includes payment of child support, and indeed men who do not pay child support often justify this on the grounds that the children are not actually theirs. Sumati Dubey (1995), interviewing a sample of American men who refused to pay child support, found that 13% of men claimed they did not pay because they did not believe the children involved were theirs. In their study of Albuquerque men, Kermyt Anderson, Hillard Kaplan, and Jane Lancaster (2007) found that a man was almost five times more likely to divorce his wife (or leave his girlfriend if they were not married) when he had low paternity confidence in a child than if he was convinced the child was his. Simply by divorcing women, men reduce their investment in children, because men often do not live with children after divorce and do spend less time with and money on them afterward. Is there any evidence that, apart from divorce, men take steps to reduce investment in children whom they suspect are not theirs?

Yes, there is. Cross-culturally, men in some societies have greater paternity confidence than men in other societies, because the rules of the culture allow men greater control over female sexuality. Cultures with higher paternity confidence tend to exhibit greater levels of paternal investment in children. When paternity confidence is low, a man's heirs are more likely to be his sister's children than his own, because a man has a certainty of being related to his sister's children but only a possibility of being related to his own putative offspring (Flinn 1981; Gaulin and Schlegel 1980; Hartung 1985). For example, John Hartung (1985), using data on seventy societies, finds that those with avuncular inheritance—in which men's heirs are their sister's children rather than their own—are much more likely to have a probability of paternity that is moderate or less (seventeen cultures) than high (three cultures). Conversely, societies in which men's heirs are their sons are much more likely to have high paternity probability (forty-five cultures) than moderate or less (five cultures). Cross-cultural studies also show that men are more likely to provide birth-related investment— activities that help the mother during pregnancy and childbirth and improve the odds of child survival—when paternity confidence is high (Huber et al. 2004).

Studies that have compared behaviors within a single society have also found support for the idea that reduced paternity confidence leads to reduced investment in offspring. Coren Apicella and Frank Marlowe (2004), in a study of men in London, England, report that men's investment in children is positively correlated with perceived resemblance to children, a possible proxy for paternity confidence. A telephone sample of men living in Knoxville, Tennessee, found that men were more involved with children if they had greater "paternity certitude" (Fox and Bruce 2001), although details about this measure were not provided. And the aforementioned study of Albuquerque men found that men spent less time with children and were less involved in children's educational progress if the men had doubts they were the children's fathers, even controlling for the effects of divorce on paternal involvement (K. G. Anderson, Kaplan, and Lancaster 2007). Lastly, pregnancies for which Albuquerque men doubted they were responsible were more likely to be aborted than pregnancies for which men accepted paternity (K. G. Anderson, Kaplan, and Lancaster 2006). Thus, not only do perceptions of paternity influence a man's interactions with a child throughout the child's life, these perceptions influence whether the child is even born.

The Costs and Benefits of Paternity Ambiguity

When studying behavior from an evolutionary perspective, both the costs and benefits of a trait must be evaluated to determine whether the trait would be favored by natural selection. This chapter has focused mostly on the costs of nonpaternity, specifically costs as defined from the male perspective. Yet it is worthwhile to question whether there are potential benefits as well. Surely someone must benefit from paternal ambiguity, or else it would not be such a widespread concern.

Many societies have a vastly different understanding of conception and paternity than those of industrialized societies. Many native South American cultures believe in partible paternity: a child can have more than one biological father (Beckerman et al. 1998). Ache hunter-gatherers of Paraguay, for example, recognize two types of fathers. There is the "real" father of the child, that is, the one who was engaged in sexual intercourse with the mother prior to her first missed menstrual period (K. Hill and Hurtado 1996). The Ache call this man "the one who put (the child) in" (K. Hill and Hurtado 1996, 274). They also recognize secondary fathers, men who had sex with the mother but were not likely to be the "real" father. This situation of ambiguous paternity, with multiple men potentially being the father of the children, was quite widespread among precontact Ache, with 63% of children having one or more secondary fathers.

Conventional wisdom might suggest that children with more than one potential father would receive less male investment and, in traditional high-mortality environments, be more likely to die in childhood. Yet it turns out that children benefit from having more than one father, at least in traditional neotropical societies. Stephen Beckerman and others (1998) report that among the Barí of Colombia and Venezuela, only 68% of children survive to age fifteen. They found that children with secondary fathers were 2.28 times more likely to reach age fifteen than children without secondary fathers. Similarly, Ache children who have one primary and one secondary father have greater survivorship than children with only a primary father (K. Hill and Hurtado 1996). But there are apparently dilution effects from having too many fathers; among the Ache, children with two or more secondary fathers had higher mortality rates than children with only one secondary father. The mechanisms by which multiple fathers may increase child survivorship are poorly understood, though they probably include greater provisioning for the mother, as well as greater social protection of the child. Among the Ache, for example, orphan children were more likely to be buried alive when an important man died than were children with surviving parents. Having a potential father who could speak out on your behalf might mean the difference between life and death. Reduced paternity confidence might pay off in evolutionary terms if the benefits (in terms of increased offspring survivorship) outweigh the costs (the possibility of investing resources in a child that is not one's offspring).

Reduced paternity confidence might also be beneficial if it is associated with greater overall fertility. Male mating strategies are complex and variable, but they are often characterized as a simple dichotomy: "quantity," in which men invest resources in maximizing the number of sexual partners, with minimal investment in children, versus "quality," in which men maximize investment in offspring rather than in the acquisition of mates (for example, Belsky, Steinberg, and Draper 1991; Draper and Harpending 1982, 1988). Men who adopt a "quantity" mating strategy are more likely to obtain sexual partners who themselves are less choosy and more promiscuous, thus undermining the men's paternity confidence. As noted above, K.G. Anderson, Kaplan, and Lancaster (2007) report that men living in Albuquerque, New Mexico, were more likely to have low paternity confidence in a pregnancy if the pregnancy was unplanned or if the couple was not married, conditions that are more likely to occur in short-term mating relationships. Jeanne Regalski and Steve Gaulin (1993) report that allegations of paternal resemblance to newborns by maternal kin are more likely for firstborn children and for newer relationships, suggesting that those circumstances might be associated with lowered paternity confidence (and thus greater reinforcement of paternity confidence from maternal kin).

On similar grounds, we might expect paternity confidence to vary with birth order. The first child a couple has together might have reduced paternity confidence if the relationship is fairly new. Alternatively, nonpaternity might increase for later-born children. Men may be reluctant to dissolve a union following the birth of a later child who is associated with low paternity confidence if doing so would punish not only the last-born child but also earlier children who are associated with high confidence (see MacDougall-Shackleton and Robertson 1998 for a similar argument for avian clutches). Yet there are very few data on the relationship between paternity and birth order. Schacht and Gershowitz (1963) report higher nonpaternity among first-borns and last-borns in Michigan, while Ricardo Cerda-Flores and others (1999) find no relationship between birth order and nonpaternity in Mexico.

If male mating strategy covaries with nonpaternity, this might explain a pattern we discern in the paternity confidence data presented above. Why are men with low paternity confidence so likely to underestimate their actual probability of paternity, while men with high paternity confidence are generally correct in their assessment of paternity? Perhaps men with high and low paternity confidence use different cues to assess paternity. Possibly men who adopt a "quantity" mating strategy have a priori assumptions about paternity confidence; such a man may be overly suspicious of his mate's fidelity, perhaps despite overwhelming evidence to the contrary, and he may use low paternity confidence as an excuse to reduce investment in her and the child. The fitness costs these men face (through poorer outcomes for each child, due to the decreased investment each child receives) may be offset through increased fertility from multiple mates. No one has yet researched the relationship between male mating strategies and beliefs about paternity, though this is clearly an interesting area that deserves attention.

What about the female perspective? This chapter has focused primarily on the costs, along with a few possible benefits, associated with reduced paternity confidence for males. What costs and benefits do females receive from engaging in behavior that reduces paternity confidence? Apparently females experience benefits from this behavior, because if every female were completely sexually faithful, there would be no reason to write this chapter. Females engage in multiple matings for a variety of reasons (Gangestad 2006; Hrdy 2000). Females may receive tangible benefits, such as increased offspring survivorship among South American Amerindian groups (reviewed above) or direct investment like food, money, and gifts from multiple suitors. A female may also mate with multiple males to obtain "good genes" for her offspring, if an extrapair male has better genetic quality than the one she is partnered with, as well as to increase genetic variability among her offspring, which may increase the odds of at least some of her children surviving.

Yet there are also costs to women who engage (or appear to engage) in promiscuous sexual behavior. Males are vigilant about such behavior and are likely to punish it with reduced investment in offspring, abandonment of both the woman and her children, and violence, perhaps even death. It is for this reason—the potential costs associated with nonpaternity—that the issue of nonpaternity is fraught with often unrecognized ethical perils. Because nonpaternity is fundamentally about sexual infidelity, knowledge of nonpaternity reveals a conflict of interest between men and women (and the children involved). Many circumstances may reveal nonpaternity without a paternity test being involved. (For example, if an individual is seeking a transfusion or an organ donation, a chart with the family members' blood types may reveal a case of nonpaternity through incompatible blood types.) If researchers or medical professionals discover a case of nonpaternity, are they obligated to reveal it to the man involved? Some medical ethicists, recognizing that revealing nonpaternity to putative fathers may have strong negative effects on their relationships with wives and children, often argue against disclosing nonpaternity, framing it as an issue of women's confidentiality (Lisker et al. 1998; Wertz, Fletcher, and Mulvihill 1990). Others, however, have argued that withholding information on nonpaternity from men is unethical, on the grounds that men always have the right to know if they have been cuckolded (Wright et al. 2002). Surveys of medical practitioners in many nations reveal that the current consensus is not to tell the father (Lucassen and Parker 2001; Wertz, Fletcher, and Mulvihill 1990). Some medical ethicists have concerns that even asking questions about nonpaternity may raise doubts in a man's mind or prompt him to take a paternity test, which may uncover an undiscovered case of cuckoldry and thus break up a heretofore happy marriage and home. Even men themselves express ambiguity toward paternity tests. In a sample of American college students, men were much more likely than women to support the suggestion that paternity tests should be mandatory (Hayward and Rohwer 2004). And yet, half of men did not agree with this suggestion. When pressed for an explanation, many expressed the sentiment that "ignorance is bliss" (Hayward and Rohwer 2004, 246).

These ethical quandaries are beyond the scope of this book, but they are worth raising. Paternity confidence clearly matters to men, and knowledge of female infidelity can be extremely damaging to men's relationships with their partners and their children. And yet, as we have surveyed the literature on nonpaternity in this chapter, we see that all is not doom and gloom. While cuckoldry does happen and some men unknowingly raise children that are not theirs, this phenomenon is not as widespread as many people believe. When a woman identifies a man as the father of her children, she is generally right. Men will continue to fret about female infidelity and nonpaternity—and in some cases they are right to do so. Yet, alternatively, they might take some reassurance from the finding that, in general, if a man thinks he is the father of his children, he probably is.

6

Father Involvement, Father Absence, and Children's Outcomes

Male investment in children is a key component of many models of human evolution. As we discussed in Chapter 1, the basic argument is that male investment is favored by natural selection because the man's investment increases the survival and well-being of his children, thus increasing his reproductive fitness. The benefit children receive from male investment is the focus of nonevolutionary models of male care as well; sociologists, economists, psychologists, social workers, and others generally assume that the reason men assist in raising children is because of the positive impacts this has on children. This assumption is so fundamental and intuitive that it may perhaps seem inappropriate to examine it critically. And yet questions must be asked: What effects do men have on children? Do the benefits of male parental care vary cross-culturally? Are the patterns we observe in the United States valid across societies, and did they hold true in the nonindustrialized societies that characterized all human populations until about two hundred years ago?

Perhaps the most straightforward means of assessing whether men benefit children is to examine what happens to children when men are absent. In the United States, rising divorce and nonmarital birth rates have resulted in a significant fraction of children growing up in single-parent households. In 1970, 85% of American children under eighteen lived with two parents. By 2006, only 67% of children under age eighteen lived with two parents, versus 23% living with a single mother and 5% living with a single father (U.S. Census Bureau 2007b). That two-parent figure actually undercounts biological father absence, because it includes families composed of a biological mother and a stepfather. Also, cross-sectional measures don't give a true sense of how many children will experience father absence, because some children are currently living with two biological parents who will divorce or separate before the children are eighteen, while children currently living with a stepfather lived at one point in a single-mother household. A study by Patrick Heuveline, Jeffrey Timberlake, and Frank Furstenberg Jr. (2003) examined American family arrangements from birth through age fifteen and estimated that 51% of children will spend part of their lives with a single parent. The study also found that over their first 15 years of life, American children can expect to spend 2.7 years living with a single mother, versus 9.9 years living with both biological parents, and 2.4 years in other living arrangements. Furthermore, the amount of time spent with a single mother varies tremendously according to the mother's marital status at the time of birth. Children whose parents were married at the child's birth will spend 1.3 years, on average, living with single mothers; children whose parents were unmarried but living together will spend 4.0 years with a single mother; children whose parents were unmarried and not living together will spend 8.6 years with a single mother.

It is important to note that single parenthood and father absence are not unique to the United States, although rates of single-mother families were greater in the United States than in any of sixteen European countries examined in the study by Heuveline and his colleagues. For example, children in Germany and Austria will spend about 39% of their lives living with a single parent, as opposed to 26% in Finland, 15% in Spain, and 11% in Italy.

Several important differences between industrialized and traditional societies may influence men's impact on children. First, while father absence in industrialized societies is primarily due to nonmarital births and divorce, among less-developed societies paternal death may be a common reason for father absence. Second, childhood mortality is a rare outcome in the United States and other industrialized societies but is much more common in less-developed countries. As a result, studies in industrialized societies rarely examine child mortality as an outcome of parental investment. Third, polygyny is illegal in Western societies but is widespread in developing countries. Polygyny results in reduced male involvement with offspring even if the parents are not divorced, because men must split their time between multiple wives. Lastly, as we reviewed in Chapter 2, cultural attitudes toward men's involvement with children vary greatly, and in some societies men's direct contact with young children is limited or discouraged. All of these factors suggest that we may see different patterns of male invest-ment in nonindustrialized societies than in industrialized societies, and thus variation across societies in the effects of male investment on chil-dren's outcomes.

Men's Impact on Child Survival

Perhaps the most fundamental way a parent can impact children is in terms of survival itself. We begin with the question, do men influence whether their children live or die, and if so, how much difference do they make? Because infant mortality rates are fairly low in industrial-ized societies, the effect of paternal involvement on offspring has not received extensive attention. One American study linked birth certifi-cates to mortality data sets for the state of Georgia and assumed that children with no father listed on the birth certificate were less likely to be involved with their biological fathers (Gaudino, Jenkins, and Rochat 1999). The study found that children born to unmarried mothers with no father listed on the birth certificate were 2.5 times as likely to die within a year of birth as children born to married women listing a fa-ther. That rate is also higher than that of unmarried women who list fathers on the birth certificate, whose children are 1.4 times as likely to die as married women listing fathers. Those figures do not control for differences in background characteristics, which is important because unmarried mothers are more likely to live in poverty and to not receive prenatal care, raising the possibility that it is socioeconomic status and not lack of a named father that is driving this result. Gaudino and col-leagues performed a statistical analysis that controlled for maternal fac-tors (such as age, marital status, education, smoking during pregnancy) and pregnancy factors (such as duration of pregnancy, birth weight, and medical complications) and found that children with no father listed on the birth certificate were still 2.0 times as likely to die as chil-dren whose fathers were listed on their birth certificates. Thus, even in industrial societies where infant mortality rates are low, father absence may be associated with increased child mortality.

What about less-developed societies, where rates of infant and child-hood mortality are much higher? Do fathers help increase childhood survival in the premodern conditions that characterized most of hu-man history? Frank Marlowe (2001) found no relationship between the percentage of the diet contributed by men and subadult mortality among hunter-gatherers, suggesting men's provisioning does not improve child survival. Other studies have examined whether father's presence or absence influences children's mortality. Among Ache hunter-gatherers of Paraguay, the major cause of death during the precontact forest period (before the Ache were settled on reservations in the 1970s) was violence, that is, death by the hands of other Ache or by non-Ache Paraguayans, with illness a distant second cause of death (K. Hill and Hurtado 1996). For example, 56% of children ages zero to three who died did so from violence, while for children ages four to fourteen the rate is 74%. Among adults who died, 46% of ages fifteen to fifty-nine and 33% of ages sixty and older died from violence. A large fraction of children's deaths was due to homicide from other Ache, specifically from the cultural practice of burying a child alive at the funeral of an important adult male. Most of the children who died this way were under age five, often injured or ill. Many were orphans, and the Ache "admitted a strong negative feeling towards children with no father who would 'be constantly begging for food'" (K. Hill and Hurtado 1996, 68). In a statistical analysis of mortality among Ache children ages zero through nine, Kim Hill and Magdalena Hurtado (1996) found that children whose fathers were alive were 1.1 times less likely to die than children whose fathers had died. Additionally, children whose parents had divorced were 1.09 times more likely to die than children whose parents were married. Father absence thus leads to greater mortality among Ache children. Hill and Hurtado attribute the protective effect of fathers to their role in maintaining male coalitions that resulted in decreased violence against their children. Among the Ache, at least, fathers appear to protect children from mortality risks.

The relationship between father absence and increased child mortality among the Ache may not be generalizable across preindustrial settings. Rebecca Sear and Ruth Mace (2008) recently reviewed forty-five studies in traditional or historical populations (including the Ache) that examined the relationship between the presence or absence of specific kin and children's survival. They found, not surprisingly, that mothers are very important; in all twenty-eight studies that had relevant data, children whose mothers had died were more likely to die themselves than were children whose mothers were alive. Sear and Mace also reviewed twenty-two studies that examined whether a father's death influenced child mortality. In 68% of these studies fathers had no apparent influence on children's survival. The other 32% found that when fathers died, children were more likely to die—though the effect was not as strong as for mothers, and the effect was shorter (in one study, child mortality increased for only one month following the death of a father). One Ethiopian study even had contradictory effects, with paternal death associated with increased mortality for sons but decreased mortality for girls.

Sear and Mace (2008) also looked at the effect of other relatives on child mortality. They found that grandmothers are generally, though not universally, helpful. The presence of maternal grandmothers was associated with improved child survival in 69% of studies, and paternal grandmothers in 53% of studies. Grandfathers, from either side of the family, had virtually no effect on child survival. Older siblings—so-called helpers at the nest—were associated with increased survival in 83% of studies, though the sample was small (only six studies).

Sear and Mace's work suggests that while fathers do have a positive effect on children's survival in some societies, the effect is not universal. Grandmothers appear to be as important as fathers, if not more so, in increasing child survival. Why are fathers not more important? Sear and Mace note that the studies they reviewed focus on child mortality, an extreme outcome that often occurs within the first few years of life. As we have noted in earlier chapters, men are often not directly involved in child care for infants and young children. Their absence may have less effect on children because their care is more easily substitutable; others can take their place should they die. The extent to which other kin can replace fathers is likely to vary by ecology, and it is possible that fathers are more important among hunter-gatherers than among agriculturalists, because the latter, with stable locations and higher fertility, are more likely to have kin present who can substitute for fathers (Draper and Harpending 1988).

Men's Impact on Children's Development and Later Outcomes

Growth, development, maturation, health status, psychological well-being—these are some of the life-course outcomes that are likely to be influenced by parental investment. They may not be as dramatic or unambiguous as mortality, yet they all influence subsequent behaviors and outcomes as children age. For example, a child who experiences extreme nutritional stress at a young age may experience stunting (very short height for age) and will never fully recover at later ages even if his or her diet improves. What influence do men have on these processes?

The impact of fathers on growth and development may begin even before the child is born. In the study of Georgia birth certificates mentioned above, babies with no father listed on the birth certificate were more likely to be underweight and to be born prematurely, factors that put them at a disadvantage right from the start (Gaudino, Jenkins, and Rochat 1999).

Father absence also affects outcomes for children later in life. A large body of literature suggests that children who grow up in single-mother households are more likely to drop out of school and complete less schooling, to exhibit disruptive and other so-called delinquent behaviors (including substance abuse), to earn less money as adults, to have poorer physical and mental health as adults, and to be more likely themselves to experience nonmarital births and union dissolution or divorce as adults (reviewed in Sigle-Rushton and McLanahan 2004).

While the apparent relationship between father absence and childhood outcomes appears compelling, it has been criticized on many counts. One major criticism concerns the issue of self-selection: because people choose the family structure they live in, unobserved variables may be responsible for any observed relationship between family structure and any particular outcome. A simpler way of stating this is that the people who live in absent-father/single-mother situations may differ in important (and perhaps unobservable) ways from people who live in two-parent households. In a hypothetical example, suppose parents who are in very poor health are both less likely to get married and more likely to have children in poor health. Thus any observed correlation between family structure and children's health outcomes is really driven by the health status of the parents, which is not something that is measured in most demographic data sets.

Testing whether the relationship between father absence and children's outcomes is due to self-selection is possible but requires more-detailed data and more-advanced statistical techniques than are available to many studies. When these tests have been done, the negative effect of father-absent family structures typically decreases, sometimes substantially (Amato and Gilbreth 1999; Sigle-Rushton and McLanahan

2004). But even with these more-complicated methods, a negative relationship between father absence and children's outcomes typically remains.

Father absence is a very gross measure of paternal investment in children. There is certainly a great deal of variation, even among men who live with children, in the degree to which fathers interact with and invest in their children. Men who do not live with their children may nonetheless invest in them. There are also many less tangible dimensions of father/child interactions, such as emotional closeness or quality of the relationship. Studies examining the long-term effects of more-nuanced measures of male parental investment and children's outcomes generally find greater paternal involvement translates into better cognitive, behavioral, social, and psychological outcomes for children. The negative effects of father absence are dampened when more-detailed dimensions of nonresident father involvement with children are included in the analysis, but less involvement still typically means poorer outcomes (for example, Amato and Gilbreth 1999). One recent review examined eighteen longitudinal studies that measured father involvement at an earlier age and then revisited the children to record outcomes at a later age; seventeen of these studies found that father involvement had a positive effect on the children's development (Sarkadi et al. 2007). One study with a nationally representative sample of "intact" families used father involvement at ages eleven to sixteen to predict children's outcomes at ages seventeen to twenty-two (Harris, Furstenberg, and Marmer 1998). The study found that greater father involvement earlier in life was associated with higher educational attainment, lower delinquency rates, and lower psychological distress among children. Another study, using a nationally representative sample of adolescents with nonresident fathers, found that teenagers with stronger ties to nonresident fathers have fewer behavioral problems (King and Sobolewski 2006). These studies confirm that paternal care is not an all-or-nothing phenomenon; the amount of care provided by men, not simply whether they provide any at all, has important consequences for children.

One provocative idea that has gained increasing support and attention over the past several decades is that male investment early in life may influence the timing of sexual maturity among children, as well as their adult reproductive strategies (Draper and Harpending 1982, 1988; Belsky, Steinberg, and Draper 1991). The model suggests that father absence and childhood psychosocial stress are indicators that low-quality parental investment is sufficient to raise offspring and that offspring use those indicators as cues in developing their own life-history trajectory. Simply put, if you grow up in a context where developmental cues suggest that high-quality male investment is not necessary for successful reproduction, then it makes sense (from an evolutionary point of view) to accelerate puberty and start reproducing earlier. Alternatively, if your environmental cues suggest that high-quality parental investment is important, you should delay puberty, which both lets you receive such investment for a longer time period and gives you more time to find an appropriate high-quality mate.

The relationship between childhood father absence and earlier sexual maturity has been examined in a large number of studies, receiving support from most of them (reviewed in Ellis 2004). The studies overwhelmingly find that father absence is associated with earlier sexual maturation among girls, though a handful of studies found no effect or even a delayed relationship between father absence and sexual maturation. Virtually all studies have focused on daughters, with only a handful examining sexual maturation among sons; we thus know little about whether the model holds true for boys. One of the few studies that has examined males found limited effects of father absence on the timing of first reproduction among Ache and Mayan men (Waynforth, Hurtado and Hill 1999). Most studies have focused on populations of European descent (including the United States and New Zealand); studies that include multiple ethnic groups (for example, Quinlan 2003) rarely present results separately by race. Thus we know little about the applicability to nonindustrialized or nonwhite populations. Nearly all of these studies use retrospective measures of childhood stressors and sexual maturation, making it more difficult to determine causality and to tease out the effects of potentially confounding variables.

Our opinion is that the effect of father absence on age at sexual maturity is real but fairly small. The effect size is often a difference of a month or two, which does not translate into tremendous differences in lifetime reproductive success. What is probably more important is the effect of father absence on reproductive behavior in certain socioecological conditions. Differences in adult sexual behavior—for example, in the duration and number of sexual relationships—may translate into meaningful long-term differences across individuals. So far this effect has received less attention that the putative effect of father absence on age at sexual maturation.

Fathering from a Distance

The evidence reviewed above suggests that father absence is associated with a suite of altered outcomes for children, most of them socially perceived as negative. The literature often does not distinguish among non-coresident fathers, implicitly treating them as if they were all equally low-investing deadbeats who have abandoned their responsibilities to their children. The reality, of course, is more nuanced; many fathers continue to invest in their children even after their relationship with the children's mother comes to an end. The transition to nonresidential father is a difficult one for many men, who struggle with the change from being "fathers" to "visitors" in their children's lives (Leite and McKenry 2002). In the following section we ask what factors influence male involvement following divorce or union dissolution. Do men invest less in children following divorce, and if so, why?

In industrialized societies such as the United States, a significant fraction of children do not live with both biological parents. Because adult mortality is relatively uncommon in these populations, these living arrangements result primarily from the end of the relationship between the biological parents, rather than from widowhood. (These arrangements include married couples who are legally divorced, married couples who are separated, unmarried couples who once cohabited but no longer live together, and unmarried couples who never lived together. For convenience, we will refer to this state as "divorced," but it is important to bear in mind that this term encompasses a broader range of relationships.)

As reviewed in Chapter 3, divorce is hardly unique to modern industrialized societies. Divorce occurs in nearly every society in the Standard Cross-Cultural Sample, most commonly due to infidelity and sterility (Betzig 1989). While in the contemporary United States children typically remain with their mother upon divorce, in other societies this is not necessarily the case. In many patrilineal cultures (in which genealogical connections are reckoned solely through the male line), children remain with the father and are part of his lineage in the event of divorce. Additionally, in the United States and Europe children historically often remained with fathers and not mothers if a marriage ended; for example, in colonial America men almost invariably retained custody of their children following divorce, while following widowhood, a woman could lose custody to a male relative of her husband (Mason 1996). In recent years in the United States, paternal custody and joint custody following union dissolution have increased, though they still represent the minority of postmarital living arrangements. In 2005 there were 13.6 million single parents living with children under twenty-one in the United States, 84% of whom were mothers (Grall 2007). Among hunter-gatherers, children typically reside with mothers following divorce. For example, among the Aka of central Africa, 21% of children ages zero to fifteen live with their mother (or mother and stepfather) but not their father, versus 5% who live with their father (or father and stepmother) but not their mother (B. S. Hewlett 1991b). In the case of groups like the Aka, single parenthood is frequently due to parental mortality rather than divorce, so the higher rate of maternal residence reflects the greater mortality observed among males. Among the Ache of Paraguay, 25% of children age fifteen have experienced parental divorce, while 20% have experienced paternal death (Hurtado and Hill 1992). Even though postmarital residence patterns are not universally biased toward mothers, from a numerical perspective many of children in the world—perhaps hundreds of millions—are living with their mothers while their biological fathers live elsewhere.

Thus men are often faced with the problem of how to invest in their genetic children who no longer live with them and how much investment to provide. It should be noted that this is essentially a human conundrum. Among virtually all birds and mammals in which males provide parental care, the male's investment in the offspring ceases with the termination of a reproductive union between two partners; mate desertion is equivalent to the cessation of paternal investment (Davies 1991). Human males, however, may continue to invest in their genetic offspring following divorce or parental separation. Over the centuries many criteria have been proposed to distinguish humans from nonhuman animals. Many of these have fallen by the wayside as studies have revealed that our species is not as unique as we had once thought. (For example, we now know we are not the only species that can make and use tools, that can hunt cooperatively, that shares food, and that can recognize itself in a mirror, etc.) One definition we have never seen proposed for humanity, but which seems to be applicable, is this: *humans are the species in which males continue to invest in offspring after the parents cease to be in a sexual relationship.*

So how do men invest in children who no longer live with them? Obviously, men who do not live with their children necessarily spend less time with them. One nationally representative sample of American nonresident fathers found that approximately half (52%) of fathers in the study saw their children several times per year or less, while the other half saw them several times a month or more (Manning and Smock 1999). Similar visitation frequencies occur in Canada: 49% of nonresident fathers visited their children weekly or biweekly, versus 51% who saw them monthly or on holidays only or less (Juby et al. 2007). In retrospective estimates of how much time fathers spent with children between the ages of five and twelve, men in Albuquerque, New Mexico, who were in a relationship with the child's mother at the time reported spending 20 hours per week with the child, while fathers who were no longer with the child's mother spent only 9.5 hours per week (K. G. Anderson, Kaplan, and Lancaster 1999).

Similar patterns occur outside of North America. In Cape Town, South Africa, high school students in a black township reported spending time with their genetic fathers with whom they reside about 199 days per year, versus about 22 days per year for genetic fathers they used to live with and only 6 days per year for genetic fathers they have never lived with (K. G. Anderson, Kaplan, Lam, et al. 1999). Among many hunter-gatherers, male investment in children of former mates is very low because men and their ex-wives often reside in different camps. For example, Lawrence Sugiyama and Richard Chacon (2005) collected data on household composition of children among the Yora, who practice horticulture and hunting and gathering in Amazonian Peru. Among twenty-four children with two living parents, eighteen (75%) were living with both of them. Two children (8.3%) were living with the mother alone, and three (13%) with the mother and stepfather. One child (4%) was living with more distant kin. None were living with the biological father but not the mother. To the best of our knowledge, no one has yet examined men's investment in children from former mates living in the same camp or vicinity among subsistence-level societies.

Lack of proximity to children is likely to be an important cause of decreased care for forms of parental care whose costs are greatly increased by distance or lack of contact. You cannot hug or share food with a child who does not live with you, at least not on a daily basis, and men spend less time with children the farther away from them they live (Manning, Stewart, and Smock 2003). Other forms of investment are possible even if men do not spend time with their children. For example, phone calls and e-mails may increase following marital dissolution and may help maintain close emotional bonds between men and their nonresidential children—although evidence suggests that such forms of contact tend to decrease over time following divorce (for example, Juby et al. 2007).

Forms of investment that are not tied to proximity may also decrease following divorce. Perhaps the most salient form of postdivorce paternal investment in industrialized societies is child support. Parents who live with a child automatically share their income with that child, but parents who live apart from the child may not (for example, Lin and McLanahan 2007). Child support, whether legally mandated or paid through informal arrangements, is the major way in which men invest financially in their nonresident children. In the United States in 2005, 7.8 million custodial parents had arrangements to receive financial support from noncustodial parents, and 92% of those were formal legal arrangements (Grall 2007). Altogether, custodial mothers received $22.4 billion in child support in 2005 (Grall 2007). By any measure, this represents a substantial investment by men in their children.

Many men are happy to pay child support and to maintain other connections with their nonresident children. And yet a significant fraction of men do not make these investments willingly. Many men who have child support obligations either pay no support or only part of what they are supposed to pay. In the United States in 2003, 23% of custodial mothers who were supposed to receive child support did not receive any payments, while 32% received only partial payments; only 45% received the full amount awarded (U.S. Census Bureau 2007b). By some estimates, men could afford to pay nearly 40% more child support than they currently do—as much as $32 billion dollars more— if all eligible women received child support awards and if men paid child support obligations in full (Sorenson 1997).

Over the past several decades an increasingly elaborate government bureaucracy has grown in the United States to oversee child support enforcement and collection, spending tremendous amounts of time and money to do so. Many states have tried innovative approaches to increase child support payments, yet rates of child support compliance have remained roughly flat for at least three decades. Richard Freeman and Jane Waldfogel (2001) report that 59% of children living with custodial mothers and no father received child support in 1978, versus 62% in 1995, while Timothy Grall (2007) reports the percentage of custodial mothers with child support agreements as 60% in 1994 and 61% in 2005. This is a 2% increase over twenty-seven years, a fairly negligible amount. Comparing across states, Freeman and Waldfogel (2001) find that states that spend more money on child support collection and that have more laws enforcing child support have greater child support compliance, but this is an expensive way to produce results. Furthermore, I-Fen Lin (2000) reports that if men think their child support award is fair, they will pay it; further governmental involvement (such as garnishing wages) does not increase their compliance. It is only men who view their awards as unfair (58% of men in Lin's sample) whose compliance is increased by methods such as withholding child support payments from their wages.

Forms of postmarital financial investment in children besides child support are also likely to decrease after divorce. A study of men living in Albuquerque, New Mexico, measured whether men provided any financial support to children (excluding child support) for attending college (K. G. Anderson, Kaplan, and Lancaster 1999). Because of the positive relationship between father presence and educational attainment, genetic children were more likely to have attended college if the man was still married to their mother (61%, versus 43% for genetic children whose parents were divorced). Those genetic children who did attend college were more likely to get money for college from their fathers if their parents were still together than if they were not (75% versus 55%). The study also asked about financial expenditures on children in specific categories—like clothing, gifts, hobbies, etc., but excluding food, housing, and child support. For both children zero to seventeen and those eighteen to twenty-four years old, men reported spending greater amounts of money on genetic children of current mates than genetic children of former mates (K. G. Anderson, Kaplan, and Lancaster 1999). Similar results were observed for men's financial expenditures on black high school students in Cape Town, South Africa: men spent more on school fees and on miscellaneous expenditures (gifts, money for hobbies, and pocket money) to genetic children if they currently lived with them than if they did not, although there was no difference in the amount of money men spent on clothing (K. G. Anderson, Kaplan, Lam, et al. 1999).

Explanations for Decreased Investment by Nonresident Fathers

American society attaches moral significance to a man's willingness to support his children, and nonresident fathers who do not pay child support are judged negatively and often labeled "deadbeat dads." Men realize they are responsible for supporting their children even if the relationship with the mother ends and both parents have moved on to new relationships. In one national study of new parents, over 90% of both men and women agreed that a nonresident father is obligated to pay child support even if the mother has a new partner, and over 97% agreed that a nonresident father is obligated to pay child support even if he has a new baby with another partner (Lin and McLanahan 2007). Most men honor their obligations; as we have seen, 77% of custodial mothers receive some form of child support payments from absent fathers (U.S. Census Bureau 2007b). Yet the child support glass could also be characterized as only half full, because over half of men with child support obligations do not pay the full amounts they owe. Why are many men resistant to paying child support?

Experts offer numerous explanations for why men invest less in children following divorce. Some of these are proximate explanations of the phenomenon. For example, nonresident fathers may have less money to spend on children because of the fixed costs of maintaining a household. Put simply, it is more expensive for two adults to maintain independent households than to have one joint household (Weiss and Willis 1985). Thus, divorced parents may effectively have less income to spend on children, because the proportion of their income that goes toward housing, food, and so forth, may be higher than when they were married or cohabiting.

Not surprisingly, a man's income is a strong predictor of whether he pays child support; men who are better able to pay child support are more likely to do so (Lin 2000; Manning, Stewart, and Smock 2003). The demographic composition of families has changed in the United States; while several decades ago most nonresident fathers had once been married to the mothers of their children, now an increasingly large proportion of children are born out of wedlock, sometimes to parents who have never lived together (Case, Lin, and McLanahan 2003). The relatively flat rate of child support compliance over the past several decades is attributable in part to the fact that unmarried mothers, who are less likely to obtain child support awards and less likely to receive the full amount of their awards, account for an increasing proportion of births over the years. Furthermore, the younger fathers who are associated with unmarried births are more likely to have less education and lower incomes and thus less ability to pay. Nonmarital births may also be associated with weaker social bonds between parents, as well as weaker legal protection for mothers once the relationship ends (Case, Lin, and McLanahan 2003).

As we discussed above, physical proximity plays a role in men's involvement with children. In addition to certain forms of investment being difficult or impossible if the man and the child are physically apart, proximity may increase investment by strengthening emotional bonds between men and their children. Both child support and involvement with children have been found to increase when the physical distance between men's and children's residences is less (Manning, Stewart, and Smock 2003; Seltzer 1991), and some studies (though not all) have found that men who visit their children more frequently are more likely to pay child support (for example, Juby et al. 2007; Sonenstein and Calhoun 1990). Men who do not provide child support often cite lack of access to their children as a reason for nonpayment (Dubey 1995), and there is a widespread perception that mothers will block visitations from men who do not pay child support. One recent national study found that over 86% of both men and women felt that fathers have a right to see their children even if these fathers cannot afford to pay child support; men and women were equally likely to agree with this statement (Lin and McLanahan 2007). However, less than 40% of either men or women felt that men who can afford to pay child support but who don't nonetheless have the right to see their children.

The causality of the relationship between nonresident men's proximity to children and their investment in them is not clear, as Todd Shackelford, Viviana Weekes-Shackelford and David Schmidt (2005) have recently noted. Do men who live near their children choose to invest more in them, or do men who plan to invest more in their children choose to live closer to them? Shackelford, Weekes-Shackelford and Schmidt (2005) posit that men who pay more child support may visit their nonresidential children more frequently in order to monitor how the mother is spending the money. Men's inability to dictate how child support is spent by the children's mother may influence how willing they are to pay it. Yoram Weiss and Robert Willis (1985) suggest that a man may reduce financial investment in a child because this form of male care is channeled through the child's mother, who may allocate it for other purposes. Weiss and Willis argue that married men and women can monitor each other's allocations to make sure resources are being distributed to children in the manner they both agree on. Once the parents divorce, however, each parent no longer needs to take the preferences of the noncustodial parent into account and can instead allocate resources as he or she sees fit. If, for example, only twenty-five cents of every dollar in child support goes toward the child, it costs the man four dollars to increase expenditures on his child by one dollar—a very inefficient transfer of resources that may result in the man curtailing his child support altogether (Willis 1999). This tendency may explain why positive and friendly relationships between ex-spouses are associated with greater child support compliance (Kurdek 1986)—perhaps the father trusts, or can better monitor, that the mother is spending the money appropriately if they are on good terms.

In South Africa, child support is called "maintenance" (while "child support" refers to governmental support for single mothers). Following divorce, both parents, as one researcher has reported, "must continue to maintain their children in proportion to their respective means" (Gallinetti 2006, 206). Similar obligations are incumbent upon unmarried parents of a child, "even though the father has no inherent rights to guardianship, custody and access to the extramarital child" (Gallinetti 2006, 207). Fathers in South Africa, as in the United States, have ambivalent attitudes toward paying maintenance. Grace Khunou (2006) notes that fathers "seem happy to pay maintenance if they are satisfied that it is being used for the benefit of their children. But many question whether their maintenance payments are being used for this purpose, especially when their ex-partners are in good jobs, and appear to be living lavish lifestyles" (272).

Another possible way to approach the decrease in male investment following divorce is to explain the problem away by claiming that male investment in children does not actually decrease when a marriage or relationship ends. This explanation may sound counterintuitive, perhaps even ridiculous, but very little research has measured involvement with children by the same men both before and after divorce. Instead, studies measure involvement by a group of men who are currently in relationships with their children's mothers and by a separate group of men who are no longer in relationships with their children's mothers. But what if men who are divorced differ from men who are not? Suppose, for example, that women are more likely to divorce men who are poor providers or uninvolved fathers or who otherwise provide lower levels of care for their children than the mothers feel is appropriate. If this is the case, low levels of male parental care may actually be a cause of divorce rather than a result of it (K. G. Anderson, Kaplan, and Lancaster 1999). This proposition turns the accepted causal arrow on its head but is worth investigating further. In a study of Dutch households, Matthijs Kalmijn (1999) found that families in which men were more involved in parental care had more stable marriages, because "the wife is happier if the husband is strongly involved with the children" (409). And Lawrence Kurdek (1986) reports that among American families with low levels of conflict before divorce, men are more involved with children than are men among whose families had high levels of predivorce conflict, though he has no data on men's predivorce level of investment. More studies along this line are needed, because the hypothesis has not yet been rigorously tested.

One indirect way of looking at whether this selection effect is at play—if men who are good investors stay in relationships while poor investors (or wives of poor investors) end them—is to see whether it matters if the man ever lived with the child or if living with the child longer is associated with greater investment levels. One possible explanation for this effect, if it exists, is that men who live with children longer develop greater emotional bonds with them. But it is also possible that duration of the relationship is a proxy for investment level before divorce, the idea being that women will end relationships with poor investors sooner—and really poor investors might not even reach the point of living with the mother. Married and cohabiting men may have different levels of investment, because marriage implies greater levels of commitment between partners (which may result in greater commitment between fathers and children as well).

Some data support this idea, though it has not yet received extensive empirical examination. Using a nationally representative sample of American children, Sandra Hofferth and Kermyt Anderson (2003) found that cohabiting biological fathers are less involved with children than married biological fathers for some measures (hours engaged with the child, warmth of relationship with the child) but not others (hours available to the child, number of activities done with the child). Andrea Beller and John Graham (1986) report that never-married fathers (which includes men who never lived with their offspring) are less likely to pay child support than men who had ever been married. In their study of Albuquerque men, Kermyt Anderson, Hillard Kaplan, and Jane Lancaster (1999) find essentially no effect of the number of years men lived with children on financial expenditures on children by non-residential fathers, though there is an effect on children's college attendance among nonresident children, so that children who lived with men longer before divorce are more likely to go to college. Elizabeth Peters and others (1993), using a national sample of fathers, report that men with greater predivorce involvement with children are more likely to comply with child support agreements. Outside of the United States, black high school students in Cape Town, South Africa, report that nonresident genetic fathers spend more time with them the longer they had lived together (K.G. Anderson, Kaplan, Lam, et al. 1999). However, there is no relationship between coresidential history and money spent on those students by nonresident genetic fathers.

Another way of looking at whether selection effects are responsible for the apparent differential investment in genetic children of current and previous unions is to examine investments by men who have children in both categories. Do men who have children from both current and previous unions invest equally in them all? Virtually no work has been done on this, partly because few studies use measures of investment that are comparable for both resident and nonresident children. (Child support, for example, is only paid to nonresident children, while the amount of time spent with a child is severely constrained by proximity.) In the aforementioned sample of Albuquerque men, Kermyt Anderson, Hillard Kaplan and Jane Lancaster (n.d.) looked at how much money (excluding child support) men reported spending on genetic children ages zero to twenty-four, by current and previous mates. When comparing average expenditures by men on children from current relationship with expenditures by men on children from previous relationship—that is, comparing across men—they found large differences, with men spending the most on children from current relationships. When Anderson and his colleagues compared expenditures by men who have genetic children by both current and previous partners—that is, comparing within men—they found children from former unions still received less money than did children from current unions. In fact, the difference in what children received was larger when comparing within men than comparing across men. This finding suggests that observed differential investment in genetic children of current and former relationships is not simply due to differences between the fathers of each type of child.

Another explanation for decreased male investment in children following divorce comes from evolutionary theory. Evolutionary theory posits that organisms experience fundamental trade-offs between mating effort and parental effort (Low 1978; Trivers 1972). That is, time, money, and other resources can be devoted to the acquisition of sexual partners and the maintenance of such relationships (mating effort) or to the production of and investment in offspring (parental effort). In general, effort allocated to acquiring mates cannot be used to increase offspring quality, and vice versa. However, the trade-off between mating and parental effort may be relaxed under certain circumstances (K. G. Anderson, Kaplan, and Lancaster 1999; Smuts 1985). Although most models of male parental care assume (though this assumption may not be explicitly stated) that men invest in children primarily because the investment has some impact on the children, men may not be doing it solely for the children's benefit. When individuals choose mates at least in part on the mates' ability to invest in offspring, then investment in offspring may increase the probability of obtaining or retaining a mate or of improving the quality of the relationship. Because human females should prefer as mates men who invest in their children, the extent to which a man invests in the children of his current mate may influence his relationship with that mate. By providing care to the children of their mates, men can influence both the quality and the duration of their relationships with their mates, above and beyond the effects the care has on the well-being of the offspring themselves.

Seen from this perspective, male parental care can thus be a form of mating effort as well as parental effort; it can influence both the man's relationship with the child's mother and the welfare or fitness of the recipient offspring. Mary La Cerra (1994) provides some support for mating effects of parental behavior. She showed men and women slides of opposite-sex models doing different things and asked her subjects to rate the models as a prospective date, sexual partner, marital partner, friend, or neighbor. She found that female subjects reacted positively to pictures of men interacting positively with a child and rated these men more highly as a prospective date, sexual partner, or marital partner than the women rated men who stood alone. She also found that women reacted negatively to men ignoring a crying baby. Women were not judging men's general compassion or helpfulness, because they did not react to images of men providing assistance to the elderly or vacuuming. Male subjects, in contrast, were indifferent to whether women were pictured with children or ignoring crying babies.

This hypothesis provides a possible explanation for decreased financial investment in children following divorce—including the resistance of some men to making child support payments. For genetic children of current mates, men are not simply investing in children for the children's sake alone; they are motivated, in part, by the impact the investment has on the child's mother. This investment is thus a combination of parental and mating effort, and we expect to see the highest levels of investments in these children. When the relationship with the mother ends, there is no more mating effort component to male parental care; the investment is solely parental effort. Natural selection will still favor male investment in offspring if it has a positive impact on offspring well-being, but at reduced levels because the man is no longer investing in the relationship with the child's mother, and he has reallocated the mating component portion of his investment in that child into new areas of mating effort. Thus, when the relationship with the child's mother ends, a man is likely to reallocate the proportion of his investment that was mating effort into the establishment and maintenance of new mating relationships.

This model of male parental care as mating effort offers an explanation for why men invest less in genetic children of previous mates than they do in genetic children of current mates. Due to trade-offs regarding resource allocation, money and time used for one purpose cannot be used for something else. The levels of investments that men are inclined to provide in genetic offspring following divorce conflict with the levels that the children's mothers might expect or prefer. This tension is reflected in child support levels as well, which are typically determined using the income shares model, requiring noncustodial parents to share the same proportion of their income with their children as they would have spent had they remained living with them (Hanson et al. 1996). This rule obliges men to pay their genetic children by former mates the same amount as the men would pay genetic children of current mates, compelling men to direct a significant portion of their mating effort budget into non-mating relationships, thereby decreasing their ability to attract or maintain subsequent mates. Perhaps the perceived unfairness that many men report regarding their child support obligations results in part from of the trade-offs between mating and parental effort men experience as a result of paying child support.

One prediction of the mating effort model is that men who invest highly in children after divorce will be less likely to attract and retain new partners and have future children (K. G. Anderson, Kaplan, and Lancaster 1999). In Trinidad, Mark Flinn (1992) found that men who were single were more likely to interact with their nonresident children than men who had a new mate. In the United States, some studies have found that men who pay child support—either willingly or through legal compulsion—are less likely to remarry (Bloom, Conrad, and Miller 1998) or to form new sexual partnerships (Huang and Han 2007), while other studies find that men who have new children are less likely to pay child support (Manning and Smock 2000; Manning, Stewart, and Smock 2003). Kermyt Anderson (n.d.) found that American men who pay child support are less likely to have subsequent children. However, David Bloom, Cecilia Conrad, and Cynthia Miller (1998) found that among fathers who remarry, child support has no effect on fertility within subsequent marriages. Susan Stewart, Wendy Manning and Pamela Smock (2003) report that paying child support has no effect on whether men form new unions, while Kermyt Anderson (n.d.) found that unmarried men who pay child support are actually more likely to get married, a counterintuitive effect that is perhaps explained as child support being an honest signal of a man's reliability and quality. Consider a woman with a choice between marrying two single men with children, one a deadbeat dad and the other a reliable payer of child support. The deadbeat dad may have more disposable income, but who is going to be more likely to honor his commitment to her—and to pay child support if it eventually comes to that? She may be better off choosing the man who pays his child support obligations, even though he has less money to spend on her, because this is a marker of his willingness and ability to commit to investing in offspring.

We have focused on the positive factors of fatherhood and the negative consequences of father absence. It is worth noting, however, that father absence is not always a bad thing. Some men are abusive or neglectful, poor parents at best and psychologically and physically hurtful parents at worst. In these cases, children—and their mothers—are probably better off not having these men play an active role in their lives.

In summary, we have seen that while men have weak effects on child survival (especially relative to the effects of mothers), they exert significant influences on many later childhood outcomes. Most studies focus on father absence rather than on more fine-grained measures of paternal investment, but this coarse measure is relevant because father absence is widespread in pre- and postindustrial societies, with half of American children living in a father-absent household at some point during their childhood. We have explored the role of selection effects—whether families in which fathers have left might differ in important respects from families in which fathers stay. This is likely to be true, but even taking that into consideration, men have important effects on children, and men invest less in their offspring following divorce. Investment is curtailed following divorce for many reasons, but we call particular attention to the suggestion that when the relationship with the child's mother was intact, men may have invested in children as a form of mating investment instead of solely as a benefit for the children. This explanation may provide some insight into why roughly half of men with child support awards do not pay their full child support obligations. This insight is not provided as an excuse for the behavior of "deadbeat dads." Rather, we propose this suggestion from the perspective that understanding the motivations of men's parental behaviors (or lack thereof) is an important first step to explaining and possibly altering the behaviors themselves.

7

The Makings of a Stepfather

The focus of this book so far has been on men's involvement with their genetic offspring. And yet fatherhood can occur in broader contexts; men also interact and invest, sometimes at very high levels, in children who are not theirs. Perhaps the most widespread example of this relationship is the stepfather, that is, a man who occupies some sort of parental role to the children of his current spouse or partner. In this chapter we'll examine the stepfather relationship in more detail. What kinds of investments do men make in stepchildren? How do men's relationships with stepchildren differ from those with genetic children? What factors influence men's relationships with their stepchildren? Why do men become stepfathers, and what are the consequences, both for children and for the men themselves?

First off, what is a stepfather? For the purposes of this discussion, we will define a stepfather as a man who parents the children who were conceived from a previous relationship of his current mate. In other words, although the children's mother is his current partner, he cannot be the genetic father of these children. The role of stepparent is a concept distinct from adoption, in which a couple may jointly choose to parent a child who is unrelated to either of them, and distinct from fostering, in which a couple may parent children who are related to them, though not their own offspring (see Chapter 3). Being a stepfather is also distinct from nonpaternity, in which a man's partner has a child who is supposed to be his but may not be (see Chapter 5). A key feature that distinguishes stepfathers from other types of fathers is that the parenting aspect is present from the start of the relationship with the mother, rather than being something that develops later. Men who contemplate entering a relationship with a woman who already has children have to decide up front if they are going to be a stepfather or not.

142

The relationship between stepparents and stepchildren is often characterized as difficult (Daly and Wilson 1998) and results to some extent from a conflict of interest between the principals involved. Two biological parents share a similar perspective on their joint children—they both benefit from investments in the children—but in a stepfamily, investments that benefit the children may be favored by the biological parent but not the stepparent, resulting in a conflict of interest. Stepfathers and stepchildren do not share genes, do not share a personal history, and may resent one another because of the demands each makes on the person who is their intersection point, the mother of the child.

From an evolutionary perspective, raising stepchildren—investing in offspring who do not carry any of your genes—seems counterintuitive. Consider two males, one who raises only his own genetic offspring, and another who raises only other males' offspring. Clearly the first male is the one who will leave more descendents in future generations (which is what evolution all about). And yet we find that stepparenting, while not the norm among nonhuman animals, is not unheard of. Many studies, mostly in birds, have reported cases in which incoming males tolerate or provide care for existing offspring of female mates (Rohwer 1986), while experimental studies, performed mostly on bird species, have demonstrated that when a resident parent is removed, the replacement parent provides care for (or at least tolerates) the existing young (Rohwer, Herron, and Daly 1999). Similarly, olive baboons will interact with and help protect the young of their female "friends," providing care to infants who are unlikely to be the males' own offspring. Several other primate species exhibit similar patterns of care, based more on mating relationship with the mother than probable genetic relatedness to the infant (Smuts and Gubernick 1992).

How common is stepparenting among humans? How many men are stepfathers, and how many children live with stepfathers? It is more difficult to find an answer to this question than you might think. Survey and census data often have not distinguished between different types of parent/child relationships in a household, lumping them all into the category of "own" children (Moorman and Hernandez 1989). While we can pull up statistics about the number of children living with two adults, we may not be able to easily identify the fraction who live with a parent and a stepparent versus two biological parents or two adoptive parents. More attention has been paid to this distinction in recent years, and some data sets now allow us to identify specific relationships. Recent estimates suggest that 62% of American children ages zero through seventeen live with two genetic parents, while 7% live with a biological parent and a stepparent (Federal Interagency Forum on Child and Family Statistics 2007). Most American children who live with a stepparent live with a stepfather; currently this group is about 6%, or roughly one in every eighteen children (Federal Interagency Forum on Child and Family Statistics 2007). In Europe, the proportion of couples living with stepchildren ranges from 12% in Slovenia to 32% in Germany (Heuveline, Timberlake, and Furstenberg 2003).

We get a slightly different perspective when looking at stepfamilies across the life course. A cross-sectional measure will underestimate the number of children who will live with stepfathers during their lifetime, because some children currently living with both parents or with a single mother will eventually live with a stepfather. Larry Bumpass, Kelly Raley, and James Sweet (1995) estimate that 30% of American children will spend time living in a stepfamily. Patrick Heuveline, Jeffrey Timberlake, and Frank Furstenberg Jr. (2003) calculate that American children ages zero to fifteen will spend an average of 1.9 years (or 13% of their childhood) living with a mother and a stepfather.

Conventional wisdom may suggest that stepfamilies are an innovation of modern life, resulting from rates of nonmarital birth and divorce that have increased enormously over the past several decades. While it's true that these factors have contributed to a tremendous growth in stepfamilies in contemporary industrialized societies, stepparents are not a modern invention. Divorce and adult mortality in traditional societies commonly resulted in paternal absence (see Chapter 6), and remarriages often created stepfamilies. Among the Aka hunter-gatherers of central Africa, 18% of children ages eleven to fifteen live with a mother and stepfather, and another 6% live with a father and stepmother (B. S. Hewlett 1991b). Among the Yora of Peru, 15% of children with at least one living parent, and 12.5% of children with two living parents, live with a stepfather (Sugiyama and Chacon 2005). Among !Kung hunter-gatherers of southern Africa, almost all children remain with their mother following divorce, and if she remarries, they will call her new husband "father," though they can identify their "real" father if they are asked (Howell 2000). Similarly, Hadza hunter-gatherers in Tanzania tend to identify stepfathers as fathers (Marlowe

1999a). Precise estimates of stepparent frequency are not available for many societies, because researchers tend to focus more on maternal bonds and also because researchers do not distinguish stepparents from biological parents (B. S. Hewlett 1991a). But we know that stepfamilies existed in traditional societies, and in many cultures they were not uncommon.

How Do Stepfathers Measure Up as Parents?

There is an ongoing debate regarding the role of stepfathers. Are they supposed to replace the child's biological father or simply fulfill a new role in the child's life? Because industrialized societies like the United States have relatively low adult mortality rates, children's biological fathers are likely to be alive (although some may play a minimal role in their children's lives). What factors influence men's involvement with stepchildren, and how do stepfathers measure relative to biological fathers?

Psychologists, sociologists, and other social scientists have approached the study of stepfamilies from many different theoretical perspectives. Susan Stewart (2007) lists twenty-seven distinct theoretical approaches applied to stepfamilies, a list that she notes is not exhaustive. In an influential paper, Andrew Cherlin (1978) argued that remarriage is an incomplete institution, subject to a certain degree of social and cultural ambiguity, because the "rules" of second marriages are not as standardized and entrenched as the norms regarding first marriages. Stepfamilies are a subset of this incomplete institution, with the result that the role of a stepparent is by its very nature ambiguous. This ambiguity is reflected, for example, in the lack of standardized terms people use for stepparents; children may refer to their stepfathers as their stepdad, as "Dad," by the stepfather's first name, or sometimes as simply "that guy." Cherlin's model has attracted much attention, as well as criticism, and despite the fact that it is widely cited, the model has been subject to very little empirical testing (Stewart 2007).

Are stepfathers replacement fathers? Expectations regarding men's roles toward their own children are fairly well defined, and in countries like the United States legal mechanisms are in place, including enforced child support, to ensure that biological fathers invest in their children. But what are stepfathers' roles? There is much less agreement about this, especially in regard to men's expected level of investment in stepchildren and involvement in disciplining stepchildren, though the general consensus is that stepfathers are not expected to do exactly what "real" fathers do (Coleman, Ganong, and Cable 1996).

From an evolutionary perspective, we would expect men to be less involved with stepchildren. As a general rule among species exhibiting parental care, individuals who preferentially allocate resources to their genetic offspring obtain greater fitness benefits than individuals who allocate resources to unrelated individuals (Alexander 1974). Parents exhibit "discriminative parental solicitude"; that is, they possess well-developed psychological and behavioral mechanisms that generally result in their time and resources being preferentially directed toward genetic offspring (Daly and Wilson 1998). Thus we would expect stepparents, on average, to invest less in stepchildren than in genetic children. This decision isn't necessarily conscious on the stepfathers' part. A simple rule of thumb, such as "bond more closely with children you knew as infants," would be sufficient to ensure less care for stepchildren, because stepparents are typically not present during a stepchild's infancy. So, compared with genetic parents, how do stepparents invest in children?

At one point, observing increasing divorce rates and nonmarital birth rates, sociologists anticipated that an increase in remarriage rates would help children by replacing their absent fathers with stepfathers, who would pick up the slack regarding reduced investments in children (Cherlin and Furstenberg 1994). Yet it turns out that stepfathers are not a replacement for genetic fathers, and in terms of many outcomes, stepchildren are much more like children living with single mothers than children living in households with two biological parents (Case, Lin, and McLanahan 2001; McLanahan and Sandefur 1994). The poorer outcomes associated with stepchildren may be due to several factors working together, such as receiving fewer investments from a stepparent and spending a portion of their lives in single-parent households with fewer resources.

In terms of direct parental care, many studies have shown that stepchildren typically receive less investment from stepfathers than from coresident genetic fathers. Kermyt Anderson, Hillard Kaplan, and Jane Lancaster (1999) found that men living in Albuquerque, New Mexico, spend less money on coresident stepchildren than on coresident genetic children and spend less time with coresident stepchildren. Stepchildren are less likely to go to college than genetic offspring of current mates, and among those who do go to college, stepchildren receive less money for college (K. G. Anderson, Kaplan, and Lancaster 1999; Zvoch 1999). In a national sample of households, Sandra Hofferth and Kermyt Anderson (2003) find that, compared with coresident genetic children, stepchildren receive fewer investments from stepfathers along several measures, including the amount of time men spend with stepchildren, the number of activities they do together, and the warmth of their relationship.

Reduced investment by stepfathers has been observed outside of the United States as well. Anthropologist Frank Marlowe (1999a) observed interactions between men and children up through age eight among Hadza hunter-gatherers in Tanzania and found that Hadza men spend more time being near, playing with, communicating with, and nurturing biological children than stepchildren. Some of the differences are extreme; for example, Hadza men simply never played with stepchildren. Marlowe also found that stepfathers brought back less meat from hunting than biological fathers did, and the more stepchildren a man had, the less meat he acquired. In Trinidad, Mark Flinn (1988) observed that men spent significantly less time interacting with their stepchildren than with their genetic children. At a black township high school in Cape Town, South Africa, students self-reported spending less time with stepfathers than with coresident genetic fathers (K. G. Anderson, Kaplan, Lam, et al. 1999). Students in this study also self-reported that genetic fathers spend more money on school-related expenditures than stepfathers do. Other variables showed no significant difference between step- and genetic children; regardless of genetic relatedness, men were equally likely to help resident children with homework and to provide money for their clothes and miscellaneous expenditures.

The Darker Side of Stepparents

Stepparents have a bad reputation. They make numerous appearances in the Grimm Brothers' fairy tales, for example, and when they're not trying to outright poison their stepchildren or lose them in the woods, stepparents verbally and psychologically abuse them and make them do the bulk of the household chores.

Cross-culturally, such Cinderella tales are common; in fact, the very word "step" derives from an Old English word meaning "to deprive or bereave" (Daly and Wilson 1988, 85). The conflict of interest between biological parents and stepparents may result in negative consequences for children. Infanticide directed toward stepchildren occurs frequently in nonhuman species as well. Sievert Rohwer, Jon Herron, and Martin Daly (1999) note that a stepparent has three options when entering a mating relationship that brings with it preexisting offspring: kill them, tolerate them, or actively invest in them. For many animals, infanticide by an incoming male brings the mother back into a fertile state, thus increasing the male's reproductive success (Hrdy 1979; Rohwer, Herron, and Daly 1999). But what about human stepparents, outside of fairy tales? Are stepparents associated with greater violence against children?

The unfortunate answer is yes. Martin Daly and Margo Wilson (1988) summarized results from several databases focusing on extreme childhood outcomes, namely, child abuse and homicide. They focused on these outcomes not because they are common or typical but because they are less likely to be underreported—particularly homicide, which rarely goes unobserved. Both child abuse and child death occur more frequently among very young children—ages when children are both the least able to defend themselves (or leave the abusive situation) and more susceptible to serious injury. Controlling for the child's age, Daly and Wilson (1988) found that children were between forty and one hundred times more likely to be abused or murdered if they lived in a stepfather household than if they lived in a two-biological-parent household. These startling results have been corroborated through subsequent analysis of other data sets (for example, Daly and Wilson 2001).

Although Daly and Wilson's work focuses on data from Western industrialized nations, the so-called Cinderella effect has been documented elsewhere. In an observational study in Trinidad, Flinn (1988) found that men were more likely to behave agonistically toward stepchildren than toward genetic children, a behavior category that includes any form of physical or verbal conflict, as well as screaming or crying that is likely to have been the result of conflict. Flinn also found that stepchildren go out of their way to avoid contact with stepfathers: children under twenty with stepfathers were much more likely to live with their grandparents instead of their mothers than were children without a stepfather, while young adults over twenty were much more likely to have emigrated from their village if their mothers coresided with stepfathers. The propensity of children and young adults to avoid living with stepfathers is probably due to increased conflict, reduced investment, or perhaps both. This increased conflict is reflected in both greater levels of stress hormones in stepchildren than in genetic offspring and poorer health outcomes for stepchildren, as Mark Flinn and Barry England (1997) documented among children living in the Caribbean nation of Dominica. Though he did not document conflict with stepfathers, Marlowe (2005b) found that Hadza children were much more likely to be held by a mother or maternal grandmother when a stepfather was present than when a genetic father was present. The mother or grandmother may have been compensating for the stepfather's reduced level of care, relative to that of the genetic father—and may also have been safeguarding the child as well.

Some people have misinterpreted Daly and Wilson's results to infer that stepfathers are homicidal maniacs bent on beating to death the children entrusted to their care. This characterization is both untrue and unfair. Some men form very close bonds with their stepchildren—as close as any biological father's could be—and the vast majority are generally tolerant of their stepchildren. Extreme outcomes such as death are rare. For example, one 1976 data set used by Daly and Wilson (1988) reported only 279 homicides, 43% of which occurred at the hands of stepfathers. Because at that time only about 1% of American children lived with a stepfather, this suggests a tremendous increase in homicide risk resulting from stepfather coresidence. However, the vast majority of stepfather households in the United States experienced no homicides at all. The greater mortality rates observed for stepchildren result not from a deliberate plan of "first thing we'll do, let's kill all the stepkids," to paraphrase Shakespeare, but rather from a combination of factors: stepfathers have fewer "brakes" on aggressive behaviors toward unrelated children; stepfathers preferentially direct care, resources, and protection toward genetic offspring and away from stepchildren; and perhaps the very presence of stepchildren and the conflicts of interest they induce between parents result in more arguments and fights that end in lethal outcomes (Daly and Wilson 1998).

How Real Are These Findings?

The negative aspects associated with stepfathers—including decreased investments in and poorer outcomes for stepchildren—have been questioned by some researchers, who note that most studies do not compare the behaviors of the same men toward both their biological children and their stepchildren but rather compare a group of men with biological children against a separate group of stepfathers. But what if men who marry women with children (that is, stepfathers) differ in important ways from men who marry women without children? If this is the case, then differential treatment of and investment in children may be due to the different qualities of the men providing the care rather than to their biological relationship to the children per se.

One way to see if this is the case is to examine the investment in children who live in blended families, that is, families in which a parent lives with both genetic offspring and stepchildren. This kind of family most commonly occurs when a man forms a union with a woman who already has children, and then this man goes on to have one or more genetic children with her. The households will thus contain half siblings who share the same mother but have different fathers. Men living in blended families may not be representative of all men; presumably women prefer to have children with men who have already demonstrated their willingness and ability to provide care to the women's existing children (K. G. Anderson 2000). If we compare how men in blended families interact with both stepchildren and genetic children, any differences observed must be due to the relationship with the child and not differences in the quality of the investor, because it's the same man in both cases. Several studies, all using samples of American households, have looked at men's investments in children in blended families (K. G. Anderson, Kaplan, and Lancaster n.d., Case, Lin and McLanahan 2001; Hofferth and Anderson 2003). They all find that, for most measures, differences between stepchildren and genetic children in blended families decrease substantially and in some cases disappear, suggesting that some of the differences observed between genetic and stepchildren are indeed due to differences between the men investing in them and not to the relationship per se. However, for most variables significant differences do remain, although they are smaller, suggesting that biological relatedness is still important. We can thus conclude that stepchildren and genetic children do indeed receive different levels of paternal investment, even when investment comes from the same men, though some of the differences we see are also due to unobserved differences between stepfathers and genetic fathers.

Proximate Influences on Stepparental Care

Although stepfathers on average invest less in stepchildren than in genetic children, there is a lot of variation among stepfathers in how much care they provide or how much they enjoy being a stepfather. William Marsiglio (1991) found that while many stepfathers have negative perceptions of the stepparenting experience, many also feel positively toward the experience. For example, while 29% of men felt the statement "It is harder to love stepchildren than it is to love your own children" was somewhat true or definitely true, 52% felt it was somewhat false or definitely false. And while 29% of men felt the statement "Having stepchildren is just as satisfying as having your own children" was definitely or somewhat false, 55% felt it was somewhat or definitely true. Some men are as close to their stepchildren as they could possibly be to their own genetic offspring, while others barely tolerate, or are openly hostile to, their stepkids. To some extent, this variation probably reflects psychological differences across men, for example, in their ability to bond with children and in their aptitude toward parenting. Measuring these differences is generally outside the scope of the type of demographic data sets we've been drawing on here, but there are a few proximate influences on men's relationships with their stepchildren that we can examine in more detail.

Few men live with their stepchildren from the children's birth. Most children who become stepchildren will generally live with their genetic father for a while and then experience some time living with a single mother before a stepfather joins the household. Stepchildren are thus generally older, on average, than children living with a genetic father (for example, Hofferth and Anderson 2003). It seems reasonable to assume that the younger a child is when a man becomes a stepfather, the easier it will be for the man to bond with that child. It is typically easier for anybody, male or female, to bond with a cute infant than, say, a sullen teenager. Therefore, we should expect the age of the child when the man entered his or her life to influence his investments in the child: the younger the child, the more closely they will bond, and thus the greater the investments the child will receive. The few studies that have examined this relationship have found little or no support for the hypothesis, however (K. G. Anderson, Kaplan, and Lancaster 1999; K. G. Anderson, Kaplan, Lam, et al. 1999; Flinn 1988).

Another area that might influence men's interactions with stepchildren is gender. Among genetic offspring, men tend to interact more with boys than girls (see Chapter 2), and we might expect the same to hold true for stepchildren. Few studies have examined this directly, because few studies have looked at investments in stepchildren by themselves; these investments are usually pooled together (and contrasted) with those made in genetic offspring. Douglas Downey (1995) examined investments in education and educational outcomes in a sample of American eighth graders living in stepfamilies. He found no effect of the child's gender on involvement with stepparents or on children's outcomes. Marsiglio (1991) found no effect of gender on the self-reported quality of a man's relationship with coresident stepchildren. In South Africa, gender has no effect on men's time involvement with or financial expenditures on stepchildren, except that these men spend more money on school expenditures for stepdaughters than for stepsons (K. G. Anderson, Kaplan, Lam, et al. 1999). In Trinidad, men appear to have similar levels of agonistic interactions with both stepdaughters and stepsons. For stepdaughters the rates do not change with age, but men's interactions with stepsons become increasingly aggressive with age, so that men are much more agonistic toward teenage stepsons than preadolescents ones (Flinn 1988).

Another factor that may influence a man's interactions with stepchildren is his marital status, that is, whether he is married to the children's mother or simply living with her. The increase in cohabiting unmarried partners has changed the very nature of stepparent relationships over recent decades. Stewart (2007) notes that "traditional" stepfamilies form when a pair of divorced individuals, at least one of whom has children, marry each other. More recent stepfamilies may form in other ways, however; couples may live together without being married, or marriage may involve at least one partner who has never have been married before (Stewart 2007). Marital status may influence investment in children in several ways. First, unmarried parents may have lower income and less education and thus have fewer resources to invest in offspring. Even controlling for differences in socioeconomic status, couples who marry may differ from couples who do not in unobservable ways. Marriage implies a significant degree of long-term commitment; even though half of all marriages eventually end, when most people get married, they tend to believe the marriage is going to work. This greater commitment associated with marriage may be reflected in increased investments in offspring. Also, unmarried fathers may not have the legitimacy and responsibility of married fathers—especially in the case of stepfathers (Hofferth and Anderson 2003). For all of these reasons, we would expect to see unmarried stepfathers make lower investments in children than would stepfathers who are legally married to the children's mother.

In what by this point in the chapter has becoming a recurring theme, very few studies have addressed this point. Stewart (2007) reviewed three decades' worth of research on stepfamilies and found that 85% of the studies focused only on married couples. Several studies suggest marriage does result in greater involvement by stepfathers. Lynn White (1994) found that men had a better relationship with, had more contact with, and were more likely to give help to a stepchild if they were married to the child's mother. Similarly, in the sample of Albuquerque men, Kermyt Anderson and others found married stepfathers spend more money on stepchildren than unmarried stepfathers do, controlling for the man's income and education (K. G. Anderson, Kaplan, and Lancaster n.d.). Yet a number of other studies have found no difference between marital versus cohabitating stepfamilies. Marsiglio (1991) found that marital status did not influence either the stepfather's perception about having a positive fatherlike role or the quality of his relationship with his oldest stepchild. Hofferth and Anderson (2003) examined involvement with children by married and unmarried biological fathers and stepfathers and found no clear pattern regarding the relationship between marital status and stepfather investment: there was no significant difference in overall time involvement, the number of activities performed together, or the warmth of the relationship, while unmarried stepfathers actually had more time available for stepchildren than married stepfathers did.

Thus, while we might expect men's involvement with stepchildren to be influenced by the duration of their relationship, by the child's gender, or by the man's marital status (that is, whether the man is legally married to the child's mother), the evidence supporting each of these predictions is at best equivocal. We have reviewed the levels of men's investments in stepchildren—how much they invest. What about why they invest? Let us turn to a biosocial perspective on stepfathers and ask the question, why do men invest in stepchildren at all?

A Biosocial Perspective on Stepfathers

While stepfathers invest in children less than in genetic children, they nonetheless invest about as much in stepchildren as fathers do in non-resident genetic offspring (K. G. Anderson, Kaplan, and Lancaster 1999; K. G. Anderson, Kaplan, Lam, et al. 1999). That's a fairly substantial amount of investment, given that these stepchildren are not the men's own offspring. Perhaps we should describe the stepfather glass as half full rather than half empty.

Why do men become stepfathers? Why do men invest as much as they do in children who aren't theirs? Perhaps some men simply like raising children and don't really care if they parent their own or somebody else's. That may be true for some men, but as a general explanation for the prevalence of stepfathers, it is unsatisfactory, because, as we have discussed, stepfathers both invest less in their stepchildren than genetic fathers do and are more likely to abuse or even kill them than genetic fathers are.

Approaching the question from an evolutionary perspective leads us to compare the costs and benefits of being a stepparent. The costs include time and resources invested in another man's offspring. When we view only the costs, it seems unlikely that natural selection would favor being a stepparent. And yet there are presumably benefits derived from being a stepfather as well. Barbara Smuts (1985), discussing baboons, suggests that males provide care and protection for unrelated infants because these males receive reciprocal benefits from the infants' mothers. One potential benefit of being a stepfather is that investing in stepchildren allows a male to create and maintain a relationship with the children's mother (K. G. Anderson, Kaplan, and Lancaster 1999; Rohwer, Herron, and Daly 1999). We discussed at some length in Chapter 6 how parental care for offspring can be a form of mating effort. In fact, because stepchildren do not carry a man's genes, his investment in stepchildren can be only mating effort. All else being equal, women with children who are no longer in a relationship with the children's father should prefer a new partner who likes and willingly invests in her children, or at least tolerates them, over one who is actively hostile. Investing in stepchildren may both help men obtain mates and increase the quality or duration of men's relationships with the children's mothers.

Sometimes just the presence of the mother is enough to induce better behavior from stepfathers. Flinn (1988) found that men in Trinidad were much less likely to have agonistic interactions with stepchildren when the children's mothers were present than when the mothers were out of view, while the presence or absence of the mother did not influence men's agonistic interactions with genetic offspring.

Viewing stepparental care as mating effort implies that once the relationship with the mother has ended, stepfathers will cease most investment in stepchildren. Virtually no one has examined men's relationships with stepchildren after divorce; the existing research on postdivorce investment has focused almost exclusively on genetic offspring (see Chapter 6). In a study of beliefs about men's obligations to children following divorce, Lawrence Ganong, Marilyn Coleman, and Deborah Mistina (1995) found that "former stepfathers were almost universally seen as no longer obligated towards stepchildren. In fact, this is the clearest consensus found in this study" (313). In their study of Albuquerque men, K. G. Anderson, Kaplan, and Lancaster (1999) collected data on men's investments in stepchildren of both current and former partners. The results were as predicted: while men spent roughly as much money on stepchildren of current unions as they did on genetic children of previous unions, they spent essentially nothing on stepchildren of previous unions. Stepchildren of previous mates were also much less likely to attend college than stepchildren of current mates, and if stepchildren of previous mates did attend college, they were much less likely to get money from their former stepfathers. These are the only empirical measures of stepchildren from previous relationships that have come to our attention.

In many different ways, men engage in mating effort without investing in stepchildren. So why should men bother with stepchildren at all? Why not skip mothers with children altogether and focus the search for potential partners solely on women without children? In fact, many men do seek women without children, but the laws of supply and demand dictate whether they can achieve this goal (K. G. Anderson 2000). In cultures where divorce and nonmarital births are rare, most women looking for a spouse will not yet have children, and most men can marry without becoming a stepfather. When divorce and nonmarital births are common—as in contemporary American and European society—a large fraction of women seeking a spouse will bring children in tow. For many men, the choice is not between marrying a woman with or without children but between marrying a woman with children or not marrying at all (K. G. Anderson 2000). Investing in (or at least tolerating) stepchildren is the price many men are willing to pay to acquire a partner.

Stepfathers and Fertility

Do men substitute stepchildren for their own children? Specifically, if a man becomes a stepfather, does he forego reproduction within that marriage and raise stepchildren instead? How does the presence of stepchildren influence marital fertility? Several studies have found that stepchildren may decrease fertility within marriage (reviewed in Stewart 2002). Stewart (2002), using a nationally representative sample of American households, found that childbearing intentions decreased as the number of stepchildren increased; men with more stepchildren were less likely to desire new biological children within their marriages. However, she also found that actual fertility patterns were not suppressed by the presence of stepchildren. Kermyt Anderson (2000) examined this question using another nationally representative sample of American households. Because of the limitations of the data, he could only examine stepchildren within marriages; stepchildren occurring from cohabitating relationships, in which men live with an unmarried partner and her children, could not be identified in the data. In examining the probability of a birth occurring within a marriage, Anderson found that men with one stepchild were actually more likely than men with no stepchildren to father a child. There was no difference in fertility rate between men with two stepchildren and men with no stepchildren, while men with three stepchildren were less likely than men with no stepchildren to have a child. It is almost as if men with one stepchild were eager to supplement that stepchild with a genetic child by the same mother—and in fact some research has suggested that couples with stepchildren will have a child together to strengthen and validate their marital bond (Stewart 2005).

In the same study, Anderson also examined the total lifetime number of genetic children men had fathered, for men ages forty-five and older. For men who had ever been married, fertility decreased with each additional stepchild they had parented over their lifetimes, relative to men who had never had stepchildren. Men with one or two stepchildren each had about 0.8 fewer genetic offspring than men with no stepchildren, while men with three stepchildren had about 1.6

fewer offspring than men with no stepchildren. These numbers suggest that perhaps stepfathers do pay a fertility penalty for raising stepchildren. However, when compared to the alternative situation of never marrying, stepfathers seemed to be at an advantage. Men who had married without stepchildren had 2.76 more genetic offspring than did never-married men. Men who had raised one or two stepchildren over their lives had about 2 more births than did never-married men, while men who had raised three stepchildren had about 1.1 more births over their lifetimes than never-married men did. If the choice is between marrying a woman with children versus never marrying, men will have higher reproductive fitness if they become stepfathers.

In conclusion, the relationship between stepfathers and stepchildren is characterized by conflicts of interest as well as ambiguity regarding the roles men should play. Men invest less in stepchildren than in genetic children, but nonetheless men do invest substantial amounts in their stepoffspring. One explanation for this relatively high level of investment is that men are investing not in the children themselves but in the relationship with the children's mother. Proximate factors such as coresidence history, gender, and marital status do not appear to have a strong influence on the relationship with the stepchild. Stepfathers often go on to have genetic offspring within the new relationship, and while men who raise stepchildren tend to have fewer genetic offspring then men who marry women without children, stepfathers have much higher fertility than men who never marry at all. An evolutionary perspective provides some insight into why the stepfather/stepchild relationship can be so difficult—and also why so many men nonetheless are willing to give it a try.

8

Having it All?
Fatherhood, Male Social
Relationships, and Work

We commonly hear discussions of the challenges women face balancing work and family life. The discussions frequently highlight incompatibilities between care of young children and paid labor. These are large and important issues and ones previously addressed by evolutionary-informed social scientists (for example, Browne 2002; Hrdy 1999).

Our focus in this chapter is to consider analogous issues in men. Do men experience trade-offs between paternal investment and their work and broader social lives? Can fathers have all they desire: a combination of social status and resources obtained through their work, meaningful relationships with other men, and sufficient involvement in day-to-day family routines? We can begin pondering these questions with a focus on the lives of—who else?—nineteenth-century evolutionary theorists Charles Darwin and Alfred Russel Wallace. These men together gave us the theory of evolution by natural selection and, as we shall see, some insights into whether men can have it all. (Many, many excellent books on both Darwin and Wallace have been published; much of the following discussion draws on Quammen [2006] and Wallace [1905].)

In his early twenties, trying to find his place in the world, Charles Darwin undertook a five-year voyage aboard the HMS *Beagle*. During his travels around the globe, he collected fossils and cataloged tremendous biological diversity; in the years to follow, he became convinced of the fact of evolution—that species changed over time—and he eventually conceived of natural selection, a theory to explain the observed facts. Darwin's travels also laid the groundwork for a family. Darwin returned home a minor celebrity, writing a best-selling book about his adventures and natural history discoveries, meeting the intellectual luminaries of his day, and establishing his reputation as a first-rate naturalist. But it was not a complete life. In his late twenties, he determined to marry and have children. His career trajectory apparent, and with a comfortable allowance granted by his father, Darwin now sought to balance that achievement with his own family. After some deliberation, he sought the hand of his wealthy cousin, Emma Wedgwood, of the Wedgwood china family. It was a fertile union: Emma bore ten children, seven of whom survived to reach adulthood. Charles became a settled family man. He worked from home, studying and writing diligently in the study of the estate he purchased. Rarely traveling, in part because of illness but also because of family considerations, he never left the United Kingdom again.

But Darwin did combine family life with experiments. In an 1877 paper titled "A Biographical Sketch of an Infant," Darwin truly melded his fatherly ways with his scientific ones. He wrote, *"Moral Sense.—* The first sign of moral sense was noticed at the age of nearly 13 months: I said 'Doddy (his nickname) won't give poor papa a kiss,—naughty Doddy'. These words, without doubt, made him feel slightly uncomfortable; and at last when I had returned to my chair, he protruded his lips as a sign that he was ready to kiss me; and he then shook his hand in an angry manner until I came and received his kiss" (291).

Despite quite distinct upbringings—Wallace was born in Wales and raised in a working-class outskirt of London, in contrast to Darwin's childhood among the landed gentry—Alfred Russel Wallace's work and family life exhibit some parallels to Darwin's. In his mid-twenties, Wallace began his formidable international travels, first in Brazil for four years and later for another eight years in southeast Asia. His own boating adventures included losing, thanks to a ship fire and the need to bail out, almost all of the field notes and specimens acquired during his Brazilian work. Still, his collection of insects, skeletons, and pelts helped finance further voyages. The collections also fueled his scientific gains, including the co-discovery of natural selection. Wallace's reputation grew, though his finances were never on entirely firm ground. Amid his intellectual contributions, he too later established a family, though not until suffering a failed first attempt at marriage. His first proposal of marriage to a "Miss L——" was declined, later followed by her acceptance a year later and then her change of heart, when she again declined Wallace's proposal, leaving him to remark in his autobiography, "The blow was very severe, and I have never in my life experienced such intensely painful emotion" (Wallace 1905, 410.) After that episode, at the age of forty-four, Wallace married Annie Mitten in England. They had three children, two of whom survived beyond childhood. He continued to publish, edit, and give talks, to try to pay the family's bills (he also received a small government pension that Darwin helped him secure), but the number of days he spent in distant forays decreased.

At least three themes concerning, work, family, and male relationships in Darwin's and Wallace's lives stand out. The first is that they undertook dangerous, extensive, and ultimately fruitful work early in their adult lives. This work helped them establish the reputations and resources that made their later lives possible. Second, their status and career prospects were largely on course before they married and had children. Darwin and Wallace had already proved their worth as men, something that a potential bride (and her family) might appreciate. Third, they continued working throughout their family years, but in ways more compatible with it (working from home, minus the international travel). Family involvement also consumed some of the time they had previously spent with other men, suggesting a trade-off between the two social worlds. These themes appear to apply quite broadly to men, not just to famous natural historians. Indeed, in Darwin's prescient prose, his list of the pluses and minuses of marriage, jotted down in July 1838 before his engagement to his cousin Emma Wedgwood, included items suggestive of a trade-off between work, manly pursuits, and family: "Children—(if it Please God)—Constant companion, (& friend in old age) who will feel interested in one,—object to be beloved & played with.——better than a dog anyhow.—Home, & someone to take care of house—Charms of music & female chit-chat.—These things good for one's health.—*but terrible loss of time*" (Darwin 1838).

One way to examine these same issues of male work, family, and social relationships among today's men is with time allocation and social network data. These are quantitative data profiling how people spend their time and with whom, data acquired, for example, by asking how many hours today one spent engaged in paid labor versus caring for young children versus watching television. These kinds of time allocation and social network data can be obtained from retrospective questionnaires. This information can also be obtained from time-diary studies, in which subjects record their activities each day, perhaps while the day is unfolding or at the end of the day. And sometimes anthropologists obtain time data by observing people in their daily activities (for example, by following an individual around and noting at regular intervals what behaviors the person is engaged in—hunting, gathering, childcare, etc.). The specific methods by which behavior is measured may vary across studies, but regardless of the method, we can ask the question, what do such data reveal about men's work, family, and social lives?

Marriage itself has strong effects on men's time allocation, even before children arrive. Using a nationally representative sample of U.S. men, Steven Nock (1998) found that married men spend less time with friends or in bars but increased time with relatives, at church, or with co-workers. A more recent nationally representative U.S. time allocation study enables us to address shifts in men's time allocation in response to family life (Knoester and Eggebeen 2006). In this study, the arrival of a new coresidential child corresponded with a decrease in overall contact with extended family members, though more support was received from them. Men's overall socializing and leisure time decreased, while their participation in service organizations increased. Paid work hours increased significantly for new fathers. As a father's youngest coresidential child increased in age, men reported increases in socializing, including socializing with other family members.

In this same U.S. study, several alterations in men's time allocation also appeared when men fathered a new nonresidential child (that is, a child by a partner the man does not live with). These men's interactions with extended family increased, the men received more family support, and their social activities increased (rather than decreased, as is the case for men with coresidential children).

A smaller study of 137 couples in rural North Carolina, recruited prior to the birth of a first child, helps to further flesh out alterations in men's lives with the onset of fatherhood (Bost et al. 2002). In this study, participants reported on their social networks four times: when their partners were pregnant, three months postpartum, one year postpartum, and two years postpartum. Across this time span, men's family network sizes declined from about 5 members to 4, but their friendship networks dropped from approximately 2 to 1.25. The frequency of contact with family initially increased three months postpartum but declined thereafter. The frequency of contact with friends decreased postpartum.

Through a series of cross-sectional time allocation studies begun in 1965 and continued through the new millennium, we can see how men's time allocation changes across forty years in the United States (Bianchi, Robinson, and Milkie 2006). Those data reveal that men's time allocated to direct childcare remained relatively constant from 1965 to 1985, at approximately two and a half hours a week. However, that contribution has substantially risen in recent decades, to approximately seven hours weekly. Closer analyses demonstrate that men have continued to engage in more interactive fun activities (for example, sports) with children than women have, but what stands out is men's increased time given to changing diapers and cleaning and feeding children. Moreover, U.S. men have increased the amount of time devoted to household activities such as cleaning the dishes. Men's hours devoted to paid labor have remained constant across these forty years. The increases in U.S. men's time allocation to direct childcare and household tasks partially (but not completely) compensated for shifts in their wives' time allocation across these decades, with wives reducing time spent on household activities, providing relatively consistent time allocation to direct childcare, and showing substantial increases in hours spent in paid employment. It is quite difficult to separate men's and women's time allocation in this data set, as the efforts of men and women are pooled in a sexual division of labor (see Chapter 3); alterations in men's time allocation to some extent occur because they compensate for shifts in women's time allocation.

Men in many societies are under increasing pressure to be both good providers and highly involved fathers. In a 1999 national survey in the United States, 49% of people born before 1946 felt that both parents should be equally involved in raising children; for people born between 1965 and 1981, 82% felt that caregiving should be equally split (Bianchi, Robinson, and Milkie 2006). This increase in expectations has led to increasing difficulties in finding the right balance between work and family. A separate American survey found that men and women both feel that they spend less time with their family and more time working than they would prefer (Jacobs and Gerson 2004). As a result, fathers are much more likely than non-fathers to experience conflicts in balancing work, personal life, and family life; to experience interference between job and family; and to feel used up at the end of the work day. Jerry Jacobs and Kathleen Gerson (2004) used statistical modeling to predict whether people experience "negative spillover," a composite measure that basically indicates whether an individual's job prevents them from having sufficient time for themselves or their family. Not surprisingly, men and women who have children under eighteen were both much more likely to experience negative spillover.

Several larger cross-national studies provide similar types of data concerning men's time allocation and social networks. These studies vary in whether they contrast effects of marriage on men's lives or, additionally, reveal effects of fatherhood. In one of the largest and earliest international studies of this kind, Szalai (1972) compiled 1960s time allocation data from twelve nations, largely from Europe. In this compilation, married men spent less time with friends and relatives as well as less time with work colleagues, compared with unmarried men. In an international study of work, the more children married men have, the more their paid work hours tend to increase (Lee, McCann, and Messenger 2007).

Drawing on data collected between 1985 and 1992 from nine countries, such as Italy, Canada and the United States, on men aged eighteen to thirty-four, Anne Gauthier and Furstenberg Jr. (2002) found that partnered men spent less time engaged in social leisure than single men did, and in three countries, partnered men devoted more hours to work than single men did. Furthermore, and most important to the present discussion, fathers spent less time in social leisure, compared with partnered non-fathers, and in four of these countries fathers worked more hours than partnered non-fathers. In the United States, partnered fathers worked 0.8 hours more per day than did partnered non-fathers.

All these time allocation and social network data are well and good, but they hardly capture the scope of human diversity. How do male work, family, and social relationships play out in small-scale societies of hunter-gatherers, horticulturalists, or pastoralists? Very few studies have addressed this question. Raymond Hames (1992) examined time allocation in four Yanomamo villages. In two of the villages he found that men spent more time engaged in productive labor (such as gardening) as their number of dependent children increased. Using cross-sectional data on Tsimane forager-horticulturalists in Bolivia, Michael Gurven and others (Gurven et al. 2009) found that the amount of time men engage in wage labor and in fishing increases with fertility. Gurven and his colleagues (Gurven et al. 2009) interpret this to indicate that Tsimane who work harder have more children, but acknowledge that the causal arrow could be reversed, such that having more children induces Tsimane men to work harder.

Men's Time Allocation in Subsistence Societies

To further address men's time allocation in non-Western societies, we will examine men's time allocation patterns using data from six societies in which people earn their living primarily through subsistence activities (see Appendix tables 1 and 2). These are new results that have not been presented elsewhere, but we feel the question of men's time use in traditional societies has received sufficiently scant attention to warrant the inclusion of new data analysis in this chapter.

These time allocation data come from quantitative behavioral scans, in which an individual is followed and, at regular intervals (such as every thirty minutes), his or her current activity is recorded by the researcher. A record might read thus: 10:00 AM—direct childcare; 10:30 AM—working in garden; etc. One advantage of this method is that it provides an estimate of behaviors recorded by an observer, not filtered through the subject (who may introduce biases). Because the observations are taken at regular intervals, they can be used to construct measures of absolute and relative time allocation. This method is very useful for making quantitative comparisons. For example, we can compare time spent in childcare by women, men, and children or by fathers and non-fathers with and without their own children; we can also examine whether time spent varies by age, number of children, etc. Observational data collection of this sort is typically restricted to daylight hours and thus gives us an estimate of time allocation during daytime only.

Field-workers in different societies generally use their own activity codes for observed behaviors, tailoring the codes to the specific socio-ecology they are working in. For example, the activities we might expect to encounter in a pastoralist society, in which cattle herds are the main form of wealth, might differ from the behaviors commonly seen in an Amazonian mixed forager/horticulturalist society, in which most food comes from manioc (cassava) grown in gardens or meat hunted in the jungle. However, in an effort coordinated by Allen Johnson and colleagues, researchers in a number of societies converted their specific time activity codes into a set of standardized codes, allowing comparisons across cultures. These files are available through the HRAF, or Human Relations Area Files (A. Johnson and O. R. Johnson 1988). We will first briefly introduce the six societies whose data are used in the present analysis and then outline the standardized time allocation codes, before delving into what these data can tell us about the time use of fathers among people living in traditional societies. (For further details on the study methodology, see K. G. Anderson, Gray, et al. n.d.)

Ethnographic Background of the Six Societies in the Sample

1. The Efe are full-time hunters and gatherers living in the Ituri Forest in northeastern Zaire (now the Democratic Republic of the Congo) (Bailey and Peacock 1988). They hunt exclusively with bows and arrows and exchange foraged resources for cultivated goods (particularly manioc and peanuts) with their agriculturalist Lese neighbors. The Efe do not grow food themselves, though they do occasionally work in Lese gardens. About 65% of the Efe's calories come from agricultural foods, and 14% from gathered plants, 13.5% from honey, and 8.5% from hunted meat. Monogamy is the primary marriage system, with only 3% of marriages being polygynous.

2. The Kipsigis are an agropastoralist group living in southwestern Kenya (Borgerhoff Mulder, Kerr, and Moore 1997). They farm maize and millet (both making up about 60% of calories consumed) and raise cattle, goats, and sheep for milk, blood, and meat. Surplus maize is often sold for cash. Polygyny is widespread among the Kipsigis, with 52% of marriages being polygynous.

3. The Madurese are agriculturalists living in the island of Madura in Indonesia (G. Smith 1995). Over 92% of their calories come from maize, manioc, and rice, and tobacco is grown as a cash crop. In addition, cattle are raised, primarily for draft labor and for dung. Because of centuries of cultivation, virtually no forested land exists in the Madurese region. Only 2% of marriages are polygynous.

4. The Machiguenga of Shimaa practice mixed horticulture and hunting and gathering in the tropical rainforest of Peru (A. Johnson and O. R. Johnson 1988). Gardens provide over 90% of the calories in their diet, and they grow primarily manioc and maize. Most families have a few chickens and ducks, but the Machiguenga also engage in bow-and-arrow hunting as well as in fishing. Over a quarter (27%) of marriages are polygynous.

5. The Ye'kwana are Amazonian horticulturalist-foragers living in Venezuela (Hames 1993). About 75% of their diet (by weight) comes from manioc and plantain, both of which they grow themselves. They

also hunt, using bows and arrows and shotguns, and fish. Polygyny occurs at low levels (about 12% of marriages).

6. The Yukpa of Yurmutu are Amazonian horticulturalists living in Venezuela (Paolisso and Sackett 1988). About 65% of their calories are derived from maize, bananas, and plantains, with taro and arrowroot comprising another 27%. Coffee is also grown as a cash crop, and the Yukpa's diet is supplemented by hunting and fishing, as well as by foods purchased through coffee sales. Only 8% of marriages are polygynous.

Standardized Time Allocation Codes

The codes used for each society differed, both in the specific activities researchers captured as well as in the detail of the coding. Every research team used at least dozens of behavior codes; some used hundreds. The standardized behavior codes regroup these various coding schemes into about sixty specific behavior codes, which are organized into ten main areas; we will briefly describe these main areas (see Appendix table 1) because they will feature prominently in our analysis. *Commercial activities* are behaviors geared toward the production of money or trade goods, activities such as raising cash crops, selling or bartering, or wage labor. *Food production* includes agricultural activities, gathering, hunting, fishing, and herding. *Eating* includes food consumption activities. *Housework* including tidying and cleaning chores, including fetching water and fuel. *Individual activities* include nonsocial behaviors that do not fit well into other categories; individual activities include hygiene, idleness, napping, individual religious observance, etc. *Manufacturing* includes making or repairing clothes, implements, roads, traps, etc. *Food preparation* includes cooking food or processing it for storage or later consumption. (Two other standardized code activities—activities "away from the community" and "other" [for activities that do not fit well into any of the above activity codes] are grouped together into a single *all else* category for the present analysis.)

The family of standardized activity codes labeled *social activities* includes activities that are characterized by social exchanges, that is, activities involving more than one person. This is the only group we will disaggregate into its component behaviors, because we are especially interested in some of them. In particular, we will examine *childcare*, which includes direct childcare, such as holding, washing, dressing, etc. (This measure does not include indirect forms of childcare such as passive babysitting.) *Education* includes teaching or learning activities in a social context. *Care of a non-child* is just that, care of an adult, and this category also includes being cared for. *Ritual* activity includes group ceremonial, ritual, or political activities. *Recreational* activity includes watching or being involved in social entertainment activities. *Chatting* includes socializing, chatting, or visiting. Lastly, *unknown social* activity includes other forms of social activity, type unknown.

The time allocation codebooks contain demographic data for most of the individuals in the time allocation data set. From these, we created variables indicating the sex, age, and fertility of each person in the data set. Our main research question is whether men's time use differs for fathers and non-fathers, and thus for the present analysis we have restricted the data to men ages seventeen through fifty-four, the ages during which men are most likely to have dependent offspring. Men whose fertility was unknown were excluded from the analysis. The data set used for the present analysis (see Appendix table 1) contains 12,518 scan observations of 196 men from six societies. We used these scans to calculate for each man in the data set the average percentage of scans that fell into each of the time use categories summarized above. Thus, for example, one Efe man spent 13.7% of his observed time in commercial activities, 22% in food production, 4.7% eating, etc. The unit of analysis is thus an individual man in the data set.

Before we proceed with the results of our study, it is worth noting a few limitations of the data. The scan sampling methodology means that only one behavior is captured at a time, even though in practical terms people are often doing multiple things at once. For example, a person might be working in his garden and chatting with his neighbor simultaneously. In those cases, the researchers usually coded whichever behavior was more prominent or more important. As we have noted above, samples were gathered only from dawn the dusk, that is, during daytime hours, and thus do not capture the frequency of behaviors throughout the evening, when some activities, such as direct childcare, might be more common among individuals who are engaged in economically productive activities during the day. The standardized data codes also do not indicate with whom the actor is interacting; thus, for childcare, for example, we cannot say whether an individual is interacting with his own or with others' children. (Many if not all of the researchers collected such data, but it is not available in the standardized data set.) Finally, the time scans record how often people engaged in a given activity but do not measure how hard they worked at it. One man may spend less time hunting than another, for example, but if the first is a better hunter, he might actually bring home more meat in less time. This lack of detail in level of work may be an issue if fathers work more efficiently than non-fathers, but measuring this difference is beyond the scope of the data.

Results: Men's Time Allocation in Six Societies

Men's time allocation varies tremendously across the six cultures in the study, as befits their different subsistence ecologies and marriage systems. (Appendix tables and 1 and 2 provide detailed descriptive statistics; we will summarize the highlights here.)

Averaging across societies, we see that men in these cultures spend most of their time in food production (20.9% across societies), chatting (14.6%), commercial activities (13.2%), and individual activities, such as grooming, napping, or doing nothing (11.1%). Those four categories alone account for 59.9% of men's time.

As noted earlier, social activity is the only broad grouping that we have disaggregated into its component time categories, in large part because we are especially interested in one particular social interaction, childcare. Men spend very little time on childcare—only 0.8% of daytime hours, on average. This figure may seem low, but recall that this is active childcare, not more passive forms of childcare, such as availability or proximity, and it is care for children of all ages, not just infants. As we reviewed in Chapter 2, men in most cultures spend very little time directly holding children, a pattern our data support.

Do the time-activity patterns of fathers differ from those of men without children in these cultures? We can compare time allocation for fathers and non-fathers in four of the six societies. (The Madurese and Ye'kwana are excluded from table 2 because all of the men sampled have children.) The results suggest that time patterns do vary by fatherhood status for many activities. Fathers spend about 16% of their time in commercial activities (such as raising cash crops, selling, or bartering, etc.), while non-fathers spend only 6.9% of their time attempting to earn money. This is one of the largest differences we observe between fathers and non-fathers. Time spent in food production also varies by fatherhood status, but not in the way we would have expected: non-fathers spend significantly more time (23%) growing crops, fishing, or hunting than fathers do (19%).

Fathers and non-fathers also differ in their use of social time. As expected, fathers spend more time on childcare than non-fathers do, although even fathers spend little more than 1% of their time directly caring for children. Social time spent acquiring or giving education, information, or socialization varies tremendously by fatherhood status, with non-fathers spending over 12% of their time on this form of social activity, while fathers spend less than one half of one percent. At a nearly 12% mean difference, this is the largest single way in which fathers and non-fathers spend time differently. Non-fathers also have more time for chatting and socializing (18% versus 15% for fathers). Fathers spend more time than non-fathers in other social activities or unknown social activities—about 11% versus 6%. It is difficult to draw much of a conclusion about this final category, because we lack details about precisely what activities fall under these "none of the above" categories, which also include time spent away from the community.

Finally, we wanted to examine whether men's time use changes as their fertility increases. Statistical analyses (not presented here) suggest there is no significant relationship between men's parity (number of children) and most measures of time allocation. Four measures of time use were correlated with men's parity, however. For three of these, the relationship between fertility and time use is positive: as their number of children increases, men spend more time in commercial activities, in other social activities, and in unknown social activities. One form of time use shows a negative relationship with fertility: men with more children have less time for "all else," a catchall category that includes any forms of time use not captured under the other categories.

These results suggest that the answer to our question, do fathers in subsistence-level societies use time differently from non-fathers? is a qualified yes. Most activities, such as eating, household activities, individual activities, manufacturing, and food preparation, exhibit little variation by paternal status or parity. The key domains in which fathers and non-fathers differ are economic productivity and social behavior. Fathers spend more time than non-fathers in commercial activities, childcare, and "other" and "unknown" social activities, while non-fathers spend more time in food production, social educational activities, and chatting. In this sense, fatherhood impinges on men in subsistence cultures in fairly similar ways to men in industrialized societies: fathers work harder and have less time for certain kinds of socializing than non-fathers do.

Major Themes of Fatherhood and Time Use

What themes stand out in these kinds of time allocation and social network studies? A major conclusion is that while men's work hours do exhibit differences depending on whether these men have children, these differences, while real, are relatively small. The main reason for that pattern is that men's continued work throughout prime adult years is taken as a given. Work serves as one of the main avenues through which men establish their relative social status (other avenues may include affiliations in religious groups, political abilities, and so forth). The status (and self-worth) derived from men's work makes sense when we view this as a human equivalent of a primate male's striving for the status that confers reproductive benefits. Indeed, much of men's value to their long-term mates and their children derives from the resources men provide, and only a select set of circumstances would favor men's voluntarily withdrawing from the paid workforce postpartum (more on those circumstances below). Fathers clearly do not exhibit the same time allocation challenges mothers face, nor do men show dramatic fluctuations in work centered on parenting.

All that being said, what variation in time allocated to work men do exhibit depending on parental status appears responsive to a host of factors. And these factors may help explain why in some contexts men's work hours increase whereas in other contexts they remain the same. If a man's wife leaves the paid workforce postpartum without paid governmental leaves or additional financial support from kin, men may increase their work hours to help allay some of the lost income; this pattern may characterize some U.S. fathers, for example. Among the hunter-gatherer Hadza of northern Tanzania, women's foraging returns tend to decline during the initial year or two postpartum; husbands appear to help make up for the resource losses by increasing the amount of calories they acquire during this "critical period" of male provisioning (Marlowe 2003).

The scant data available on men's social networks suggest that family life commonly entails a reduction in men's leisure time, particularly leisure time spent with other men. Men's social lives focus more on family at the expense of time previously spent with male friends and kin. The time when this change is most dramatic occurs during the initial transition from bachelorhood to marriage and fatherhood. For example, among Efe foragers, single young adult men spend much of their time with other men, but after marriage they spend more time in proximity to their wives than to anyone else (Bailey and Aunger 1990). Darwin himself, in his 1838 note listing the pros and cons of marriage, lamented the loss of the "conversation of clever men at clubs" that marriage would entail. Perhaps there are subtle fluctuations in men's social networks, fluctuations depending on the age of their children, but these are dwarfed by the initial entry into family life and the way children eventually move out from under men's care. The main time allocation trade-off fathers appear to face, then, is one between leisure activities spent with other men versus direct interactions with a wife and young children. To the degree these are mutually exclusive, as suggested by some of the data reviewed above, men cannot quite have it all.

Cross-culturally, other circumstances may influence men's time spent with children. When fraternal interest groups—groups of related males—are socially important, these can favor men's continuing to spend the bulk of their prime adult years together at the expense of more intimate marital relationships and direct care of children (J. Whiting and B. Whiting 1975; D. R. White and Burton 1988). Fraternal interest groups arc important wherever high rates of intergroup aggression prevail among small-scale societies, as throughout much of the Amazon Basin or the Papua New Guinea Highlands. Indeed, in many Highland New Guinea societies, such as the Sambia, men view women as pollutants, and strict rules limit cross-gender contact and interactions; this view is perhaps culturally sensible if emotional investment in a wife could compromise a man's ability to form the strong male-male relationships required to protect his family and community in the face of high rates of intergroup violence. In addition, powerful fraternal interest groups commonly arise among pastoralists. If a man's wealth resides in his livestock, he might form strong male-male bonds useful in defending these stores of wealth, as well as in stealing these mobile resources from enemies. The strength of these male-male bonds may come at the expense of more intimate family time and relationships.

To summarize, in societies characterized by strong male-male bonds, weak marital relationships, and little direct paternal care, the nature of male work, family, and social relationships differs from that of other societies. Men in societies that emphasize male-male bonds experience less of a shift in their male-male relationships after marriage and father-hood. These men may also face little need to adjust their work hours postpartum, particularly to help at all in direct childcare. In extreme cases, such as the sex-segregated Bedouin of the Negev or some High-land New Guinea communities, the trade-off in men's allocation appears to fall in favor of investment in male-male relationships in place of intimate family life.

All the male work, family, and social relationship patterns discussed so far paint quite broad societal strokes. That is, among all men in a given society such as the United States or the Sambia of New Guinea, we have attempted to characterize the impacts of family life on men's time allocation and social networks. Clearly, though, a variety of other factors impinge upon these general characterizations. What are some of the additional factors shaping men's work, family, and male-male social relationships both within and between societies?

One set of considerations is that men may face different work, fam-ily, and male-male relationships equations, depending on their status, wealth, and physical attractiveness. A model based on mating markets (see Chapter 3) might predict that individuals who rank higher than their spouses will have a bargaining advantage, allowing the higher-ranked individuals to invest less in their partners or their children. This prediction has not been tested in any great detail but has received some empirical support. Among Mayan men living in Belize, David Wayn-forth (1999) found that men's retrospective time allocation differed depending on their facial attractiveness: on their last day not working, more-attractive men spent more time engaged in mating effort and less time with relatives. Similarly, in a sample of American college students, Steve Gangestad and Randy Thornhill (1995) found that men who were more symmetrical—a trait that is correlated with phenotypic quality and attractiveness—invested less time in their relationships with women and also sexually pursued other women more, relative to men who were less symmetrical (a trait correlated with being less attractive). Further support comes from Nock (1998), who found, using multi-variate regression on a sample of American men, that as men's ranking on the marriage market declines, they work more weeks per year.

Another important variable is the nature of the job market. The days in which colonial men farmed and raised families on the same land, as subsistence agriculturalists around the world have done, are diminishing. Indeed, approximately half the world's population now lives in urban settings, a rapid rise from only around 20% at 1900 (Heymann 2006). In their place is arising unpredictable paid labor that entails commutes or migrations, with or without entire families moving. With moves, families may be extracted from extended kin networks that otherwise would provide help. These transformations in work and family life often leave working parents without a strong safety net. As one consequence, 27% of families in Mexico, 48% of families in Botswana, and 19% of families in Vietnam reported having had to leave a child younger than age five either at home alone or in the care of an unpaid older child (Heymann 2006).

Another consequence of global shifts in the labor market is that men may live apart from their wives and children for extended periods, in the pursuit of the resources their families need. That separation may be seasonal (as, for example, when Jamaican hotel employees work summers in U.S. resorts) or extend over years (as, for example, when construction workers' residency status prohibits easy returns to a native country). These migratory labor patterns may result in children being sent to live with other relatives while one or both parents seek employment. Throughout Africa, for example, children are commonly fostered with kin, because of wide-ranging labor migration. In South Africa, over 30% of black children live in households that are composed primarily of half siblings, grandparents, aunts, uncles, cousins, or more distant kin (K. G. Anderson 2005). The negative effects of living with distant relatives are partially offset by the higher income in these foster households, suggesting that parents are preferentially placing their children with families who can afford to invest in their offspring. Nonetheless, South African children fostered with more distant kin are further behind in school, have less money spent on their clothes, and are less likely to receive medical care when sick. One study in Cape Town, South Africa, found that 13.6% of black children were nonorphaned foster children, a figure that is roughly equivalent to the number of nonfostered orphans (K. G. Anderson and Beutel n.d.). Migration for economic reasons reduces parents' ability to invest in children and often has negative consequences for the children involved.

Yet another consequence of global labor market shifts is that mothers' and fathers' time may be less pliable if a family emergency arises. If a paid employer refuses to allow parents to leave work to tend to children, particularly if other alternate caregivers such as grandmothers or daycare centers are unavailable, parents' economic productivity may be strained. In an extensive study of international work and family concerns, including interviews with men in Mexico, Botswana, Vietnam, the United States, Honduras, and Russia, fully 27% of men said they had lost pay when caring for a sick child (Heymann 2006). Moreover, 28% of fathers reported losing job promotions or experiencing difficulties in retaining jobs because of a sick child, and 44% of men said they had faced work difficulties while caring for a sick child or performing other caregiving.

Another factor impacting men's work, family, and relationship lives is governmental policy. This effect is apparent in the recent history of paternal leaves. Sweden was the first country to provide for paternity leave; since 1974 Sweden has allowed new fathers to take time off from work to help care for their children (O'Brien, Brandth, and Kvande 2007). By 2006 in Norway, fathers were given six weeks of paternity leave during the first year of their newborn's life, time that could not be transferred to the child's mother. Approximately sixty countries, including these Scandinavian ones, provide paternity leaves that are at least partially paid, meaning that men continue to draw at least part of their regular salary while away from work. In countries such as Australia and the United States, where paternity leaves are not paid, men's economic circumstances may impact their leaves: Australian men often use paid vacation time immediately postpartum, and poorer Australian men take shorter leaves after the birth of a child (Whitehouse, Diamond, and Baird 2007). Adrienne Burgess and Sandy Ruxton (2000) report that British men take an average of two days off after a child's birth, with a third of these men taking eight days or more; most of this is informal leave, via sick days, rather than formal paternity leave.

If you are a father looking for the best paternity leave policy, perhaps you should move to Iceland. Fathers are given three months, mothers three months, and both parents another three months of paternal leave that they can divide as they wish (for example, two months for the mother, one for the·father) during the first year and a half of their child's life (O'Brien, Brandth, and Kvande 2007). While on leave, parents are paid 80% of their prebirth salary. Parents are entitled to another thirteen weeks of unpaid annual parental leave. How are Icelandic men responding to such policies? As many as 90% of fathers take parental leave, for an average of 97 days, just over half of the 180 days that mothers take.

Psychological Dimensions of the Work-Family Trade-off

Throughout this chapter, we have portrayed the impacts of fatherhood on men's time allocation and social networks, and some of the reasons accounting for these patterns. The data, however, do not tell us how men evaluate the allocation decisions they face. Do men feel stressed by trying to balance their work and family lives? Do fathers such as Darwin and Wallace express sadness at a loss of time spent in leisure with other men? To answer these questions, we need to move beyond numbers and make use of other kinds of data, such as qualitative data obtained from interviews and participant observation.

In an international study of predominantly male managers from eighteen countries, including Latin American, east Asian, and European samples, researchers attempted to quantify work-family pressure (Spector, Allen, and Poelmans 2005), which was measured with a set of questions concerning issues like "demands my work makes on relationships with spouse/children." Respondents indicated measurable work-family pressures across the samples, with levels highest in Taiwan and Hong Kong and lowest in Australia and the United Kingdom. Interestingly, in only three samples (the United States, the United Kingdom, and Australia) were work hours significantly and positively correlated with work-family pressures. Work-family pressures were not consistently correlated with number of children, though these pressures quite consistently leaned toward poorer job satisfaction, poorer mental well-being, and poorer physical well-being. Such data suggest that male managers are commonly strained in the attempt to have it all.

Talk to fathers and they may articulate the challenges involved in balancing their work and family lives. In 2001, Peter Gray interviewed approximately one hundred Swahili men in Kenya about their work and family lives as part of his dissertation research (P. B. Gray, unpublished data). One theme that sticks out from those interviews is how commonly men described the challenges of successfully providing the resources (particularly Kenyan shillings) their wives and children needed. For their wives to cook the meals all the family ate, men needed to provide them with money to purchase food; for their children to attend the schools that would enhance their prospects in life, men needed to largely cover the costs of requisite school fees and of uniforms and other school supplies. In a market economy with unpredictable labor, everything eventually costs money, and men expressed concerns over being able to meet these perceived obligations. The link between a man's work and the income generated from it clearly impacted the success a man achieved in meeting his family's needs, and his own self-worth. Yet it was still not clear whether fathers perceived less opportunity to spend time with other men or other kinds of trade-offs.

These Kenyan perspectives are far from isolated. Japanese men describe their love for their children but also the reasons they choose to stay late at work or develop business relationships on a golf course rather than spend time with their children (Ishii-Kuntz 1993). Men from a working-class San Francisco Bay neighborhood recount the meaning of their work and family lives (Townsend 2002). These U.S. men sought success at work, in part to help provide each of their families with a house and other material requirements (part of what Townsend calls "the package deal"). The men juggled issues such as how far to commute to work in relation to the cost of a house, and the quality of the public school district in which their children would enroll. The men connected their work to their self-worth and family well-being. In their responses, we find a subtlety and an individualized emotional struggle that may not manifest in quantitative time allocation data, and a response that says that men strive to find their way through work, family, and male-male relationship trade-offs.

So where does this foray into work, family, and male-male relationships leave us? Some key messages extracted along our journey include the following. Men do face a juggling act of work, family, and male-male relationships, but that act is quite distinct from the one women face. Men's work remains a relative constant across parenting; men's work hours may display subtle shifts, such as increases in the postpartum period or with increasing numbers of children, but we do not find the long-lasting declines in economic work that many women experience. Indeed, that is hardly an option for most men. One of the reasons they were selected as mates was their provisioning abilities, and men as social primates also tend to strive for the status that success at work commonly provides. Apart from work, however, men's time spent in leisure activities with other men often declines with marriage and fatherhood, especially during the initial transition from life as a bachelor to that of a family man. Some exceptions to that pattern may occur where fraternal interest groups are particularly strong. Herein lies the main time allocation challenge many fathers face: a trade-off not between work and family time but between investment in relationships with other adult men through shared leisure activities versus direct involvement in intimate family life. Still, men's family time may be modulated, to some degree, by work factors such as mode of subsistence and wife's employment. Because the waking time men spend in direct childcare tends to be relatively modest across and within societies, these adjustments do not appear to generate pronounced trade-offs between work and direct childcare. Men's own voices suggest that the desire to "have it all" entails challenges, but the trade-offs men face are inherently different from those experienced by women.

9

The Descent of Dad's Sexuality

A man encounters a spirit child during sleep and directs it to his wife to help her conceive. A man's fluid mixes with menstrual blood to make a new life. A man's sperm penetrates a woman's egg to form a fertilized egg that might grow into a full-blown fetus. As these anecdotes reveal, humans have conceived many ways of describing the links between sex and fatherhood. A biomedical understanding is the latest and the one built on a foundation of science. Because this biomedical understanding is so recent, however, we are left with fundamental questions concerning how humans (and other animals) have been able to conceptualize the links between sex and reproduction. This is but the first of various facets of paternal sexuality that we address in the present chapter. As a major focus, we consider how men's sexual behavior changes after conception (the word "descent" in the chapter title forecasts those changes) but also address a variety of other issues concerning links between fatherhood and sexual life.

Cross-Cultural Conception Beliefs

Are men universally believed to play some physiological role in conception? Do men contribute some essential physical essence to create a life? In the majority of human societies in which conception beliefs have been documented by anthropologists, links are made between male substances and conception. Suzanne Frayser (1985, 286) observes that 62% of twenty-six societies for which she had data posit some physiological basis for conception. Typically a physiological basis means that during intercourse men provide some sort of fluid—semen—that contributes to a successfully pregnancy. According to these conception beliefs, the mixing of male semen with female bodily fluids, usually menstrual blood, accounts for the cessation of menstruation once conception has occurred. This belief does not lead to sex during menses, however. In fact, menses tends to be the one period of a woman's ovulatory cycle when coital frequency is universally low (Ford and Beach 1951). Many cultures believe that sex outside of menses enables the combination of a woman's blood (that would otherwise flow during menses) with a man's semen to beget a new life.

Many of these conception beliefs do not assume that a single male orgasm is sufficient for conception (Frayser 1985; Gregersen 1994). Repeated male ejaculation may be required for conception to take place and for a pregnancy to continue. Repeated ejaculation may clog up the womb, allowing male fluids to coalesce with menstrual blood to establish a pregnancy, a belief shared among Solomon Islanders and the Wogeo of New Guinea, among other societies. If a Chimbu woman in New Guinea becomes pregnant after having sex only a few times with her husband, the woman is suspected of having sex with other men.

The exceptions to a male physiological contribution to conception have been largely confined to aboriginal Australia and New Guinea (Gregersen 1994). Anthropologists working in nineteenth-century Australia recorded native beliefs suggesting that conception took place when a spirit child was channeled into a woman. A man did not need to ejaculate into a woman to establish a pregnancy. These beliefs were also recorded among societies such as the Aranda and Trobriand Islanders. Unfortunately, later scholarship has not fully resolved whether these "beliefs" were actually believed. The concept of a spirit child may have been metaphor even to locals, with semen a necessary component after all. Among the Tiwi of northern Australia, for example, a man must first dream of a child and then have intercourse with the child's mother for conception to occur (Goodale 1971).

If a male physiological contribution to reproduction is typically recognized, little evidence suggests that conception has been explicitly linked to midcycle physiology, when females are capable of becoming pregnant. An egg lasts only around one day after ovulation, and sperm can survive around two to four days after ejaculation, meaning that intercourse must occur during the fleeting days that a viable egg and sperm can meet (Wilcox et al. 2004). Instead, conception beliefs typically suggest that intercourse at any time apart from menses tends to foster conception. Among Hadza hunter-gatherers of Tanzania, about half of men and women believe that conception is most likely to occur shortly after menstruation, with the timing of conception spread across the cycle among remaining respondents (Marlowe 2004).

A few studies suggest, contrary to common conception beliefs, that human female proceptivity (the active seeking of sex) and sexual activity may exhibit cycle-related changes, including peaks in sexual behavior around the time of ovulation (reviewed in Brewis and Meyer 2005). Among the Huli of New Guinea, a society characterized by spatial segregation between spouses and beliefs that men are polluted by contact with their wives, couples are supposed to have sex only on days eleven to fourteen of the wife's ovulatory cycle (Wardlow 2008). These are very close to the actual days a woman can conceive. This Huli case is remarkably unusual, however. In two of the best-designed studies involving North American pair-bonded (but childless) females, increases in intercourse frequency occurred in the days prior to and around ovulation (Bullivant et al. 2004; Wilcox et al. 2004). These studies included urine collection for hormone assay and cycle phase assignment, making them more accurate than standard question-based cycle phase inferences (for example, assuming that ovulation takes place about fifteen days after a woman reports her last menses began). It takes a well-designed study to find these subtle effects, and as we shall see, they appear to be small compared to the alterations in sexual behavior undertaken during pregnancy and the postpartum period.

Taking some of these early and variable conception beliefs and related sexual behavior together, we can see several patterns appear. Conception is typically linked with sex, and a male contribution in the form of his semen. Linking sex with reproduction confers paternity upon a male mate. Repeated intercourse also favors attribution of paternity to a consistent partner rather than to a brief extrapair fling. Little evidence suggests that conception has been explicitly linked to midcycle female physiology, however. Rather, the belief is that intercourse at any time apart from menses tends to foster conception. There may be cycle-related shifts in sexual behavior, including increased female proceptivity and sexual activity around the time of ovulation, but these effects appear to be subtle and inconsistently detected. More striking are reductions in sexual behavior during menses and largely consistent sexual access during the remainder of a cycle.

Biomedical Approaches to Conception

As a counterpart to these ethnographic examples of conception beliefs, biomedical research has increasingly revealed the intimate details of conception. The combination of egg and sperm to create a zygote is a familiar example of this scientific understanding. How do males play their part in conception?

Males begin producing sperm at puberty. The onset of sperm production is less dramatic in males than menarche, or first menstruation, in females. Male pubertal onset can be identified in several ways—for example, by measuring increases in the size of males' testes, asking males when they had their first "wet dream" (an ejaculation during sleep), or observing increases in reproductive hormones such as luteinizing hormone (LH) (Worthman 1999). In the United Kingdom, male pubertal onset, as indexed by elevations in LH, is around 11.5 years. That is younger than in many other societies. Among the Kikuyu of Kenya, LH surges begin around age 12.5, and among the hunter-gatherer Hadza of Tanzania, LH increases begin around age 15. Nutritional availability, activity patterns, and disease loads appear to contribute to the variation in male pubertal onset, including decreases in male age of puberty in places such as the United States.

Male sperm production begins before males are "men." That is, a scrawny teenage male can produce sperm even before he has fully developed the secondary sexual characteristics, such as upper body musculature and facial hair, that distinguish him as an adult (Bribiescas 2006). The reason for early sperm production appears to be physiological cost: sperm are cheap (but muscles aren't). Sperm can be produced using a small proportion of a male's energetic budget, enabling his capacity to fertilize a female on the off chance he has a reproductive opportunity. This context contrasts with that of females, in which secondary sexual characteristics such as breasts begin to develop before gametes are produced, a reflection of the much greater female physiological requirement for reproduction.

Sperm production occurs continuously during a man's postpubertal life. A cycle of sperm production takes approximately ninety days and begins to unfold in the recesses of the testes. Within the Sertoli cells, immature sperm begin their journey, moving onto the epididymis and vas deferens, where they mature before eventually being stored in accessory organs before ejaculation. Along this course, a sperm is honed for its task: because it must travel (rather than wait for an arriving female gamete), it contains few organelles (no cytoplasm, just a few mitochondria providing a bit of energy) and has a tail attached to aid its travels. A sperm is a streamlined gene machine. Millions of them are eventually released together at orgasm, with a rare one finding genetic immortality, the rest becoming evolutionary dead ends. In any event, demise comes quickly: mature ejaculated sperm survive only two to four days.

The semen ejaculated along with sperm contains lots of helpful things: fructose, which provides an energy source, to help fuel the sperm toward an egg; bicarbonates, which help neutralize the acidic vagina, in order to pave the way to conception; prostaglandins, which may help foster smooth muscle contractions and lower immune responses in female reproductive tracts, to help sperm on their way to an egg; and prostate-specific antigen (PSA), made famous as a molecular marker of prostate cancer risk, which also helps liquefy semen after ejaculation, giving sperm contained in it a chance to swim rather than remain stuck (Dixson 2009). Semen even contains hormones such as testosterone and estrogen, which are capable of absorption through the vaginal wall, leading some to speculate whether semen might have psychological effects on women (Gallup, Burch, and Platek 2002). These ancillary compounds aid the male initiative to create a new life. Interestingly, semen quality (for example, the percentage of sperm that are motile) produced from intercourse surpasses that from masturbation, suggesting that reproduction can enhance sexual function (Shackelford, Pound, and Goetz 2005).

Semen parameters (and the primary and accessory sexual organs that produce them) reflect, in part, the specifics of our ancestors' mating ways. As highlighted in earlier chapters, most of human reproduction occurs within contexts of long-term mating relationships. The consequence is that human reproductive physiology reflects relatively low pressures of sperm competition, or competition between sperm of different men within a female's reproductive tract. Human men, unlike many mammalian males subject to intense sperm competition, produce lots of poor-quality sperm, possess sperm with small midpieces, and have modestly sized seminal vesicles used to produce the bulk of semen (Dixson 1998). A comparison with our closest living relatives—chimpanzees and bonobos, who have both relatively large testes and stronger sperm competition—illustrates our derived reproductive physiology.

While the gametes must be aligned for conception to take place, it is readily apparent that almost all attempts at conception are failures. That is the norm. Besides the obvious superfluous production of sperm (of which all but one or two out of millions must fail in a given attempt), a variety of other reasons explain failed conceptions upon ejaculation. Some of these too are obvious: a female partner was not of reproductive age (postmenopausal), reproductive status (was not cycling, perhaps immediately after giving birth), was not in the fertile time in the ovulatory cycle, or was sterile (as the result, say, of a sexually transmitted infection). Infertility research indicates that approximately 30% of cases are traceable to a "male contribution," suggesting that a variety of male factors appear to contribute to different fertility outcomes (Bentley and Mascie-Taylor 2000).

The male contribution to infertility may trace to problems with a man's sperm. In the course of sperm production, mutations inevitably arise. A mutated sperm may have too many of a given type of chromosome or exhibit other problems with a specific locus on a chromosome. Either way, mutations tend to be bad things, even if occasionally they give rise to something helpful and new. Mutations present in sperm also tend to increase with paternal age, in part because the mutation-control machinery functions less efficiently with advancing age (Tarin, Brines, and Cano 1998). As a result of gametes gone awry, men provide the bulk of mutations present in the next generation.

Male sperm problems may be not just genetic, however, but also epigenetic. The term "epigenetic" refers to molecular modifications to genes (Jablonka and Lamb 2005). For example, a gene may be methylated (have a methyl group added to it) during an organism's development, because of environmental exposure. One of the most fascinating examples is the variable methylation of the glucocorticoid receptor in newborn rat offspring, resulting from the kinds of maternal care they receive (Weaver et al. 2004). Because the glucocorticoid receptor is involved in the body's stress response, methylation patterns can alter the individual's subsequent expression of that gene in ways related to its early social experience. Even more striking, these methylation patterns not only are retained throughout an individual's lifetime but may also be passed to subsequent generations. This passing on of methylation patterns represents a kind of inheritance of acquired characteristics.

What does that have to do with male sperm? It is unclear what proportion of the "male contribution to infertility" and lesser fertility challenges occur thanks to genetic versus epigenetic causes. The assumption has been that genetic causes are primary. New research on environmental endocrine disruptors suggests that epigenetic causes should be considered too. Rat males treated with vinclozolin, which has antiandrogen properties, exhibit alterations in methylation that can be detected (and that result in their being shunned as mates) three generations later (Crews et al. 2007).

What about other reasons why semen may fail to fertilize? Problems with any of the accessory compounds may be important. If a man has his prostate gland, a key accessory gland producing semen components, removed for reasons such as prostate cancer, how much does that impact his ability to fertilize an egg? To our knowledge, this question has not been answered in the scientific literature. However, the removal of male accessory glands in other species, such as hamsters, does compromise their fertility (Chow and O 1989).

Another reason for infertility may be male-female incompatibility. We are accustomed to thinking of personality incompatibility in our day-to-day social experiences. But sometimes our molecules just can't get along with those of someone else. An example of this would be Rh incompatibility. If an Rh- woman (lacking the Rhesus allele) has a child with an Rh+ mate and the child acquires the Rh+ allele from the father, the mother may develop Rh+ antibodies if exposed to the fetus's blood (for example, at birth). Later-born Rh+ fetuses are then at increased risk of maternal immune attack and death. In a global mating market, most Chinese are Rh-, while most Europeans Rh+; reproduction between Chinese women and European men might activate responses if it were not for biomedical intervention (that is, giving pregnant women at risk anti-D immunoglobulin). Indeed, cases of Rh incompatibility in the United Kingdom alone declined from 46 out of 100,000 in 1969 to 1.6 out of 100,000 in 1990, thanks to intervention (Bittles and Matson 2000).

Somehow, fertilization occurs with or without the involvement of spirits. Suppose that zygote survives, thrives, and develops into a fetus. It survives the harsh cut of spontaneous abortion (30–70% of recognized pregnancies appear to be aborted by a human female's body [Ellison 2001; Bentley and Mascie-Taylor 2000]), and the pregnancy becomes established. What does this mean for the male partner's sexuality? That is a question central to this chapter and probably to many fathers.

Of Human Pair-Bondage

If that male partner were a gorilla, his sex life with his pregnant female partner would decline for the duration of her pregnancy and also post-partum (see Campbell et al. 2007). As a reproductive male, he might have several other partners in his polygynous family unit in different reproductive states, so perhaps his overall sex life would not fall entirely dormant, just close to it. If that male partner were a gibbon or sia-mang, his sex life might continue or slightly wane during his partner's pregnancy but plummet postpartum. Indeed, observing wild white-handed gibbons in Thailand, Claudia Barelli and others (2008) found that females continued to engage in sex during gestation, but only one of seven lactating females engaged in sex, meaning that a male part-ner's sexual life descended too.

What about the sex life of fathers among our closest living relatives, chimpanzees and bonobos? Because the social context of chimpanzee and bonobo sexual activity differs from ours, fathers' sexual activity is modified minimally by conception. Suppose a male chimpanzee fathers a child: his ongoing sexual activity is tied more to his dominance status and the availability of other, fertile females than it is to a single female's reproductive changes. Indeed, the better question in such a case is, how well does a given male even "know" he has fathered a given off-spring? By relying on cues such as having had sex with a female who subsequently gave birth, he may intuit that the resulting offspring could be his. Recent field data provide some evidence suggesting that chim-panzee paternal relationships are sometimes recognized, and similar evidence is emerging from field data on gorillas, baboons, and rhesus monkeys, suggesting that these relationships are also recognized some-times (Lehmann 2008). At any rate, chimpanzee and bonobo male sexuality is not tied to a long-term partner's reproductive state.

Human sexuality is less stifled than that of other mammals that form long-term bonds. For the relatively few mammalian species that also form long-term reproductive relationships, male sexual activity tends to be concentrated during the times a female is cycling, before waning dramatically during pregnancy and postpartum (Kleiman 1977). Hu-mans often continue their sex lives in these partnerships even when a woman becomes pregnant, though cross-cultural variation in these patterns exists, as we will see. Still, a robust feature of human socio-sexuality is that married men (and women) engage in sex more than their single counterparts do. This is true in countries like the United States (Laumann et al. 1994) as well as around the globe. In Mali and Brazil, for example, 70% of married men but only 30% of single men reported having sex in the past four weeks; in the Philippines, again about 70% of married men but a stark 20% of single men reported sex during the past four weeks (Wellings et al. 2006).

Notably, those patterns in sexual activity according to marital status hold up despite declines in sexuality with relationship duration. The variety of sexual experiences, intercourse frequency, and often sexual satisfaction tend to decline with the duration of a long-term partnership such as marriage. These patterns suggest a "honeymoon effect." Without children, a couple may explore a wider array of sexual behaviors, like oral sex, as part of courtship functions and without the demands of children nagging at them. At the early stages of romantic relationships, the sex drive of both partners may be at its highest (Baumeister 2000), only to change into a different relationship dynamic (again, more on that in the next chapter). These types of effects are probably quite widespread. In a recent German study of 1,865 students aged nineteen to thirty-two, men reported reduced coital frequency and decreased sexual satisfaction with relationship duration (Klusmann 2002). Men's desire for sex remained relatively constant across relationship duration, whereas women's desire for sex decreased, leading to enhanced discrepancies (Klusmann 2002). Even among captive callitrichid monkeys, courtship frequency decreases with the duration of a pair-bond, revealing that such changes are not restricted to humans (French and Schaffner 2000).

Effects of Pregnancy on Paternal Sexuality

How does a partner's pregnancy impact a man's sexuality? In a comprehensive review of fifty-nine sexuality studies published between 1950 and 1996, almost all conducted in the United States and western Europe, sexual behavior changed across a woman's pregnancy (Von Sydow 1999). Coital frequency tended to remain high the first semester, was quite variable the second trimester, but dropped considerably the third trimester. Positions for intercourse also changed: during the third trimester, couples primarily engaged in sex with the male-from-behind and partners side-by-side. In a particularly detailed study of German sexual practices, decreases in intercourse were apparent across gestation, but so too were decreases in male breast stimulation of a partner, oral sex (by both partners), manual stimulation of the genitals (by both partners), and French-kissing (Von Sydow, Ullmeyer, and Happ 2001).

A broader survey of international cross-cultural patterns reveals even more variation in sexual behavior during a woman's pregnancy. From a sample of sixty societies around the globe, 70% permitted marital intercourse to continue early in a pregnancy (Ford and Beach 1951, 222). That percentage remained relatively high through the middle of pregnancy (60% of the societies allowed intercourse during the fifth month of pregnancy) before dropping steadily. By the seventh month of gestation, 50% of these societies allowed intercourse, but only 25% did during the ninth month of gestation. The primary reasons behind the plummet in marital intercourse during the advancement of a pregnancy were concerns over the fetus's health—concerns that it not be harmed during intercourse.

In this same survey, rules concerning marital intercourse suggested a sexual double standard. The intercourse of wives was restricted, but commonly men were permitted additional sexual outlets. As Clellan Ford and Frank Beach write (1951), "All save two of the twenty-one societies that forbid coitus throughout the greater part of pregnancy are polygynous and the man may have access to other wives who are not pregnant" (223) If a man has only one wife, often he is given sexual allowances with other, unmarried women while his wife remains pregnant.

In some societies, sex during pregnancy is thought to serve valuable fertility functions. For example, among the Aka of Central African Republic, pregnant women actively solicit sex from their husbands, even repeatedly, during the night, with the thought that the man's semen helps the fetus to grow (B. L. Hewlett and B. S. Hewlett 2008). Aka report having sex several times a night, viewing sex as pleasurable but also "work" in the service of successful reproduction. Similar beliefs in the value of gestational sex are shared in other parts of sub-Saharan Africa (Gregersen 1994). Among many native Amazonian societies, all men having intercourse with a pregnant woman are thought to contribute to a fetus's conception and growth (Beckerman and Valentine 2002). In some societies, sex during advanced pregnancy is thought to facilitate the birth process, for example, by softening the vagina for delivery. Given the recognized function of prostaglandins, which are contained in semen, to facilitate dilation of the cervix, there may be a physiological basis to these late-gestation intercourse-birth connections.

Sex during pregnancy can also be linked with social functions. If a woman values her relationship with a partner, she may engage in sex with him to facilitate continued investment in her and their offspring. Continued sex, especially when situated in a complementary cultural context, may establish paternity and in turn paternal investment. Among South American societies such as the Kulina of Brazil, pregnant women mating with multiple men establish each partner as a father of the child, a practice useful in obtaining resources such as fish and game meat for herself and her child (Beckerman and Valentine 2002). Moreover, a woman's strategic use of sex may be easier in the early stages of pregnancy than postpartum, when her physiology is oriented toward maternal investment and an infant demands her attentions. For his part, a male sexually satisfied by his female partner may be less likely to seek extrapair sex during her pregnancy.

Effects of Fatherhood on Men's Sexuality

The birth day arrives. Ultimately a product of sex, the arrival of a newborn may have large impacts on a couple's ongoing sexual life. Providing cross-cultural evidence of these postpartum patterns of sexuality, a large study including pair-bonded, reproductive-aged women from thirteen countries (for example, Guinea, Haiti, Peru) relied on questionnaire responses to identify cycle phase and sexual activity (Brewis and Meyer 2005). While women were cycling, no increases in sexual behavior occurred around the time of ovulation, although sexual behavior decreased during menses. Several factors associated with reduced sexual behavior were being older, breast-feeding, having more children, and being involved in a polygynous (rather than monogamous) union. These are not isolated findings, as we shall see.

The impacts of parenting on sexual behavior may be best appreciated by first considering the effects of pregnancy, birth, and lactation on a female partner. These profound life-history shifts in women alter their sexuality, with major ramifications for their male partners' sexuality. After all, pregnancy and lactation entail enormous endocrine changes in females (Ellison 2001). These endocrine changes function to promote a successful pregnancy and postpartum maternal investment in the form of maternal bonding and lactation. These alterations, especially postpartum, modify female sexuality. Female bodies in these states have already undertaken the path toward reproduction, so the shift away from sexuality makes sense.

After the baby is born, how do female endocrine shifts undercut a woman's libido (Greenspan and Gardner 2001)? Estrogen levels, which have skyrocketed during pregnancy, plummet to baseline levels. Testosterone levels may experience modest changes. Testosterone levels may be lower among breast-feeding women compared with non-breast-feeding mothers (Alder and Bancroft 1988). Progesterone levels drop from the high levels of pregnancy to baseline. If a mother breast-feeds her newborn, then nipple stimulation and suckling by the infant stimulate oxytocin and prolactin release. These hormonal changes matter: the reduced estrogens diminish vaginal lubrication, making intercourse potentially more painful; because estrogens and androgens are the prime movers behind female libido, the drop in estrogens and potentially androgens can diminish a woman's desire for sex; and prolactin inhibits ovarian steroid hormone production, providing another breast-feeding–related brake on resumption of a woman's cycling (Bancroft 2005). Altogether, a woman's postpartum body is primed to use her limited energy reserves to invest in her current offspring rather than to prepare for the next one.

Other maternal alterations matter too. Changes in female body image with pregnancy may impact a woman's perceived attractiveness and self-esteem, altering her desire for intimacy (Pastore, Owens, and Raymond 2007). The wear and tear of birth itself accounts for a doctor's advice to wait at least a few weeks to months for the resumption of intercourse. Indeed, if birth occurs by cesarean section, this can delay sexual activity for the initial months postpartum, but without apparently longer-standing effects (G. Barrett et al. 2005). The intimacy a mother experiences with a baby may crowd out physical proximity with the baby's father. It is no surprise, then, that the arrival of a baby heralds alterations in a couple's relationship (more on that in the next chapter), including patterns of sexual activity.

Human sexual behavior diminishes after the birth of a child. A father's sexual life does indeed descend. As summarized in Von Sydow's (1999) review of the same fifty-nine sexuality studies drawn largely from the United States and western Europe, "compared with the prepregnancy period, coital frequency is reduced in most couples during the first year after the birth" (23). A variety of factors contribute to the decline in postpartum sexual behavior (De Judicibus and McCabe 2002). Marital quality is positively correlated with resumption of sexual activity postpartum, with higher-quality marriages linked to earlier and more frequent sexual activity. The fatigue resulting from infant care diminishes postpartum sexuality. Breast-feeding also inhibits resumption of sexual behavior postpartum (more on this below).

Taboos against postpartum sexual activity in a broader sample of societies demonstrate even more variation in postpartum sexual behavior. In some societies, a woman is expected to engage in intercourse postpartum as soon as the scars of birth heal—within a matter of weeks to a couple of months. In the United States, for example, doctors typically "taboo" intercourse for four to six weeks postpartum. In other societies, taboos against a woman engaging in postpartum sex with her husband can extend for two or three years. Putting some numbers on these patterns, Frayser's (1985, 318) cross-cultural survey finds some sort of postpartum sex taboo present in thirty-eight out of forty-one societies. The duration of these taboos varies: 34% last one to five months; 27%, six months to a year; 17%, one to two years; and 15% of these, more than two years. Longer durations tend to be found in sub-Saharan Africa and shorter durations in Europe. Widespread sexual restraints on postpartum women and men occur in indigenous South America. Among the Mehinaku of Brazil, a man is expected to live in seclusion, abstaining from sex, for about one year after the birth of the man's child (Gregor 1985). What accounts for such variation?

The duration and frequency of breast-feeding help account for some of this variation. Throughout human evolutionary history, mothers have nursed their offspring for several years. Among human hunter-gatherers, for example, mothers commonly nurse their offspring for two to four years, with supplementary foods typically introduced during the first year of lactation (Ellison 2001; Kelly 1995). Lactation provides important nutritional, immunological, and psychological benefits. The energetic costs of lactation are also significant—requiring even more calories than gestation does. Thus, a nursing mother faces an energetic trade-off should she both lactate and gestate at once. Consequently, as one study notes, "the reason given for insisting upon sexual abstinence after parturition is the prevention of another pregnancy in the belief that this would be dangerous to the welfare of the present child. Should conception take place while the baby is nursing, the mother's milk supply would diminish and the growing child would have to be prematurely weaned" (Ford and Beach 1951, 226). As the contraceptive effects of lactation wane, then, requiring a nursing woman to avoid intercourse prevents her from undertaking this energetic trade-off.

The duration of breast-feeding has been shortened—even eliminated altogether—in some societies, making an important contribution to the resumption of postpartum sexual behavior. In the United States, breast-feeding rates reached their nadir in 1971, when only 24% of women breast-fed their babies at all, in part thanks to the introduction of infant formulas marketed as modern and progressive (J. H. Wolf 2003). Both of the authors of this book were born during these times: one of us (Anderson, born in 1970) was breast-fed, while the other (Gray, born in 1972) was not. Rates of breast-feeding have increased somewhat in the United States, to 70% of mothers breast-feeding after birth and 36% breast-feeding at six months. Yet these rates are quite low compared with other parts of the world. Ninety-four percent of Bangladeshi and 50% of Ugandan mothers are still breast-feeding twenty to twenty-three months postpartum (UNICEF 2007). Why does all of this matter? Because the endocrine and physical aspects of breast-feeding can diminish a woman's libido and can also delay a woman's desire to engage in sexual behavior. In a detailed study of 570 U.S. women and 550 of their partners, Janet Hyde and others (1996) found that breast-feeding women reported lower sexual desire than non-breast-feeding women. The effects of breast-feeding also impacted paternal sexuality: men whose partners were breast-feeding reported lower sexual satisfaction, both one month and four months postpartum.

As we have seen, lactation and birth-spacing concerns help motivate female postpartum sex taboos. Are men subject to the same variation in postpartum taboos? The short answer to that question is no. Men tend to have greater postpartum sexual license than women. Fathers tend to have alternative sexual outlets that allow them to resume intercourse, even if their lactating wives are subject to constraints on intercourse. Polygynous marriage helps in this regard: in societies that permit polygynous marriages, taboos against sexual behavior postpartum tend to occur over a longer time span than in societies permitting only monogamous marriages. In a polygynous society, a man may have other wives with whom he can have intercourse.

Even if other wives are not available, other sexual outlets may be available. These may be unmarried women with whom fathers have short trysts or longer-standing affairs. As an illustration of such patterns, unusually detailed quantitative data from southwest Nigeria speak to the importance of postpartum sex taboos and male sexual partnerships. Here, in a sample of 3,204 men, taboos yielded significant delays in the resumption of intercourse with their postpartum wives (Lawoyin and Larsen 2002). Rural monogamous men reported average resumption of sexual activity at eighteen months, rural polygynous men at twenty-four months, urban monogamous men at six months, and urban polygynous men at twelve months. So having multiple wives did delay postpartum sexual activity in both urban and rural populations. Of alternative partners, approximately 60% of monogamously married men reported none (that is, they were temporarily celibate while following postpartum sex taboos), while approximately 33% of polygynously married men reported none, indicating that male postpartum abstinence is less common in polygynous unions. Of the 40% of monogamous men who reported sex with other partners, the majority of these (around 70%) were with one "regular" partner, with the remainder reporting nonregular or multiple partners. A few of those nonregular or multiple partners were likely prostitutes.

Men may pay for sex as one means of maintaining postpartum sexuality. A global survey of prostitution use reveals variation, with 9–14% of men in different parts of Africa reporting to have engaged in "sex in exchange for money, gifts, or favors" in the past year (Wellings et al. 2006). Rates of paid sex were 11% in China and Hong Kong, 6–7% in the Caribbean, and 1–3% in the Middle East, among other places. While these data do not enable disentangling prostitute access postpartum, they do indicate that prostitutes can serve as sexual outlets to men in some parts of the world. One of us (Gray) lives forty-five minutes from Pahrump, Nevada, where legal brothels operate: how many of their clients are postpartum fathers? We don't know, but other U.S. data indicate that a substantial proportion (27–60%) of men accessing prostitutes are married, and the rationales men give for utilizing prostitutes include a partner's constrained sexuality (for example, their partners are pregnant or not interested in certain types of sexual behavior) (Sawyer et al. 2001).

Why do men seek sexual outlets during a partner's pregnancy or in the postpartum period? The most common reason appears to be sexual dissatisfaction, a dissatisfaction that increases according to changes in a partner's desires (Allen et al. 2005). Men may even maintain a high degree of marital satisfaction while seeking extrapair partnerships, suggesting that desires for sex can be disconnected from emotional investment in a partner. That men are willing to seek extrapair partners even if their wives disapprove suggests the power of these motives (Jankowiak, Nell, and Buckmaster 2002). Certainly, other factors may matter, such as a man's age, relationship duration, and so forth—among the Tsimane of Bolivia, for example, younger men with fewer children are the most likely to engage in extramarital sex (Winking, Kaplan, et al. 2007)—but the main reason appears traceable to sexual concerns. Interestingly, men's rationale for seeking additional sexual partners also tends to differ from women's: poor marital quality and low perceived support from a male partner are more common reasons for women seeking additional partners (Allen et al. 2005).

Several other facets of postpartum sexual function warrant attention, but it's difficult to say much about them, given the available data. One issue is how postpartum sexual behavior compares after the birth of a first child with that of later children. Do couples having more children ever regain their prepartum vigor? What about couples who choose not to have more children? Broadly speaking, patterns of postpartum sexual behavior, to the degree that they do increase with time, should reflect prepartum patterns of sexual function. At the societal level, this means that couples who have aloof marital relationships and tense sex in the first place (for example, the Mae Enga of New Guinea) will not find their sexual relationships altering in emotional tenor after children are born. Similarly, patterns of sexual behavior such as oral sex and emphasis on the importance of female orgasm within a society or a given couple prepartum will likely predict their later postpartum presence, even if overall sexual function is down regulated. A baby's birth is not likely to herald a birth in sexual novelty.

Clearly, men experience alterations in their sexual behavior with their pregnant and postpartum partners. But how do we disentangle the effects of women's from men's contributions to this diminished sexuality? If much of the shifts in parental sexuality can be accounted for from a female perspective, is there any additive effect of down-shifted paternal sexual motivation? One way to address these issues is to simply ask men about their libido and whether it changes. Another way is to tap measures of male libido that do not entail negotiations with a sexual partner. Measures of masturbation frequency, utilization of pornography, and use of paid sexual services such as prostitution can provide these sorts of diagnostic windows (Symons 1979). To be sure, there is variation in the social acceptance of such outlets. Views concerning male masturbation illustrate this variation: in some societies, male masturbation is entirely disapproved of, in others it is generally disapproved of except among unmarried adolescents, and in still others it is viewed as a normal facet of adult male sexual functioning (Ford and Beach 1951). Nevertheless, when unencumbered behavioral evidence of male libido (such as male masturbation) is permitted, this kind of evidence can provide important motivational insights.

What do such data suggest? According to Von Sydow's (1999) review, male sexual interest remains strong until the third trimester, when it tends to wane. Postpartum, approximately 20% of men experience diminished libido even up to a year later. In a sample of U.S. couples, the percentage of men (43–45%) who reported masturbating at each of four time points (the second trimester of partner's pregnancy and one month, four months, and twelve months postpartum) was invariant (Hyde et al. 1996), comparable to findings from German men (Von Sydow, Ullmeyer, and Happ 2001). However, assuming that coital frequency has declined among these U.S. and German subjects, an invariant masturbation frequency actually implies a downturn in male sexual function across this span (men are not responding to decreased intercourse with increased masturbation). As a compelling nonhuman primate counterpart, common marmoset "family males" (breeding males in a family group) did not experience spikes in testosterone (which is indicative of a courtship response) when exposed to ovulatory smells of unrelated females, whereas paired and single males did (Ziegler, Schultz-Darken et al. 2005). So there is at least some evidence of downturns in the sexual motivation of paternal males.

We are aware of only inferential data concerning prostitute use like that discussed above, and we know of no data on pornography consumption according to paternal status. Therefore, even if we can think of some ways to assess whether male libido changes with fatherhood, few relevant data are available to address this issue. This gap in knowledge goes much further too. We can find no data on the patterns of sexual behavior among stepfathers or among gay male fathers. Predictions can be hazarded—that newly arrived stepfathers may engage in more sex than genetic fathers do or that sex among gay fathers will be reduced less than that of lesbian mothers or heterosexual controls—but no data can be mined to test these predictions.

The few signs available suggest that changes in male libido are modest compared with those occurring in women postpartum. This observation underlies exaggerated conflicts over desire for sex postpartum. Even if sex differences in sexual desire exist generally, these differences are enhanced by shifts in physiology and behavior after the arrival of a baby. Such conflicts of sexual interest also help account for patterns of extra-pair partnerships. The period after the birth of a child can represent a dangerous one for couples, especially in relatively young relationships. Conflicts over sexual desire can underlie motivations to seek alternative sexual partners.

Behind Closed Doors

If paternal sexual function is dampened, there are still other challenging facets of paternal sexuality. Some of these challenges relate to our species' unusual proclivity to have sex in private. When is the last time you saw a couple having sex in the grocery store or at a party you hosted? When is the last time you saw pets, animals in a zoo, or animals you saw "in the wild" having sex in plain view? Exactly. Our pattern of private sexual behavior probably relates to our unusual social system entailing multiple pair-bonded couples embedded in multimale, multifemale social groups: sex in private in such contexts might diminish effects of sexual arousal and jealousy, compared with sex in public. Our use of clothing where it is not necessary to cover our genitals (for example, at beaches around the world) probably speaks to similar considerations.

However our desire for sex in private arose, it presents challenges to a couple seeking to resume sexual activity in the midst of other adults and children. Sex in plain view is usually not permitted. That taboo does not exist for other species. Mother nonhuman primates commonly engage in naked sex in open view, including in view of their own offspring. A male gorilla can also copulate during daylight hours with a mate without being chastized by group members.

The sex-in-private human challenge is especially salient to new parents. Cross-cultural research on human sleeping arrangements reveals that the typical pattern is for a mother to sleep next to a nursing offspring, with the father variably present or absent from this immediate dyad. In a study of 186 preindustrial societies, there was not a single one in which mothers slept apart from infants (see McKenna, Mosko, and Richard 1999). These cross-cultural patterns of sleeping arrangements apply to hunter-gatherers. Among hunter-gatherer societies such as the !Kung, Ache, Hadza, or Tiwi, mothers sleep next to their infants, whom they nurse typically for two to four years before weaning. Nighttime sleeping proximity facilitates nursing. This pattern is also typical of Old World monkeys and apes: mothers sleep with offspring whom they nurse on demand.

So fathers may or may not sleep next to their partners in these circumstances, and in either case an infant is present. On top of that, the social contexts of human sleeping arrangements commonly mean that other family members, from older children to other adults, inhabit the same sleeping space. Picture an Inuit igloo brimming with family members and maybe a few guests. Imagine further an Amazonian enclosure containing around fifty hammocks filled with sleeping friends and family.

Several solutions to sex occur in these social circumstances (Frayser 1985; Gregersen 1994). One resolution is to have sex discreetly. Couples can have quiet sex utilizing positions (like the male from behind) other than the missionary position, which is the most prevalent cross-culturally. This practice of discreet intercourse appears to be common among couples sleeping in social circumstances, such as when the !Kung engage in nocturnal sex near a fire with children nearby. Couples can also seek alternative locations in which to have sex (as in a nearby forest in daytime). In addition, couples may segregate infants and toddlers in their own sleeping spaces, apart from private adult space (as in some Western societies).

We get around this problem, at any rate. Our sex-in-privacy tendencies also present an interesting challenge to children's developing sexuality: our young, unlike those of other primates, do not have ready occasion to witness public acts of sex. Unlike a curious chimpanzee, say, who can watch its mother to learn about sexual practices, human young must find out these things through other avenues. Maybe a human father needs to communicate with his children about these issues in ways that would not be necessitated under the social lives of other primates. Imagine the conversation: "Son, because you have not had occasion to witness your mother and I openly engaging in sex throughout your life, you're old enough now that we should talk about this. You see, when menstrual blood mixes with semen."

Another facet of sexuality is also linked to privacy issues: parent-child incest (A. P. Wolf and Durham 2005). Why would a parent have sex with his or her child? Surely natural selection would have acted against any such dispositions. The genetic costs of breeding between close relatives (particularly full siblings or parents and offspring) have been demonstrated, with most costs appearing through the expression of deleterious recessive alleles (Bittles 2005).

When parent-child incest occurs, several considerations help make sense of its patterning. These matings occur almost exclusively between father-daughter pairs rather than mother-son pairs. This fact appears to implicate a more generalized male libido, stronger mother-offspring early social attachment, and the greater reproductive costs of inbreeding to females compared with males. Several factors appear to increase the likelihood of father-daughter incest. The most important should not, by now, surprise us: the abusers are usually unrelated to the female victim (that is, the abuser is a stepfather or the mother's boyfriend). Among approximately eight thousand Finnish adolescents, sexual abuse by stepfathers was fifteen times more common than sexual abuse by genetic fathers (Sariola and Uutela 1996). Given the importance of paternity certainty in predicting facets of paternal investment (see Chapter 5), we should also expect that male-initiated incest should be contingent on perceived low paternity certainty (Tal and Lieberman 2007), although data are not available to directly test this hypothesis.

Even when genetic relatives do engage in incest, these behaviors too are patterned. Male relatives committing incest may have had little caregiving contact with a female, especially when she was an infant or child, preventing inhibitions against incest to develop. Akin to the "Westermarck hypothesis" (Westermarck 1891), which postulates that shared early social experience prohibits the development of siblings' sexual desires for each other, fathers caring for their young children may develop sexual aversions to them. Additionally, fathers engaging in incest may also have something relatively uncommon in our evolutionary history and across cultures—privacy. Back to those sleeping arrangements as indications of the availability of privacy: incest is frowned upon, so it takes opportunities for it to take place away from view, and variable social worlds create more or fewer such opportunities.

So concludes our descent into the sex lives of fathers. While perhaps reaching a low point with a discussion of incest, we have considered conception beliefs, patterns of sexual behavior during pregnancy and the postpartum period, and other facets of paternal sexuality. While men's sexuality may be changed with fatherhood, we might ask about other dimensions of change. With the transition to fatherhood, surely the brain—the main organ of sex—is changed by more than just sex. What broader psychological and physiological shifts do men undergo with fatherhood? We will explore these issues in the next chapter.

10

Babies on His Brain

A baby can change a man's mind. Take Peter Gray's mind as an example. After having two young girls, he finds himself perceptive of the cries and squirmings of little ones, whether in a grocery store, in an airplane, on a playground, or in a coffee shop. Babies surrounded him in all of these same places before he became a father. Yet somehow he did not perceive them. It wasn't until he had his own children that babies entered his brain—and his social vision. He's probably not alone. In a study that measured changes in pupil area (an index of a person's social orientation) in response to looking at pictures of various things, babies elicited no changes in men's eyes, and mothers and babies together barely altered men's eyes, yet either type of image noticeably altered women's eyes. So what did modify men's attention? Men's pupils opened up at the sight of naked women (Eibl Eibesfeldt 1989, 255).

In this chapter, we focus on two issues concerning the effect of babies on the male brain. First, what are the psychological impacts of parenting on men? As men transition into fatherhood, they experience a variety of changes in their emotional life and quality of life, and we want to describe and understand these changes. Second, what are the physiological mechanisms underlying the psychological and behavioral transitions associated with fatherhood? In what is essentially a new science of human fatherhood, we can begin to tease apart the physiological substrates underlying these transitions to fatherhood. Grab a place in a functional imaging machine, listen to infant cries, and watch your brain respond to these infant stimuli. Or let researchers measure your hormone levels while you interact with a baby. These are some of the ways that we can begin revealing the proximate mechanisms underlying our responses to babies.

199

Emotional Impacts of Fatherhood

Impending fatherhood can elicit a variety of emotional responses. Often these are positive. Fatherhood serves as a social marker of full adult achievement in many societies: you are not a complete man unless you have fathered children. Among the Sambia of New Guinea, a "fully masculine" man has fathered children, and in many circum-Mediterranean societies the ultimate litmus test of manhood is impregnating one's wife (Gilmore 1990). In these contexts, the recognition of a partner's pregnancy and a man's own fatherhood can be validating. If a child is desired, the recognition of impending fatherhood also tends to be positive. The arrival of a child is awaited eagerly and with excitement.

The expectation of a child's arrival can also cause mixed emotions. Several qualitative studies of men's prepartum lives illustrate the vagaries of prepartum life. Through interviews with U.K. men, sources of ambivalence during a partner's pregnancy centered on how men would perform as fathers, on how having the child would affect lifestyles, and on how marital relationships would change (Donovan 1995). In a different study entailing interviews with prospective U.K. fathers, additional sources of ambivalence emerged, as one study notes: "While the pregnancy generated positive feelings it also precipitated worries and concerns. These were mainly in response to the demands of the pregnancy, what it signified in terms of its potential effects on the health of the partner and unborn, its impact upon the conjugal relationship and other siblings, financial commitment, accommodation space, prospective parenthood, antenatal preparation and maternal care" (Brennan, Marshall-Lucette, et al. 2007, 27).

Several biomedical studies have tracked the emotional lives of men pre- and postpartum, and sometimes in contrast with control "nonfather" men (reviewed in E. E. Bartlett 2004; Brennan, Ayres, et al. 2007). What do biomedical studies find concerning the emotional lives of would-be fathers? Jacqueline Clinton (1987) studied about 150 Wisconsin men, both expectant and nonexpectant, across the course of a year. During the first trimester, expectant fathers reported greater irritability and more colds than nonexpectant men. While no differences appeared in the second trimester, during the third trimester, expectant fathers reported more weight gain, restlessness, and insomnia. In a study of about 160 Australian men, participants contrasted their health symptoms during a partner's pregnancy with those they experienced prior to their partner's pregnancy. The main symptoms affected were sleep disturbances, lack of energy, diminished libido, appetite changes, and aches/pains (cited in E. E. Bartlett 2004). In a 1960s U.K. study investigating physical symptoms of over 500 men, a higher percentage (57%) of men whose partners were pregnant experienced pregnancy symptoms, compared with men whose partners were not pregnant (46%) (Trethowan and Conlon 1965). The pregnancy symptoms men commonly reported included anxiety, loss of appetite, and nausea. Symptoms were most severe during a partner's first and third trimester, a pattern that appears quite common and seems to reflect responsiveness to a newly recognized pregnancy (in the first trimester) and concern over the partner's well-being and the challenges of an expanding family (in the third trimester).

The main emotional change takes place during the first few months postpartum. In a 1987 study of pre- and postpartum Wisconsin fathers contrasted with control non-fathers, Jacqueline Clinton investigated a battery of emotional and health outcomes. Postpartum, fathers exhibited more fatigue, irritability, headaches, difficulties concentrating, insomnia, nervousness, and restlessness, but no differences in backaches, depression, or colds compared with controls (Clinton 1987, 65). Other studies elicit men's emotional ups and downs during early postpartum life; interviews with Australian fathers suggest that men struggled to cope with changes in a relationship with a mate, with demands of work, and with ambivalence over their interactions with an infant (Barclay and Lupton 1999).

In the face of family turmoil, men commonly exhibit postpartum depression. Because paternal postpartum depression is relatively little appreciated, we consider it in some detail. In a meta-analysis of twenty relevant studies, all from North America, western Europe, or Australia, rates of postpartum male depression varied from 1% to 26% (Goodman 2004). Variation in the timing of assessment, the ways depression was assessed, the study populations, and other factors help account for this wide-ranging variation, and almost all of the studies had sample sizes of less than one hundred men. Still, several key patterns stood out from this analysis. Perhaps the most important finding was that the largest risk factor for men experiencing postpartum depression was whether their partners also displayed it. Between 24% and 50% of men reported postpartum depression if their partner also had postpartum depression.

In perhaps the most rigorous investigation yet of male postpartum depression, a nationally representative study of approximately five thousand U.S. families revealed that 10% of fathers with nine-month-old infants exhibited clinically significant rates of depressive symptomatology (Paulson, Dauber, and Lieferman 2006). That rate was less than that of postpartum female depression in the same study (14%) but twice the expected rate of male depression among non-father controls (Paulson, Dauber, and Lieferman 2006). Male depression in the study was also associated with less male involvement in parenting behaviors such as reading to a child.

As research in male postpartum depression grows, so too do factors helping account for its variation. Apart from a partner's own depression, a variety of additional factors appear linked to variable rates of male postpartum depression. Stepfatherhood is associated with a higher rate of postpartum male depression than genetic fatherhood is (Deater-Deckard et al. 1998), but that effect disappears when adjusting for other factors associated with depression, such as male education, age, social support and network, and a partner's lack of affection. A history of depression, poor relationship quality with a partner, young paternal age, and poor health status of an offspring may also be linked with increased postpartum depression (Johns and Belsky 2007). Poverty appears linked with male depression, with higher rates of paternal depression among more economically challenged men (E. A. Anderson, Kohler, and Letiecq 2005). When the time between births is short, this too can amplify problems in family relationships.

Importantly, it is unclear whether men experience elevated postpartum depression in broader cross-cultural perspectives. Almost all studies are restricted to Western samples. While cross-cultural data on women's postpartum depression have recently emerged, the same kinds of data are lacking for fathers (see Halbreich and Karkun 2006; Oates et al. 2004). Thus, at this time, we are unable to determine whether fathers experience postpartum depression in various cultural contexts and, if this is the case, whether predictors such as the quality of a marital relationship help account for variation. We are sorely lacking data from small-scale societies in South America, Africa, and elsewhere. We suspect that future research will someday find that male postpartum depression exists in these wider social contexts too.

Still, in light of the available depressing evidence, why have children in the first place? The weight of depression may be counterbalanced by other factors. Roy Baumeister (1991) finds that despite reductions in marital satisfaction postpartum, men and women commonly find their lives enriched. Life has more meaning, even with a crying baby in hand. Furthermore, that decline in marital satisfaction may not be eternal: Catherine Hakim (2003) found that after children left the home (admittedly, a long time after birth), marital satisfaction rebounded. And from an evolutionary perspective, the reason why men strive to father children is that, in doing so, they attend to nature's bottom line: reproductive success. A father may feel compelled to sacrifice for his children because it feels right, and in this course he enables his genes to survive another generation. Our offspring are, quite literally, reproductive successes.

Several large Danish studies speak further to the favorable sides of fatherhood. In a twin study consisting of over 2,000 men (Kohler, Behrman, and Skytthe 2005), subjects responded to the question, "How satisfied are you with your life, all things considered?" The presence of children, especially first-born sons, led to slightly more positive responses. The effect of parenting in this study was small compared with the effect of partnership status (partnered men reported much larger, more positive responses compared with unpartnered men) yet still indicated an upside for children. In addition, a huge study of approximately 390,000 Danes investigated the effects of parenting on suicide risk; two-thirds of the approximately 18,000 suicides taking place between 1981 and 1997 were males, consistent with the finding that most suicides around the globe involve males (Qin and Mortensen 2003). Across all men, fathering five or more children or having a child aged two or younger was associated with reduced risk of committing suicide. When fathers are split into those involved in cohabiting relationships and those who are not, among cohabiting fathers, having more children was protective against suicide; among single fathers, who typically lived apart from their children, having more children was associated with increased suicide risk.

Couvade in Cross-Cultural Perspective

Against the backdrop of these recent forays into fatherhood and mental health, earlier scholarly research on prenatal and postnatal changes in men's psychology and behavior traces to a substantial literature on the so-called couvade (Elwood and Mason 1995). The etymology of "couvade" derives from a French word suggesting "hatching" or "brooding." Findings of this couvade literature relate to male psychological transitions occurring alongside fatherhood. The idea is that men experience symptoms prior to and shortly after a partner's pregnancy during the development of a paternal role. While study of the couvade traces back to the anthropologist Edward Tylor's work during the nineteenth century, ongoing research has been conducted largely by two disparate intellectual communities: anthropologists and biomedical scientists. Academic study of the couvade has used inconsistent definitions, time frames (prepartum versus postpartum, variable lengths postpartum), symptomatology (emotions, physical effects), and so forth, making much of the scholarship unstandardized. The couvade literature has given rise to some sensible and testable accounts of paternal transitions but also to some strange ones: Felix Bohem (cited in Brennan, Ayres, et al. 2007) suggested that men experience couvade symptoms because of a latent, unattainable desire to give birth.

All that being said, there are some interesting features of the couvade literature that help shed light on the psychological transformations men experience with fatherhood. The couvade research also covers cross-cultural terrain, providing much-needed insight into the patterns and function of men's paternal transitions around the world. In a study of 172 Thai men whose wives were pregnant, these men described couvade symptoms quite similar to those identified in Western societies (cited in Brennan, Ayres, et al. 2007). Common symptoms included poor concentration, anxiety, fatigue, and sleep alterations. Couvade symptomatology has also been addressed in a study of 300 Chinese married men. The majority (68%) of those husbands whose wives were pregnant (in the third trimester) reported more pregnancy symptoms than men whose wives were not pregnant (Tsai and Chen 1997). The anthropological scholarship suggests that the couvade appears in a variety of societies but primarily in two regions: aboriginal South America and southeast Asia. More ink has been spilled on South America, a trend we continue here too.

Throughout much of aboriginal South America, fathers are subject to a variety of late pregnancy and postpartum taboos and psychological effects resembling those experienced by their partners. Men may be confined for days to months, shift from a meat-heavy diet to a vegetarian one late in a partner's pregnancy and postpartum, be restricted from engaging in subsistence practices, and claim to report physiological symptoms. Among the Witoto of northwestern Amazonia, for example, "the husband rests for a week or more in his hammock, observes food taboos, and receives the congratulations of his friends while the new mother is almost ignored. During this couvade, which is practiced until the child's navel is healed, he cannot eat meat or touch his weapons" (K. E. Paige and J. M. Paige 1981, 189).

What are the functions of couvade behavior (Elwood and Mason 1995; R. L. Munroe, R. H. Munroe, and Whiting 1973)? Numerous functions have been advanced, but several stand out as more reasonable, given current understanding of human behavioral biology. One broad function is that the couvade fosters male emotional commitment to a partner and child, thus favoring continued investment in them. By this logic, men experience "sympathy" with a partner's pregnancy and postpartum period, sympathy that leads men to experience similar feelings of nausea and fatigue. This function presumably has physiological substrates that encourage emotional commitment and thereby continued investment in the offspring. This account links both proximate (physiological bases of couvade) and ultimate (function) causation. Unfortunately, because descriptive accounts of the emotional experiences—and not just symptom reports and behavioral transformations—of men are typically lacking in the relevant cross-cultural literature, we cannot determine how reliably the posited psychological changes unfold.

A second broad function is that the couvade serves as a social signal, potentially in several ways. By men marking their fatherhood experience with behavioral and psychological adjustments witnessed by others, paternity is conferred upon those men experiencing the couvade. Indeed, in native South American societies recognized for the possibility of "multiple paternity," any man, even a married man, who has had intercourse with a pregnant or postpartum woman is supposed to publicly engage in couvade behaviors (K. E. Paige and J. M. Paige 1981). Recognized as fathers, all such men have a responsibility to help care for the offspring thereafter.

As an extension of this second function, the couvade experience may legitimize a partnership within the broader community, thus having signaling value outside the immediate family. Consistent with this view, couvade constraints that reduce the ability of a couple to feed themselves for days, weeks, or even longer inherently demand that others provide sustenance during these times. As part of a legitimizing process, extended family or a broader portion of the local community may provide that support. As an illustration of this function, Laura Rival (1998) contends that the couvade serves this latter social function—legitimizing a reproductive union within the longhouse community—among the Huaoroni of Ecuador. The longhouse community, by witnessing and supporting the constrained couple, effectively says, "We sanction your union and the baby it has produced."

Cross-cultural perspectives on the couvade suggest it cannot be divorced from a larger social context like those described here. Karen Paige and Jeffery Paige (1981) make a compelling point that the couvade is more prevalent among matrilocal societies than among patrilineal, patrilocal ones. To be sure, cultural inertia must play a large role in the geographic distribution of the couvade, given its prevalence in a few regions such as Amazonia. More than that, however, a sensible rationale based on the matrilineal versus patrilineal basis of a society accounts for the presence or absence of the couvade. The idea is that among patrilineal, patrilocal societies men commonly provide bride wealth or some other compensation for acquiring a wife, and in the course of doing so also acquire rights to sexual access and the resulting children. Among matrilocal societies, a man enters a woman's and her kin's terrain, often without providing the same sort of compensation for reproductive rights inherent in the formation of a long-term bond. Men's unions and the offspring born from them may thus benefit from the social signaling that occurs during the couvade.

Impacts of Children on Parents' Relationship Quality

While this couvade literature suggests behavioral transformations with fatherhood, what about other changes? Father's emotional barometers are not the only thing adjusting postpartum. So too are men's marital relationships. The arrival of baby tends to go hand in hand with declines in a couple's relationship quality. A meta-analysis of ninety studies, drawn largely from North American and western European samples, found that parents experienced lower marital satisfaction than non-parents do (Twenge, Campbell, and Foster 2003). The effect was slightly larger for women, especially mothers with infants, but the effect held for men too and was not related to the age of their children. Other variables "moderating" the relationships between marital satisfaction and parenting were socioeconomic status and the time a study was conducted. Couples of higher socioeconomic status who were studied more recently exhibited greater deficits of marital satisfaction associated with parenting. Married fathers in Beijing, China, reported lower marital satisfaction than married non-fathers, providing some evidence that the postpartum marital declines described among Western societies may apply more widely (P. B. Gray, Yang, and Pope 2006).

A variety of factors may contribute to postpartum declines in relationship satisfaction. In Chapter 9, we saw how conflicts over sexuality are amplified after birth, and these may serve as a postpartum sore point. Findings from the meta-analysis above (Twenge et al. 2003) suggest that a waning in pronatalist outlooks in places like the United States help contribute to greater reductions in marital satisfaction associated with parenting among couples studied more recently. To the degree socioeconomic status is linked with greater freedom in one's (and a couple's) behavior, the intrusion of a demanding baby may be perceived more negatively. Challenges to a couple's communication abilities, including the lack of time for spending leisurely time together, appear to play a role too. Jay Belsky and John Kelly (1994) found that communication strategies were linked with changes in marital satisfaction in their longitudinal study of parents in Pennsylvania.

Physiological Effects of Fatherhood: The Neuroendocrine System

With all of these emotional and social changes, what is happening "under the skin"? This question concerns the physiological substrates underlying men's transition to fatherhood. This issue is a natural complement to the focus on the psychology of fatherhood discussed so far in this chapter. To begin addressing that question, we need to cover some basics of the neuroendocrine system. It is the workings of this system that illuminate the physiological effects of fatherhood.

The neuroendocrine system consists of the interlinked nervous and endocrine systems (Breedlove, Rosenzweig, and Watson 2007; Ellison and Gray 2009; Nelson 2005). The function of this system is to integrate information both within and outside an organism and then use that information to guide appropriate behavioral responses for its environment. The system can work across variable speeds and specificities too, with neurons enabling rapid and direct communication between parts of the body and with hormones permitting more diffuse signaling throughout the body and over slower paces. To put some flesh on these concepts, suppose a father holds a child, acquiring sensory information through touch, smell, hearing, and visual pathways. His brain integrates that information with brain areas devoted to memory and emotion. Neural pathways favor responses suitable for the moment: facilitating release of hormones that travel throughout the body to foster integrated behavioral responses, for example, or allowing the man to make a conscious decision to continue holding the child. Effectively, the neuroendocrine system serves as the body's primary means of engaging sensory, cognitive, emotional, and motor mechanisms to enable the kinds of behavior, such as childcare or mating, that enhances an organism's survival and reproductive success.

Evolution is a tinkerer, and natural selection has "discovered" that by tinkering with the neuroendocrine system, it is possible to alter a species' and indeed an individual's behavioral tendencies, including family proclivities. Beginning with highly conserved neuroendocrine mechanisms, evolution can adjust brain tissue development, the affinity of a receptor to bind a specific neuorotransmitter, or the structure of a peptide hormone, among other possibilities. Since life evolved once on this planet, the neuroendocrine machinery of all life forms has the deepest of shared ancestry, helping account for why the progesterone in a woman is like that of a yam (which helped in the creation of the first birth control pills) or why the pharmacological drugs that work on us (for example, selective serotonin reuptake inhibitors) also commonly work on our distantly related pets, like cats and dogs. Yet from those basics, nature can throw some switches to alter the specifics of these processes in ways suitable for more specific selective pressures, including family ones.

When it comes to the neuroendocrine mechanisms of paternal care, we will see shortly how many of these processes have been illustrated through intricate and invasive research on small rodents known as voles, as well as through less invasive work on humans. Before we fully jump into this story, however, a few other concepts deserve attention. One is that the mechanisms of paternal care are effectively parasitic tweakings of preexisting neuroendocrine substrates. Sometimes it appears that mechanisms of paternal care take the systems operating in females and co-opt them for males (for example, the effects of the hormone prolactin). In other cases, it seems that the system alters male-specialized circuitry (for example, the effects of the hormone vasopressin). In still other examples, the relevant mechanisms appear more generalized before being coaxed into aiding in paternal care (for example, the functions of the vagus nerve or prefrontal cortex). Lastly, the evolutionary story likely entails not a conscious process of natural selection, as we have pretended, but developmental plasticity, that is, the potential for change across a life span (West-Eberhard 2003). Put another way, the relevant mechanisms provide for species-specific and even individual tendencies. But the specifics of an organism's interaction with its environment during development will shape how these tendencies play out, enabling a range of outcomes—such as a rhesus monkey male, who in the wild would never provide paternal care, doing so in a captive setting (H. J. Smith 2005). Effectively, a push toward paternal care during development can create a new environment favoring the evolution of heritable neuroendocrine mechanisms that in turn increase the tendencies toward paternal care.

Sensing a Baby

Babies can reach their fathers through several sensory modalities. This is the first step toward making impacts on fathers' neuroendocrine systems and in turn shaping paternal behavior. Among most mammals, including various rodent species on which the majority of paternal physiological research has been conducted, smell factors heavily into how an offspring impacts its father. This insight is as apparent as noticing a mouse's or rat's relatively large, wet nose (by which the father smells various things, including its pups). Human reliance on smell is diminished greatly, compared with that of our nonhuman relatives. This diminished reliance on smell manifests in various ways, including our relatively smaller olfactory bulbs, and recent comparative genomics research reveals a reduction in the reliance on smell among our ancestors—even compared with chimpanzees.

All that being said, Peter Gray can still remember the intoxicating smell of his first baby's forehead. For the first several weeks of her life, his daughter exuded a profound, glorious smell that he could breathe in at close distance. Given the cross-cultural variation in paternal proximity to infants, much less in hygiene and other factors, this experience may not be widely generalizable; it may be something of an evolutionary holdover, and more functional in maternal-offspring dyads, but the experience does raise several issues concerning smell and fatherhood.

Can human fathers recognize their offspring by smell? Sometimes. Studies have revealed that blindfolded fathers (unlike mothers) could not recognize their offspring by smell when allowed to smell their babies' heads. If given a shirt worn by the baby, however, a father could identify that of his own baby. When fathers of older children (aged six to fifteen) were asked to identify by smell who had worn shirts placed inside a container, they correctly recognized thirty-one out of forty-two children (Weisfeld et al. 2003). However, the fathers in this latter study preferred the scents of unrelated females over those of their daughters, a finding the authors suggested fits with incest avoidance.

In a more recent study of thirty-nine Dutch fathers who had children around nine years of age, two-thirds of the fathers were able to identify their children's smells (Dubas, Hiejkoop, and Van Aken 2009). Paternal recognition of children's smells was positively associated with paternal investment, affection, and attachment. Fathers who recognized their children's smells ignored their children less than fathers unable to recognize their children's smells did. Results from this study do not enable determining whether smell recognition favors or is instead a reflection of paternal care. Yet the data do suggest that smell may continue to infuse paternal physiology, at least to some degree.

Visual cues provide important infant lifelines to fathers. This is hardly surprising, given the importance humans place on vision for navigating our social worlds. We possess a dedicated face-recognition neural circuitry, enhanced facial musculature that allows a breadth of expressiveness, and newborns keen on seeking eye contact with a caregiver (Cozolino 2006). We even possess a different sort of eye (which, unlike those of other primates, exhibits a vivid contrast between the white of the eye and the pupil), which arguably may have arisen to enhance our capacities for visual communication. Given our sensory worlds, how does vision shape paternal physiology? As noted in Chapter 5, a father may seek and be given visual confirmation of a child's resemblance to him. This visual alignment suggests that a man's investment is being channeled into his genetic offspring rather than those of another man.

Further illustrating the importance of vision to paternal physiology, Steven Platek and others (2004) constructed a virtual paternal world by computer-morphing facial photographs of non-fathers and non-mothers with those of three unrelated babies. The researchers then asked these men and women a host of questions concerning their likely paternal investment in the morphed and unmorphed children's images. Across the positive investment items—for example, "Which one of these children would you spend the most time with?"—the men preferentially selected the morphed children's images more often that did the women. When men and women were subject to fMRI in a similar photo-morphing scheme, men also displayed different neural activity than women did when faced with morphed versus unmorphed stimuli. More specifically, men exposed to the morphed photos exhibited increased left frontal cortical activation, which is thought to be involved in an inhibitory process. The implication is that facial resemblance matters more to men than it does to women in anticipating parental investment, and this sex difference has observable neural substrates.

Touch can have powerful physiological effects. We know these effects when someone scratches our backs or rubs our feet. Touch can have physiological effects on the "toucher" as well as the "touched." The levels of cortisol (a stress hormone) in depressed mothers declined after they touched their infants (Onozawa et al. 2001). Dog lovers playing with and scratching dogs for about fifteen minutes experienced elevations in beta-endorphins as well as in hormones, including oxytocin and prolactin (Odendaal and Meitje 2003). If playfully rolling around with a dog can have these effects on people, it is little surprise that touching and holding an infant can have physiological effects too.

Just a few days postpartum, fathers were able to identify their infants by touch alone (not looking) (Kaitz et al. 1994). In a sense, the feel of our baby makes its mark on our minds. Research with titi monkeys suggests further links between touch and the brain, particularly the somatosensory cortex. The somatosensory cortex forms a strip along the front portion of the parietal lobe in the brain. It contains a miniaturized map of our body's experience with the world, with enlarged areas for our faces, fingers, genitals, and toes. Among titi monkeys, in which males devote an inordinate amount of time tending their young, portions of the somatosensory cortex are enlarged in association with enhanced hand and forelimb touch (Padberg, Disbrow, and Krubitzer 2005).

Paternal proximity may activate several sensory pathways in the course of linking a father's physiology with his child. A man sees and hears his infant. He holds his child's hand. The child's mother is often present too, fostering a family atmosphere. Imagining an intimate sensory world like this one, however, we step back to consider the variable paternal roles men fulfill around the globe. Among some societies, such as the Thonga of Africa, men avoid all forms of touch with their young children. In the vast majority of societies, fathers spend relatively little time directly interacting with their infants and toddlers during day hours but perhaps more time with older children, including sons. At the other extreme, among the Aka, fathers are within reach of infants the bulk of the day as well as the night.

While there is variation in paternal proximity (and hence fathers' sensory experiences with children) during daylight, what about during sleeping times? Even if men spend relatively little time with their young children during day hours, sleeping arrangements commonly place father and child closer together and may contribute to the formation of an attachment between them. A father may awaken to his child's movements and cries. Perhaps that same father loses sleep but gains an enhanced bond. Research has barely scratched the surface of this interesting interface, however. In a preliminary study of thirty-two U.K. children, those children who had co-slept with parents had lower cortisol levels than those children who had not (Waynforth 2007). This study suggests an impact of sleeping arrangements on children. However, there is no research investigating the effects of sleeping arrangements on paternal physiology.

Babies and Brain Imaging

Through various sensory pathways, babies can crawl into our brains. New brain imaging studies reveal some of the specific neural pathways taken by these baby stimuli (reviewed in Swain et al. 2007). In these types of studies, subjects are put inside a scanner (for example, an fMRI machine) and given standardized stimuli, such as photos of children and adults, to determine which areas of the brain respond with heightened activity. Brain areas associated with elevated activation also shed insight on the cognitive and emotional processes that make up paternal psychology and behavior. If emotional centers of a father's brain light up in response to an infant's face, we infer that part of the way a baby elicits paternal care is by pulling on these emotional strings. Furthermore, these imaging studies also reveal ways in which information about a baby can be coordinated with other information in the brain to generate integrated neuroendocrine responses. If the hypothalamus is activated by baby stimuli, we might imagine how this could lead to release of hormones from the hypothalamus, which would in turn initiate hormone release from the pituitary gland, which in turn would travel throughout the body to help coordinate an individual's behavior.

The first of these types of imaging studies compared patterns of neural activation among parents and non-parents, including men and women, to infant cries (Seifritz et al. 2003). The parents exhibited more pronounced neural responses in the right amygdala to infant crying than to infant laughter. The amygdala is a small brain structure active in emotional processing, especially the processing of fear. So the interpretation of this infant cry activation could be that parents experience the cry as emotionally salient, and the cry perhaps induces a vigilance response.

James Swain and others (2007) have conducted fMRI studies of fathers exposed to both visual and auditory stimuli. Men responded differently to cries of their own versus other infants. Those men listening to cries from their own infants experienced increased activation in several brain areas, including the hypothalamus, hippocampus, midbrain, and anterior cingulate. The activation of the hypothalamus is striking because, as noted above, of its role transducing neural information into release of hormones that can in turn have effects on further hormone release throughout the body (for example, the hypothalamus's releasing a hormone, GnRH, that in turn stimulates the pituitary gland to release luteinizing hormone, which in turn increases testosterone release from the testes). The hippocampus plays an important role in long-term memory formation, suggesting that it may play a role in the neural distinction between one's own and another person's baby. The midbrain consists of the superior and inferior colliculi as well as the substantia nigra; to find the midbrain more activated is interesting because the substantia nigra contains dopaminergic neurons associated with psychological reward.

Activation of the anterior cingulate cortex in the fMRI studies is also notable. The anterior cingulate rests at the intersection between the emotional (limbic) and higher cognitive (neocortex) functions (Cozolino 2006). It appears to play a broad role in social orientation. The cingulate cortex appears to have evolved among animals involved in parental care (animals that include a very distant ancestor of ours). By linking emotional activation with higher association areas, an organism is better able to evaluate the emotional significance of its social world, including an offspring in its charge. So the increased activation of fathers' anterior cingulate cortices in response to their own babies' cries suggests an enhanced social attention and evaluation in progress.

Fathers displayed increased neural activity in specific brain areas when exposed to photos of babies compared with photos of houses (Swain et al. 2007). This observation suggests that babies impact the brain differently than do inanimate objects. While that may hardly surprise anyone, the details of neural activation are more compelling. Some of the areas more activated by babies include the thalamus, anterior and middle cingulate, and midbrain. Some of these areas, such as the anterior cingulate, thus overlap with ones activated by infant cries. The patterns of activation also make some sense. The thalamus serves as a relay station for neural information, and babies appear to generate more information transit than houses do. The anterior cingulate appears capable of facilitating social evaluation equally for infant visual and auditory stimuli.

Interestingly, fathers' brains also responded differently to images of their own babies compared with images of unrelated babies. The brain areas more highly activated by a father's own baby photos were almost exactly the same ones activated when men were viewing babies compared with houses. The inference is that babies activate the brain differently than houses do, and fathers' own babies are more salient stimuli than unrelated babies are.

Hormones and Paternal Care: Lessons of the Voles

Several of the paternal imaging studies above reveal activation of brain structures (for example, the hypothalamus) involved in hormone release. Moreover, some of those areas responding to paternal stimuli also contain specific hormone receptors—molecules that bind hormones such as vasopressin or prolactin. These observations suggest that hormones are involved in the regulation of paternal behavior.

Leave it to voles (small, furry rodents) to illustrate some of the specific ways in which hormones facilitate paternal behavior. Because the lessons of the voles are immensely useful in our understanding of hormones and paternal care generally, including how we conceptualize this area in humans, we discuss these rodents in some detail. Elegant experimental research has been conducted on several sister species of voles, species differing in mating system and paternal care. Through comparisons of the neuroendocrine substrates of closely related species characterized by long-term pair-bonding and considerable paternal care on one hand (for example, prairie voles) and by polygynous mating relationships and little paternal involvement on the other (for example, montane voles), proximate mechanisms underlying these behavioral proclivities have been revealed. Much of the story centers on the vasopressin system.

Males tend to have higher vasopressin levels than females do. While we commonly recognize sex differences in steroid hormone levels (for example, levels of estradiol, progesterone, testosterone), the sex difference in vasopressin is less recognized, even though vasopressin levels (and densities of the hormone receptors to which it binds) are modulated by androgens such as testosterone (Carter 2007). Effects of vasopressin are also more pronounced in males, suggesting this hormone warrants more attention for its roles in sexually dimorphic behavior.

What are the physiological effects of vasopressin (H. K. Caldwell et al. 2008)? Vasopressin is classically recognized for two functions: increasing blood pressure and acting as an antidiuretic. It also serves to psychologically and behaviorally activate an organism, especially a male, in response to the appropriate stimuli. A male competitor, a courtship opportunity, a helpless rodent pup—these may elicit a vasopressin response, including potentially adaptive psychological effects of heightened anxiety and enhanced social memory, both of which may prime a male's readiness and physiologically mark the importance of the interaction. To exert its effects, vasopressin is bound to one of three receptor types: AVP1a, AVP1b, and AVP2, each of which has a different distribution in the body. For our purposes, it is notable that AVP1a receptors are found in several key brain structures, including the ventral pallidum, itself involved in "reward" pathways. The links between vasopressin and reward pathways, which themselves rely on the neurotransmitter dopamine, enables linking a vasopressin response to a social stimulus like a mate or pup with a positive emotional association.

Experiments with prairie and montane voles reveal differences in the distribution of AVP1a receptors in their brains (Carter 1998; Young and Wang 2004). These differences have been traced to differences in the promoter region of the AVP1a receptor gene. Most remarkable have been the results of transgenic experiments—those which involve moving a gene from one species into another—demonstrating that expression of the AVP1a receptor in the normally polygynous montane vole's forebrain can lead to enhanced interest in spending time with a single female partner, thereby facilitating partner preferences and likely pair-bonding (Lim and Young 2006). Similar results have been found in normally polygynous mouse and other vole species (Lim and Young 2006). Stop and think about these results for a moment. The introduction and expression of a single gene—one involved in the vasopressin system—has proven capable of behaviorally altering a male's family life. Such exciting research has spurred interest in the roles of hormones, neurotransmitters, and neural pathways in human male social behavior too. Ethical and logistical constraints mean that we often cannot perform the kinds of experiments on humans that can be done on lab rodents like these voles. We do not know if human transgenic experiments involving the AVP1a receptor would alter family proclivities. Yet nonhuman animal research like this can serve as a rich source of testable hypotheses for less invasive human research.

Testosterone and Human Male Family Life

In the world of hormones and paternal care, the so-called challenge hypothesis represents a wonderful example of nonhuman animal research influencing human research. The hypothesis posits that male testosterone levels increase in reproductively relevant contexts; consequently, male-male competition and courtship may elicit adaptive increases in testosterone levels, while involvement in long-term bonds and paternal care may be linked with lower testosterone levels (Wingfield et al. 1990). The hypothesis originally integrated a body of research on North American migratory birds, including dark-eyed juncos and song sparrows, whose males commonly exhibit peak testosterone levels during spring male-male competition and courtship but decreased testosterone levels after forming long-term bonds and raising offspring. In some cases, injecting birds in the wild with synthetic testosterone could also affect family life behaviors, including reductions in feeding rates but increases in courtship of extra-pair mates (Ketterson and Nolan 1999).

An obvious question spurred by the challenge hypothesis is, do human males involved in long-term affiliative pair-bonds and/or paternal care have lower testosterone levels? The data on human male testosterone and family life have been piling up recently, including data from a variety of international samples, enabling us to address that question. The short answer is that in samples of men living in the United States and Canada, men involved in long-term relationships like marriage and fatherhood almost uniformly have lower testosterone levels than their single and childless counterparts. However, outside North America, the answer is muddier, probably in good measure because of the cross-cultural variation in human family relationships. Let's walk through some of the key findings in this research on men's testosterone and family relationships.

Among North American testosterone and pair-bonding studies, ten of eleven have found lower testosterone levels among men involved in committed relationships such as marriage (P. B. Gray and Campbell 2009; Van Anders and Gray 2007). In the earliest of these studies, Alan Booth and James Dabbs (1993) showed that among approximately four thousand U.S. Army veterans, men's testosterone levels were higher if they had never married, had ever divorced, had separated, or had had extramarital sex. In a longitudinal study of approximately four thousand U.S. Air Force veterans, Mazur and Michalek (1998) observed that married men had lower testosterone levels, but also found that men's testosterone increased around the time of divorce. Research among Harvard undergraduates and Harvard Business School students revealed that men involved in a long-term committed relationship, whether married or not, had lower testosterone levels than unpaired men. A study on Canadian men revealed that men involved in either same-city or long-distance relationships had lower testosterone levels than single men.

In the first study considering sexual orientation, testosterone, and men's relationships, testosterone levels of Canadian gay men involved in relationships were not different from those of gay men not involved in relationships, although paired heterosexual men had lower testosterone levels than unpaired heterosexual men (Van Anders and Watson 2006). In this same study, testosterone levels of heterosexual women did not differ according to relationship status, whereas paired lesbians had lower testosterone levels than unpaired lesbians. The inference from this study is that being paired to a woman (but not a man) appears to be associated with lower testosterone levels, for both men and women.

Several North American studies also point to lower testosterone levels among fathers. In a study of Canadian men undergoing the transition to fatherhood, men's testosterone levels shortly after birth were 33% lower than shortly before birth (Storey et al. 2000). In a different Canadian sample, of sixty-seven men, fathers had lower testosterone levels than control non-fathers (Fleming et al. 2002). Men's testosterone levels, whether they were fathers or not, were also negatively related to their sympathy and desire to respond to tape-recorded infant cries. In other words, men with lower testosterone levels were more paternally responsive. Put these testosterone and fatherhood data together with the other North American studies, and we find a consistent link between lower testosterone and men's involvement in affiliative pair-bonds and paternal care.

Step off the North American continent, and the links between testosterone and men's family relationships become less clear. In only three of seven studies outside North America do we find that monogamously married men have lower testosterone levels compared with those of their unmarried counterparts (reviewed in P. B. Gray and Campbell 2009). For example, among urban Bangladeshi men, testosterone levels did not differ depending on whether men were married. Results regarding testosterone and polygyny have also differed. Among Swahili on the Kenyan coast, men married to two wives had higher testosterone levels than other men. This result was not replicated among Ariaal pastoralists, however: in fact, older, polygynously married Ariaal men had lower, rather than higher, testosterone levels compared with older, monogamously married men.

Several international studies have also tested whether fathers outside of North America have lower testosterone levels. In four of six such studies, fathers had lower testosterone levels than controls did. Married fathers in Beijing, China, had lower testosterone levels than married non-fathers or unmarried men (P. B. Gray, Yang, and Pope 2006). Fathers in urban Jamaica had lower testosterone levels than single controls did, although this effect was largely and surprisingly due to the lowest levels of "visiting fathers" (fathers who live separately from their partner and child) rather than "coresidential fathers" (P. B. Gray, Parkin, and Samms-Vaughan 2007). Fathers in urban Bangladesh, in contrast, did not have lower testosterone levels compared with married non-fathers or single men.

What accounts for some of these globally discrepant results? Perhaps a major factor underlying the variable patterns is the cross-cultural variation in men's family relationships. These studies outside of North America encompass a range of family contexts, including ones in which polygyny is common and acceptable, ones in which fathers may spend little time with their infants and toddlers, and ones in which extramarital affairs may be less stigmatized.

To illustrate the importance of social context, and its likely helping to account for these cross-culturally variable data, we can compare findings from two human societies living in the same northern Tanzania bush. Here, the Hadza live as hunter-gatherers, and men engage in relatively frequent interaction with their children. The neighboring Datoga are pastoralists with a high degree of polygyny and less paternal involvement with young children. Based on differences in family life, researchers predicted that Hadza fathers would have lower testosterone levels than single men, but no differences in testosterone levels would be found between Datoga fathers and non-fathers (Muller et al. 2009). Once the researchers asked men about their family relationships and collected saliva samples from which testosterone levels were measured, the results supported the predictions. Indeed, Hadza fathers, but not Datoga fathers, had lower testosterone levels compared with controls. So given the social context of fatherhood, we might generally expect where men engage in a reasonable degree of direct interaction with young children during day hours and perhaps also during co-sleeping, men may be more likely to have lower testosterone levels.

Hormones and Human Paternal Care: Vasopressin, Prolactin, and More

While the birds helped inspire research on human testosterone and family life, let's go back to the rodents to ask what further insights they might offer concerning the possible hormonal correlates of human paternal care. The vole work described above suggests we ought to be testing for links between vasopressin and paternal care. Experimental research on male voles shows that simultaneously blocking the effects of vasopressin and oxytocin can compromise paternal care (Bales et al. 2004). Rodent work has also suggested a conceptual bridge between androgenic hormones, such as testosterone, with other hormones, like vasopressin. In an integrative model of social affiliation derived primarily from experimental rodent research, Richard Depue and Jeannine

Morrone-Strupinsky (2005) suggest that there are interactions between the social context of an organism and the facilitatory roles for gonadal steroids such as testosterone that in turn can have facilitatory roles on peptide hormones like vasopressin. Hormones such as vasopressin play important integrative functions in part through their effects on dopaminergic reward pathways in brain structures such as the ventral pallidum. Depue and Morrone-Strupinsky (2005) also postulate important roles for endogenous opioids in the continuation of a relationship. Let's draw on these concepts to ask about vasopressin and human male family life.

The only study investigating vasopressin and human paternal care is the Jamaican one previously described (P. B. Gray, Perkin, and Samms-Vaughan 2007). In this study of Jamaican fathers and control nonfathers, vasopressin levels did not differ according to whether men had children. Among the twenty-seven fathers in the study, however, the age of their youngest children was negatively correlated with the fathers' urinary vasopressin levels. In other words, the younger the child a father had, the higher his vasopressin levels. That finding resonates with the recent report in common marmosets that age of youngest offspring and fathers' AVP1a receptor density in the prefrontal cortex were negatively correlated (Kozorovitskiy et al. 2006). In this Jamaican sample, vasopressin levels were positively correlated with blood pressure. Based on that link with blood pressure, along with nonhuman research on psychological and behavioral effects of vasopressin, we can offer interpretations of this preliminary study. Fathers interacting with younger children may have higher vasopressin levels for several reasons: responding to unpredictable and potent infant stimuli like cries, carrying and holding their young, and experiencing greater anxiety and promoting social memory.

Prolactin has been linked with paternal care in numerous vertebrates (Nelson 2005). If males play important roles caring for offspring, one of the most consistent hormonal correlates of this care is elevated prolactin. In species as diverse as emperor penguins, wolves, meerkats, ringdoves, and common marmosets, involved males exhibit prolactin increases associated with offspring care. Even that paragon of paternal investment—the pipefish, containing a pouch in which he incubates eggs before "giving birth"—develops that brood pouch under the stimulation of prolactin (Stolting and Wilson 2007).

Although the name "prolactin" refers to its classical function of lactation support (literally, "promoting lactation"), this hormone, secreted from the anterior pituitary, serves a variety of functions, including ones related to offspring care. Prolactin promotes adaptive weight gain and anxiety and inhibits reproductive function, all good things if one is focused on providing extensive care of dependent offspring rather than on looking for mates (Sobrinho 2003). Under the right sex steroid hormone milieu, along with nipple stimulation, a man can also produce small amounts of milk under the influence of prolactin (Bribiescas 2006). Relatively few men have pursued this breast-feeding potential, despite the potential to revolutionize paternal involvement. However, several human studies have also investigated links between prolactin and paternal care.

The first of these human studies, published in 2000, initiated a new era in human hormones and fatherhood research (Storey et al. 2000). Although researchers had linked elevated prolactin levels with fatherhood in common marmosets almost twenty years earlier, no human study on this subject had been published until the new millennium dawned. In this study of thirty-four highly invested Canadian men recruited from prenatal classes, men's prolactin levels were highest shortly before the birth of their offspring. Across samples collected before and after birth, men who reported concern when listening to tape-recorded infant cries had higher prolactin levels than less-concerned men. Those men reporting two or more pregnancy symptoms, such as nausea and fatigue, also had higher prolactin levels. Results of this study thus suggested links, like those among other paternal vertebrates, between prolactin and human paternal care. Additionally, the findings were relatively rare in bridging the psychology and physiology of fatherhood. It was not just that men's prolactin levels were associated with infant cries but also that some of the couvade symptoms discussed earlier in this chapter could also be linked with paternal physiology.

In a different study of Canadian men, fathers listened to either "control" background noise or the tape-recorded pain and hunger cries of unrelated infants (Fleming et al. 2002). The experienced fathers listening to the infant cries experienced acute increases in prolactin levels, compared with experienced fathers listening to control noise or inexperienced fathers listening to control noise or the same cries. Fathers with higher prolactin levels tended to respond with more alertness and positive feelings to infant cries. Among fathers listening to the infant cries, their prolactin levels were positively associated with experience in changing diapers and holding babies.

In a third study investigating prolactin and human paternal interactions, the same Jamaican men described above participated (Gray et al.

2007). The prolactin levels of men were measured before and after a twenty-minute session during which fathers interacted with their partners and youngest children and single non-fathers sat quietly. The prolactin levels of single men dipped during this period, whereas prolactin levels of fathers remained relatively flat across the test session. The result was different prolactin profiles according to paternal status. The contrast between single non-fathers and fathers was largely due to "visiting fathers," a result mirroring the testosterone results in the same sample. This study, like the two Canadian ones, suggests that paternal interactions, including exposure to infant cries, can affect men's prolactin levels.

Non-human research has inconsistently pointed to the roles of oxytocin or cortisol in paternal care. Oxytocin is typically viewed in other animals as fostering social affiliation and inhibiting the stress axis, including cortisol release (Carter 1998). What about oxytocin's role in humans? In the same Jamaican study, no links between paternal status or age of youngest child and urinary oxytocin levels were found. Interestingly, however, one study did observe a link between oxytocin and human male pair-bonding: Karen Grewen and others (2005) found that in a study of thirty-eight couples who had been in a committed relationship for at least one year, both men and women with higher relationship quality had higher oxytocin levels. No differences in cortisol levels occurred with respect to paternal status or offspring age in the Jamaican study. Of two Canadian hormone and fatherhood studies, one (Berg and Wynne-Edwards 2001), but not the other (Fleming et al. 2002), observed lower cortisol levels among fathers compared with non-father controls. Alison Fleming and others (2002) also found that fathers holding their infants experienced transient increases in cortisol levels. From these sparse and inconsistent preliminary data, perhaps we would anticipate the potential for fathers to experience transient increases in oxytocin during warm interactions with children (comparable to the human-dog study mentioned above, though not observed in this preliminary Jamaican study) and variable acute cortisol responses depending on the infant stimuli (for example, increases in response to cries but lowered levels during calm times). Indeed, Ann Frodi and others (1978) discovered that fathers experienced greater cardiovascular responses to premature infant cries and faces, just one illustration of the ways that variable child stimuli are likely to elicit variation in paternal physiological responses.

By now, all of our brains, whether we are fathers or not, are steeped in babies. We have covered a lot of ground in attempting to address the two primary questions of this chapter concerning the psychological and physiological impacts associated with human fatherhood. We have found that men undergo a variety of psychological changes, ranging from excitement to anxiety, a heightened sense of life's worth to depression. We have seen that babies foster these variable psychological impacts by reaching through various sensory modes to affect men's neural and hormonal underpinnings. The specific ways in which all of these processes unfold depend on the sociocultural context.

Despite the amount of terrain we have covered this chapter, we can point to numerous roads researchers have yet to travel. We have said nothing about the ways development impacts the physiology of human paternal responses, an omission caused by the lack of available data. We have said nothing about genetic bases of paternal behavior. In this case, a modest amount of work has suggested that genetic differences contribute to some variation in paternal care (Pérusse et al. 1994); one might imagine that newly discovered polymorphisms, or genetic variants, in the human vasopressin or oxytocin receptor contribute small but additive amounts to variation in paternal behavior (see Walum et al. 2008). We have said nothing about variation in couvade symptoms, much less in paternal physiology, depending on whether men are step- or biological fathers, simply because there are no relevant data, whether among Western societies or among broader cross-cultural samples. We have also yet to formally link some of the core psychological transitions with fatherhood—such as risk of postpartum depression and reduced marital quality—with the physiological bases of paternal responses discussed in the latter half of this chapter. We can clearly underscore large gaps in our knowledge of the psychology and physiology of human fatherhood. Still, the progress made in recent years has been fast (note that the majority of studies cited in this chapter were published since 2000), and that pace will likely just get faster as babies continue to encroach upon our brains.

11

Health and the Human Father

The past few years have given birth to a new dimension of fatherhood studies: health. While in previous chapters we have considered the effects of fatherhood on men's time allocation, sexuality, physiology, and more, it is an altogether new leap to ask how fatherhood may impact men's health. Illustrating this nascent tie, the prestigious *Journal of the American Medical Association* published a 2006 article titled "Fatherhood as a Component of Men's Health" (Garfield, Clark-Kauffman, and Davis 2006). The relevant literature cited in that topical review was small, and the evolutionary and cultural issues so central to this book ignored. Clearly, there is great room to shed light on the health manifestations of fatherhood. The present chapter represents our attempt at just such an effort—to pull together a wide-ranging set of concepts and data sets that collectively address health and fatherhood. Like so many good things in evolutionary biology, we find ourselves drawn to Darwin while beginning this endeavor.

Darwin, Sexual Selection, and Male Mortality

Darwin spelled out the basics of sexual selection in his aptly titled 1871 classic *The Descent of Man, and Selection in Relation to Sex*. He highlighted two key facets of sexual selection in the book. In the case of intrasexual selection, he focused on male-male competition, the outcomes of which could be found abundantly in nature, including in our own species. Male Irish elk have huge antlers to foster success in male-male battles, stag beetles have large horns for the same purpose, and elephant seal males have three times the fatty and muscular bulk of females in order to throw their weight around against other males. In contrast, intersexual selection refers to one sex choosing members of

224

the opposite sex as mates. In terms of intersexual selection, Darwin emphasized female choice of male mates. The process of female choice could give rise to seemingly nonfunctional or even deleterious characteristics like the flamboyance of the peacock's train or the wild beauty of a male sage grouse's dance.

What does sexual selection have to do with fatherhood and health? The ways in which males strive for reproductive success have consequences for their morbidity (patterns of illness) and mortality (death). This quite broad claim provides a bridge between male reproductive strategies and central facets of health.

Take elephant seals as an example. During a recent drive along the California coast, one of us (Gray) observed beaches covered with these giants. In the world of an elephant seal, males compete for reproductive opportunities largely by attempting to control portions of the beaches sought by females (Le Bouef and Reiter 1988). A successful male gains reproductive access to many females at the expense of many other males. Success is achieved through loud calls, smashing chests against other males, and snagging other males with sharp teeth. Males do not give an ounce of paternal care—that's not part of the reproductive equation. Indeed, a "successful" male elephant seal father may be the one who does not accidentally roll over his offspring. Consequences of this reproductive dynamic are that males are much heavier than females, males battle more viciously against members of their own sex than do females, relatively few males reproduce compared with females, and, most important for our present purposes, males suffer a notably higher rate of mortality than do females. All that sexual selection takes its toll on the ultimate criterion of health: risk of mortality.

Elephant seals are not alone in this regard. While approximately 90% of bird species are socially monogamous and provide paternal care, these behavioral tendencies occur among only around 5% of mammalian species (Trivers 1972). These facts make it more difficult to tease apart some of the phylogenetic impacts on relative male mortality, especially if we wish to focus on animal species studied for extensive periods of time in the wild. That being said, it appears that male behavioral strategies for achieving reproductive success modulate relative mortality risk. In a review of the subject, Tim Clutton-Brock and Kavita Isvaran (2007) tabulate relative male-female mortality risk across various social vertebrate species studied at length in the wild. In the set of socially monogamous species, from beavers to the barnacle goose, male mortality risks are reduced compared with the risks of socially polygynous species like red deer (elk), African lions, and black-tailed prairie dogs. In another set of analyses, the more polygynous the species, the greater the relative male mortality. In other words, male mortality rates (indexed against female mortality rates) are higher in species in which individual males have several female mates. While that elephant seal male must face an extreme of polygyny in the hope of leaving a reproductive successor, that socially monogamous, family-oriented male dwarf mongoose exhibits a mortality profile little different from that of dwarf mongoose females across most reproductive years.

Because this is a discussion of mortality profiles, what about causes of death? Darwin's views on the subject, in addition to our own discussion thus far, might lead one to think that the bulk of excess male mortality lies on the field of battle—the direct consequence of violence. That may not be true, however. We should entertain at least three broad causes of death: violence, compromised immune function, and energetics (that is, alterations in energetic status, including starvation).

In a study of thirteen closely related sets of organisms differing in mating system (for example, social monogamy versus polygyny), Sarah Moore and Kenneth Wilson (2002) find that in eleven of them males of the more polygynous species have higher rates of parasitism. In other words, males of polygynous species appear to be more prone to the deleterious health effects of parasitism. The greater risk of parasitism, in turn, might be attributable to the compromised immune function of socially strapped males. In the face of male-male challenges, males may prioritize energetic investment in behavioral competition to a point that immune defenses are weakened. These views might contribute to the magnitude of male mortality risk according to mating systems.

Still, it is a tricky business to disentangle causes of death. Males of the same species with greater parasitism may be the same males who not only battle more (and thus incur more festering wounds, which challenge their immune systems) but also encounter more parasites (through longer day ranges and larger body sizes). These may be the same males who forego a meal for a reproductive opportunity, only to suffer the ill consequences of negative energy balance at later times. We can thus acknowledge the difficulties of sorting out causes of death (and lesser health challenges) but still find it useful to conceptually parse causes into behavioral, energetic, and immune ones. We will draw up a related conceptual scheme for considering human data.

Shifting closer to home, with research on captive nonhuman primates, the magnitude of male-female mortality risk varies across mating systems and paternal care. Consistent with broader patterns, males of more polygynous species, such as chimpanzees, gorillas, and orangutans, die at higher rates than do females of the same species (Allman et al. 1998). Because these mortality profiles still hold in captivity, when male-male battles are minimized, the fact that these differentials remain is quite striking. Even with access to veterinary care, males still find ways to die earlier and more often than females.

Importantly, in the same male-female mortality profile analyses, gibbons and siamangs exhibit no notable sex differences in mortality (Allman et al. 1998). Males and females die at about equivalent rates in captivity. These tendencies conform to their mating systems: these species tend to be socially monogamous, although males invest relatively little in offspring care.

Saving the best for last, what about relative mortality profiles among titi monkeys and owl monkeys, small South American monkeys characterized by social monogamy and intensive paternal care? You might guess that these latter species buck the mammalian trend. You would be right. Male titi monkeys and owl monkeys survive, rather than die, at higher rates than females of their same species in captivity (Allman et al. 1998). These species provide excellent evidence that variation in male reproductive behavior can translate into benefits quantified in survival.

Human Mortality: Sex Differences and Effects of Family Life

All of this sexual selection and comparative research sets up the human data. Males tend to die at higher rates than females in almost every population studied (www.who.int). The few exceptions are places such as Afghanistan, where societal biases against females prevail, including selective infanticide of females. Otherwise, from Japan to Denmark, Colombia to the United States, males die at higher rates than females do. The magnitude of this sex difference is modest compared with some of the more polygynous species, however. Our mortality profiles do not look like those of an elephant seal. With a modest degree of polygyny, embedded in pair-bonds and paternal care, our evolutionary past makes sense of this magnitude.

The overall sex difference in human mortality covers up interesting age-related patterning. Suggesting that males are designed for shorter, deadlier lives, males die at higher rates than females from the moment of conception onward (Kraemer 2000). Even before a baby is born, males are more likely to have died in the womb. That trend only continues after birth. And it ramps up in at least one, if not two, other periods of life.

Around adolescence, the magnitude of male excess mortality spikes, in large part thanks to male risk-taking behavior (Wilson and Daly 1985). These are the ages of reckless traffic accidents and deadly escalated behavioral confrontations. In the United States, this amplified male mortality risk means that men in their twenties are four times as likely to die as women, in part because of committing suicide seven times more often and dying in car accidents three times as often (Kruger and Nesse 2006). Across a sample of twenty countries, men in their twenties die at higher rates than women (Kruger and Nesse 2004). At extremes, men in Colombia die five times as often, and men in Sweden only three times as often, as women in their twenties. Lest we wonder whether these differentials hold among small-scale societies of hunter-gatherers and horticulturalists, Barry Hewlett (1991) notes that Aka forager men in their young twenties die four times as often as young females, largely because of accidents (for example, falling out of a tree while attempting to obtain honey), and that higher violent death rates among other societies such as the Yanomami make maleness risky wherever one looks.

At later ages (in middle age), another spike in excess male mortality occurs (Allman 1999). This later-age excess male mortality appears largely attributable to failings in male cardiovascular health (Allman 1999). Those physiological tolls have added up, with men around age fifty suffering increased relative mortality thanks especially to heart attacks.

Marital life can moderate the negative impacts of being a male. Just when male and mortality risk were beginning to sound synonymous, we see a way in which life is kinder, gentler, and healthier. In the United States, for example, even though males die at higher rates than females across prime adult years, the magnitude of this sex difference is damp-ened if one is married. In 1999 data, whether men aged fifteen to twenty-four were married or not did not alter relative male mortality, but at all later ages married men had lower excess mortality compared with their never-married male counterparts (Kruger and Nesse 2006).

These U.S. data are not isolated. Similar patterns hold across the sixteen countries in which Peifeng Hu and Noreen Goldman (1990) were able to summarize data. In all of these countries, married men had lower mortality rates than single men did. Moreover, married men displayed lower mortality than either widowed or divorced men. As illustrations, single or divorced Japanese men had three times the relative mortality as married men, and in the Netherlands single or divorced men had approximately twice the relative mortality as married men.

These international data on male marital status and mortality also raise several important considerations. The first is teasing apart cause from correlation. If married men live longer than their single counterparts, is that because of inherent characteristics of the men who married (fewer genetic risk factors, fewer detrimental early life development impacts, more desirable mates because of better health or resources) or because of alterations in risk factors for mortality occurring with marriage (engaging in less risky behavior, eating better, and so forth), or some combination thereof? Thanks to the availability of a few longitudinal studies, in which men's health was traced in and out of marriage, at least part of the effect can be attributed to marital transitions in risk factors. In a longitudinal study of over a quarter million U.S. male and female citizens aged forty-five to sixty-four, married men had lower mortality compared with other men (N. J. Johnson et al. 2000). Similarly, among Danish men and women in their fifties, sixties, and seventies, an eight-year longitudinal study revealed that, even after controlling for potential confounding variables such as smoking status, married and cohabiting men died at lower rates than unpaired men (Lund et al. 2002). The most reasonable interpretation is that the outcomes of studies like these represent a combination of psychosocial alterations, with marriage interacting with preexisting factors.

A second issue is the meaning of "marital status" in the available studies and for broader analytical purposes. Until quite recently in places like the United States, it would be a foreign concept to marry but not reproduce. In one Japanese sample, 98% of married men had fathered children (Ikeda et al. 2007). These considerations suggest that, especially for older data sets, including Hu and Goldman's 1990 international marriage and mortality study, "marital status" may be masking effects of both marriage and fatherhood on men's mortality. It may be impractical to try disentangling the two—they really go hand in hand. Yet we may wish to isolate, if possible, independent effects of marriage and fatherhood on men's health and mortality. It is only with new studies—and with studies remaining to be conducted—that we can conceptualize and attempt to measure differential effects of marriage versus fatherhood (Kendig et al. 2007).

Only a handful of studies explicitly address the effects of fatherhood on male mortality. Findings of these studies are mixed. Among samples of British peerage and Finnish men, mortality rates of fathers did not differ from those of non-fathers (cited in Jasienska et al. 2006). A more recent study of all Finnish men born between 1935 and 1958 revealed that men with two children had mortality comparable to that of men with more than two children, but lower mortality than men without children or only one child (Grundy and Kravdal 2008). A large study of more than half a million Swedish men aged twenty-nine to fifty-four found that fatherless men in long-term cohabiting relationships had 1.7 times the all-cause mortality as their cohabiting father counterparts (Weitoft, Burstrom, and Rosen 2004). Furthermore, among fathers, those in long-term cohabiting relationships and with lone custody of children had 1.7 times the mortality risk, and those in similar cohabiting relationships but without custody had 3.6 times the mortality risk, as cohabiting fathers. In a study of approximately five thousand U.S. men comprising a nationally representative study of households, fathers exhibited significantly lower mortality rates (K. R. Smith and Zick 1994). However, another U.S. study of affluent older men living in southern California found no difference in mortality according to whether men had fathered children (Friedlander 1996). In a rare study of a small-scale population of recent hunter-gatherers, there was a trend for Ache fathers of Paraguay with more living children to have lower mortality risk (K. Hill and Hurtado 1996).

In an interesting twist on paternal effects on mortality, Grazyna Jasienska and others (2006) took up this issue in a study of historical Polish records collected from parishes. Among fathers of sons, there was no relationship between number of offspring and mortality risk. Among fathers of daughters, however, the more girls born, the lower the mortality risk. These Polish findings differed from those of other samples. In rural Bangladesh, the more surviving sons a man has, the lower his mortality, but daughters exerted no effects on paternal mortality (Hurt, Ronsmans, and Quigley 2006). Paternal mortality did not differ according to sex ratios of offspring among the Sami reindeer herders of Scandinavia or among men in Utah (Harrell, Smith, and Mineau 2008). All this variation in paternal mortality leads us to ask what factors account for it.

Human Male Family Life: Causes of Morbidity and Mortality

These studies of fatherhood and mortality leave aside the causes of death. A few studies have investigated effects of fatherhood on mortality stemming from causes such as prostate cancer and cardiovascular disease. These studies also fail to tell a clear picture. In meta-analysis of prostate cancer etiology (disease processes), fatherhood was not linked with altered risk of mortality (Dennis and Dawson 2002). However, in the most detailed study investigating the effects of fatherhood on prostate cancer risk, different results emerged. In a study of all Dutch men born between 1935 and 1988, fathers who had one child had the highest prostate cancer risk, and men with two to four children had almost comparable risk; however, childless men had 0.80 the relative risk of men with one child, and men with six children had only about half the relative risk of men with one child (Jorgensen et al. 2008).

In the Framingham U.S. heart study, researchers investigated the effect of parity (number of children) on cardiovascular health risk (Haynes, Eaker, and Feinleib 1983). There emerged a statistical trend in which the more children a man fathered, the higher his risk of cardiovascular disease. However, among U.K. men aged sixty to seventy-nine, men with two children had the lowest risk of coronary heart disease (Lawlor et al. 2003). In a large Swedish study of all-cause mortality and fatherhood, data were also given according to specific causes of death (Weitoft, Burstrom, and Rosen 2004). Long-term cohabitating non-fathers had 1.6 times the risk of heart attacks compared with long-term cohabitating fathers.

To focus on chronic diseases like prostate cancer and heart disease and their association with fatherhood appears to be getting a long way from elephant seals battling or titi monkeys caring for their young. We can step back and ask about risk factors contributing to variable causes of death associated with male family life. Here, we take up several risk factors, which we classify as behavioral risk-taking factors; energetic (diet, activity patterns, sleep) factors; and mental health factors. In considering these types of risks, we can better envision possible etiologies underlying the human mortality profiles discussed above.

Do fathers engage in less behavioral risk taking? To be more specific, are fathers involved in fewer traffic accidents, in less drug and alcohol use, and in less male-male competition resulting in morbidity and mortality counts? Sadly, very few data enable us to answer this question directly. In one of the exceptions, the previously described Swedish fatherhood and mortality study (Weitoft, Burstrom, and Rosen 2004) revealed that long-term cohabiting fathers had lower mortality risk attributed to addictions, external violence, and lung cancer but not lower risk attributed to traffic injuries or suicides, compared with long-term cohabiting non-fathers. Among Swedish fathers, noncustodial fathers had especially elevated mortality risk stemming from suicides, addictions, falls, and poisonings.

Marital status is consistently linked with differences in behavioral risk taking. In Chapter 8 we saw that men tend to engage in fewer male group social activities after steeping themselves in marital and fatherly life. Associated with that behavioral tendency are lower rates among married men of crime, pathological gambling, scholarly and artistic creativity (Gray et al. 2004), cigarette smoking, alcohol and drug consumption (Power, Rodgers, and Hope 1999; Broman 1993), and same-sex homicides (Daly and Wilson 1999). We even find lower success among the top one hundred male professional tennis players (Farrelly and Nettle 2007). The rationale put forth for the reduction in male-male homicides and tennis success among married men is that after pairing with a mate, men may experience some reduction in the competitive urges that make them sensitive to the kinds of slights of honor eliciting violent responses or to the demands of rising to a competitor's challenge on the athletic courts. A wrong look by another adult male seeps in less when your social vision includes a mate and offspring.

Interestingly, these kinds of behavioral differences associated with marital status are also linked with advancing male age (Daly and Wilson 1988). It thus appears that male competitive urges, surging in adolescent to motivate male engagement in the dangerous reproductive world (and fostering those increased early adulthood mortality risks), wane as men successfully attain the status and resources enabling them to acquire mates and reproduce, and in turn adopt less risky behavioral strategies. The result is that male risk-taking behaviors appear to be attenuated with both age and involvement in male family life. High-quality family involvement may serve as preventative medicine.

Turning to energetics, let us start with a perspective that may seem awkward to those of us fattening in the comfort of an office chair, doughnuts in reach. Contrary to this energetically cushy lifestyle, most of life's food-getting ways entail trials and tribulations. Most animals, male or female, spend the bulk of their waking hours seeking, eating, and digesting the foods that keep them alive. Even then, we can appreciate how sexual selection might prioritize male mate-seeking at the cost of starvation. Take red deer as an example. A significant risk of male mortality during winter months is starvation (Clutton-Brock, Guinness, and Albon 1982), a senseless cause of death that results when males focus less on eating fall foliage than on mating with females in heat.

In the human realm, energetic concerns may be one means through which health and mortality differentials linked with fatherhood arise (Sear 2006). In subsistence societies, where food availability is a concern, better male fat reserves may be a mark of energetic privilege. These reserves may indicate that a male has succeeded in locally appropriate economic endeavors (for example, by being a good hunter or farmer) or in acquisition of such resources through his social networks, which perhaps have expanded with adult age. The fat reserves might also indicate the luxury of reduced energy expenditure, that is, his finding others to do some of the hard work he used to do (such as sending younger herd boys to take his livestock to water and pasture). However the case, markers of energy reserve may be positive health indicators. Indeed, among rural men in the Gambia, heavier men have lower mortality in addition to more wives and more children (Sear 2006).

If we do not live in a subsistence society, energetic considerations may be turned on their head: we're becoming too fat. Taking in too much energy, not using enough, we are currently witnessing an epidemic of obesity spreading throughout many parts of the developed and developing world. Perhaps fatherhood contributes to these energetic equations.

So what do the data suggest about alterations in men's diets after fatherhood? According to nationally representative U.S. data, fathers eat more total and saturated fat (Garfield, Clark-Kauffman, and Davis 2006). Among older married men living in Australia, Finland, and the

Netherlands, fathers did not consume more fruit in wintertime than non-fathers did (Kendig et al. 2007). In some societies practicing couvade, including some of those discussed in the previous chapter, fathers may be subject to food taboos during a partner's pregnancy or the postpartum period. Among the Witoto of South America, for example, postpartum fathers are prohibited from eating meat (K. E. Paige and J. M. Paige 1981). Still, these prohibitions are limited in time and unlikely to have major health impacts. Reviewing much of the limited but relevant evidence, Hal Kendig and others (2007) suggest that marital status differences in behavior are more powerful generally than parental status. Across the board, we suspect that men's diets improve with marriage—and such improvements are largely maintained with fatherhood. In light of continued sexual divisions of labor around the world, men's involvement in family life probably helps keep them better nourished than they otherwise would be. Indeed, when one of us (Gray) interviewed Swahili men in Kenya concerning their work and family lives, several single men specified a wife's cooking as a reason they wished to marry.

In Chapter 8, covering shifts in men's time allocation with fatherhood, we found that fathers commonly devote less time to male-male group socializing, and in some societies, such as the United States, fathers also engage in fewer athletic activities. Reductions in men's activities may have variable health relevance. If men are living in a subsistence society, a reduction in energy expenditure may be viewed favorably. Rather than needing to roam in search of resources, burning fuel in the process, a man with a more sedentary lifestyle may preserve valuable resources that enable better immune functioning. A more sedentary life may be a good thing. But flip the social context to a world of nutritional excess, and that same sedentism may be a negative. In that world, increases in sedentism associated with fatherhood may have deleterious health consequences. When body composition is altered (more on that momentarily), chronic disease risks may be elevated. Beneficial effects of physical activity on cardiovascular and immune function are diminished.

In a review of the relationship between parenting and physical activity, Kai Bellows-Riecken and Ryan Rhodes (2008) identified twenty-five studies, of which eight included men, primarily from North America and Australia. In meta-analysis, Bellows-Riecken and Rhodes identified an overall reduction in physical activity with parenting (for both men and women) but were not able to calculate a separate effect for males alone, given study design constraints. Still, when we look at results of specific studies, it appeared that in most, but not all, studies fathers had lower activity levels than non-fathers. As an illustration, in a study of over thirteen thousand Australian men, fathers had 1.6 times the risk of being "insufficiently active" of non-fathers.

Any new parent, especially a mother, knows all too well that a baby serves as an insult to sleep. If fathers also suffer sleep deficits, then alterations in sleep patterns can serve as another pathway through which fatherhood impacts a man's health. Sleep disruptions can alter anabolic and maintenance functions, meaning these disruptions can also be viewed from an energetic perspective. Recent research reveals how sleep deprivation can alter metabolism, with effects including elevated evening cortisol levels and reductions in insulin sensitivity. Sleep deprivation can alter levels of anabolic hormones, including growth hormone and testosterone.

Do fathers suffer the kinds of sleep modifications that might foster these types of physiological impacts on health? Unfortunately, we do not have a straightforward answer. We suspect that most fathers around the world do incur sleep deficiencies and alterations in waking/sleeping rhythms associated with the arrival of a newborn, but direct data are not available to buttress this suspicion. Given the cross-cultural patterns in sleep arrangements discussed in Chapter 2, fathers are commonly in proximity to newborns during sleep times, meaning that these men would be subject to infant cries and movements. In the Jamaican study described in the previous chapter, coresidential fathers reported 5.7 hours of sleep the previous night, visiting fathers 6.7 hours, and single non-fathers 7.7 hours, suggesting that fatherhood, at least in this study of fathers with young children, was associated with alterations in sleep patterns (P. B. Gray, Parkin, and Samms-Vaughan 2007). Among Japanese men, the number of hours of sleep during a partner's late pregnancy and four to five weeks postpartum was not altered, but their sleep rhythms—that is, waking, duration of sleep bouts—were (Yamazaki et al. 2005). Helping reduce the impacts of fatherhood on sleep, many of these Japanese men began sleeping apart from their partners and infants, an explicit recognition of young children's impacts on parents' sleep.

In considering the available data on paternal differences in diet, activity patterns, and sleep, we can also consider measures that sum these various impacts. From an energy economy perspective, the outcome of energy in and energy out is energy balance, measurable in terms of weight loss or gain. And over the longer haul, the energetic bottom line can be measured with energy status, including weight or measures of specific components of weight, such as fat. These energetic considerations allow us to ask whether fathers gain weight compared with non-fathers or whether fathers are fatter than control men. These are important questions because we know that weight and fatness are some of the best predictors of a variety of health outcomes. In industrial societies, a higher body mass index (or BMI, a crude index of fatness measured as an individual's weight in kilograms divided by his height in meters squared) predicts increased risk of heart attacks, type 2 diabetes, and prostate cancer, among other outcomes (for example, www .who.int). These negative weight-related effects tend to be even more pronounced for measures of "central" fat deposition—or fat deposited in the belly. Larger waist circumferences tend to be even more powerful predictors of chronic health problems than overall measures of body weight or fatness.

Data addressing differences in men's weight and/or body composition associated with marital status are more available than data associated with fatherhood (reviewed in Sobal, Rauschenbach, and Frongillo 2003). In the bulk of available studies, married men tend to have higher BMIs compared with single men. This tendency is found in Polish men, for example, but not in Jamaican men (Ichinohe et al. 2006). Longitudinal studies suggest that changes in marital life can alter body weights, meaning that at least part of the effect is due to differences in lifestyle factors in addition to preexisting factors. In a nationally representative U.S. study, men who remained unmarried over a ten-year year time span gained around five pounds, whereas unmarried men who married gained about eleven pounds (Sobal, Rauschenbach, and Frongillo 2003).

In a study of Wisconsin men described previously (Clinton 1987), men self-reported whether their weight changed during a partner's pregnancy. Expectant fathers experienced more unanticipated weight gain during a partner's third trimester compared with non-father controls (Clinton 1987). As it turns out, these were not the only Wisconsin males who appeared to experience weight increases during a partner's pregnancy. Among captive colonies of common marmosets and cotton-top tamarins housed in the University of Wisconsin's National Primate Research Center facility, expectant fathers experienced weight increases (Ziegler et al. 2006). Across a partner's five-month pregnancy, common marmoset fathers' weights increased about 8%, whereas weights of control non-fathers decreased by a few percent. Among cotton-top tamarins, expectant fathers' weights increased about 4%, while weights of control non-fathers decreased slightly. Recalling that males of both these monkey species form long-term bonds with mates and provide extensive paternal care, we find it striking that they gain weight in anticipation of childcare—and we cannot blame television watching or reduced team sports participation for the effect. This weight gain may be adaptive, however, by helping a father pack on a few more pounds, which he will subsequently burn while helping carry and care for his newborns.

If we try to focus on associations between central fat and fatherhood, we are left with but one study that has considered this relationship. In a large study of 783 Dutch men in their twenties, fathers had higher waist circumferences but not different BMIs compared with non-fathers (Nielsen et al. 2007). The differences in waist circumference in this study were attributable in part to the more sedentary lifestyles of fathers.

Health and Human Male Family Life: A Synthesis

So how can we integrate these data on fathers' body composition with other evidence, to provide a coherent story of health and fatherhood? Like other facets of family life, men's behavior is most visibly altered by marriage, with fatherhood continuing or perhaps slightly altering the shifts that are set in motion by marriage. In this vein, in no studies do we find evidence of men's weight declining with increasing involvement in family life; rather, marriage tends to be associated with increased weight and perhaps fatness, both in subsistence societies and in large nation-states, and fatherhood may only continue those trends. That extra bulk may be advantageous in subsistence societies but not in a world of obesity and chronic diseases, such as heart disease and prostate cancer. Moreover, the increase in body weight and fatness associated with male family life appears to reflect, in part, alterations in activity patterns. The available evidence suggests that men's lives tend to become more sedentary with marriage and possibly additionally so with fatherhood. Sleep alterations associated with fatherhood may contribute to changes in body composition. The nutritional data suggest, if anything, that married life is associated with healthier diets, not to mention reductions in alcohol consumption.

Add it all up, and these sorts of lifestyle transitions contribute to the mortality patterns we discussed earlier this chapter. The more dramatic and consistent effects of family life on male mortality profiles occur with transitions in marital status (for example, getting married or divorced). Separate effects of fatherhood are mixed, and even when present they are not as strong as the effects of marital status. Part of the reason why is likely due to the improvements in diet and so forth with marriage, even in the face of countervailing factors (such as elevated BMIs, which might predispose men to chronic disease). A major part of the reason may be that affiliative bonds with a long-term mate have powerful, protective effects on men's physiology and well-being. Men can be drawn from a competitive male-male world into a more empathetic one when they are embedded in an affiliative marriage, a relationship perhaps marked by lower testosterone levels, higher oxytocin levels, and other physiological effects. This marital transition tends to go hand in hand with reductions in male-male physical competitiveness and behavioral risk taking, providing further benefit. It is against this potential beneficial effect of male involvement in long-term affiliative pair-bonds that we can situate further shifts in male family life. For one example, when a man leaves that relationship (that is, divorces), the negative health impacts associated with divorce appear consistent with the loss.

Fatherhood appears to have both protective and deleterious impacts on men's health. The parenting of young children tends to negatively impact marital quality, meaning that men lose some of the beneficial effects of affiliative pair-bonds. Male mental health may suffer, especially if his partner is also struggling with mental health difficulties. Sleep and sexual challenges may exacerbate these difficulties. Young children, particularly those in daycare, can also serve as disease vectors (for example, Hillis et al. 1992), presenting a father with greater exposure to transmissible diseases. The outcome of these types of issues is that fathers of young children may have compromised health.

Yet as those same children age, men's health may rebound. The strains of caring for young children wane. Those children may provide social and material support to aging parents. Perhaps an older father, living somewhere without a Social Security check to cash, is supported partly by the sons or daughters he raised to adulthood. Put all of these health and fatherhood variables together, and maybe observations like the following make sense. As shown in a U.S. study of approximately five thousand adults, the effects of fatherhood altered across a man's life and his children's ages (see E. E. Bartlett 2004, 163). In this large U.S. study, among married men aged forty years or younger, 8.9% of fathers but only 1.1% of married men without children rated their health as fair or poor. In the same study, among married men aged forty-one to sixty-four, 16.5% of married fathers with children but 22.7% of married men without children rated their health as fair or poor. Similarly, in an Australian study, fathers of preschool-aged children reported worse health than fathers did of older children (Hewitt, Baxter, and Western 2006). These data suggest that earlier in life fatherhood may be a drain on a man's health, but that same relationship may have later, beneficial effects. This pattern appears to be the overarching perspective on fatherhood and health.

Age, Health, and Fatherhood

Still, health and aging tend to spiral together. We all know this from personal experience, and we have a sense why evolutionary biology has forged this link. We thus wish to underscore at some length the relevance of male age to discussions of health and fatherhood. Several theories in evolutionary biology account for age-related investment in various bodily functions, from immune function to cognitive function, from reproductive function to muscle maintenance (Austad 1997; Carey and Tuljapurkar 2003). "Disposable soma" theories suppose that the body's pattern of maintenance and disrepair track survival and reproductive functions that vary with age. If you have a good chance of surviving in the near future, and even reproducing, then it pays a body to maintain itself (and we see this as maintenance of better health). If you live in a high-mortality world, and one with few reproductive prospects in the near future, then your body may invest in itself accordingly (so you would live fast, die soon in an attempt to reproductively succeed in these harsh conditions). We recall that these same types of logic were employed earlier in this book, when we discussed developmental influences on paternal care.

Evidence from various species suggests that natural selection can shape age-related functions in accordance with disposable soma theories (Austad 1997). Bats live longer than similarly sized mammals, in large part because their ability to fly gives them relatively lower mortality rates. Tortoises live exceptionally long lives thanks to the low adult mortality rates they experience by wearing on their backs protection against predators and by continuing to reproduce at advanced ages.

What does all this have to say about health and fatherhood? It suggests that paternal age should itself be a prominent variable in the discussion. Males may be "optimized" to reproduce at certain ages, meaning that their paternal functioning may be slow to warm up and may decline after a peak. We suggest that this is in fact the case for us humans and that recent evolutionary circumstances extend this optimal range of fatherhood, both at the low and high ends, effectively creating a "mismatch" between evolutionarily relevant and current potential ages of fatherhood.

Age-related male reproductive output among hunter-gatherers like the !Kung or Ache helps give us a sense of the "optimal age of fatherhood" from an evolutionary perspective (Tuljapurkar, Puleston, and Gurven 2007). Among the !Kung, ages of fatherhood range between twenty and sixty, with the shape of paternal output steadily rising and falling at a peak centered in the early thirties. This pattern reflects the fact that men reproduce primarily in long-term reproductive unions, tend to be a few years older than their wives, take some years after puberty to be considered socially eligible and worthwhile mates, and so forth. Similarly, among the Ache of Paraguay, men's reproductive output ranges from the late teens to early sixties, with a peak centered around age forty.

Now contrast those hunter-gatherer data with male paternal output in other societies, including polygynous west African ones (for example, the Gambia) or a nation-state dictating monogamy (for example, historical Canada of the 1930s [Tuljapurkar, Puleston, and Gurven 2007]). High rates of polygyny in Gambia result in both delays and extensions of male reproductive output: peak male reproductive output occurs among men at around age fifty and continues until men are around eighty. In Canada, in contrast, men's reproductive output is concentrated between age twenty and forty, with a sharper rise and faster fall than that of either hunter-gatherer or other types of societies. In Canada, men have fewer children, have them spaced closer together, and end their reproductive careers at younger ages. Both in these Gambian and Canadian data, not to mention data from various other sources, we can get a sense of how contemporary patterns of age-related fatherhood may be "mismatched" with an evolutionary-relevant context.

A hunter-gatherer teenage father, for one, would be rare. Ages of paternal onset, traced to the kinds of energetic factors discussed in Chapter 9, would prevent a male from reaching an earlier puberty. A teenage male, yet to prove his social value as a productive hunter, honey collector, or otherwise, would also be shunned as a mate in favor of more proven, older men. Developmental data also suggest that a teenager's brain may not be designed for the responsibilities of family life: new neural imaging data reveal that the prefrontal cortex, involved in impulse control and social evaluation, among other cognitive functions, continues developing into the midtwenties (Cozolino 2006; Gogtay et al. 2004). Psychological data indicate that teenage fathers are more prone to paternal mental health challenges, including elevated risk of postpartum depression. Perhaps these kinds of consequences of teenage fatherhood are not surprising; our ability in the West to overcome energetic and social brakes against teenage fatherhood are evolutionarily novel.

At the other end of the age spectrum, we can carry fatherhood into advanced ages. Our bodies may not be optimally designed for these evolutionarily novel older ages. Take male age-related sexual function, for example. In Chapter 9, we observed that mutation rates of sperm increase with paternal age. The quality of various semen parameters—from sperm concentration to sperm morphology to sperm motility—fades with age, particularly after age fifty-five (Levitas et al. 2007). Male libido declines with advanced ages. As vendors of the popular pharmaceutical Viagra discovered in the 1990s, men crave the ability to suppress the erectile problems they face, especially at advanced ages. Research with the pastoralist Ariaal of northern Kenya revealed that men's erectile problems increased notably from the sixties onward, suggesting that age-related erectile problems occur in subsistence societies too, and not just in Germany, Singapore, or the United States (P. B. Gray and Campbell 2005). Why, according to these various measures, does male sexual function decline at advanced ages?

An evolutionary answer, beckoning to the disposable soma theories of aging, can be situated with the hunter-gatherer reproductive data. Put simply, our hunter-gatherer male ancestors were not regularly reproducing beyond their sixties, meaning that selection did not favor maintenance of peak reproductive function beyond these years. Even if we can overcome this evolutionary past today, we should not be surprised to find older fatherhood more challenging. That is true as much in the mechanics of reproduction (the ability to impregnate a partner) as it is in the strength to do the things fathers do (hold, protect, model behavior). Older fathers play less with their children, and that hardly seems surprising in a mismatched world. The ability of a ninety-year-old man in India to father his twentieth or so child (he had a hard time recalling the precise number of his children when asked) is an evolutionary novelty.

In summary, although the study of fatherhood and health is quite recent, we can begin to see some underlying patterns. There exists a link between male social behavior, sexual selection, and relative male:female mortality. In species with less competitive and more paternal load placed upon males, relative male mortality risk seems to be attenuated compared with that of females and of other species. Among humans, males typically suffer elevated mortality risk compared with females across all ages, but male family life appears to modify the magnitude of this risk, with protective effects of marriage and with both negative and positive impacts of fatherhood. These mortality differentials appear to represent a combination of energetic effects (for example, weight and fatness), alterations in behavior (for example, risk taking), and psychological factors (for example, elevated postpartum depression). Evolutionary mismatches between the ages at which men father children also appear relevant to understanding health challenges posed by fatherhood. Still, this nexus of health and fatherhood, like so many other facets of fatherhood, is subject to great flux. In the next, and last, chapter we touch upon some of the new trends in fatherhood, including the impacts of changing family contexts and assisted reproductive technologies for extending the meaning of "fatherhood" into new terrain.

12

Rewriting the Manual

We have just about completed our evolutionary tour of human paternal care. Here, we summarize some of the key themes that have emerged from the book. After this brief synopsis, we turn to some of the ways in which the book on fatherhood is being rewritten. These nods to the transformations in fatherhood are hardly complete; they are, however, vivid examples of some of the changes under way in the ongoing definition of fatherhood.

Some Central Paternal Lessons

Men and women have formed reproductive unions for a long time. Men have been involved in caring for their children for a long time. Men's involvement in family life thus represents a central feature of human behavior that did not appear just yesterday. When we contrast our species' paternal ways to male behavior in other mammals, other primates, and our closest living relatives, chimpanzees and bonobos, we realize how unusual it is for mammalian males to be so involved in family life and infer that these patterns were derived recently in human evolution. Best guesses based on the available paleoanthropological, hunter-gatherer, and other data are that long-term, primarily socially monogamous reproductive partnerships emerged within the past 2 million years but that the complete modern human family suite (including, for example, an expanded sexual division of labor) did not fully emerge until modern humans evolved in Africa around 150,000 years ago.

Are fathers who are involved with their children really necessary? Raising this huge question at the end of this book may seem silly, but answering it in part invokes the tremendous amount of variation in human paternal care (more on this variation in a moment). As scholars like Sarah Hrdy (2009, 1999) have argued, human mothers appear to require care from others to successfully raise their children. Our species' lot is different from that of most mammals (for which single mothering is the rule), including our close relative the orangutan, whose females in part cope with single motherhood by spacing out their babies in the wild every six to seven years on average. Yet a variety of caregivers can assist human mothers, and fathers are just one part of that social equation. Grandmothers, aunts, older siblings, other mates, the government—all of these may serve important subsidiary roles in providing assistance to mothers. When the specifics of these caregiving contexts play out, fathers are called consistently into assistance. If grandmothers are around, fathers may spend less time in direct care but may make up for that by investing more resources to help provide food, a home, and advantages to children climbing a competitive social ladder. If fathers opt out entirely, other kin step in (a function served by public assistance and welfare in state societies, where extended kin networks are less central to survival). So the bottom line is that additional care appears necessary for human children and that often fathers are the most important (or close to it) of these additional caregivers.

Human paternal care clearly exhibits a remarkable amount of variation, both across and within societies. This variation hinges on a host of variables that, once we think more about them, make sense as pivots of paternal care. Because men typically reproduce in long-term unions, their paternal care necessarily is viewed with respect to both a child's mother and the child itself. A man tends to be better invested in his children when he has a better relationship with their mother. That holds true both across societies and within them. For example, men are more prone to postpartum depression when their partners are also depressed. A man's parenting experiences are entangled in his mate's.

Men also tend to channel their limited time and energy in other sensible ways. Depending on the economic specifics of a society, circumstances may favor greater or lesser paternal care. Hunter-gatherer fathers spend more time in direct care of young children than pastoralist fathers do, in part because of lower polygyny rates, more emotionally close marriages, less need to maintain male-male alliances for purposes of resource defense, and so forth. Around most of the world, the main contributions of fathers may lie in providing material—paying school fees, earning money for a home, assisting a son with bride price—rather than in devoting lots of time to direct childcare. And the role of fathers serving as central moral agents and protectors has diminished in most places because the state or other outside influences have partly usurped these roles, making men's investment better channeled through other means.

A massive amount of evidence indicates that men care about paternity, wanting to invest in the children they (rather than attractive neighbors) may have fathered, and that men's investment is commonly sensitive to whether they have fathered a given child or not. This tendency holds as much for providing direct care of a child as for helping pay a son's or daughter's college expenses. Still, some men appear willing to invest in children who aren't their own, especially if that helps maintain reproductive access to the children's mothers, a situation many stepfathers encounter.

Put many of the contingencies of paternal care together, and it does seem like men commonly pursue behavioral strategies ensuring the survival and reproductive success of their offspring in specific contexts. Yet sometimes a man can't have it all. Some degree of male-male time may be mutually exclusive to tending to young children; child care requires a trade-off, in other words. Men's very health may suffer in the initial years of caring for a young child, but those sacrifices have longer-term benefits: children who have been started on a path to health and social success, and fathers earning later health and mortality benefits. A father may also face the trade-off of either channeling his limited resources to help lots of children be born but with less investment in each or having fewer children but with more investment in each—a quality versus quantity trade-off.

These are significant challenges indeed. No wonder, then, that we have touched upon the various ways that fatherhood impacts men's sexuality, psychology, physiology, and health. Men's sexuality may decline with the arrival of a child, though the availability of alternate sexual outlets (such as other wives) plays an important role in the specifics of these changes. Men may experience couvade symptoms, which are suggestive of a psychological adjustment with impending or realized fatherhood. Men respond to sounds, smells, and visual stimuli associated with their children. Recent imaging data reveal some of the specific neural circuits activated by these stimuli and the hormonal correlates of fatherhood, include lower testosterone and elevated prolactin. As fathers ourselves, the authors of this book have firsthand experience undertaking some of these same transformations, although we are also cognizant of how our experiences do not fully generalize to fathers everywhere.

Transforming Fathers: An International Project

The face of fatherhood internationally, as always, is diverse. Yet that paternal diversity is moving in some different directions (Borstein 2005; Hennon and Wilson 2008; Lamb 2004; Roopnarine and Gielen 2004). The fathers of small-scale hunter-gatherer or subsistence horticulturalist economies removed from outside influences are waning in number. There are fewer rural fathers relying on help from their children to run the family farm and modeling behavior, especially to their sons, that illustrates how to get the work done. Fathers are moving in different directions in part because of shifts in international trade and competitive labor markets, the expansion of formal education, the increase in urbanization, and the global media explosion, among other factors.

To compete in a global labor market, a man may need to build his "stock" through education, experience, and the need to capitalize on opportunities to find work. The competitive scene may require him to be more mobile, to spend years upon years striving for prosperity, to seek ways to achieve social and financial success. Because men are social primates, these orientations may come naturally. Yet they may also have consequences for the realization of fatherhood.

While some men may succeed beyond Darwin's wildest imagination (men such as computer guru Bill Gates, the wealthiest human as of spring 2009, the father of three children, and creator of the well-endowed Bill and Melinda Gates Foundation), many other men struggle. Some of these men may slowly make their way toward paternity, but only after lengthy waits, which lead to late ages of pair-bond formation and fatherhood. This pattern is part of a global trend toward later ages of first marriage and first reproduction.

Many men's social and economic prospects leave them as undesirable mates, meaning they will never be worthwhile family contributors. Especially in higher education, men are beginning to lag behind women. In the extreme, in the Caribbean, approximately 75% of people earning degrees are women; (see http://web.worldbank.org, accessed

Nov. 4, 2009) the less-educated men often have fewer economic prospects and may not be viable, long-term contributors to family life, given the costs of living. Accordingly, partnerships tend to be shorter lived and less often formalized by marriage. These patterns are growing increasingly common throughout the world, not just in the Caribbean. The percentage of children born to unmarried parents is on the rise internationally. Stepfathering is increasingly common because of more frequent mate shifting.

Parents are also having fewer children in most corners of the world. The costs of parents competing in the international labor market help explain part of this effect. The costs of raising children to compete in a similar environment are another. As parents ourselves, the authors of this book contemplate the expenses of housing, transportation, and education for our own children. Sure, we could each have fifteen children if we didn't care about their prospects for social success, but because we also want them to enjoy such opportunities, having two children makes for a better trade-off. The expenses of raising children mean that many parents simply cannot afford to raise more than one or two or three if they want their children to have a chance at social success. Is it any wonder that people increasingly view pets as emotional substitutes for small children?

With geographic mobility, fewer family members may be close at hand to help, especially to parents juggling the challenges of caring for really young children. This greater distance from extended family may place greater importance on fathers' stepping up to provide direct childcare, in addition to providing resources like money. Fathers may, in a city removed from other relatives, be more directly involved in the birth of their children, in spending time with their young children, and in serving as a social resource for the children's mother.

One of the consequences of these trends is that the rainbow of human family diversity looks ever more colorful. Some fathers are among the most involved ever seen in evolution (men providing high levels of direct and indirect care, without needing to worry about male alliances for group defense), whereas other men provide no care at all. More children today are raised in households of mixed paternity, and these kinds of households may be marked by differential child treatment by fathers who maintain investment priority in their own genetic children. More cases of paternal investment entail a spatially removed father—cases in which, after separating from his partner, a man faces decisions of whether or how much to invest in step- and genetic children with whom he no longer lives. A growing fraction of households include gay fathers (Berkowitz and Marsiglio 2007). While until quite recently most gay fathers had their children during marriages before separating from their wives, there is now a growing trend for gay men to become fathers through adoption (or in a small number of cases, noted below, through technologically assisted reproduction). The expansion of gay fatherhood is particularly fascinating from a mammalian perspective: while male mammals may specialize in mating effort compared with female specializations in parenting effort, it is notable that many gay men want to have and raise children (even when not facing the reproductive constraints of female choice).

Legislating Fatherhood

With all of these changing trends in fatherhood, how must a bureaucracy respond? The changing face of fatherhood presents challenges and opportunities to the bureaucratic systems in which we live. Issues such as paternity leaves, custody decisions, paternal financial support, and more all require legislative decisions. Here, we simply highlight legislation in one country, emphasizing the case in the United States, though appreciating that similar issues increasingly apply around the globe.

The increasing accuracy and acceptability of paternity tests has led to two roughly orthogonal trends in legislative and judicial involvement in fatherhood. First, there is a trend toward legislatively increasing men's involvement with their children. Second, there is a trend toward government's involvement in officially ending the paternal relationship altogether.

Many industrialized nations have experienced an increase in the proportion of births that occur outside of marriage. While many of these nonmarital births are to couples who live together, 15.6% of first births in the United States are to unmarried couples living apart (Martinez et al. 2006). This trend, along with the general increase in divorce that has occurred over the past four decades, has led to a growing number of children living in homes without fathers. Increasingly, courts and legislatures are focusing on men who were unmarried at the time their children were born and putting pressure on these fathers to increase their involvement with, and investment in, these children.

An important method of achieving this goal is through the establishment of paternity. Paternity, in this sense, means the identification of a legal father of a child. This meaning is very distinct from the biological definition of paternity that we have used elsewhere in this book, which refers to whether a putative father of a child is the biological father. Paternity, in a legal sense, does not have to be established for a married woman; her husband is automatically assumed to be the father of her child. For unmarried couples, however, paternity needs to be established, and governments have invested a lot of time and effort into increasing the number of fathers listed on birth certificates, or otherwise legally identified, of children of unwed mothers. For example, in 2002, 33.8% of births in the United States were to unmarried women; paternity was established for 74% of them (U.S. Congress 2004).

Increasing effort has been made to identify fathers in the hospital, when they are most likely to visit a non-coresidential, nonmarital child. Federal law requires that hospitals must provide fathers the opportunity to voluntarily acknowledge paternity at the time of birth (U.S. Department of Health and Human Services 1997). Many men embrace their paternal role willingly; this group includes the majority of unmarried fathers, most of whom live with their children's mothers. Some men, however, are skeptical about whether they are in fact the fathers of the children in question and hesitate to acknowledge paternity. In such cases, all states require a paternity test (for example, Case 1998), the use of which to establish paternity was strongly encouraged by the 1988 Family Support Act (Miller and Garfinkel 1999).

Nearly everyone agrees (despite, in some cases, weak or insubstantial supporting evidence) that having fathers involved with children enriches the children's lives and well-being. Thus the stated justification of many lawmakers for the substantial bureaucratic resources devoted to paternity establishment is that when men take responsibility for their children, children benefit in numerous ways. Cynics might also note that children without legal fathers are more likely to end up on public welfare; by establishing paternity and targeting men for child support payments, states also reduce their welfare burden.

There is some debate, however, concerning the effectiveness of legislatively requiring men to assume paternal responsibilities. Can a man be made to parent if he does not want to? Despite increased legislative power to enforce child support obligations, child support compliance has remained fairly flat in the United States for decades. Men who believe their child support award is fair usually pay it willingly, while strong-arm techniques (such as withholding wages and tax returns) may be necessary to increase compliance only from men who feel their child support payments are unduly high (Lin 2000). Miller and Garfinkel (1999) found that the use of genetic testing did not increase paternity establishment rates, while other state policies to increase paternity establishment (such as automatic withholding of child support and "long-arm" statues granting states the ability to establish paternity for men living in other states) had the intended effect.

Programs that encourage men to voluntarily acknowledge paternity may have a greater impact on men's involvement with children than programs that use genetic testing to identify otherwise unwilling fathers. Ronald Mincy, Irwin Garfinkel, and Lenna Nepomnyaschy (2005), using a national sample of so-called fragile families (that is, couples who are unmarried at the time of birth), find the men who acknowledge paternity in the hospital are more likely to pay child support, to have continued contact with their children, and to have overnight visits with their children than do men whose paternity was not established until after the mother had left the hospital. A study in Maryland also found that after four years, men who voluntarily acknowledged paternity were much more likely to still be paying child support than men whose paternity was initially contested (Ovwigho, Head, and Born 2007).

Many questions remain unanswered, but the answer to the question, can laws increase men's involvement with children? is, perhaps, yes— but only if they are willing to. Programs that encourage men to acknowledge paternity for nonmarital children do seem to have a positive impact, but only among men who are willing to acknowledge their paternity without dispute.

In the opposite direction, another major trend in the legislation of paternity is the increase in the state's ability to dissolve the paternal relationship. Under the Seven Seas rule, it was virtually impossible for a man to deny responsibility for the children his wife bore (Rudavsky 1999). Even when technology was developed that could identify nonpaternity, courts were extremely reluctant to use it. In a famous example, in 1943 the silent film star Charlie Chaplin was named as the father of a child by an actress named Joan Barry, with whom he admitted having had a brief sexual relationship. Blood tests showed that he could not possibly be the father—but these were not admissible as evidence in court, and he was ordered to pay child support.

Beginning in the 1950s, American courts began to allow biochemical evidence of nonpaternity to be used in divorce proceedings (Rudavsky 1999). The use of DNA paternity tests is now widespread, and they are increasingly being used to absolve men of any responsibility for children. Men whose marriages dissolve after many years may request (or demand) a paternity test, and the general inclination is that if the test proves they are not the fathers of their putative children, these men are not to be held responsible for child support.

There is perhaps a perception that paternity tests are being used by men as a means of "getting back" at their spouses during angry divorce proceedings. Accusations of promiscuity and infidelity can indeed be very painful and slanderous to women, and the mere ordering of a paternity test by a man sends a clear message to his soon-to-be ex-wife. Increasingly, paternity tests are being requested by married men who are not undergoing divorce proceedings, without the mother contributing a sample (Wenk, Houtz, and Korpisz 2007). One suspects that in many cases, these clandestine tests are a prelude to divorce.

However, paternity tests can also be used by women to separate their children from their ex-husbands—sometimes with the result that men who wished to be involved with their children postdivorce find themselves legally barred from contact on the grounds that these men are not the biological fathers (Hirczy 1993). The potentially negative effects of paternity tests on marriage and family are a key reason most courts were once reluctant to admit them as evidence, even though "dismantling the family, ironically, was the one thing upon which the two warring ex-spouses could agree" (Rudavsky 1999, 128).

The use of paternity tests to annul the paternal relationship raises important questions about the nature of fatherhood. Is fatherhood simply genetic relatedness? Is it right for courts to formally sever a paternal bond? These are not easy questions to answer. On the one hand, many people feel it is wrong to require men to pay child support for children who aren't theirs. On the other hand, it seems callous of men to dissolve years of demonstrated warmth and responsibility toward children based on a single biochemical marker. Apparently some judges are refusing to let men off the hook that easily and insisting that, DNA test or no, men have some responsibility to the children they had helped raise, even if those children do not carry their genes. That appears to be a minority opinion, however, and the general trend is that judges are willing to absolve men from paternal responsibility if they are not the fathers of their putative children.

It's ironic that the same technology—highly accurate paternity tests based on DNA polymorphisms—is being used for diametrically opposed ends: establishment of paternity at the start of a child's life (for nonmarital births) and disestablishment of paternity later in a child's life (primarily for marital births, upon divorce). Several authors have commented that the use of this technology has, to a certain extent, outpaced the ethical discussion surrounding such use (for example, Lucassen and Parker 2001; Rudavsky 1999). Currently, in Australia there are discussions about whether paternity tests should be required at birth for all children, regardless or marital status, or required before any child support award is granted. A balance needs to be struck between potentially destroying otherwise strong family bonds and honoring men's right to know about their biological descendents (and children's right to know about their biological ancestry). Clearly there are no easy answers to these questions. But the widespread availability of technology may end up with de facto solutions being imposed, whether or not a society reaches a consensus about which resolution is the most appropriate.

Assisting Reproduction

The changing landscape of paternity testing has dramatic technical parallels in the world of assisted reproduction. Treatments for infertility are rapidly challenging the possibilities and meaning of "reproduction." Easy headliners are a seventy-year-old woman from India giving birth in 2008 or a Virginia sperm donor and doctor "fathering" at least thirty-five children by spreading his seed. Many of these issues are covered in a wonderful book on the topic by Liza Mundy (2007), and this book serves as the basis for much of the material below. Many of these new technologies reconfigure male roles in reproduction.

The application of assisted reproductive technologies is transforming male infertility. Earlier in the book we commented on the fact that "male factor infertility" contributes a major share of couples' infertility problems, but these male factors are increasingly resolvable through use of assisted reproductive techniques. For example, if a male can't get sperm out of his seminiferous tubules to ejaculate on his own or if his sperm even after ejaculation aren't able to fertilize an egg, medical intervention may alleviate some of these challenges. Sperm can often be obtained surgically or though electroejaculation (even from men with spinal cord injuries). Ever since the first test tube baby was born in the United Kingdom in 1978, doctors have been increasingly able to mix sperm with an egg in a test tube, allow fertilization to occur, and then transplant the fertilized egg back into a uterus. Now doctors can also inject an individual sperm directly into an egg through intracytoplasmic sperm injection (ICSI).

What are the consequences of these new medical technologies? For one, these technologies enable bypassing problems with male tubing (for example, scarring that prevents sperm from being ejaculated). These technologies also enable bypassing some of the molecular barriers to insemination (for example, female immune responses to a male's sperm). However, these techniques also allow genes in sperm that otherwise would not have inseminated an egg to do just that. The result is an increase in genetically based deleterious health conditions such as cystic fibrosis among children born through ICSI. Assisted reproduction today will mean more assisted reproduction among children born through aid of these technologies.

Another consequence is that these medical technologies raise fundamental questions about the meaning of fatherhood. Suppose, as is increasingly the case, that a single woman approaching the decline of her fertile years seeks to become pregnant through use of a donor's sperm. She does not have a social father present to help but has friends and family committed to helping her. How do we apply the concept of "father" to the sperm donor? Should sperm donors' identities be revealed to children when they are old enough to contemplate their conceptions? What might the reaction of a man be upon discovering he is a father eighteen or nineteen years after the ejaculation that led to the conception? What are the impacts of not having a social father present to care for the child, particularly if a son is born? Exactly these sorts of discussions have been and will continue to be subject to vigorous debate. Countries are enacting legislation to specify legal outcomes in these cases. In Australia, for example, anonymous sperm donations are no longer feasible; moreover, sperm donors can no longer be paid, leading to the unsurprising outcome that the numbers of available sperm donors have plummeted.

To take another example from this new reproductive world, what does assisted reproduction mean for gay men? A gay couple seeking to have children must seek help from others. The ways gay men are navigating pathways to parenting reveal the powerful tug of paternity.

Having a possible genetic paternity link to children is commonly preferred over adoption of unrelated individuals. So this preference pushes gay couples into fertility clinics, if they have the money to afford the expense of assisted reproduction. Los Angeles serves as the epicenter of assisted reproduction for gay men. A number of clinics help connect men with both a gestational surrogate (a woman who will gestate fertilized eggs) and an egg donor. Interestingly, different women are typically chosen for these purposes because of their different backgrounds (for example, a slightly older, generous woman is chosen as a surrogate, and a younger woman is chosen as an egg donor in part because of her looks and education). But then how does a gay couple decide about the sperm side of reproduction? In one report, gay men's sperm were mixed together in a test tube to create a genetic lottery, with the winner subsequently determined when the semen was mixed with an egg. Creating a mix of eggs fertilized by both men's sperm and then transplanting one or two of these eggs into a uterus provides another sort of genetic paternity lottery. (This raises issues of sperm competition, which we touched on in earlier chapters.) The fascinating point is that genetic paternity bears an important role in these processes.

Another side of these assisted reproductive technologies is that for the first time in human evolutionary history, a woman can gestate a fetus created from another woman's egg. This technology can create a host of novel social dilemmas. What if a woman requires an egg donor but her husband's sperm suffice? Suppose the other woman's egg and his sperm are allowed to meet in a lab and the egg is fertilized, transplanted into the wife's uterus, and then gestated to term. Should the parents reveal the varied parental origins to their child? If such children know about their origins, will they treat their relationships to their birth mothers differently, or even try to contact egg donors? Does the dynamic of the father, but not the mother, serving as a genetic progenitor affect the psychology of the parents' attachment to the child or the relationship between the couple? In some cases, the answer to these questions appears to be yes. One woman raising a child conceived with her husband's sperm and another woman's egg told the journalist Liza Mundy, "If I never met her [the egg donor], it won't feel like my husband is having a child by her" (Mundy 2007, 99).

Apart from these assisted reproductive techniques, other medical treatments are altering the paternal landscape. One of the most substantial, judging by pharmaceutical sales and prescriptions, began in

1998 with a little blue pill. The release of Viagra and related drugs to treat erectile dysfunction raised the possibility of many men enhancing their sex lives and perhaps becoming fathers when they otherwise wouldn't have. Older men, hardest hit with erectile dysfunction, have been the main beneficiaries. No one knows how many of them have become fathers because of these pills, though it would be fascinating to know, particularly in societies where older men are married to younger, reproductive-aged women.

Finally, the increasing use of ultrasound to check on a fetus facilitates several major changes in fatherhood. The amplified heartbeat, the first photo (in black and white, as in the early days of photography), the first view of a new life—all this is increasingly taking place before birth, thanks to the use of ultrasound technology. These sides of ultrasound technology speed up the process by which a father sees, contemplates, and responds to and bonds with his child. Who needs to wait until the birth? The ability to determine with good (though not 100%) accuracy the sex of the fetus also makes for some novel parental outcomes. A father can begin fantasizing about roughhousing with a son even while the son is attached to a placenta. Parents may also decide to opt out of the birth bargain if the sex of the fetus doesn't match their wishes. This practice has been particularly common in India and China, even though it is illegal, as a means of aborting further investment in a less-desired female fetus. So even the sex ratio of a society can be impacted by these reproductive technologies (later favoring females, who will have a greater chance to select among a surplus of males—see our discussion on this topic in Chapter 3).

Perhaps the greatest irony made possible by assisted reproductive technologies is that you no longer need to be alive to reproduce, as gametes can be frozen and stored for years. While the ultimate in Darwinian currency is survival and reproductive success, we have broken the link between effective survival and reproduction. There are now cases in which the sperm from a deceased spouse were used to fertilize an egg in vitro and create a postmortem child. A father's legacy lives on in unexpected and miraculous ways, and this new medical marvel once again rewrites the story of human fatherhood.

Appendix

Table 1. Descriptive statistics on time allocation for six subsistence societies

	Efe	Kipsigis	Madurese	Machiguenga	Ye'kwana	Yukpa	Signif.
N (men)	13	128	22	16	12	5	
N (obs)	2,184	4,367	1,133	568	4,095	169	
Observations	168	34	52	36	341	34	
Number of children	0.62	2.96	2.05	2.75	3.33	2.20	NS
Men with no children	69.2%	43.8%	0.0%	25.0%	0.0%	20.0%	***
Time allocation							
Commercial activities	2.1%	15.0%	28.0%	0.3%	1.0%	2.9%	***
Food production	28.51%	19.01%	21.61%	32.29%	20.38%	11.76%	***
Eating	5.60%	4.73%	1.11%	10.04%	3.76%	8.33%	***
Housework	0.98%	0.89%	3.09%	1.40%	2.99%	3.95%	***
Individual activities	33.40%	5.85%	21.03%	17.80%	10.55%	22.38%	***
Manufacturing	9.03%	9.30%	5.48%	17.22%	11.13%	5.57%	**
Food preparation	2.08%	1.21%	0.77%	1.34%	0.94%	3.89%	+
Social activities							
Childcare	0.58%	0.80%	1.54%	0.49%	0.53%	1.51%	NS
Education	0.50%	6.78%	0.00%	1.61%	0.29%	0.00%	+
Care of a non-child	0.33%	0.81%	0.51%	1.60%	0.87%	1.20%	NS
Ritual	0.12%	1.24%	3.94%	0.30%	1.53%	1.54%	***
Recreation	6.66%	0.72%	0.00%	1.84%	3.79%	4.61%	***
Chatting	2.21%	19.27%	6.11%	5.87%	8.37%	8.62%	***
Other social	0.00%	2.23%	0.26%	2.38%	0.14%	0.06%	*
Unknown social	0.00%	8.84%	0.00%	0.00%	0.02%	0.00%	***
All else	7.89%	3.30%	6.52%	5.52%	33.73%	23.66%	***

* p < 0.0533   ** p < 0.0133   *** p < 0.00133   + p < 0.10

257

Table 2. Men's time allocation by fatherhood status, four subsistence societies

	Fathers (N = 92)	Non-fathers (N = 70)	Signif.
Commercial activities	16.12%	6.93%	***
Food production	19.16%	23.10%	+
Eating	5.77%	5.00%	
Housework	0.95%	1.15%	
Individual activities	9.79%	9.71%	
Manufacturing	10.02%	9.85%	
Food preparation	1.59%	1.09%	
Social activities			
Childcare	1.11%	0.34%	*
Education	0.47%	12.24%	***
Care of a non-child	1.15%	0.47%	+
Ritual	0.96%	1.21%	
Recreation	1.52%	1.31%	
Chatting	14.64%	18.37%	+
Other social	2.65%	1.15%	*
Unknown social	8.56%	4.90%	*
All else	5.54%	3.18%	

Note: Madurese and Ye'kwana excluded from this analysis because all of the men sampled are fathers.
* p < 0.0533   ** p < 0.0133   *** p < 0.00133   + p < 0.10

References

Adimora, A. A., V. J. Schoenbach, D. M. Bonas, F. E. A. Martinson, K. H. Donaldson, and R. T. Stancil. 2002. "Concurrent sexual partnerships among women in the United States." *Epidemiology* 13: 320–327.

Aiello, L. C., and Wheeler, P. 1995. "The expensive-tissue hypothesis." *Current Anthropology* 36:199–221.

Alder, E., and J. Bancroft. 1988. "The relationship between breastfeeding persistence, sexuality and mood in postpartum women." *Psychological Medicine* 18: 389–396.

Alemseged, Z., F. Spoor, W. H. Kimbel, R. Bobe, D. Geraads, D. Reed, and J. G. Wynn. 2006. "A juvenile early hominin skeleton from Dikika, Ethiopia." *Nature* 443: 296–301.

Alexander, R. D. 1974. "The evolution of social behavior." *Annual Review of Ecology and Systematics* 5: 325–383.

Alexander, R. D., J. L. Hoogland, R. D. Howard, K. M. Noonan, and P. W. Sherman. 1979. "Sexual dimorphisms and breeding systems in pinnipeds, ungulates, primates, and humans." In *Evolutionary Biology and Human Social Behavior: An Anthropological Perspective,* ed. N. A. Chagnon and W. Irons, 402–435. North Scituate, Mass.: Duxbury Press.

Allen, A. S., D. C. Atkins, D. H. Baucom, D. K. Snyder, K. C. Gordon, and S. P. Glass. 2005. "Intrapersonal, interpersonal, and contextual factors in engaging in and responding to extramarital involvement." *Clinical Psychology: Science and Practice* 12: 101–130.

Allman, J. 1999. *Evolving Brains.* New York: Scientific American.

Allman, J., A. Rosin, R. Kumar, and A. Hasenstaub. 1998. "Parenting and survival in anthropoid primates: Caretakers live longer." *Proceedings of the National Academy of Sciences* 95: 6866–6869.

Amato, P. R., and J. G. Gilbreth. 1999. "Nonresident fathers and children's well-being: A meta-analysis." *Journal of Marriage and the Family* 61: 557–573.

Ambach, E., W. Parson, and C. Brezinka. 2000. "Superfecundation and dual paternity in a twin pregnancy ending with placental abruption." *Journal of Forensic Sciences* 45: 181–183.

Anderson, E. A., J. K. Kohler, and B. L. Letiecq. 2005. "Predictors of depression among low-income, nonresidential fathers." *Journal of Family Issues* 26: 547–567.

Anderson, K. G. 2000. "The life histories of American stepfathers in evolutionary perspective." *Human Nature* 11: 307–333.

———. 2005. "Relatedness and investment in children in South Africa." *Human Nature* 16: 1–31.

———. 2006. "How well does paternity confidence match actual paternity? Results from worldwide nonpaternity rates." *Current Anthropology* 48: 511–518.

———. n.d. "Does paying child support reduce men's subsequent remarriage and fertility?" Unpublished manuscript, Department of Anthropology, University of Oklahoma.

Anderson, K. G., and A. M. Beutel. n.d. "Are orphans and fostered children less likely to be in school? Evidence from South Africa." Unpublished manuscript in preparation.

Anderson, K. G., A. Case, and D. Lam. 2001. "Causes and consequences of schooling outcomes in South Africa: Evidence from survey data." *Social Dynamics* 27: 37–59.

Anderson, K. G., P. B. Gray, J. Henrich, M. Borgerhoff Mulder, and C. Moody. n.d. "Time allocation across the life course in subsistence ecologies." Unpublished manuscript.

Anderson, K. G., H. Kaplan, D. Lam, and J. B. Lancaster. 1999. "Paternal care by genetic fathers and stepfathers II: Reports by Xhosa high school students." *Evolution and Human Behavior* 20: 433–451.

Anderson, K. G., H. Kaplan, and J. B. Lancaster. 1999. "Paternal care by genetic fathers and stepfathers I: Reports from Albuquerque men." *Evolution and Human Behavior* 20: 405–431.

———. 2006. "Demographic correlates of paternity confidence and pregnancy outcomes among Albuquerque men." *American Journal of Physical Anthropology* 131: 560–571.

———. 2007. "Confidence of paternity, divorce, and investment in children by Albuquerque men." *Evolution and Human Behavior* 28: 1–10.

———. n.d. "Do men in blended families invest more evenly in children?" Unpublished manuscript, Department of Anthropology, University of Oklahoma.

Anderson, K. G., and B. S. Low. 2003. "Nonmarital first births and women's life histories." In *The Biodemography of Human Reproduction and Fertility*, ed. J. Rodgers and H. P. Kohler, 57–86. Boston: Kluwer Academic Publishers.

Andersson, M. 1994. *Sexual Selection*. Princeton, N.J.: Princeton University Press.

Apicella, C. L., and F. W. Marlowe. 2004. "Perceived mate fidelity and paternal resemblance predict men's investment in children." *Evolution and Human Behavior* 25: 371–378.

Aristotle. 1908. *Nicomachean Ethics.* Trans. W. D. Ross. Oxford, Clarendon Press. http://www.ilt.columbia.edu/publicATIONS/artistotle.html (accessed 11/21/08).

Austad, S. N. 1997. *Why We Age.* New York: Wiley.

Bailey, R. C., and R. Aunger. 1990. "Humans as primates: The social relationships of Efe Pygmy men in comparative perspective." *International Journal of Primatology* 11: 127–146.

Bailey, R. C., and N. R. Peacock. 1988. "Time allocation of Efe Pygmy men and women of the Ituri Forest, Zaire." *Cross-Cultural Studies in Time Allocation.* Vol. 3. Ed. A. Johnson. New Haven, Conn.: Human Relation Area Files.

Baker, R. R., and M. A. Bellis. 1995. *Human Sperm Competition: Copulation, Masturbation and Infidelity.* London: Chapman and Hall.

Bales, K. L., A. J. Kim, A. D. Lewis-Reese, and C. S. Carter. 2004. "Both oxytocin and vasopressin may influence alloparental behavior in male prairie voles." *Hormones and Behavior* 45: 354–361.

Ball, H. L., E. Hooker, and P. J. Kelly. 2000. "Parent-infant co-sleeping: Fathers' roles and perspectives." *Infant and Child Development* 9: 67–74.

Bancroft, J. 2005. "The endocrinology of sexual arousal." *Journal of Endocrinology* 186: 411–427.

Barclay, L., and D. Lupton. 1999. "The experiences of new fatherhood: A socio-cultural analysis." *Journal of Advanced Nursing* 29: 1013–1020.

Barelli, C., M. Heistermann, C. Boesch, and U. H. Reichard. 2008. "Mating patterns and sexual swellings in pair-living and multimale groups of wild white-handed gibbons, *Hylobates lar.*" *Animal Behaviour* 75: 991–1001.

Barrett, G., J. Peacock, C. R. Victor, and I. Manyonda. 2005. "Cesarean section and postnatal sexual health." *Birth* 32: 306–311.

Barrett, L., R. Dunbar, and J. Lycett. 2002. *Human Evolutionary Psychology.* Princeton, N.J.: Princeton University Press.

Bartlett, E. E. 2004. "The effects of fatherhood on the health of men: a review of the literature." *Journal of Men's Health and Gender* 1: 159–169.

Bartlett, T. 2007. "The hylobatidae: Small apes of Asia." In *Primates in Perspective,* ed. C. J. Campbell, A. Fuentes, K. C. MacKinnon, M. Panger, and S. K. Bearder, 274–289. New York: Oxford University Press.

Bateman, A. 1948. "Intrasexual selection in *Drosophila.*" *Heredity* 2: 349–368.

Baumeister, R. F. 1991. *Meanings of Life.* New York: Guilford Press.

Baumeister, R. 2000. "Gender differences in erotic plasticity: The female sex drive as socially flexible and responsive." *Psychological Bulletin* 126: 347–374.

Beall, C. M., and M. C. Goldstein. 1981. "Tibetan fraternal polyandry: A test of sociobiological theory." *American Anthropologist* 83: 5–12.

Becker, G. S. 1991. *A Treatise on the Family.* Enlarged ed. Cambridge, Mass.: Harvard University Press.

Beckerman S., R. Lizzarralde, C. Ballew, S. Schroeder, C. Fingelton, A. Garrison, and H. Smith. 1998. "The Barí partible paternity project: Preliminary results." *Current Anthropology* 39: 164–167.

Beckerman, S., and P. Valentine. 2002. *Cultures of Multiple Fathers: The Theory and Practice of Partible Paternity in Lowland South America*. Gainesville, FL: University Press of Florida.

Beller, A. H., and J. W. Graham. 1986. "Child support awards: Differentials and trends by race and marital status." *Demography* 23: 231–245.

Bellows-Riecken, K. H., and R. E. Rhodes. 2008. "A birth of inactivity: A review of physical activity and parenthood." *Preventive Medicine* 46:99–110.

Belsky, J., and J. Kelly. 1994. *The Transition to Parenthood*. New York: Delacorte.

Belsky, J., L. Steinberg, and P. Draper. 1991. "Childhood experience, interpersonal development, and reproductive strategy: An evolutionary theory of socialization." *Child Development* 62: 647–670.

Bentley, G. R., G. Jasienska, and T. Goldberg. 1993. "Is the fertility of agriculturalists higher than that of nonagriculturalists?" *Current Anthropology* 34: 778–785.

Bentley, G. R., and C. G. N. Mascie-Taylor. 2000. *Infertility in the Modern World*. Cambridge: Cambridge University Press.

Berg, S. J., and K. E. Wynne-Edwards. 2001. "Changes in testosterone, cortisol, and estradiol levels in men becoming fathers." *Mayo Clinic Proceedings* 76: 582–592.

Berkowitz, D. and W. Marsiglio. 2007. "Gay men: Negotiating procreative, father, and family identities." *Journal of Marriage and Family* 69: 366–381.

Bernhardt, E. M. 2004. "Cohabitation or marriage? Preferred living arrangements in Sweden." *sdf-puzzle*, no. 4: 1–10. http://www.oif.ac.at/sdf/sdf_04_2004.html (accessed 11/22/08).

Bernhardt, E. M., and F. K. Goldscheider. 2001. "Men, resources, and family living: The determinants of union and parental status in the United States and Sweden." *Journal of Marriage and Family* 63: 793–803.

Berrin, K. 1978. *Art of the Huichol Indians*. San Francisco: Fine Arts Museums of San Francisco.

Betzig, L. 1989. "Causes of conjugal dissolution: A cross-cultural study." *Current Anthropology* 30: 654–676.

Betzig, L., and P. Turke. 1992. "Fatherhood by rank on Ifaluk." In *Father-Child Relations: Cultural and Biosocial Contexts*, ed. B. S. Hewlett, 153–176. New York: Aldine de Gruyter.

Bianchi, S. 2000. "Maternal employment and time with children: Dramatic change or surprising continuity?" *Demography* 37: 139–154.

Bianchi S., J. P. Robinson, and M. Milkie. 2006. *Changing Rhythms of American Family Life*. New York: Russell Sage.

Bishai, D., N. Astone, L. Argys, R. Gutendorf, and C. Filidoro. 2006. "A national sample of US paternity tests: Do demographics predict test outcomes?" *Transfusion* 46: 849–853.

Bittles, A. H. 2005. "Genetic aspects of inbreeding and incest." In *Inbreeding, Incest, and the Incest Taboo,* ed. A. P. Wolf, and W. H. Durham, 38–60. Stanford: Stanford University Press.

Bittles, A. H., and P. L. Matson. 2000. "Genetic influences on human infertility." *In Infertility in the Modern World-Present and Future Prospects,* eds. G. Bentley and C. G. N. Mascie-Taylor, 46–81. Cambridge: Cambridge University Press.

Blanchard, R. 2008. "Review and theory of handedness, birth order, and homosexuality in men." *Laterality* 13: 51–70.

Bliege Bird, R., E. A. Smith, and D. W. Bird. 2001. "The hunting handicap: Costly signaling in human foraging strategies." *Behavioral Ecology and Sociobiology* 50: 9–19.

Bloom, D. E., C. Conrad, and C. Miller. 1998. "Child support and fathers' remarriage and fertility." In *Fathers Under Fire: The Revolution in Child Support Enforcement,* ed. I. Garfinkel, S. S. McLanahan, D. R. Meyer, and J. A. Seltzer, 128–156. New York: Russell Sage Foundation.

Blurton Jones, N. G., F. Marlowe, K. Hawkes, and J. F. O'Connell. 2000. "Paternal investment and hunter-gatherer divorce rates." In *Adaptation and Human Behavior: An Anthropological Perspective,* ed. L. Cronk, N. Chagnon, and W. Irons, 69–90. New York: Aldine.

Boehm, C. 1999. *Hierarchy in the Forest.* Cambridge, Mass.: Harvard University Press.

Bongaarts, J. 1978. "A framework for analyzing the proximate determinants of fertility." *Population and Development Review* 4: 105–132.

Boone, J. L. 2002. "Subsistence strategies and early human population history: An evolutionary ecological perspective." *World Archaeology* 34: 6–25.

Booth, A., and J. M. Dabbs Jr. 1993. "Testosterone and men's marriages." *Social Forces* 72: 463–477.

Borgerhoff Mulder, M. 1987. "On cultural and reproductive success: Kipsigis evidence." *American Anthropologist* 89: 617–634.

———. 1998. "The demographic transition: Are we any closer to an evolutionary explanation?" *Trends in Ecology and Evolution* 13: 266–270.

Borgerhoff Mulder, M., A. T. Kerr, and M. Moore. 1997. "Time allocation among the Kipsigis of Kenya." *Cross-Cultural Studies in Time Allocation.* Vol. 14. Ed. A. Johnson. New Haven, Conn.: Human Relation Area Files.

Borstein, M., ed. 2005. *Handbook of Parenting.* 5 vols. Mahwah, N.J.: Lawrence Erlbaum.

Bost, K. K., M. J. Cox, M. R. Burchinal, and C. Payne. 2002. "Structural and supportive changes in couples' family and friendship networks across the transition to parenthood." *Journal of Marriage and Family* 64: 517–531.

Bradley, B. J. 2008. "Reconstructing phylogenies and phenotypes: A molecular view of human evolution." *Journal of Anatomy* 212: 337–353.

Brédart, S., and R. M. French. 1999. "Do babies resemble their fathers more than their mothers? A failure to replicate Christenfeld and Hill (1995)." *Evolution and Human Behavior* 20: 129–136.

Breedlove, S. M., M. R. Rosenzweig, and N. V. Watson. 2007. *Biological Psychology.* Sunderland, Mass.: Sinauer.

Brennan, A., S. Ayers, H. Ahmed, and S. Marshall-Lucette. 2007. "A critical review of the Couvade syndrome: The pregnant male." *Journal of Reproductive and Infant Psychology* 25: 173–189.

Brennan, A., S. Marshall-Lucette, S. Ayers, and H. Ahmed. 2007. "A qualitative exploration of the Couvade syndrome in expectant fathers." *Journal of Reproductive and Infant Psychology* 25: 18–39.

Bressan, P., and M. F. Dal Martello. 2002. "Talis pater, falis filius: Perceived resemblance and the belief in genetic relatedness." *Psychological Science* 12: 213–218.

Bressan, P., and M. Grassi. 2004. "Parental resemblance in 1-year-olds and the Gaussian curve." *Evolution and Human Behavior* 25: 133–141.

Brewis, A., and Meyer, M. 2005. "Demographic evidence that human ovulation is undetectable (at least in pair bonds)." *Current Anthropology* 46: 465–471.

Bribiescas, R. 2006. *Men: Evolutionary and Life History.* Cambridge, Mass.: Harvard University Press.

Broman, C. L. 1993. "Social relationships and health-related behavior." *Journal of Behavioral Medicine* 16: 335–350.

Brott, A. A. 2001. *The Expectant Father.* 2nd ed. New York: Abbeville.

Brown, S. L. 2000. "Union transitions among cohabitors: The role of relationship assessments and expectations." *Journal of Marriage and the Family* 62: 833–846.

Buchan, J. C., S. C. Alberts, J. B. Silk, and J. Altmann. 2003. "True paternal care in a multi-male primate society." *Nature* 425: 179–181.

Buckle, L., G. G. Gallup Jr., and Z. A. Rodd. 1996. "Marriage as a reproductive contract: Patterns of marriage, divorce, and remarriage." *Ethology and Sociobiology* 17: 363–377.

Bullivant, S. B., S. A. Sellergren, K. Stern, N. A. Spencer., and S. Jacob. 2004. "Women's sexual experience during the menstrual cycle: Identification of the sexual phase by noninvasive measurement of luteinizing hormone." *Journal of Sex Research* 41: 82–93.

Bumpass, L. L., and H. Lu. 2000. "Trends in cohabitation and implications for children's family contexts in the United States." *Population Studies* 54: 29–41.

Bumpass, L. L., R. K. Raley, and J. A. Sweet. 1995. "The changing nature of stepfamilies: Implications of cohabitation and nonmarital childbearing." *Demography* 32: 425–436.

Bumpass, L. L., J. Sweet, and A. Cherlin. 1991. "The role of cohabitation in declining rates of marriage." *Demography* 53: 913–927.

Burgess, A. and S. Ruxton. 2000. "Men and their children." In *Social Policy and Social Justice,* ed. J. Franklin, 114–133. New York: Polity.

Buss, D. M. 1989. "Sex differences in human mate preferences: Evolutionary hypotheses tested in 37 cultures." *Behavioral and Brain Sciences* 12: 1–49.

Buss, D. M., T. K. Shackelford, L. A. Kirkpatrick, and R. J. Larsen. 2001. "A half century of mate preferences: The cultural evolution of values." *Journal of Marriage and Family* 63: 492–503.

Caldwell, H. K., H. J. Lee, A. H. Macbeth, and W. S. Young. 2008. "Vasopressin: Behavioral roles of an 'original' neuropeptide." *Progress in Neurobiology* 84: 1–24.

Caldwell, J. 1976. "Toward a restatement of demographic transition theory." *Population and Development Review* 6: 225–256.

Campbell, C. J., A. Fuentes, K. C. MacKinnon, M. Panger, and S. K. Bearder, eds. 2007. *Primates in Perspective.* New York: Oxford University Press.

Carey, J. R., and S. Tuljapurkar, eds. 2003. *Life Span: Evolutionary, Ecological, and Demographic Perspectives,* New York: Population and Development Review Supplement Series.

Carnahan, S. J., and M. I. Jensen-Seaman. 2008. "Hominoid seminal protein evolution and ancestral mating behavior." *American Journal of Primatology* 70: 939–948.

Carter, C. S. 1998. "Neuroendocrine perspectives on social attachment and love." *Psychoneuroendocrinology* 23: 779–818.

———. 2007. "Sex differences in oxytocin and vasopressin: Implications for autism spectrum disorders?" *Behavioral Brain Research* 176: 170–186.

Case, A. 1998. "The effects of stronger child support enforcement on nonmarital fertility." In *Men in Families: When Do They Get Involved? What Difference Does It Make?,* ed. A. Booth and A. C. Crouter, 191–215. New York: Lawrence Erlbaum.

Case, A., I. Lin, and S. McLanahan. 2001. "Educational attainment of siblings in stepfamilies." *Evolution and Human Behavior* 22: 269–289.

———. 2003. "Explaining trends in child support: Economic, demographic, and policy effects." *Demography* 40: 171–189.

Caspari, R., and S-H. Lee. 2004. "Older age becomes common late in human evolution." *Proceedings of the National Academy of Sciences* 101: 10895–10900.

Cerda-Flores, R. M., S. A. Barton, L. F. Marty-Gonzalez, F. Rivas, and R. Chakraborty. 1999. "Estimation of nonpaternity in the Mexican population of Nuevo Leon: A validation study with blood group markers." *American Journal of Physical Anthropology* 109: 281–293.

Chagnon, N. 1988. "Life histories, blood revenge, and warfare in a tribal population." *Science* 239: 985–992.

Chandra, A. 1998. "Surgical sterilization in the United States: Prevalence and characteristics, 1965–95." *Vital and Health Statistics* 23 (20): 1–33.

Cheney, D. L., and R. M. Seyfarth. 2007. *Baboon Metaphysics: The Evolution of a Social Mind.* Chicago: University of Chicago Press.

Cherlin, A. J. 1978. "Remarriage as an incomplete institution." *American Journal of Sociology* 84: 634–650.

———. 2008. *Public and Private Families: An Introduction.* 5th ed. New York: McGraw Hill.

Cherlin, A. J., and F. F. Furstenberg Jr. 1994. "Stepfamilies in the United States: A reconsideration." *Annual Review of Sociology* 20: 359–381.

Chisholm, J. S. 1996. "The evolutionary ecology of attachment organization." *Human Nature* 7: 1–38.

Chisholm, J. S., V. K. Burbank, D. A. Coall, and F. Gemmiti. 2005. "Early stress: Perspectives from developmental evolutionary ecology." In *Origins of the Social Mind,* ed. B. J. Ellis and D. F. Bjorklund, 76–107. New York: Guilford.

Chow, P. H., and W. S. O. 1989. "Effects of male accessory sex glands on sperm transport, fertilization and embryonic loss in golden hamsters." *International Journal of Andrology* 12: 155–163.

Christenfeld, Nicholas J. S., and E. A. Hill. 1995. "Whose baby are you?" *Nature* 378: 669.

Claxton-Oldfield, S., T. Garber, and K. Gillcrist. 2006. "Young adults' perceptions of their relationships with their stepfathers and biological fathers." *Journal of Divorce and Remarriage* 45: 51–61.

Clay, M. M. 1989. *Quadruplets and Higher Multiple Births.* London: Mac Keith Press.

Clinton, J. F. 1987. "Physical and emotional responses of expectant fathers throughout pregnancy and the early postpartum period." *International Journal of Nursing Studies* 24: 59–68.

Clutton-Brock, T. H. 1991. *The Evolution of Parental Care.* Princeton, N.J.: Princeton University Press.

Clutton-Brock, T. H., F. Guinness, and S. Albon. 1982. *Red Deer: Behavior and Ecology of Two Sexes.* Chicago: University of Chicago Press.

Clutton-Brock, T. H., and K. Isvaran. 2007. "Sex differences in ageing in natural populations of vertebrates." *Proceedings of the Royal Society of London B: Biological Sciences* 274: 3097–3104.

Clutton-Brock, T. H., and A. C. J. Vincent. 1991. "Sexual selection and the potential reproductive rates of males and females." *Science* 351: 58–60.

Coleman, M., L. H. Ganong, and S. M. Cable. 1996. "Perceptions of stepparents: An examination of the incomplete institutionalization and social stigma hypotheses." *Journal of Divorce and Remarriage* 26: 25–48.

Cowlishaw, G., and R. Mace. 1996. "Cross-cultural patterns of marriage and inheritance: a phylogenetic approach." *Ethology and Sociobiology* 17: 87–97.

Cozolino, L. 2006. *The Neuroscience of Human Relationships.* New York: W. W. Norton.

Crews, D., A. C. Gore, T. S. Hsu, N. L. Dangleben, M. Spinetta, T. Schallert,

M. D. Anway , and M. K. Skinner. 2007. "Transgenerational epigenetic imprints on mate preference." *Proceedings of the National Academy of Sciences* 104: 5942–5946.

Daly, M., and M. I. Wilson. 1982. "Whom are newborn babies said to resemble?" *Ethology and Sociobiology* 3: 69–78.

————. 1988. *Homicide.* New York: Aldine.

————. 1998. *The Truth about Cinderella: A Darwinian View of Parental Love.* New Haven, Conn.: Yale University Press.

Daley, M. and M. Wilson. 1999. "Darwinism and the roots of machismo." *Scientific American Presents* 10:8–14.

————. 2001. "An assessment of some proposed exceptions to the phenomenon of nepotistic discrimination against stepchildren." *Annales Zoologici Fennici* 38: 287–296.

Darwin, C. R. 1838. "This is the Question Marry Not Marry" [memorandum on marriage]. The Complete Works of Charles Darwin Online. http://darwin-online.org.uk/content/frameset?viewtype=text&itemID=CUL-DAR210.8.2&pageseq=1 (accessed 11/26/2008).

————. 1871. *The Descent of Man, and Selection in Relation to Sex.* Princeton, N.J.: Princeton University Press.

————. 1877. A biographical sketch of an infant. *Mind. A Quarterly Review of Psychology and Philosophy* 2: 285–294.

Davies, N. B. 1991. "Mating systems." In *Behavioural Ecology: An Evolutionary Approach,* ed. J. R. Krebs and N. B. Davies, 263–294. London: Blackwell Scientific.

Davis, J. N., and M. Daly. 1997. "Evolutionary theory and the human family." *Quarterly Review of Biology* 72: 407–435.

Davis, K., and J. Blake. 1956. "Social structure and fertility: An analytic framework." *Economic Development and Cultural Change* 4: 211–325.

Deater-Deckard, K., K. Pickering, J. F. Dunn, J. Golding, and the Avon Longitudinal Study of Pregnancy and Childhood Study Team. 1998. "Family structure and depressive symptoms in men preceding and following the birth of a child." *American Journal of Psychiatry* 155: 818–823.

De Judicibus, M. A., and M. P. McCabe. 2002. "Psychological factors and the sexuality of pregnant and postpartum women." *Journal of Sex Research* 39: 94–103.

Dennis, L. K., and D. V. Dawson. 2002. "Meta-analysis of measures of sexual activity and prostate cancer." *Epidemiology* 13: 72–79.

Depue, R. A., and J. V. Morrone-Strupinsky. 2005. "A neurobehavioral model of affiliative bonding: Implications for conceptualizing a human trait of affiliation." *Behavioral and Brain Sciences* 28: 313–395.

Digby, L. J., S. F. Ferrari, and W. Saltzman. 2007. "Callitrichines: The role of competition in cooperatively breeding species." In *Primates in Perspective,* ed. C. J. Campbell, A. Fuentes, K. C. MacKinnon, M. Panger, and S. K. Bearder, 85–106. New York: Oxford University Press.

Dixson, A. F. 1998. *Primate Sexuality.* Cambridge: Cambridge University Press.

———. 2009. *Sexual Selection and the Origins of Human Mating Systems.* New York: Oxford University Press.

Doblhammer, G., and J. Oeppen. 2003. "Reproduction and longevity among the British peerage." *Proceedings of the Royal Society of London B: Biological Sciences* 270: 1541–1547.

Donovan, J. 1995. "The process of analysis during a grounded theory study of men during their partners' pregnancies." *Journal of Advanced Nursing* 21: 708–715.

Downey, D. B. 1995. "Understanding academic achievement among children in stephouseholds: The role of parental resources, sex of stepparent, and sex of child." *Social Forces* 73: 875–894.

Draper, J. 1997. "Whose welfare in the labour room? A discussion of the increasing trend of fathers' birth attendance." *Midwifery* 13: 132–138.

Draper, P., and H. C. Harpending. 1982. "Father absence and reproductive strategy: an evolutionary perspective." *Journal of Anthropological Research* 38: 255–273.

———. 1988. "A sociobiological perspective on the development of human reproductive strategies." In K. B. MacDonald, ed., *Sociobiological Perspectives on Human Development,* 340–372. New York: Springer-Verlag.

Dubas, J. S., M. Hiejkoop, and M. A. G. van Aken. 2009. "Parent-progeny olfactory recognition and parental investment." *Human Nature* 20.

Dubey, S. N. 1995. "A study of reasons for non-payment of child-support by non-custodial parents." *Journal of Sociology and Social Welfare* 22: 115–131.

Durham, W. H. 1991. *Coevolution: Genes, Culture, and Human Diversity.* Stanford, CA: Stanford University Press.

Duvander, A-Z. 1999. "The transition from cohabitation to marriage: A longitudinal study of the propensity to marry in Sweden in the early 1990s." *Journal of Family Issues* 20: 698–717.

Eaton, J. W., and A. J. Mayer. 1953. "The social biology of very high fertility among the Hutterites: The demography of a unique population." *Human Biology* 25: 206–264.

Eibl-Eibesfeldt, I. 1989. *Human Ethology.* New York: Aldine.

Einon, D. 1998. "How many children can one man have?" *Evolution and Human Behavior* 19: 413–426.

Ellis, B. J. 2004. "Timing of pubertal maturation in girls: An integrated life history approach." *Psychological Bulletin* 130: 920–958.

Ellison, P. T. 2001. *On Fertile Ground.* Cambridge, Mass.: Harvard University Press.

———. 2003. "Energetics and reproductive effort." *American Journal of Human Biology* 15: 342–351.

Ellison, P. T., and P. B. Gray, eds. 2009. *Endocrinology of Social Relationships.* Cambridge, Mass.: Harvard University Press.

Elwood, R. W., and C. Mason. 1995. "The couvade and the onset of paternal care: A biological perspective." *Ethology and Sociobiology* 15: 145–156.

Farrelly, D., and D. Nettle. 2007. "Marriage affects competitive performance in male tennis players." *Journal of Evolutionary Psychology* 5: 41–48.

Federal Interagency Forum on Child and Family Statistics. 2007. *America's Children: Key National Indicators of Well-Being, 2007.* Federal Interagency Forum on Child and Family Statistics. Washington, D.C.: U.S. Government Printing Office.

Fisher, Helen E. 1989. Evolution of human serial pairbonding. *American Journal of Physical Anthropology* 78:331–54.

Fleming, A. S., C. Corter, J. Stallings, and M. Steiner. 2002. "Testosterone and prolactin are associated with emotional responses to infant cries in new fathers." *Hormones and Behavior* 42: 399–413.

Flinn, M. V. 1981. "Uterine vs. agnatic kinship variability and associated cousin marriage preferences: An evolutionary biological analysis." In *Natural Selection and Social Behavior,* ed. R. D. Alexander and D. W. Tinkle, 439–475. New York: Chiron Press.

———. 1988. "Step- and genetic parent/offspring relationships in a Caribbean village." *Ethology and Sociobiology* 9: 335–369.

———. 1992. "Paternal care in a Caribbean village." In *Father-Child Relations,* ed. B. S. Hewlett, 57–84. New York: Aldine.

Flinn, M. V., and B. G. England. 1997. "Social economics of childhood glucocorticoid stress response and health." *American Journal of Physical Anthropology* 102: 33–53.

Ford, C. S., and F. A. Beach. 1951. *Patterns of Sexual Behavior.* New York: Ace Books.

Fortunato, L. 2008. "A phylogenetic approach to the history of cultural practices." In N. J. Allen, H. Callan, R. Dunbar, and W. James, eds., *Early Human Kinship: From Sex to Social Reproduction,* 188–199. Oxford: Blackwell.

Fouts, H. N. 2008. "Father involvement with young children among Aka and Bofi foragers." *Cross-Cultural Research* 42: 390–412.

Fox, G. L., and C. Bruce. 2001. "Conditional fatherhood: Identity theory and parental investment theory as alternative sources of explanation of fathering." *Journal of Marriage and Family* 63: 394–403.

Frayser, S. 1985. *Varieties of Sexual Experience.* New Haven, Conn.: HRAF Press.

Freeman, R. B., and J. Waldfogel. 2001. "Dunning delinquent dads: The effects of child support enforcement policy on child support receipt by never married women." *Journal of Human Resources* 36: 207–225.

French, J. A., and C. M. Schaffner. 2000. "Contextual influences on sociosexual behavior in monogamous primates." In K. Wallen, and J. E.

Schneider, eds., *Reproduction in Context*, 325–353. Cambridge, Mass.: MIT Press.

Friedlander, N. J. 1996. "The relation of lifetime reproduction to survivorship in women and men: A prospective study." *American Journal of Human Biology* 8: 771–783.

Fries, A. B., T. E. Ziegler, J. R. Kurian, S. Jacoris, and S. Pollak. 2005. "Early experience in humans is associated with changes in neuropeptides critical for regulating social behavior." *Proceedings of the National Academy of Science* 102: 17237–17240.

Frodi, A. M., M. E. Lamb, L. A. Leavitt, W. L. Donovan, C. Neff, and D. Sherry. 1978. "Fathers' and mothers' responses to the faces and cries of normal and premature infants." *Developmental Psychology* 14: 490–498.

Gallinetti, J. 2006. "Legal aspects of fatherhood in South Africa." In *Baba: Men and Fatherhood in South Africa*, ed. L. Richter and R. Morrell, 201–215. Chicago: HSRC Press.

Gallup, G. G., R. L. Burch, and S. M. Platek. 2002. "Does semen have anti-depressant properties?" *Archives of Sexual Behavior* 31: 289–293.

Ganong, L. H., M. Coleman, and D. Mistina. (1995) "Normative beliefs about parents' and stepparents' financial obligations to children following divorce and remarriage." *Family Relations* 44: 306–315.

Gangestad, S. W. 2006. Evidence for adaptations for female extra-pairing in humans: Thoughts on current status and future directions. In S. M. Platek & T. K. Shackelford (Eds.), *Female Infidelity and paternal uncertainty: Evolutionary perspectives on male anti-cuckoldry tactics*, pp. 37–57. Cambridge, UK: Cambridge University Press.

Gangestad, S. W., and R. Thronhill. 1995. Sexual selection and relationship dynamics: Trade-offs between partner investment and developmental stability. Manuscript. Department of Pscyhology, University of New Mexico.

Garburn, N. H. 1969. *Eskimos without Igloos*. Boston: Little Brown.

Garfield, C. F., E. Clark-Kauffman, and M. M. Davis. 2006. "Fatherhood as a component of men's health." *Journal of the American Medical Association* 296: 2365–2368.

Gaudino, J. A., B. Jenkins, and R. W. Rochat. 1999. "No fathers' names: A risk factor for infant mortality in the state of Georgia, USA." *Social Science and Medicine* 48: 253–265.

Gaulin, S. J. C., and J. S. Boster. 1990. "Dowry as female competition." *American Anthropologist* 92: 994–1005.

Gaulin, S. J. C., and A. Schlegel. 1980. "Paternal confidence and paternal investment: A cross cultural test of a sociobiological hypothesis." *Ethology and Sociobiology* 1: 301–309.

Gauthier, A. H., and F. F. Furstenberg Jr. 2002. "The transition to adulthood: A time use perspective." *Annals of the American Academy of Political and Social Science* 580: 153–171.

Gauthier, A. H., T. M. Smeedeng, and F. F. Furstenberg Jr. 2004. "Are parents investing less time in children? Trends in selected industrialized countries." *Population and Development Review* 30: 647–671.

Geary, D. C., and M. V. Flinn. 2001. "Evolution and human parental behavior and the human family." *Parenting: Science and Practice* 1: 5–61.

Gilmore D. D. 1990. *Manhood in the Making: Cultural Concepts of Masculinity.* New Haven, Conn.: Yale University Press.

Gogtay, N., J. N. Giedd, L. Lusk, K. M. Hayashi, D. Greenstein, A. C. Vaituzis, T. F. Nugent III, D. H. Herman, L. S. Clasen, A. W. Toga, J. L. Rapoport, and P. M. Thompson. 2004. "Dynamic mapping of human cortical development during childhood through adulthood." *Proceedings of the National Academy of Sciences* 101: 8174–8179.

Goodale, J. 1971. *Tiwi Wives: A Study of the Women of Melville Island, North Australia.* Seattle: University of Washington Press.

Goodall, J. 1986. *The Chimpanzees of Gombe.* Cambridge, Mass.: Harvard University Press.

Goodman, J. H. 2004. "Paternal postpartum depression, its relationship to maternal postpartum depression, and implications for family health." *Journal of Advanced Nursing* 45: 26–35.

Gould, R. G. 2000. "How many children could Moulay Ismail have had?" *Evolution and Human Behavior* 21: 295–296.

Gould, S. J., and R. C. Lewontin. 1979. "The spandrels of San Marco and the panglossian paradigm: A critique of the adaptationist programme." *Proceedings of the Royal Society of London B* 205: 581–598.

Gray, J. P. 1998. "Ethnographic atlas codebook." *World Cultures* 10: 86–136.

Gray, P., and B. Campbell. 2005. "Erectile dysfunction and its correlates among the Ariaal of northern Kenya." *International Journal of Impotence Research* 17: 445–449.

———. 2009. "Human male testosterone, pair bonds, and fatherhood." In *Endocrinology of Social Relationships,* ed. P. T. Ellison and P. B. Gray, . Cambridge, Mass.: Harvard University Press.

Gray, P. B., P. T. Ellison, and B. C. Campbell. 2007. "Testosterone and marriage among Ariaal men of northern Kenya." *Current Anthropology* 48: 750–755.

Gray, P. B., J. Flynn Chapman, M. H. McIntyre, T. C. Burnham, S. F., Lipson, and P. T. Ellison. 2004. "Human male pair bonding and testosterone." *Human Nature* 15:119–131.

Gray, P. B., S. M. Kahlenberg, E. S. Barrett, S. F. Lipson, and P. T. Ellison. 2002. "Marriage and fatherhood are associated with lower testosterone in males." *Evolution and Human Behavior* 23: 193–201.

Gray, P. B., J. C. Parkin, and M. E. Samms-Vaughan. 2007. "Hormonal correlates of human paternal interactions: A hospital-based investigation in urban Jamaica." *Hormones and Behavior* 52: 499–507.

Gray, P. B., C. J. Yang, and H. G. Pope. 2006. "Married fathers have lower salivary testosterone levels than married non-fathers and unmarried men in Beijing, China." *Proceedings of the Royal Society of London B* 273: 333–339.

Greenspan, F. S., and D. G. Gardner, eds. 2001. *Basic and Clinical Endocrinology*. New York: McGraw Hill.

Gregersen, E. 1994. *The World of Human Sexuality: Behaviors, Customs, and Beliefs*. New York: Irvington Publishers.

Gregor, T. 1985. *Anxious Pleasures: The Sexual Lives of an Amazonian People*. Chicago: University of Chicago Press.

Grewen, K., S. Girdler, J. Amico, and K. Light. 2005. "Effects of partner support on resting oxytocin, cortisol, norepinephrine, and blood pressure before and after warm partner contact." *Psychosomatic Medicine* 67: 531–538.

Grundy, E., and O. Kravdal. 2008. "Reproductive history and mortality in late middle age among Norwegian men and women." *American Journal of Epidemiology* 167: 271–279.

Gurven, M., and K. Hill. 2009. "Why do men hunt? A reevaluation of 'Man the Hunter' and the sexual division of labor." *Current Anthropology* 50: 51–74.

Gurven, M., and H. Kaplan. 2007. "Longevity among hunter-gatherers: A cross-cultural examination." *Population and Development Review* 33: 321–365.

Gurven, M., J. Winking, H. Kaplan, C. von Rueden, and L. McAllister. "A bioeconomic approach to marriage and the sexual division of labor." *Human Nature* 20(2):151–183.

Haddix, K. A. 2001. "Leaving your wife and your brothers: When polyandrous marriages fall apart." *Evolution and Human Behavior* 22: 47–60.

Hakim, C. 2003. *Work-Lifestyle Choices in the 21st Century: Preference Theory*. Oxford: Oxford University Press.

Halbreich, U., and S. Karkun. 2006. "Cross-cultural and social diversity of prevalence of postpartum depression and depressive symptoms." *Journal of Affective Disorders* 91: 97–111.

Hames, R. 1992. "Variation in paternal care among the Yanomamo." In *Father-Child Relations: Cultural and Biosocial Contexts,* ed. B. S. Hewlett, 85–110. New York: Aldine de Gruyter.

———. 1993. "Ye'kwana time allocation." *Cross-Cultural Studies in Time Allocation*. Vol. 10. Ed. Allen Johnson. New Haven, Conn.: Human Relation Area Files.

Hanson, T. L., I. Garfinkel, S. S. McLanahan, and C. K. Miller. 1996. "Trends in child support outcomes." *Demography* 33: 483–496.

Harkness, S. and C. M. Super. 1992. "The cultural foundations of fathers' roles: Evidence from Kenya and the United States." In B. S. Hewlett, ed., *Father-Child Relations,* 191–211. New York: Aldine.

Harknett, K. 2008. "Mate availability and unmarried parent relationships." *Demography* 45: 555–571.

Harrell, C. J., K. R. Smith, and G. P. Mineau. 2008. "Are girls good and boys bad for parental longevity?" *Human Nature* 19: 56–69.

Harris, K. M., F. F. Furstenberg Jr., and J. K. Marmer. 1998. "Paternal involvement with adolescents in intact families: The influence of fathers over the life course." *Demography* 35: 201–216.

Hartung, J. 1985. "Matrilineal inheritance: New theory and analysis." *Behavioral and Brain Sciences* 8: 661–688.

Hawkes, K. 1991. "Showing off: Tests of an hypothesis about men's foraging goals." *Ethology and Sociobiology* 12: 29–54.

Hawkes, K., and R. Bliege Bird. 2002. "Showing off, handicap signaling, and the evolution of men's work." *Evolutionary Anthropology* 11: 58–67.

Hawkes, K., J. F. O'Connell, N. G. Blurton Jones, H. Alvarez, and E. L. Charnov. 1998. "Grandmothering, menopause, and the evolution of human life histories." *Proceedings of the National Academy of Sciences* 95: 1336–1339.

Haynes, S., E. Eaker, and M. Feinleib. 1983. "Spouse behavior and coronary heart disease in men: Prospective results from the Framingham heart study." *American Journal of Epidemiology* 118: 1–22.

Hayward, L. S., and S. Rohwer. 2004. "Sex differences in attitudes toward paternity testing." *Evolution and Human Behavior* 25: 242–248.

Heath, K. M., and C. Hadley. 1998. "Dichotomous male reproductive strategies in a polygynous human society: Mating versus parental effort." *Current Anthropology* 39: 269–374.

Helle, S., V. Lummaa, and J. Jokela. 2002. "Sons reduced maternal longevity in preindustrial humans." *Science* 296: 1085.

Helminen, P., C. Ehnholm, M-L. Lokki, A. Jeffreys, and L. Peltonen. 1988. "Application of DNA 'fingerprints' to paternity determinations." *Lancet* 1: 574–576

Hennon, C. B., and Wilson, S. M., eds. 2008. *Families in a Global Context.* New York: Routledge.

Henshaw, S. K., S. Singh, and T. Haas. 1999. "The incidence of abortion worldwide." *International Family Planning Perspectives* 25 (supplement): S30–S38.

Hern, W. M. 1977. "High fertility in a Peruvian Amazon Indian village." *Human Ecology* 5:355–368.

Hesketh, T., L. Lu, and Z. W. Xing. 2005. "The effect of China's one-child family policy after 25 years." *New England Journal of Medicine* 353: 1171–1176.

Heuveline, P., J. M. Timberlake, and F. F. Furstenberg Jr. 2003. "Shifting childrearing to single mothers: Results from 17 Western countries." *Population and Development Review* 29: 47–71.

Hewitt, B., J. Baxter, and M. Western. 2006. "Family, work and health: The impact of marriage, parenthood and employment on self-reported health of Australian men and women." *Journal of Sociology* 42: 61–78.

Hewlett, B. L., and B. S. Hewlett. 2008. "A biocultural approach to sex, love, and intimacy in central African foragers and farmers." In *Intimacies: Love and Sex across Cultures,* ed. W. Jankowiak, 7–24. New York: Columbia University Press.

Hewlett, B. S. 1991a. "Demography and childcare in preindustrial societies." *Journal of Anthropological Research* 47: 1–37.

———. 1991b. *Intimate Fathers: The Nature and Context of Aka Pygmy Paternal Infant Care.* Ann Arbor: University of Michigan Press.

———, ed. 1992. *Father-Child Relations: Cultural and Biosocial Contexts.* New York: Aldine.

———. 2000. "Culture, history, and sex: Anthropological contributions to conceptualizing father involvement." *Marriage and Family Review* 29: 59–73.

Heymann, J. 2006. *Forgotten Families: Ending the Growing Crisis Confronting Children and Working Parents in the Global Economy.* New York: Oxford University Press.

Hill, E. M., and B. S. Low. 1992. "Contemporary abortion patterns: A life history approach." *Ethology and Sociobiology* 13: 35–48.

Hill, K., and A. M. Hurtado. 1996. *Ache Life History: The Ecology and Demography of a Foraging People.* New York: Aldine de Gruyter.

Hillis, S. D., C. M. Miranda, M. McCann, D. Bender, and K. Weigle. 1992. "Day care center attendance and diarrheal morbidity in Colombia." *Pediatrics* 90: 582–588.

Hirczy, W. 1993. "A new twist in divorce paternity tests as Solomon's sword." *Journal of Divorce and Remarriage* 20: 85–104.

Hofferth, S. L., and K. G. Anderson. 2003. "Are all dads equal? Biology vs. marriage as basis for paternal investment in children." *Journal of Marriage and Family* 65: 213–232.

Holden, C. and R. Mace. 2003. "Spread of cattle led to the loss of matrilineal descent in Africa: A coevolutionary analysis." *Proceedings of the Royal Society of London B* 270: 2425–2433.

Holman, D. J., and J. W. Wood. 2001. "Pregnancy loss and fecundability in women." In *Reproductive Ecology and Human Evolution,* ed. Peter Ellison, 15–38. New York: Aldine de Gruyter.

Howell, N. 2000. *Demography of the Dobe !Kung.* 2nd ed. New York: Aldine de Gruyter.

Hrdy, S. 1979. "Infanticide among animals: A review, classification, and examination of the implications for the reproductive strategies of females." *Ethology and Sociobiology* 1: 13–40.

———. 1999. *Mother Nature: A History of Mothers, Infants, and Natural Selection.* New York: Pantheon.

———. 2000. "The optimal number of fathers: Evolution, demography, and history in the shaping of female mate preferences." *Annals of the New York Academy of Sciences* 907: 75–96.

————. 2009. *Mothers and Others: The Evolutionary Origins of Mutual Under-standing*. Cambridge, Mass.: Belknap Press of Harvard University Press.

Hu, Y., and N. Goldman. 1990. "Mortality differentials by marital status: An international comparison." *Demography* 2: 233–250.

Huang, C-C., and W-J. Han. 2007. "Child support enforcement and sexual activity of male adolescents." *Journal of Marriage and Family* 69: 763–777.

Huber, B. R., and W. L. Breedlove. 2007. "Evolutionary theory, kinship, and childbirth in cross-cultural perspective." *Cross-Cultural Research* 41: 196–219.

Huber, B. R., V. Linhartova, D. Cope, and M. Lacy. 2004. "Evolutionary theory and birth-related investments by kin in cross-cultural perspective." *World Cultures* 15: 60–79.

Hudson, V. M., and A. Den Boer. 2002 "A surplus of men, a deficit peace-security and sex ratios in Asia's largest states." *International Securities* 26: 5–38.

Hurt, L. S., C. Ronsmans, and M. Quigley. 2006. "Does the number of sons born affect long-term mortality of parents? A cohort study in rural Bangla-desh." *Proceedings of the Royal Society of London B* 273: 149–155.

Hurtado, A. M., and K. Hill. 1992. "Paternal effect on offspring survivorship among Ache and Hiwi hunter-gathers: Implications for modeling pair-bond stability." In *Father-Child Relations: Cultural and Biosocial Contexts*, ed. B. S. Hewlett, 31–55. New York: Aldine de Gruyter.

Hyde, J. S., J. D. DeLamater, E. A. Plant, and J. M. Byrd. 1996. "Sexuality during pregnancy and the year postpartum." *Journal of Sex Research* 33: 143–151.

Ichinohe, M. R. Mita, K. Saito, H. Shinkawa, S. Nakaji, M. Coombs, A. Car-ney, B. Wright, and E. L. Fuller. 2005. "The prevalence of obesity and its relationship with lifestyle factors in Jamaica." *Tohoku Journal of Experimen-tal Medicine* 207: 21–32.

Ikeda, A., H. Iso, H. Toyoshima, Y. Fujino, T. Mizoue, T. Yoshimura, Y. In-aba, A. Tamakoshi, and JACC Study Group. 2007. "Marital status and mortality among Japanese men and women: The Japan Collaborative Co-hort Study." *BMC Public Health* 7: 73.

Ishii-Kuntz, M. 1993. "Japanese fathers: Work demands and family roles." In *Men, Work, and Family,* ed. J. C. Hood, 45–67. Newbury Park, Calif.: Sage.

Jablonka, E., and M. J. Lamb. 2005. *Evolution in Four Dimensions.* Cambridge, Mass.: MIT Press.

Jacobs, J. A., and K. Gerson. 2006. *The Time Divide: Work, Family and Gen-der Inequality.* Cambridge, Mass.: Harvard University Press.

James, W. H. 1993. "The incidence of superfecundation and of double pater-nity in the general population." *Acta Geneticae Medicaeet Gemellologiae* 42: 257–262.

Jankowiak, W., M. D. Nell, and A. Buckmaster. 2002. "Managing infidelity: A cross-cultural perspective." *Ethnology* 41: 85–101.

Jasienska, G., I. Nenko, and M. Jasienski. 2006. "Daughters increase longevity of fathers, but daughters and sons equally reduce longevity of mothers." *American Journal of Human Biology* 18: 422–425.

Jeffreys, A. J., M. Turner, and P. Debenham. 1991. "The efficiency of multilocus DNA fingerprint probes for individualization and establishment of family relationships, determined from extensive casework." *American Journal of Human Genetics* 48: 824–840.

Johns, S. E., and J. Belsky. 2007. "Life transitions: Becoming a parent." In *Family Relationships: An Evolutionary Perspective,* ed. C. A. Salmon, T. K. Shackelford, 71–90. New York: Oxford University Press.

Johnson, A., and O. R. Johnson. 1988. "Time allocation among the Machiguenga of Shimaa." *Cross-Cultural Studies in Time Allocation.* Vol. 1. Ed. Allen Johnson. New Haven, Conn.: Human Relation Area Files.

Johnson, A. M., C. H. Mercer, B. Erens, A. J. Copas., S. McManus, K. Wellings, K. A. Fenton, C. Korovessis, W. MacDowell, K. Nanchahal, S. Purdon, and J. Field. 2001. "Sexual behaviour in Britain: Partnerships, practices, and HIV risk behaviours." *Lancet* 358: 1835–1842.

Johnson, N. J., E. Backlund, P. D. Sorlie, and C. A. Loveless. 2000. "Marital status and mortality: The national longitudinal mortality study." *Annals of Epidemiology* 10: 224–238.

Jones, S. 1998. "Enacted marriages and fatherhood without jural paternity: Signs of bilateral kinship among Xhosa in an Eastern Cape township." Paper presented at the annual meeting of the Association for Anthropology in Southern Africa, University of Stellenbosch, South Africa.

Jorgensen, K. T., B. V. Pedersen, C. Johansen, and M. Frisch. 2008. "Fatherhood status and prostate cancer risk." *Cancer* 112: 919–923.

Juby, H., J-M. Billette, B. Laplante, and C. Le Bourdais. 2007. "Nonresident fathers and children: Parents' new unions and frequency of contact." *Journal of Family Issues* 28: 1220–1245.

Judge, D. S., and S. B. Hrdy. 1992. "Allocation of accumulated resources among close kin: Inheritance in Sacramento, California, 1890–1984." *Ethology and Sociobiology* 13: 495–522.

Käär, P., J. Jokela, J. Merilä, T. Helle, and I. Kojola. 1998. "Sexual conflict and remarriage in preindustrial human populations: Causes and fitness consequences." *Evolution and Human Behavior* 19: 139–151.

Kaitz, M., S. Shiri, S. Danziger, Z. Hershko, and A. I. Eidelman. 1994. "Fathers can also recognize their infants by touch." *Infant Behavior and Development* 17: 205–207.

Kalmijn, M. 1999. "Father involvement in childrearing and the perceived stability of marriage." *Journal of Marriage and the Family* 61: 409–421.

———. 2007. "Explaining cross-national differences in marriage, cohabitation, and divorce in Europe, 1990–2000." *Population Studies* 61: 243–263.

Kaplan, H. 1994. "Evolutionary and wealth flows theories of fertility: Empirical tests and new models." *Population and Demographic Review* 20: 753–791.

———. 1996. "A theory of fertility and parental investment in traditional and modern human societies." *Yearbook of Physical Anthropology* 39: 91–135.

Kaplan, H., and K. Hill. 1985. "Hunting ability and reproductive success among male Ache foragers." *Current Anthropology* 26: 131–133.

Kaplan, H., K. Hill, J. Lancaster, and A. M. Hurtado. 2000. "A theory of human life history evolution: Diet, intelligence, and longevity." *Evolutionary Anthropology* 9: 156–185.

Kaplan, H., J. B. Lancaster, S. E. Johnson, and J. A. Bock. 1995. "Does observed fertility maximize fitness among New Mexican men? A test of an optimality model and a new theory of parental investment in the embodied capital of offspring." *Human Nature* 6: 325–360.

Katz, M. M., and M. J. Konner. 1981. "The role of the father: An anthropological perspective." In *The Role of the Father in Child Development,* ed. M. Lamb, 155–185. Hoboken, N.J.: John Wiley.

Kelly, R. 1995. *The Foraging Spectrum.* Washington, D.C.: Smithsonian Press.

Kendig, H., P. A. Dykstra, R. I. van Gaalen, and T. Melkas. 2007. "Health of aging parents and childless individuals." *Journal of Family Issues* 28: 1457–1486.

Kennedy, G. E. 2003. "Palaeolithic grandmothers? Life history theory and early *Homo." Journal of the Royal Anthropological Institute* 9: 549–572.

Ketterson, E. D., and V. Nolan Jr. 1999. "Adaptation, exaptation, and constraint: A hormonal perspective." *American Naturalist* 154S: S4–S25.

Khlat, M. 1997. "Endogamy in the Arab world." In *Genetic Disorders among Arab Populations,* ed. A. S. Teebi and T. I. Farag, 63–80. New York, Oxford University Press

Khunou, G. 2006. "Fathers don't stand a chance: Experiences of custody, access, and maintenance." In *Baba: Men and Fatherhood in South Africa,* ed. L. Richter and R. Morrell, 265–277. Chicago: HSRC Press.

King, V., and J. M. Sobolewski. 2006. "Nonresident fathers' contributions to adolescent well-being." *Journal of Marriage and Family* 68: 537–557.

Kleiman, D. G. 1977. "Monogamy in mammals." *Quarterly Review of Biology* 52: 39–69.

Kleiman, D. G., and J. R. Malcolm. 1981. "The evolution of male parental investment in primates." In *Parental Care in Mammals,* ed. D. J. Gubernick and P. H. Klopfer, 347–387. New York: Plenum.

Klein, R. 2009. *The Human Career.* 3rd ed. Chicago: University of Chicago Press.

Klusmann, D. 2002. "Sexual motivation and the duration of partnership." *Archives of Sexual Behavior* 31: 275–287.

Knoester, C., and D. J. Eggebeen. 2006. "The effects of the transition to parenthood and subsequent children on men's well-being and social participation." *Journal of Family Issues* 27: 1532–1560.

Knott, C. D., and S. M. Kahlenberg. 2007. "Orangutans in perspective: Forced copulations and female mating resistance." In *Primates in Perspec-*

tive, ed. C. J. Campbell, A. Fuentes, K. C. MacKinnon, M. Panger, S. K. Bearder, 290–304. New York: Oxford University Press.

Kohler, H. P., J. R. Behrman, and A. Skytthe. 2005. "Partner + children = happiness? The effects of partnerships and fertility on well-being." *Population and Development Review* 31: 407–445.

Kozorovitskiy, Y., M. Hughes, K. Lee, and E. Gould. 2006. "Fatherhood affects dendritic spines and vasopressin via receptors in the primate prefrontal cortex." *Nature Neuroscience* 9: 1094–1095.

Kraemer, S. 2000. "The fragile male." *British Medical Journal* 321: 1609–1612.

Kramer, K. L. 2005. "Children's help and the pace of reproduction: Cooperative breeding in humans." *Evolutionary Anthropology* 14: 224–237.

Kruger, D. J., and R. M. Nesse. 2004. "Sexual selection and the male:female mortality ratio." *Evolutionary Psychology* 2: 66–85.

———. 2006. "An evolutionary life-history framework for understanding sex differences in human mortality rates." *Human Nature* 17: 74–97.

Kurdek, L. A. 1986. "Custodial mothers' perceptions of visitation and support and payment of child support by noncustodial fathers in families with low and high levels of preseparation interparent conflict." *Journal of Applied Developmental Psychology* 7: 307–323.

La Cerra, M. M. 1994. "Evolved mate preferences in women: Psychological adaptations for assessing a man's willingness to invest in offspring." PhD diss., University of California, Santa Barbara.

Lam, D. 1999. "Generating extreme inequality: Schooling, earnings, and intergenerational transmission of human capital in South Africa and Brazil." PSC Research Report No. 99–439. Population Studies Center, University of Michigan.

Lamb, M., ed. 2004. *Role of the Father in Child Development*. 3rd ed. New York: Wiley.

Lancaster, J. B., and C. S. Lancaster. 1983. "Parental investment: The hominin adaptation." In *How Humans Adapt: A Biocultural Odyssey*, ed. D. Ortner, 33–65. Washington D.C: Smithsonian Press.

Laumann, E. O., J. H. Gagnon, R. T. Michael, and S. Michaels. 1994. *The Social Organization of Sexuality*. Chicago: University of Chicago Press.

Lawlor, D. A., J. R. Emberson, S. Ebrahim, P. H. Whincup, S. G. Wannamethee, M. Walker, and G. D. Smith. 2003. "Is the association between parity and coronary heart disease due to biological effects of pregnancy or adverse lifestyle risk factors associated with childrearing?" *Circulation* 107: 1260–1264.

Lawoyin, T. O., and U. Larsen. 2002. "Male sexual behaviour during wife's pregnancy and postpartum abstinence in Oyo State, Nigeria." *Journal of Biosocial Science* 34: 51–63.

Le Boeuf, B. J., and J. Reiter. 1988. "Lifetime reproductive success in northern elephant seals." In *Reproductive Success,* ed. T. H. Clutton-Brock, 344–362. Chicago: University of Chicago Press.

Lee, S., D. McCann, and J. Messenger. 2007. *Working Time around the World: Trends in Working Hours, Laws and Policies in a Global Comparative Perspective.* Geneva: International Labour Office.

Lehmann, J. 2008. "Meaning and relevance of kinship in great apes." In *Early Human Kinship,* ed. W. James, N. Allen, H. Callan, R. Dunbar, 160–167. New York: Wiley-Blackwell.

Leite, R. W., and P. C. McKenry. 2002. "Aspects of father status and postdivorce father involvement with children." *Journal of Family Issues* 23: 601–623.

Le Roux, M-G., O. Pascal, M-T. Andre, O. Herbert, A. David, and J-P. Moisan. 1992. "Non-paternity and genetic counseling." *Lancet* 340: 607.

Levinson, D. 1989. *Family Violence in Cross-Cultural Perspective.* Newbury Park, Calif.: Sage.

Levitas, E., E. Lunenfeld, N. Weisz, M. Friger, and G. Potashnik. 2007. "Relationship between age and semen parameters in men with normal sperm concentration: Analysis of 6022 semen samples." *Andrologia* 39: 45–50.

Lev-Wiesel, R. 2000. "The effect of children's sleeping arrangements (communal vs. familial) on fatherhood among men in an Israeli kibbutz." *Journal of Social Psychology* 140: 58–588.

Lichter, D. T., R. N. Anderson, and M. D. Hayward. 1995. "Marriage markets and marital choice." *Journal of Family Issues* 16: 412–431.

Lin, M. M., and L. J. Young. 2006. "Neuropeptidergic regulation of affiliative behavior and social bonding in animals." *Hormones and Behavior* 50:506–517.

Lin, I-F. 2000. Perceived Fairness and Compliance with Child Support Obligations. *Journal of Marriage and the Family,* 62(2):388–398.

Lin, I-F., and S. S. McLanahan. 2007. "Parental beliefs about nonresident fathers' obligations and rights." *Journal of Marriage and Family* 69: 382–398.

Lisker, R., A. Carnevale, J. A. Villa, S. Armendares, and D. C. Wertz. 1998. "Mexican geneticists' opinions on disclosure issues." *Clinical Genetics* 54: 321–329.

Liu, C. 2003. "Does quality of marital sex decline with duration?" *Archives of Sexual Behavior* 32: 55–60.

Lloyd, Cynthia B. and Ann K. Blanc. 1996. Children's Schooling in Sub-Saharan Africa: The Role of Fathers, Mothers and Others. *Population and Development Review* 22:265–98.

Lordkipanidze, D., T. Jashashvili, A. Vekua, M. S. Ponce de León, C. P. E. Zollikofer, G. P. Rightmire, H. Pontzer, R. Ferring, O. Oms, M. Tappen, M. Bukhsianidze, J. Agusti, R. Kahlke, G. Kiladze, B. Martinze-Navarro,

A. Mouskhelishvili, M. Nioradze, and L. Rook. 2007. "Postcranial evidence from early *Homo* from Dmanisi, Georgia." *Nature* 449: 305–310.

Lovejoy, O. 1981. "The origin of man." *Science* 211: 341–350.

Low, B. S. 1978. "Environmental uncertainty and the parental strategies of marsupials and placentals." *American Naturalist* 112: 197–213.

———. 1989. "Cross-cultural patterns in the training of children: An evolutionary perspective." *Journal of Comparative Psychology* 103: 311–319.

———. 1994. "Men in the demographic transition." *Human Nature* 5: 223–253.

———. 2000. *Why Sex Matters.* Princeton, N.J.: Princeton University Press.

Low, B. S., and Alice L. Clarke. 1992. Resources and the life course: Patterns in the demographic transition. *Ethology and Sociobiology* 13(5–6): 463–494.

Low, B. S., and J. T. Heinen. 1993. "Population, resources, and environment: Implications of human behavioral ecology for conservation." *Population and Environment* 15: 7–41.

Low, B. S., C. P. Simon, and K. G. Anderson. 2003. "The biodemography of modern women: Tradeoffs when resources become limiting." In *The Biodemography of Human Reproduction and Fertility,* ed. J. Rodgers and H. P. Kohler, 105–134. Boston: Kluwer Academic Publishers.

Lozoff, B. 1983. "Birth and 'bonding' in non-industrial societies." *Developmental Medicine and Child Neurology* 25: 595–600.

Lucasson, A., and M. Parker. 2001. "Revealing false paternity: Some ethical considerations." *Lancet* 357: 1033–1035.

Lund, R., P. Due, J. Modvig, B. E. Holstein, M. T. Damsgaard, and P. K. Anderson. 2002. "Cohabitation and marital status as predictors of mortality—an eight year follow-up study." *Social Science and Medicine* 55: 673–679.

MacDougall-Shackleton EA and RJ Robertson. 1998. Confidence of paternity and paternal care by eastern bluebirds. Behavioral Ecology 9:201–205.

MacIntyre, S., and A. Sooman. 1991. "Non-paternity and prenatal genetic screening." *Lancet* 338: 869–871.

Manning, W. D., and P. J. Smock. 1999. "New families and nonresident father-child visitation." *Social Forces* 78: 87–116.

———. 2000. "'Swapping' families: Serial parenting and economic support for children." *Journal of Marriage and the Family* 62: 111–122.

Manning, W. D., S. D. Stewart, and P. J. Smock. 2003. "The complexity of fathers' parenting responsibilities and involvement with nonresident children." *Journal of Family Issues* 24: 645–667.

Mare, R. D. 1991. "Five decades of educational assortative mating." *American Sociological Review* 56: 15–32.

Marlowe, F. 1999a. "Male care and mating effort among Hadza foragers." *Behavioral Ecology and Sociobiology* 46: 57–64.

———. 1999b. "Showoffs or providers? The parenting effort of Hadza men." *Evolution and Human Behavior* 20: 391–404.

———. 2000. "Paternal investment and the human mating system." *Behavioural Processes* 51: 45–61.

———. 2001. "Male contribution to diet and female reproductive success among foragers." *Current Anthropology* 42: 755–760.

———. 2003. "A critical period for provisioning by Hadza men: Implications for pair bonding." *Evolution and Human Behavior* 24: 217–229.

———. 2004. "Is human ovulation concealed? Evidence from conception beliefs in a hunter-gatherer society." *Archives of Sexual Behavior* 33: 427–432.

———. 2005a. "Hunter-gatherers and human evolution." *Evolutionary Anthropology* 14: 54–67.

———. 2005b. "Who tends Hadza children?" In *Hunter-Gatherer Childhoods: Evolutionary, Developmental and Cultural Perspectives,* ed. B. Hewlett and M. Lamb, 177–190. New Brunswick, N.J.: Aldine Transaction.

Marsiglio, W. 1991. "Paternal engagement activities with minor children." *Journal of Marriage and the Family* 53: 973–986.

Marsters, R. W. 1957. "Determination of nonpaternity by blood groups: A series of two hundred cases." *Journal of Forensic Sciences* 2: 15–37.

Martinez, G. M., A. Chandra, J. C. Abma, J. Jones, and W. D. Mosher. 2006. "Fertility, contraception, and fatherhood: Data on men and women from Cycle 6 (2002) of the National Survey of Family Growth." *Vital and Health Statistics* 23(26):i–142.

Mason, M. A. 1996. *From Father's Property to Children's Rights: A History of Child Custody.* New York: Columbia University Press.

Mazur, A., and J. Michalek. 1998. "Marriage, divorce, and male testosterone." *Social Forces* 77: 315–330.

McHenry, H. M. 1994. "Behavioral ecological implications of early hominid body size." *Journal of Human Evolution* 27: 77–87.

McKenna, J., S. Mosko, and C. Richard. 1999. "Breastfeeding and mother-infant cosleeping in relation to SIDS prevention." In W. R. Trevathan, E. O. Smith, J. J. McKenna, eds., *Evolutionary Medicine,* 53–74. New York: Oxford University Press.

McLain, D. K., D. Setters, M. P. Moulton, and A. E. Pratt. 2000. "Ascription of resemblance of newborns by parents and nonrelatives." *Evolution and Human Behavior* 21: 11–23.

McLanahan, S., and G. Sandefur. 1994. *Growing Up with a Single Parent: What Hurts, What Helps.* Cambridge, Mass.: Harvard University.

Melancon, T. 1982. Marriage and Reproduction Among the *Yanomamo* Indians of Venezuela. PhD dissertation, Pennsylvania State University.

Miller, C., and I. Garfinkel. 1999. "The determinants of paternity establishment and child support award rates among unmarried women." *Population Research and Policy Review* 18: 237–260.

Mincy, R., I. Garfinkel, and L. Nepomnyaschy. 2005. "In-hospital paternity establishment and father involvement in fragile families." *Journal of Marriage and Family* 67: 611–626.

Moore, S. L., and K. Wilson. 2002. "Parasites as a viability cost of sexual selection in natural populations of mammals." *Science* 297: 2015–2018.

Moorman, J. E., and D. J. Hernandez. 1989. "Married-couple families with step, adopted and biological children." *Demography* 26: 267–277.

Morgan, S. P., D. Lye, and G. Condran. 1988. "Sons, daughters, and the risk of marital disruption." *American Journal of Sociology* 94: 110–129.

Muller, M. N., F. Marlowe, R. Bugumba, and P. T. Ellison. 2009. "Testosterone and paternal care in East African foragers and pastoralists." *Proceedings of the Royal Society of London B* 276: 347–354.

Mundy, L. 2007. *Everything Conceivable: How Assisted Reproduction is Changing Our World*. New York: Anchor.

Munroe, R. L., R. H. Munroe, and J. M. Whiting. 1973. "The couvade: A psychological analysis." *Ethos* 1: 30–74.

Murdock, G. P. 1949. *Social Structure*. New York: Macmillan.

Nelson, R. J. 2005. *An Introduction to Behavioral Endocrinology*. 3rd ed. Sunderland, Mass.: Sinauer.

Nielsen, T. L., K. Wraae, K. Brixen, A. P. Hermann, M. Andersen, and C. Hagen. 2007. "Prevalence of overweight, obesity and physical inactivity in 20-to-29-year-old, Danish men: Relation to sociodemography, physical dysfunction and low socioeconomic status: The Odense Androgen Study." *International Journal of Obesity* 30: 805–815.

Nock, S. L. 1998. *Marriage in Men's Lives*. New York: Oxford University Press.

Nonaka, K., T. Miura, and K. Peter. 1994. "Recent fertility decline in Dariusleut Hutterites: an extension of Eaton and Mayer's Hutterite fertility study." *Human Biology* 66(3):411–20.

Nyambedha, Erick Otieno, Simiyu Wandibba, and Jens Aagaard Hanscn. 2003. Changing Patterns of Orphan Care Due to the HIV Epidemic in Western Kenya. *Social Science and Medicine* 57:301–311.

Oates, M. R., J. L. Cox, S. Neema, P. Asten, N. Glangeaud-Freudenthal, B. Figueiredo, L. L. Gorman, S. Hacking, E. Hirst, M. H. Kammerer, C. M. Klier, G. Seneviratne, M. Smith, A. L. Sutter-Dallay, V. Valoriani, B. Wickberg, K. Yoshida, and the TCS-PND Group. 2004. "Postnatal depression across countries and cultures: A qualitative study." *British Journal of Psychiatry* 184 (S46): S10–S16.

O'Brien, M., B. Brandth, and E. Kvande. 2007. "Fathers, work and family life." *Community, Work and Family* 10: 375–386.

O'Connell, J. F., K. Hawkes, and N. G. B. Jones. 1999. "Grandmothering and the evolution of *Homo erectus*." *Journal of Human Evolution* 36: 461–485.

Oda, R., A. Matsumoto-Oda, and O. Kurashima. 2002. "Facial resemblance of Japanese children to their parents." *Journal of Ethology* 20: 81–85.

Odendaal, J. S. J., and Meintjes, R. A. 2003. "Neurophysiological correlates of affiliative behavior between humans and dogs." *Veterinary Journal* 165:296–301.

Onozawa, K., V. Glover, D. Adams, N. Modi, and R. C. Kumar. 2001. "Infant massage improves mother-infant interaction for mothers with postnatal depression." *Journal of Affective Disorders* 63: 201–207.

Operario, Don, Lucie Cluver, Helen Rees, Catherin MacPhail, and Audrey Pettifor. 2008. Orphanhood and Completion of Comulsory School Education Among Young People in South Africa: Findings from a National Representative Survey. *Journal of Research on Adolescence* 18:173–186.

Ovwigho, P. C., V. Head, and C. E. Born. 2007. "Child support outcomes of Maryland's in-hospital paternity acknowledgement program." Family Welfare Research and Training Group, University of Maryland School of Social Work.

Padberg, J., E. Disbrow, and L. Krubitzer. 2005. "The organization and connections of anterior and posterior parietal cortex in titi monkeys: Do New World monkeys have an area 2?" *Cerebral Cortex* 15: 1938–1963.

Pagel, M. 1997. "Desperately concealing father: A theory of parent-infant resemblance." *Animal Behaviour* 53: 973–981.

Paige, K. E., and J. M. Paige. 1981. *The Politics of Reproductive Ritual.* Berkeley: University of California Press.

Paolisso, M., and R. D. Sackett. 1988. "Time allocation among the Yukpa of Yurmutu." *Cross-Cultural Studies in Time Allocation.* Vol. 2. Ed. Allen Johnson. New Haven, Conn.: Human Relation Area Files.

Paquette, D. 2004. "Theorizing the father-child relationship: Mechanisms and developmental outcomes." *Human Development* 47: 193–219.

Parker, Geoffrey A. 1970. Sperm competition and its evolutionary consequences in the insects. *Biological Reviews* 45.525–567.

Parr, Lisa A. and Frans B.M. de Waal. 1999. Visual kin recognition in chimpanzees. *Nature* 399: 647–48.

Pastore, L., A. Owens, and C. Raymond. 2007. "Postpartum sexuality among first-time parents from one U.S. academic hospital." *Journal of Sexual Medicine* 4: 115–123.

Paulson, J. F., S. Dauber, and J. A. Leiferman. 2006. "Individual and combined effects of postpartum depression in mothers and fathers on parenting behavior." *Pediatrics* 118: 659–668.

Pena, S. D. J., and R. Chakraborty. 1994. "Paternity testing in the DNA era." *Trends in Genetics* 10: 204–209.

Pérusse, D. 1993. "Cultural and reproductive success in industrial societies: Testing the relationship at the proximate and ultimate levels." *Behavioral and Brain Sciences* 16: 267–323.

Pérusse, D., M. C. Neale, A. C. Heath, and L. J. Eaves. 1994. "Human parental behavior: Evidence for genetic influence and potential implication for gene-culture transmission." *Behavior Genetics* 24: 327–335.

Peters, H. E., L. M. Argys, E. E. Maccoby, and R. H. Mnookin. 1993. "Enforcing divorce settlements: Evidence from child support compliance and award modifications." *Demography* 30: 719–735.

Petrie, M., and B. Kempenaers. 1998. "Extra-pair paternity in birds: Explaining variation between species and populations." *Trends Ecology and Evolution* 13: 52–57.

Pillsworth, E. 2008. "Mate preferences among the Shuar of Ecuador: Trait rankings and peer evaluations." *Evolution and Human Behavior* 29: 256–267.

Platek, S. M., D. M. Raines, G. G. Gallups, F. B. Mohamed, J. Thomson, T. Myers, I. Panyavin, S. Levin, J. Davis, and L. Fonteyn. 2004. "Reaction to children's faces: Males are more affected by resemblance than females are, and so are their brains." *Evolution and Human Behavior* 25: 394–405.

Plavcan, J. M. 2002. "Sexual dimorphism in primate evolution." *Yearbook of Physical Anthropology* 44: 25–53.

Plummer, T. 2004. "Flaked stones and old bones: Biological and cultural evolution at the dawn of technology." *Yearbook of Physical Anthropology* 47: 118–164.

Polesky, H. F., and H. D. Krause. 1977. "Blood typing in disputed paternity cases: Capabilities of American laboratories." *Transfusion* 17: 521–524.

Potts, M. 1997. "Sex and the birth rate: Human biology, demographic change, and access to fertility-regulation methods." *Population and Development Review* 23: 1–39.

Power, C., B. Rodgers, and S. Hope. 1999. "Heavy alcohol consumption and marital status: Disentangling the relationship in a national study of young adults." *Addiction* 94: 1477–1487.

Pritchett, L. H. 1994. "Desired fertility and the impact of population policies." *Population and Development Review* 20: 1–55.

Qin, P., and P. B. Mortensen. 2003. "The impact of parental status on the risk of completed suicide." *Archives of General Psychiatry* 60: 797–802.

Quammen, D. 2006. *The Reluctant Mr. Darwin.* New York: W. W. Norton.

Quinlan, R. J. 2003. "Father absence, parental care and female reproductive development." *Evolution and Human Behavior* 24: 376–390.

Regalski, J. M., and S. J. C. Gaulin. 1993. "Whom are Mexican infants said to resemble? Monitoring and fostering paternal confidence in the Yucatan." *Ethology and Sociobiology* 14: 97–113.

Reichard, U. H., and C. Boesch, eds. 2005. *Monogamy: Mating Strategies and Partnerships in Birds, Humans and Other Mammals.* Cambridge: Cambridge University Press.

Richerson, P. J., and R. Boyd. 2005. *Not by Genes Alone.* Chicago: University of Chicago Press.

Rival, L. 1998. "Androgynous parents and guest children: The Huaorani couvade." *Journal of the Royal Anthropological Institute* 4: 619–642.

Robbins, M. M. 2007. "Gorillas: Diversity in ecology and behavior." In *Primates in Perspective,* ed. C. J. Campbell, A. Fuentes, K. C. MacKinnon, M. Panger, and S. K. Bearder, 305–320. New York: Oxford University Press.

Rodgers, J. L., H-P. Kohler, K. O. Kyvik, and K. Christensen. 2001. "Behavior genetic modeling of human fertility: Findings from a contemporary Danish twin study." *Demography* 38: 29–42.

Rodgers, J. L., D. C. Rowe, and M. Buster. 1999. "Nature, nurture, and first sexual intercourse in the USA: Fitting behavioral genetic models to NLSY kinship data." *Journal of Biosocial Science* 31: 29–41.

Rohwer, S. 1986. "Selection for adoption versus infanticide by replacement 'mates' in birds." *Current Ornithology* 3: 353–395.

Rohwer, S., J. C. Herron, and M. Daly. 1999. "Stepparental behavior as mating effort in birds and other animals." *Evolution and Human Behavior* 20:367–390.

Roopnarine, J. L. 2005. African American and African Caribbean fathers: Level, quality, and meaning of involvement. In *The Role of the Father in Child Development, Fourth Edition* (Michael E. Lamb, ed.), pp. 58–97.

———. n.d. Paternal involvement across cultures: Implications for childhood development. Unpublished manuscript, Syracuse University.

Roopnarine, J. L., and U. P. Gielen. 2004. *Families in Global Perspective.* Boston: Allyn and Bacon.

Roughgarden, J. 2004. *Evolution's Rainbow: Diversity, Gender, and Sexuality in Nature and People.* Berkeley: University of California Press.

Royston, J. P. 1982. Basal body temperature, ovulation and the risk of conception, with special reference to the lifetimes of sperm and egg. *Biometrics* 38(2):397–406.

Rudavsky, S. 1999. "Separating spheres: Legal ideology v. paternity testing in divorce cases." *Science in Contest* 12: 123–138.

Sariola, H., and A. Uutela. 1996. "The prevalence and content of incest abuse in Finland." *Child Abuse and Neglect* 20: 843–850.

Sarkadi, A., R. Kristiansson, F. Oberklaid, and S. Bremberg. 2007. "Fathers' involvement and children's developmental outcomes: A systematic review of longitudinal studies." *Acta Paediatrica* 97: 153–158.

Sasse, G., H. Muller, R. Chakraborty, and J. Ott. 1994. "Estimating the frequency of nonpaternity in Switzerland." *Human Heredity* 44: 337–343.

Sawyer, S., M. E. Metz, J. D. Hinds, and R. A. Brucker Jr. 2001. "Attitudes toward prostitution among males: A 'consumers' report.'" *Current Psychology* 20: 363–376.

Scelza, B. A. Forthcoming. "Father's presence speeds the social and reproductive careers of sons in a contemporary Australian aboriginal society." *Current Anthropology.*

Schacht, L. E., and H. Gershowitz. 1963. "Frequency of extra-marital children as determined by blood groups." In *Proceedings of the Second International Congress on Human Genetics,* ed. L. Gedda, 894–897. Rome: G. Mendel.

Schlegel, A., and H. Barry III. 1991. *Adolescence: An Anthropological Inquiry.* New York: The Free Press.

Schwagmeyer, P. L., and D. W. Mock. 1993. Shaken confidence of paternity. *Animal Behaviour* 46:1020–1022.

Schwagmeyer, P. L., R. C. St. Clair, J. D. Moodie, T. C. Lamey, G. D. Schnell, and M. N. Moodie. 1999. "Species differences in male parental care in birds: A reexamination of correlates with paternity." *Auk* 116: 487–503.

Sear, R. 2006. "Size-dependent reproductive success in Gambian men: Does height or weight matter more?" *Social Biology* 53: 172–188.

Sear, R., and R. Mace. 2008. "Who keeps children alive? A review of the effects of kin on child survival." *Evolution and Human Behavior* 29: 1–18.

Seccombe, K., and G. Lee. 1987. "Female status, wives' autonomy, and divorce: A cross-cultural study." *Family Perspective* 20: 241–249.

Seifritz, E., F. Esposito, J. H. Neuhoff, A. Luthi, H. Mustovic, G. Dammann, U. von Bardeleben, E. W. Radue, S. Cirillo, G. Tedeschi, and F. Di Salle. 2003. "Differential sex-independent amygdale response to infant crying and laughing in parents versus nonparents." *Biological Psychology* 54: 1367–1375.

Seltzer, J. A. 1991. "Relationships between fathers and children who live apart: The father's role after separation." *Journal of Marriage and the Family* 53: 79–101.

Semaw, W., P. Renne, and J. W. K. Harris, C. S. Feibel, R. L. Bernor. 1997. "2.5-million-year-old stone tools from Gona, Ethiopia." *Nature* 385: 333–336.

Shackelford, T. K., N. Pound, and A. T. Goetz. 2005. "Psychological and physiological adaptations to sperm competition in humans." *Review of General Psychology* 9: 228–248.

Shackelford, T. K., V. A. Weekes-Shackelford, and D. P. Schmitt. 2005. "An evolutionary perspective on why some men refuse or reduce their child support payments." *Basic and Applied Social Psychology* 27: 297–306.

Sheldon, B. C. 2002. "Relating paternity to paternal care." *Philosophical Transactions of the Royal Society of London, Series B: Biological Sciences* 357: 341–350.

Shenk, M. 2005. "Kin Networks in Wage-Labor Economics: Effects on Child and Marriage Market Outcomes." *Human Nature* 16:81–114.

Shostak, Marjorie. 1981. *Nisa: The Life and Words of a !Kung Woman.* Cambridge, MA: Harvard University Press.

Shwalb, D. W., J. Nakazawa, T. Yamamoto, and J. H. Hyun. 2004. "Fathering in Japanese, Chinese, and Korean cultures." In *The Role of the Father in Child Development*, ed. M. Lamb, 146–181. Hoboken, N.J.: Wiley.

Sigle-Rushton, W., and S. McLanahan. 2004. "Father absence and child well-being: A critical review." In *The Future of the Family*, ed. L. Rainwater, T. Smeeding, and D. P. Moynihan, 116–155. Thousand Oaks, Calif: Russell Sage Foundation.

Silk, J. B. 1980. "Adoption and kinship in Oceania." *American Anthropologist* 82: 799–820.

Simmons, Leigh, W., Renee C. Firman, Gillian Rhodes & Marianne Peters. 2004. Human sperm competition: testis size, sperm production and rates of extrapair copulations. *Animal Behaviour* 68:297–302.

Simpson, S. W., J. Quade, N. E. Levin, R. Butler, G. Dupont-Nivet, M. Everett, and S. Semaw. 2008. "A female *Homo erectus* pelvis from Gona, Ethiopia." *Science* 322: 1089–1092.

Skinner, G. W. 1997. "Family systems and demographic processes." In *Anthropological Demography: Towards a New Synthesis,* ed. D. I. Kertzer and T. Fricke, 53–95. Chicago: University of Chicago Press.

Small, M. 1998. *Our Babies, Ourselves.* New York: Anchor.

Smith, G. 1995. "Time allocation among the Madurese of Gedang-Gedang." *Cross-Cultural Studies in Time Allocation*. Vol. 13. Ed. Allen Johnson. New Haven, Conn.: Human Relation Area Files.

Smith, H. J. 2005. *Parenting for Primates*. Cambridge, Mass.: Harvard University Press.

Smith, K. R., and C. D. Zick. 1994. "Linked lives, dependent demise? Survival analysis of husbands and wives." *Demography* 31: 81–93.

Smith, M. S., B. J. Kish, and C. B. Crawford. 1987. "Inheritance of wealth as human kin investment." *Ethology and Sociobiology* 8: 171–182.

Smith, R. L. 1984. "Human sperm competition." In *Sperm Competition and the Evolution of Animal Mating Systems,* ed. R. L. Smith, 601–659. New York: Academic Press.

Smock, P. J. 2000. "Cohabitation in the United States: An appraisal of research themes, findings, and implications." *Annual Review of Sociology* 26:1–20.

Smock, P. J., W. D. Manning, and M. Porter. 2005. "'Everything's there except money': How money shapes decisions to marry among cohabitors." *Journal of Marriage and Family* 67: 680–696.

Smouse, P. E., and R. Chakraborty. 1986. "The use of restriction fragment length polymorphism in paternity analysis." *American Journal of Human Genetics* 38: 918–939.

Smuts, B. B. 1985. *Sex and Friendship in Baboons.* Hawthorne, N.Y.: Aldine.

Smuts, B. B., and D. J. Gubernick. 1992. "Male-infant relationships in non-human primates: Paternal investment or mating effort?" In *Father-Child Relations: Cultural and Biosocial Contexts,* ed. B. S. Hewlett, 1–30. New York: Aldine de Gruyter.

Sobal, J., B. Rauschenbach, and E. A. Frongillo. 2003. "Marital status changes and body weight changes: A US longitudinal analysis." *Social Science and Medicine* 56: 1543–1555.

Sobrinho, L. G. 2003. "Prolactin, psychological stress, and environment in humans: Adaptation and maladapation." *Pituitary* 6: 35–39.

Sonenstein, F. L., and C. A. Calhoun. 1990. "Determinants of child support: A pilot survey of absent parents." *Contemporary Policy Issues* 8: 75–94.

Sorensen, E. 1997. "A national profile of nonresident fathers and their ability to pay child support." *Journal of Marriage and the Family* 59: 785–797.

Spector, P. E., T. D. Allen, and S. Poelmans et al. 2005. "An international comparative study of work-family stress and occupational strain." In *Work and Family: An International Research Perspective,* ed. A. Y. Poelmans, 71–86. Mahwah, N.J.: Lawrence Erlbaum.

Stewart, S. D. 2002. "The effect of stepchildren on childbearing intentions and births." *Demography* 39: 181–197.

———. 2005. "How the birth of a child affects involvement with stepchildren." *Journal of Marriage and Family* 67: 461–473.

———. 2007. *Brave New Stepfamilies: Diverse Paths towards Stepfamily Living*. Thousand Oaks, Calif.: Sage Publications.

Stewart, S. D., W. D. Manning, and P. J. Smock. 2003. Union formation among men in the U.S.: Does having prior children matter? *Journal of Marriage and Family* 65:90–104.

Stolting, K. N., and A. B. Wilson. 2007. "Male pregnancy in seahorses and pipefish: Beyond the mammalian model." *BioEssays* 29: 884–896.

Storey, A. E., C. J. Walsh, R. L. Quinton, and K. E. Wynne-Edwards. 2000. "Hormonal correlates of paternal responsiveness in new and expectant fathers." *Evolution and Human Behavior* 21: 79–95.

Strassmann, B. I. 1992. "The function of menstrual taboos among the Dogon: Defense against cuckoldry?" *Human Nature* 3: 89–131.

———. 1997. "The biology of mensturation in *Homo sapiens*: Total lifetime menses, fecundity, and nonsynchrony in a natural-fertility population." *Current Anthropology* 37(1): 123–129.

Strassmann, B. I., and A. L. Clarke. 1998. "Ecological constraints on marriage in rural Ireland." *Evolution and Human Behavior* 19: 33–56.

Stritof, S., and B. Stritof. 2008. "Cousin marriages: Marriage license laws." http://marriage.about.com/cs/marriagelicenses/a/cousin.htm (accessed 11/24/08).

Strier, K. B. 2007. *Primate Behavioral Ecology,* 3rd Ed. Boston: Allyn and Bacon.

Stumpf, R. 2007. "Chimpanzees and bonobos: Diversity within and between species." In *Primates in Perspective,* ed. C. J. Campbell, A. Fuentes, K. C. MacKinnon, M. Panger, and S. K. Bearder, 321–344. New York: Oxford University Press.

Sugiyama, L. S., and R. Chacon. 2005. "Juvenile responses to household ecology among the Yora of Peruvian Amazonia." In *Hunter-Gatherer Childhoods: Evolutionary, Developmental and Cultural Perspectives,* ed. B. S. Hewlett and M. E. Lamb, 237–261. New Brunswick, N.J.: Aldine Transaction.

Sussman, L. N. 1954. Blood grouping tests in disputed paternity proceedings. *Journal of American Medical Association* 155 (13):1143–1145.

———. 1956. "Blood grouping tests in disputed paternity proceedings and filial relationships." *Journal of Forensic Sciences* 1: 25–34.

Swain, J. E., J. P. Lorberbaum, S. Kose, and L. Strathearn. 2007. "Brain basis of early parent-infant interactions: Psychology, physiology, and in vivo functional neuroimaging studies." *Journal of Child Psychology and Psychiatry* 48: 262–287.

Symons, D. 1979. *The Evolution of Human Sexuality.* New York: Oxford University Press.

Szalai, A. 1972. *The Use of Time: Daily Activities of Urban and Suburban Populations in Twelve Countries.* The Hague: Mouton.

Tal, I., and D. Lieberman. 2007. "Kin detection and the development of sexual aversions: Toward an integration of theories on family sexual abuse." In *Family Relationships: An Evolutionary Perspective,* ed. C. A. Salmon, and T. K. Shackelford, 205–229. New York: Oxford University Press.

Tarin, J. J., B. Brines, and A. Cano. 1998. "Long-term effects of delayed parenthood." *Human Reproduction* 13: 2371–2376.

Thompson, J. L., and A. J. Nelson. Forthcoming. "Middle childhood and modern human origins." *Human Nature.*

Tinbergen, N. 1963. "On aims and methods of ethology." *Zeitschrift fur Tierpsychologie* 20: 410–433.

Townsend, N. W. 2002. *The Package Deal: Marriage, Work, and Fatherhood in Men's Lives.* Philadelphia: Temple University Press.

Trent, K., and S. J. South. 1989. "Structural determinants of the divorce rate: A cross-societal analysis." *Journal of Marriage and the Family* 51: 391–404.

Trethowan, W. H., and M. F. Conlon. 1965. "The couvades syndrome." *British Journal of Psychiatry* 111: 57–66.

Trevathan, W. 1987. *Human Birth: An Evolutionary Perspective.* New York: Aldine.

Trivers, R. 1972. "Parental investment and sexual selection." In *Sexual Selection and the Descent of Man,* ed. B. C. Campbell, 136–179. Chicago: Aldine.

Tsai, S., and C. Chen. 1997. "Somatic symptoms, stress and social support of expectant fathers (Chinese)." *Nursing Research* 5: 439–451.

Tuljapurkar, S. D., C. O. Puleston, and M. D. Gurven. 2007. "Why men matter: Mating patterns drive evolution of human lifespan." *PLoS ONE* 8: e785.

Turke, P. 1989. "Evolution and the demand for children." *Population and Development Review* 15: 61–90.

———. 1991. "Theory and evidence on wealth flows and old-age security: A reply to Fricke." *Population and Development Review* 17: 687–702.

Turke, P., and L. Betzig. 1985. "Those who can, do: Wealth, status, and reproductive success on Ifaluk." *Ethology and Sociobiology* 6: 79–87.

Turnbull, C. M. 1961. *The Forest People.* Touchstone: New York.

Twenge, J. M., W. K. Campbell, and C. A. Foster. 2003. "Parenthood and marital satisfaction: A meta-analytic review." *Journal of Marriage and Family* 65: 574–583.

UNICEF. 2007. The State of the World's Children 2008. www.unicef.org/sowe08/. Acccessed 09/01/08.

United Nations. 2008. *World Fertility Patterns 2007*. www.un.org/esa/population/publications/worldfertility2007/worldfertility2007.htm. Accessed 11/08/08.

U.S. Census Bureau. 2003. "Adopted children and stepchildren: 2000." Census 2000 Special Reports, CENSR-6RV. Prepared by R. M. Kreider. U.S. Census Bureau, Washington, D.C.

———. 2005. "Number, timing, and duration of marriages and divorces: 2001." Current Population Reports, P70–97. Prepared by R. M. Kreider. U.S. Census Bureau, Washington, D.C.

———. 2007a. "Custodial mothers and fathers and their child support: 2005." Current Population Reports, P60-234. Prepared by T. S. Grall. U.S. Census Bureau, Washington, D.C. http://www.census.gov/prod/2007pubs/p60–234.pdf.

———. 2007b. *Statistical Abstract of the United States: 2008*. 127th ed. U.S. Census Bureau, Washington, D.C., 2007. http://www.census.gov/statab/www. Accessed 11/21/2008.

U.S. Congress. House of Representatives. Committee on Ways and Means. 2004. *2004 Green Book: Background Material and Data on the Programs within the Jurisdiction of the Committee on Ways And Means*. Washington, D.C.: U.S. Government Printing Office.

U.S. Department of Health and Human Services, Office of Inspector General. 1997. "In-hospital voluntary paternity acknowledgment program: Effective practices in hospital staff training." OEI-06-95-00162. U.S. Department of Health and Human Services, Washington, D.D.

Van Anders, S. M., and P. B. Gray. 2007. "Hormones and human partnering." *Annual Review of Sex Research*, 18:60–93.

Van Anders, S. M., and N. V. Watson. 2006. "Relationship status and testosterone in North American heterosexual and nonheterosexual men and women: Cross-sectional and longitudinal data." *Psychoneuroendocrinology* 31: 715–723.

Veith, J. L., M. Buck, S. Getzlaf, P. van Dalfsen, and S. Slade. 1983. "Exposure to men influences the occurrence of ovulation in women." *Physiology and Behavior* 31:313–315.

Vermeer, H. J., and M. H. van IJzendoorn. 2006. "Children's elevated cortisol levels at daycare: A review and meta-analysis." *Early Childhood Research Quarterly* 21: 390–401.

Vining, D. R. 1986. "Social versus reproductive success: The central theoretical problem of human sociobiology." *Behavioral and Brain Sciences* 9: 167–216.

Volk, A., and V. L. Quinsey. 2002. "The influence of infant facial cues on adoption preferences." *Human Nature* 13: 437–455.

Von Sydow, K. 1999. "Sexuality during pregnancy and after childbirth: A metacontent analysis of 59 studies." *Journal of Psychosomatic Research* 47: 27–49.

Von Sydow, K., M. Ullmeyer, and N. Happ. 2001. "Sexual activity during pregnancy and after childbirth: Results from the Sexual Preferences Questionnaire." *Journal of Psychosomatic Obstetrics and Gynecology* 22: 29–40.

Wallace, A. R. 1905/1974. *My Life: A Record of Events and Opinions.* New York: AMS.

Walum, H., L. Westberg, S. Henningsson, J. M. Neiderhiser, D. Reiss, W. Igl, J. M. Ganiban, E. L. Spotts, N. L. Pedersen, E. Eriksson, and P. Lichtenstein. 2008. "Genetic variation in the vasopressin receptor 1a (AVPR1A) associates with pair-bonding behavior in humans." *Proceedings of the National Academy of Sciences* 105: 14153–14156.

Wardlow, H. 2008. "'She liked it best when she was on top': Intimacies and estrangements in Huli men's marital and extramarital relationships." In *Intimacies: Love and Sex across Cultures,* ed. W. Jankowiak, 194–223. New York: Columbia University Press.

Waynforth, D. 1999. "Differences in time use for mating and nepotistic effort as a function of male attractiveness in rural Belize." *Evolution and Human Behavior* 20: 19–28.

———. 2007. "The influence of parent-infant cosleeping, nursing, and child-care on cortisol and SIgA immunity in a sample of British children." *Developmental Psychobiology* 49: 640–648.

Waynforth, D., A. M. Hurtado, and K. Hill. 1998. "Environmentally contingent reproductive strategies in Mayan and Ache males." *Evolution and Human Behavior* 19: 369–385.

Weaver, I. C. G., C. Nadia, F. A. Champagne, A. C. D'Alessio, S. Sharma, J. R. Secki, S. Dymov, M. Szyf, and M. J. Meaney. 2004. "Epigenetic programming by maternal behavior." *Nature Neuroscience* 7: 847–854

Wedding Report Inc. 2008. Cost of Wedding. http://www.costofwedding.com (accessed 11/13/08).

Weeks, J. R. 2008. *Population: An Introduction to Concepts and Issues.* Wadsworth Publishing: New York.

Weisfeld, G. E., T. Czilli, K. A. Phillips, J. A. Gall, and C. M. Lichtman. 2003. "Possible olfaction-based mechanisms in human kin recognition and inbreeding avoidance." *Journal of Experimental Child Psychology* 85: 279–295.

Weiss, Y., and R. J. Willis. 1985. "Children as collective goods and divorce settlements." *Journal of Labor Economics* 3: 268–292.

Weitoft, G. R., B. Burstrom, and M. Rosen. 2004. "Premature mortality among lone fathers and childless men." *Social Science and Medicine* 59: 1449–1459.

Wellings, K., M. Collumbien, E. Slaymaker, S. Singh, Z. Hodges, D. Patel, and N. Bajos. 2006. "Sexual behaviour in context: A global perspective." *Lancet* 368: 1706–1728.

Wenk, R. E., T. Houtz, M. Brooks, and F. A. Chiafari. 1992. "How frequent is heteropaternal superfecundation." *Acta Geneticae Medicae et Gemellologiae* 41: 43–47.

Wenk, R. E., T. Houtz, and S. Korpisz. 2007. Paternity inclusions among suspicious spouses and their social value." *Transfusion* 47: 947–948.

Wertz, D. C., J. C. Fletcher, and J. J. Mulvihill. 1990. "Medical geneticists confront ethical dilemmas: Cross-cultural comparisons among 18 nations." *American Journal of Human Genetics* 46: 1200–1213.

West-Eberhard, M. J. 2003. *Developmental Plasticity and Evolution.* Oxford: Oxford University Press.

Westermarck, E. A. 1891. *The History of Human Marriage.* London: Macmillan.

White, D. R., and M. L. Burton. 1988. "Causes of polygyny: Ecology, economy, kinship, and warfare." *American Anthropologist* 90: 871–887.

White, L. 1994. "Stepfamilies over the life course: Social support." In *Stepfamilies: Who benefits? Who does not?*, ed. A. Booth and J. Dunn, 109–137. Hillsdale, N.J.: Lawrence Erlbaum Associates.

White, L. K. 1990. "Determinants of divorce: A review of research in the eighties." *Journal of Marriage and the Family* 52: 904–912.

White, T. D., B. Asfaw, Y. Beyene, Y. Haile-Selassie, C. O. Lovejoy, G. Suwa, G. Woldegabriel. 2009. "Ardipithecus ramidus and the paleobiology of early hominids." *Science* 326:75–86.

Whitehouse, G., C. Diamond, and M. Baird. 2007. "Fathers' use of leave in Australia." *Community, Work and Family* 10: 387–407.

Whiting, J., and B. Whiting. 1975. "Aloofness and intimacy of husbands and wives: A cross-cultural study." *Ethos* 3: 183–207.

Wiederman, Michael W. 1997. Extramarital sex: Prevalence and correlates in a national survey. Journal of Sex Research 34(2):167–174.

Wilcox, A. J., D. D. Baird, D. B. Dunson, D. R. McConnaughey, J. S. Kesner, and C. R. Weinberg. 2004. "On the frequency of intercourse around ovulation: Evidence for biological influences." *Human Reproduction* 19: 1539–1543.

Wilcox, A. J., C. R. Weinberg, and D. D. Baird. 1995. "Timing of sexual intercourse in relation to ovulation: Effects on the probability of conception, survival of the pregnancy, and sex of the baby." *New England Journal of Medicine* 333: 1517–1521.

Wilder, R. 2006. *Daddy Needs a Drink.* New York: Delacorte.

Willis, R. J. 1999. "A theory of out-of-wedlock childbearing." *Journal of Political Economy* 107: S33–S64.

Wilson, M. 1987. "Impact of the uncertainty of paternity on family law." *University of Toronto Faculty of Law Review* 45: 216–242.

Wilson, M., and M. Daly. 1985. "Competitiveness, risk-taking and violence: The young male syndrome." *Ethology and Sociobiology* 6: 59–73.

Wingfield, J. C., R. E. Hegner, A. M. Dufty Jr., and G. F. Ball. 1990. "The "'challenge hypothesis': Theoretical implications for patterns of testosterone secretion, mating systems, and breeding strategies." *American Naturalist* 136: 829–846.

Winking, J., M. Gurven, H. Kaplan, and J. Stieglitz. 2009. "The goals of direct paternal care among a South Amerindian population." *American Journal of Physical Anthropology*, 139:295–304.

Winking, J., H. Kaplan, M. Gurven, and S. Rucas. 2007. "Why do men marry and why do they stray?" *Proceedings of the Royal Society of London B* 274: 1643–1649.

Winn, S. G., A. Morelli, and E. Z. Tronick. 1990. "The infant in the group: A look at Efe caretaking practices." In *The Cultural Context of Infancy,* ed. J. K. Nugent, B. M. Lester, and T. B. Brazelton, 87–109. Norwood, N.J.: Ablex Publishing.

Wolf, A. P., and W. H. Durham, eds. 2005. *Inbreeding, Incest, and the Incest Taboo.* Stanford, Calif.: Stanford University Press.

Wolf, J. H. 2003. "Low breastfeeding rates and public health in the United States." *American Journal of Public Health* 93: 2000–2010.

Wood, B., and N. Lonergan. 2008. "The hominin fossil record: Taxa, grades and clades." *Journal of Anatomy* 212: 354–376.

Wood, J. W. 1994. *Dynamics of Human Reproduction: Biology, Biometry and Demography.* New York: Aldine de Gruyter.

Worthman, C. M. 1999. "Evolutionary perspectives on the onset of puberty." In *Evolutionary Medicine,* ed. W. R. Trevathan, E. O. Smith, and J. J. McKenna, 135–163. New York: Oxford University Press.

Wrangham, R. W., J. H. Jones, G. Laden, D. Pilbeam, and N. Conklin-Brittain. 1999. "The raw and the stolen: Cooking and the ecology of human origins." *Current Anthropology* 40: 567–594.

Wrangham, R. W., and D. Peterson. 1996. *Demonic Males.* New York: Mariner.

Wright, L., S. MacRae, D. Gordon, E. Elliot, D. Dixon, S. Abbey, and R. Richardson. 2002. "Disclosure of misattributed paternity: Issues involved in the discovery of unsought information." *Seminars in Dialysis* 15: 202–206.

Wu, L. L., L. Bumpass, and K. Musick. 2001. "Historical and life course trajectories of nonmarital childbearing." In *Out of Wedlock: Causes and Consequences of Nonmarital Fertility,* ed. L. L. Wu and B. Wolfe, 3–48. New York: Russell Sage Foundation.

Wu, Z., and T. R. Balakrishnan. 1995. "Dissolution of premarital cohabitation in Canada." *Demography* 32: 521–532.

Yamazaki, A., K. A. Lee, H. P. Kennedy, and S. J. Weiss. 2005. "Sleep-wake cycles, social rhythms, and sleeping arrangements during Japanese childbearing family transition." *Journal of Obstetric, Gynecologic, and Neonatal Nursing* 34: 342–348.

Young, L. J., and Z. Wang. 2004. "The neurobiology of pair bonding." *Nature Neuroscience* 7: 1048–1054.

Ziegler, T. E., S. L. Prudom, N. C. Schultz-Darken, A. V. Kurian, and C. T. Snowdon. 2006. "Pregnancy weight gain: Marmoset and tamarin dads show it too." *Biology Letters* 2: 181–183.

Ziegler, T. E., N. J. Schultz-Darken, J. J. Scott, C. T. Snowdon, and C. F. Ferris. 2005. "Neuroendocrine responses to female ovulatory odors depends upon social condition in male common marmosets, *Callithrix jacchus*." *Hormones and Behavior* 47: 56–64.

Zvoch, K. 1999. "Family type and investment in education: A comparison of genetic and stepparent families." *Evolution and Human Behavior* 20: 453–464.

Acknowledgments

A book, like a baby, is the result of a gestational process; periods of slow and steady growth are interspersed with bursts of frenzied activity, culminating in a small package of joy you can hold in one hand. (Lest we push the analogy too far, we are not going to claim that the process of delivering the book is anywhere near as difficult as childbirth. On the plus side, books do not need their diapers changed.)

This book was truly a fifty-fifty writing effort. (Is it not appropriate that a book on fatherhood should have two fathers?) While having two authors writing the same text would be an exercise in frustration for many, it suited us extremely well. We both benefited from immediate feedback and criticism of our writing, pushing each other to do better. This collaborative process blurred the lines between who wrote what and undoubtedly resulted in a far stronger volume than either of us could have produced on his own. We left the question of authorship unresolved until the last possible moment, ultimately deciding the order of our names by a coin toss, which Peter Gray won. We thank Liam Frink for flipping the fateful coin.

Just as parents receive extensive support from friends, families, and colleagues during pregnancy and beyond, so too have we benefited from many sources during the incubation of this project. This book is greatly enriched by their contributions; ultimately, of course, we accept final responsibility for any errors that remain. At Harvard University Press, we thank Michael Fisher for his support for this project, and Anne Zarrella for her editorial assistance. Tonnya Norwood provided excellent project management of the manuscript, and Martha Carlson-Bradley's copyediting was thoughtful and careful. We extend our heartfelt gratitude to the many generous scholars who helped improve this book in so many ways: Dan Benyshek, Ann Biddlecom, Eduardo Fernandez-Duque, Lee Gettler, Isal Guillermo, Sanjiv Gupta, Samuli Helle, Sandy Hofferth, Sarah Hrdy, Chris Lorck, Wendy Manning, Chandler Marrs, Deb Martin, Justin McLaughlin, Catherine Salmon, Brooke Scelza, Bill Schumaker, Todd Shackelford, Susan Stewart, James Swain, John Swetnam, Jen Thompson, Claudia Valeggia, and Jeff Winking. We also thank Monique Borgerhoff Mulder, Joe Henrich, Adam Moody, Carol Ember, and Robert Bailey for assistance with the time allocation data presented in Chapter 8.

We each have additional personal acknowledgments to make, and will each take a turn.

Kermyt Anderson: Hilly Kaplan exercised a profound influence on my professional development, with Jane Lancaster, Kim Hill, Magdalena Hurtado, Martin Daly and the late Margo Wilson rounding out my graduate training. As a postdoctoral fellow, my life was enriched, both personally and professionally, by Bobbi Low, Carl Simon, and David Lam. My two pairs of parents, Larry Anderson and Barb Kinsey, and Virginia and Larry Hedlund, have provided encouragement throughout my life. Of course, my deepest and most heartfelt thanks go to my wife, Ann Beutel, and our children, Keaton and Mariel, for their unconditional love and support. Without them my interest in fatherhood would have been only theoretical. I am also grateful for their patience during the many long evenings when Daddy was "working on the book."

Peter Gray: I wish to thank my scholarly parents—Rob Boyd, Joe Manson, and Nick Blurton Jones while I was a UCLA undergraduate; Frank Marlowe, Peter Ellison, Richard Wrangham, and Cheryl Knott as my PhD advisors at Harvard; Shalender Bhasin as my mentor during my postdoctoral stint in clinical endocrinology; and numerous colleagues and collaborators over the years, many of whom have shared in the joys of collecting bodily fluids with me as part of hormones and family life research: Coren Apicella, Emily Barrett, Rick Bribiescas, Terry Burnham, Ben Campbell, Rob Durette, Michelle Escasa, Dan Eisenberg, Melissa Emery-Thompson, Michelle Elekonich, Judith Flynn-Chapman, Steve Gangestad, Isal Guillermo, Fred Hadi, Brian Hare, Karen Herbst, Sam Holland, Carole Hooven, Bill Jankowiak, Julie Kachinski, Sonya Kahlenberg, Deborah Keil, Fred Kuch, Susan Lipson, Heidi Manlove, Chandler Marrs, Andy Marshall, Matthew McIntyre, Martin Muller, Lucha Pfister, Harrison Pope, Maureen Samms-Vaughan, Roxanne Sanchez, Tom Steiner, Michael Steiper, Sari van Anders, Jeff Yang, Nate Young, Sharon Young, and Toni Ziegler. I also thank my parents, David and Kay, and sister, Diana, for their lifelong love and support; the many extended family who have helped shape me and now my own children; and most of all my wife, Megan, and daughters, Sophie and Stella, for daily reminding me of the ultimate in life's meanings.

Index